# Principles of Insurance: Life, Health, and Annuities

**LOMA (Life Office Management Association, Inc.)** is an international association founded in 1924. LOMA is committed to a business partnership with its worldwide members in the insurance and financial services industry to improve their management and operations through quality employee development, research, information sharing, and related products and services. Among LOMA's activities is the sponsorship of several self-study education programs leading to professional designations. These programs include the Fellow, Life Management Institute (FLMI) program and the Fellow, Financial Services Institute (FFSI) program. For more information on all of LOMA's education programs, please visit www.loma.org.

*Statement of Purpose: LOMA Educational Programs Testing and Designations*
Examinations described in the *LOMA Education and Training Catalog* are designed solely to measure whether students have successfully completed the relevant assigned curriculum, and the attainment of the FLMI and other LOMA designations indicates only that all examinations in the given curriculum have been successfully completed. In no way shall a student's completion of a given LOMA course or attainment of the FLMI or other LOMA designation be construed to mean that LOMA in any way certifies that student's competence, training, or ability to perform any given task. LOMA's examinations are to be used solely for general educational purposes, and no other use of the examinations or programs is authorized or intended by LOMA. Furthermore, it is in no way the intention of the LOMA Curriculum and Examinations staff to describe the standard of appropriate conduct in any field of the insurance and financial services industry, and LOMA expressly repudiates any attempt to so use the curriculum and examinations. Any such assessment of student competence or industry standards of conduct should instead be based on independent professional inquiry and the advice of competent professional counsel.

# Principles of Insurance:
# Life, Health, and Annuities
## *Third Edition*

Harriett E. Jones, J.D., FLMI, AIRC, ACS

**LOMA Education and Training**
**Atlanta, Georgia**
**www.loma.org**

Information in this text may have
been changed or updated since its
publication date. For current
updates, visit www.loma.org.

**<u>LOMA 280</u> Text — Principles of Insurance: Life, Health, and Annuities**

| | |
|---|---|
| **Author:** | Harriett E. Jones, J.D., FLMI, AIRC, ACS |
| **Manuscript Editor:** | Mary C. Bickley, J.D., FLMI, CLU, AIRC, ACS, AIAA, PAHM, AAPA, ARA |
| **Exam Editor:** | Jo Ann Appleton, FLMI, ALHC, PCS, HIA, CEBS |
| **Project Manager:** | Joyce R. Abrams, J.D., FLMI, PCS, AAPA, AIRC, ARA, AIAA, FLHC, PAHM, HIA, MHP |
| **Production Manager:** | Stephen J. Bollinger, ACS |
| **Copyeditor:** | Robert Land, FLMI |
| **Indexer:** | Amy Souwan |
| **Typesetter:** | Amy Souwan |
| **Production Coordinator:** | Amy Souwan |
| **Print Buyer:** | Audrey H. Gregory, ACS |
| **Permissions Coordinator:** | Iris F. Hartley, FLMI, ALHC |
| **Administrative Support:** | Mamunah Carter<br>Natalie Sanders |
| **Cover Design:** | Kathleen Ryan, FLMI, PCS, AIRC, AIAA, ARA, PAHM |

Library of Congress Cataloging-in-Publication Data

Jones, Harriett E.
    Principles of insurance: life, health, and annuities / Harriett E. Jones.--3rd ed.
      p. cm.
    Includes index.
    ISBN 1-57974-275-0
     1. Insurance, Life--United States. 2. Insurance, Health--United States. 3. Annuities. I. Title.

HG8951.J63 2005
368.3'00973--dc22

2005040921

ISBN 1-57974-275-0

*Printed in the United States of America*

# Contents

# Part 2: Individual Life Insurance and Annuities ......... 55

# Chapter 7: Supplemental Benefits .......................................... 116

# Chapter 8: Individual Life Insurance Policy Provisions ............ 132

# Chapter 9: Life Insurance Policy Ownership Rights ................. 156

## Chapter 10: Paying Life Insurance Policy Proceeds ................. 184

## Chapter 11: Annuities and Individual
## Retirement Arrangements ........................................ 200

# Part 3: Group Insurance ......................................... 229

## Chapter 12: Principles of Group Insurance ........................... 230

## Chapter 13: Group Life Insurance ..................................... 250

# Preface

The life and health insurance and financial services industries continue to undergo dramatic changes. This textbook is designed to give readers an understanding of the basic principles that underlie the operation of life and health insurance companies and how those companies operate within the financial services industry. The text describes the products that are most widely marketed by life and health insurance companies, and it explains how those products operate.

# Acknowledgements

This textbook was created as a joint effort of professionals from insurance and financial services companies and LOMA staff. On behalf of LOMA, the authors thank all the individuals who gave their time and energy and shared their knowledge and expertise with us as we developed this textbook.

## Textbook Review Panel

LOMA's Education and Training Division has assembled a team of writers, editors, and production staff who work together closely to create educational materials such as this textbook. This staff team, however, depends on the work of industry professionals who give their time and knowledge to help ensure that LOMA's educational publications are as accurate and complete as possible. The following industry professionals reviewed the manuscript and made numerous suggestions for its improvement:

- Sandra Batten, FLMI, AIAA, ACS, PCS, Manager, Customer Services—Western Canada, Standard Life Assurance Company of Canada

- Lydia M. Boyko, FLMI, APR, Professor and Associate, Centre for Financial Services, Seneca College of Applied Arts and Technology

- Duane Clarke, FLMI, ACS, AIAA, Life Compliance Specialist, Jackson National Life Insurance Company

- Laura K. Gillenwater, FLMI, ACS, EPS & Documentation Manager, Sun Life Financial

- Josee Malboeuf, FLMI, ALHC, Vice President, Underwriting and Claims, RGA Life Reinsurance Company of Canada

- Eileen Wan, FLMI, ACS, AIAA, Consultant, Projects, Systems and Processes, Standard Life Assurance Company of Canada

# LOMA Staff

Developing a LOMA textbook is a collaborative effort of many individuals at LOMA. These individuals from LOMA's Education and Training Products staff include Mary C. Bickley, J.D., FLMI, CLU, AIRC, ACS, AIAA, PAHM, AAPA, ARA, Senior Associate, who served as Manuscript Editor; Joyce R. Abrams, J.D., FLMI, PCS, AAPA, AIRC, ARA, AIAA, FLHC, PAHM, HIA, MHP, Assistant Vice President, who served as Project Manager; and Jo Ann Appleton, FLMI, ALHC, PCS, HIA, CEBS, Senior Associate, who served as the Examinations Editor. Jane Lightcap Brown, Ph.D., FLMI, ALHC, ACS, Senior Associate, and Patsy Leeuwenburg, Ph.D., FLMI, ACS, FLHC, AIAA, ARA, AIRC, AAPA, PAHM, Senior Associate, both helped recruit members of the Textbook Review Panel. Miriam A. Orsina, FLMI, PCS, ARA, PAHM, Senior Associate helped to coordinate the materials to be included in this text with materials included in the text, *Insurance Company Operations*. Mamunah Carter, Administrative Assistant III, provided outstanding administrative support.

In LOMA's Production Department, thanks go to Stephen J. Bollinger, ACS, Production Manager, who oversaw the production of the text and Amy Souwan, Production Coordinator II/Scheduling Coordinator, who typeset the text. Consultant Robert D. Land, FLMI, ACS, served as copyeditor, and Iris F. Hartley, FLMI, ALHC, secured the necessary permissions.

Also deserving of thanks are individuals in LOMA's Information Center who provided valuable research services: Olivia Blakemore, ACS, Technical Administrator and Mallory Eldridge, Research Analyst/Writer.

Finally, special thanks go to Katherine C. Milligan, FLMI, ACS, ALHC, Vice President, and William H. Rabel, Ph.D., FLMI, CLU, Senior Vice President, both of the Education and Training Division, who provided guidance, support, and encouragement for this project.

Harriett E. Jones, J.D., FLMI, AIRC, ACS
Atlanta, Georgia 2005

# Code of Professional Ethics for LOMA Designees

Individuals earning LOMA designations shall adhere to LOMA's Code of Professional Ethics, which consists of the following canons:

- The Designee shall discharge all duties with honesty, integrity, objectivity, fairness, and professionalism.

- The Designee shall deal with others in a manner in which he or she would want to be dealt with by others.

- The Designee shall place the public interest above his or her own interest.

- The Designee shall continually strive to master all aspects of his or her business and to improve his or her professional knowledge and skills.

- The Designee shall diligently strive to ascertain clients' best interests and seek to ensure that these interests are met.

- The Designee shall respect clients' privacy and the confidentiality of information they provide, within the constraints of the law.

- The Designee shall comply with the spirit and letter of the law in all his or her activities.

- The Designee shall hold his or her professional designation proudly and seek to enhance the reputation of the designation, as well as the financial services industry, in every way.

# Introduction

The purpose of *Principles of Insurance: Life, Health, and Annuities*, Third Edition, is to describe the life and health insurance industry and the products provided by life and health insurance companies. The text is designed for students who are preparing for LOMA's FLMI Course 280 examination. Each chapter includes several features to help you organize your studies, reinforce your understanding of the materials, and prepare for the examination. As we describe each of these features, we give you suggestions for studying the material.

- **Chapter Outline.** The first page of each chapter contains an outline of the chapter. Review this outline to gain an overview of the major topics that will be covered; then scan through the chapter to familiarize yourself with the presentation of the information. Looking at the headings will give you a preview of how the various subjects relate together.

- **Learning Objectives.** The first page of each chapter contains a list of learning objectives to help you focus your studies. Before reading each chapter, review these learning objectives. Then, as you read the chapter, look for material that will help you meet the learning objectives.

- **Key Terms.** Because this is an introductory text, it requires no prior knowledge of insurance terms and concepts. Each insurance term is defined or explained when it is first used. Important terminology is highlighted in ***bold italic*** type when the term is defined and is included in a list of key terms at the end of the chapter. All key terms also are included in a comprehensive glossary at the end of the book. As you read each chapter, pay special attention to these key terms.

- **Figures and Insights.** Figures and insights that appear throughout the text illustrate the text's discussions of selected topics and amplify the text's descriptions of certain topics. Note that information contained in figures and insights may be tested on the examination for this course.

- **Glossary.** A comprehensive glossary containing definitions of all key terms appears at the end of the book. Following each glossary entry is a number in brackets that indicates the chapter in which the key term is defined. The glossary includes references to important equivalent terms, acronyms, and contrasting terms.

The text and study aids for LOMA courses may be revised periodically. To ensure that you are studying from the correct materials, check the current *LOMA Education and Training Catalog* for a description of the texts and study aids assigned for the examination for which you are preparing.

# Using LOMA Study Aids

LOMA has prepared study aids designed to help students prepare for the LOMA 280 examination. LOMA recommends that you use all of the study aids available for this course. **Studies indicate that students who use LOMA study aids consistently perform significantly better on LOMA examinations than students who do not use these study aids.**

## Test Preparation Guide

In addition to this book, LOMA's *Test Preparation Guide for LOMA 280* is assigned reading for students preparing for the LOMA 280 examination. Used along with this textbook, the Test Preparation Guide will help you master the course material. The Test Preparation Guide includes chapter review exercises, practice exam questions, a full-scale sample examination in both paper and electronic format, and answers to all of the questions in the Test Preparation Guide.

## Using the CD-ROM Accompanying This Text

The CD-ROM found on the inside back cover of this text contains a Quick Review, which gives you an overview of the materials found in this text. The CD-ROM also contains some sample insurance policies that illustrate various products described in the textbook.

## Using *LOMA's Handbook of Insurance Policy Forms*

*LOMA's Handbook of Insurance Policy Forms* is suggested reading for the LOMA 280 course. This handbook is a reference tool to provide students and other insurance and financial services industry professionals with examples of the insurance and annuity products that are described in this text. Sample policy forms include a range of individual life insurance, health insurance, and annuity products. The handbook also includes a sample group insurance master contract and a certificate of insurance provided to the individuals insured under the group contract.

# Part 1:
# Introduction
# to Insurance

# The Life and Health Insurance Industry

## objectives

*After reading this chapter, you should be able to*

- Describe the three primary types of life and health insurance products

- Distinguish among the three types of business organizations and explain why insurance companies must be organized as corporations

- Distinguish among stock insurers, mutual insurers, and fraternal benefit societies

- Describe the financial services industry and how insurance companies function within that industry

- Describe three ways in which governments influence the insurance industry

- Identify the two primary goals of insurance regulation in most countries

The life and health insurance industry plays a major role in the economy of every developed nation, and life and health insurance products are important elements of financial planning by individuals and families. This text is designed to introduce you to the life and health insurance industry and to the range of products marketed by life and health insurance companies. Figure 1.1 identifies some of the products that life and health insurers issue and sell and that we describe throughout this text.

We begin our discussion by describing insurance companies as business organizations. Next, we discuss the financial services industry and the role of insurance companies in that industry. Finally, we describe the influence that governments have on the insurance industry.

# Insurance Companies as Business Organizations

Businesses are established to produce goods or provide services that consumers want or need and then to sell those goods or services, typically for a profit. *Profit* is the money, or revenue, that a business receives for its products or services *minus* the costs it incurred to produce the goods or deliver the services. As a business, an insurance company typically has a responsibility to its owners to operate profitably.

## Types of Business Organizations

In many countries, including the United States, businesses are structured in one of three ways: (1) as a sole proprietorship, (2) as a partnership, or (3) as a corporation. A *sole proprietorship* is owned and operated by one individual. The owner receives all profits and is personally responsible for all the debts of the business. If the business fails, the owner's personal property may be used to pay the debts of the business. If the owner becomes disabled or dies, the business often cannot continue to operate.

A *partnership* is a business that is owned by two or more people, who are known as the *partners*. The partners receive the profits and are personally responsible for the debts of the business. If one of the partners dies or withdraws from the business, the partnership generally dissolves, although the remaining partners may form a new partnership and continue to operate the business.

For our discussion, we are primarily concerned with the corporate form of business. A *corporation* is a legal entity that is created by the authority of a governmental unit and that is separate and distinct from the people

**FIGURE 1.1** | Types of Life and Health Insurance Products

**Life insurance policy**

A policy under which the insurer promises to pay a benefit upon the death of a named person.

- *Term life insurance* provides a policy benefit if the insured dies during a specified period of time.

- *Cash value life insurance*, also known as *permanent life insurance*, provides life insurance coverage throughout the insured's lifetime and also provides a savings element. As premiums are paid for these policies, an accumulated savings amount—known as the policy's **cash value**—gradually builds. A policy's cash value is a valuable asset that the policyowner can use in a number of ways.

- *Endowment insurance* provides a policy benefit that is paid either when the insured dies or on a stated date if the insured lives until then. Endowment insurance has some characteristics of both term life insurance and cash value life insurance. Like term insurance, endowment insurance provides life insurance coverage for only a stated period of time. Like cash value life insurance, endowment insurance provides a savings element.

**Annuity contract**

A contract under which an insurer promises to make a series of periodic payments to a named individual in exchange for a premium or a series of premiums.

**Health insurance policy**

A policy that provides protection against the risk of financial loss resulting from the insured person's illness, accidental injury, or disability. The two major forms of health insurance coverage are as follows:

- *Medical expense coverage* provides benefits to pay for the treatment of an insured's illnesses and injuries.

- *Disability income coverage* provides income replacement benefits to an insured who is unable to work because of illness or injury.

**These products can be issued as either an individual insurance policy or a group insurance policy**

- An *individual insurance policy* is a policy that is issued to insure the life or health of a named person. Some individual policies also insure the named person's immediate family or a second named person.

- A *group insurance policy* is a policy that is issued to insure the lives or health of a specific group of people, such as a group of employees.

who own it. A corporation has two major characteristics that set it apart from a sole proprietorship and a partnership. First, a corporation is a legal entity that is separate from its owners. As a result, a corporation can sue or be sued, can enter into contracts, and can own property. The corporation's debts and liabilities belong to the corporation itself, not to its owners. The owners are not personally responsible for the corporation's debts. The second difference is that the corporation continues beyond the death of any or all of its owners. This second characteristic of the corporation provides an element of stability and permanence that a sole proprietorship and partnership cannot guarantee. Because an insurer's contractual obligations extend many years into the future, the corporation is the ideal form of business organization for an insurance company. Recognizing the importance of such stability and permanence, laws in the United States and many countries require insurance companies to operate as corporations.

## Types of Insurance Company Organizations

Even though they must be corporations, life and health insurance companies have some flexibility in how they are organized to do business. Typically, insurers are organized as stock insurance companies, mutual insurance companies, or fraternal benefit societies.

### Stock Insurance Companies

The majority of life and health insurance companies are established and organized as stock companies. A *stock insurance company* is an insurance company that is owned by the people and organizations that purchase shares of the company's stock. The investors who purchase *stock*—ownership shares—in the corporation are known as the *stockholders*. From time to time, a portion of the company's operating profits may be distributed to these stockholders in the form of *stockholder dividends*.

### Mutual Insurance Companies

Life and health insurance companies also can be organized as mutual companies. A *mutual insurance company* is an insurance company that is owned by its policyowners, and a portion of the company's operating profits are from time to time distributed to these policyowners in the form of *policy dividends*. We describe policy dividends in more detail in Chapter 9.

Before a mutual company can be formed, a certain number of policies must be sold in advance to provide the funds the company needs to begin operations. Because most people are reluctant to purchase a product from a company that does not yet exist, most mutual companies in existence today began many years ago as stock companies and later converted to mutual companies. This process of converting from a stock company to a mutual company is called *mutualization*.

Over the last few decades, many mutual companies reorganized to become stock companies through the process of *demutualization*. The primary reason a mutual insurer might wish to demutualize is that, as a stock company, it can more easily raise operating funds by selling additional shares of stock to the public. Stock insurers also have greater flexibility than mutual insurers in buying and operating other types of companies.

Even though stock insurers greatly outnumber mutual insurers, mutual insurers provide a significant amount of the life insurance in force in the United States. Figure 1.2 depicts the concentrations of stock, mutual, and fraternal companies operating in the United States in 2003. Mutual insurers account for a significant amount of life insurance in force because they generally are older and larger than stock insurers.

### Fraternal Benefit Societies

A *fraternal benefit society* is an organization formed to provide social, as well as insurance, benefits to its members. The members of such societies often share a common ethnic, religious, or vocational background, although membership in some societies is open to the general public. One of the

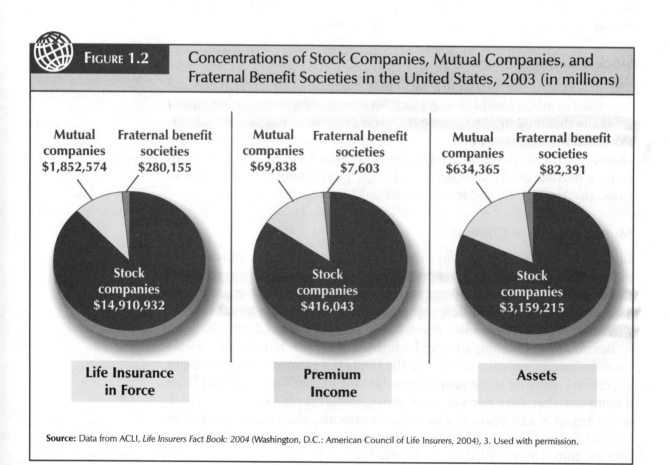

**FIGURE 1.2** Concentrations of Stock Companies, Mutual Companies, and Fraternal Benefit Societies in the United States, 2003 (in millions)

Life Insurance in Force — Mutual companies $1,852,574; Fraternal benefit societies $280,155; Stock companies $14,910,932

Premium Income — Mutual companies $69,838; Fraternal benefit societies $7,603; Stock companies $416,043

Assets — Mutual companies $634,365; Fraternal benefit societies $82,391; Stock companies $3,159,215

**Source:** Data from ACLI, *Life Insurers Fact Book: 2004* (Washington, D.C.: American Council of Life Insurers, 2004), 3. Used with permission.

legal requirements of being a fraternal benefit society is that the fraternal society must have a representative form of government—that is, the members must elect the officers of the fraternal society. Additionally, fraternal societies must operate through a lodge system whereby only lodge members and their families are permitted to own the fraternal society's insurance. In fact, applicants for insurance often become members of the society automatically once the society issues them a policy.

**FAST FACT**

By the end of 2003, residents of the United States owned $16.8 trillion of life insurance coverage.

**Source:** ACLI, *Life Insurers Fact Book: 2004* (Washington, D.C.: American Council of Life Insurers, 2004), 81.

# Insurance Companies as Financial Institutions

Insurance companies are financial institutions that function in the economy as part of the financial services industry.[1] A *financial institution* is a business that owns primarily financial assets, such as stocks and bonds, rather than fixed assets, such as equipment and raw materials. The *financial services industry* is made up of various kinds of financial institutions that help people, businesses, and governments save, borrow, invest, and otherwise manage money. The financial products provided by financial institutions help people manage income and debt, accumulate resources for their retirements, and protect themselves from financial losses resulting from unexpected occurrences such as disability, premature death, and natural disasters. The following are some of the various types of financial institutions:

- **Insurance companies** provide protection against the risk of financial loss caused by specified events. The two primary types of insurers are (1) *life and health insurance companies*, which issue and sell products that insure against financial losses that result from the personal risks of death, disability, illness, accident, and outliving one's savings and (2) *property/casualty insurance companies*, which issue and sell insurance policies to provide financial security from property damage risk and liability risk.

- **Depository institutions** accept deposits from people, businesses, and government agencies and use these deposits to make loans to people, businesses, and government agencies. Such institutions include commercial banks, savings and loan associations, savings banks, and credit unions.

- **Finance companies** specialize in making short- and medium-term loans to businesses and people.

- **Mutual fund companies** operate *mutual funds*, which are investment vehicles that pool the funds of investors and use the funds to buy stocks, bonds, and other financial instruments to create a diversified portfolio of investments.

- **Securities firms** facilitate the sale of investment instruments known as securities. A *security* is an investment instrument that represents either an ownership interest in a business (for example, a share of stock) or an obligation of indebtedness owed by a business, government, or agency (a bond, for example).

Financial institutions, including insurance companies, serve as financial intermediaries. A ***financial intermediary*** is an organization that channels funds from those people, businesses, and governments that have a surplus of funds (savers) to those who have a shortage of funds (borrowers). In the process of moving funds from savers to borrowers, financial intermediaries generate income for themselves. Insurers are financial intermediaries because they take a portion of the money that their customers pay for their insurance and invest that money in business and industry. The investments made by insurers provide funds that these businesses need to operate and expand. As shown in Figure 1.3, life insurers are among the most important institutional sources of funds provided to businesses.

The financial services industry has undergone profound changes in the past few decades. The evolution of the financial services industry is characterized by convergence, consolidation, and globalization.

## Convergence

Historically, the financial services industry was divided into distinct sectors. Banks provided banking services such as checking accounts, savings accounts, and loans. Securities firms and mutual fund companies handled investments. Insurance companies issued and sold insurance products.

Today, however, the financial services industry is characterized by ***convergence***, which is the movement toward a single financial institution being able to serve a customer's banking, insurance, and securities needs. Financial services companies have entered into each other's traditional businesses, either through expansion of operations or through mergers and acquisitions. Thus, the distinctions among financial institutions based on the products they offer have blurred.

Although certain financial services companies for some time now have been contracting with certain other financial services companies to act as third-party distributors of their products, convergence received a real boost in the United States from the passage of federal legislation in 1999. The ***Gramm-Leach-Bliley (GLB) Act***, also known as the *Financial Services Modernization Act*, removed regulatory barriers to affiliations among financial institutions.[2] The primary effect of the GLB Act is that the traditionally separate components of the financial services industry can enter into structural affiliations under the umbrella of a financial holding company, thus facilitating the distribution of one another's products.

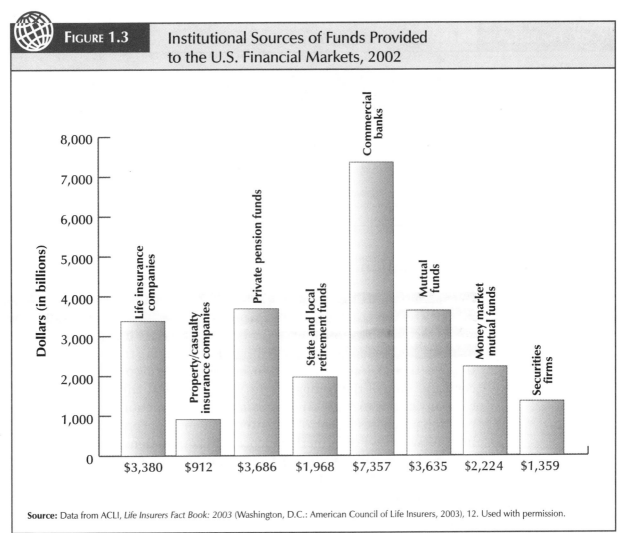

**FIGURE 1.3** Institutional Sources of Funds Provided to the U.S. Financial Markets, 2002

Source: Data from ACLI, *Life Insurers Fact Book: 2003* (Washington, D.C.: American Council of Life Insurers, 2003), 12. Used with permission.

A *financial holding company* is a company that owns and controls another company (or companies)—known as a *subsidiary* of the holding company—and conducts activities that are financial in nature or incidental to financial activities. Figure 1.4 illustrates a financial holding company structure. The various subsidiaries that are under the common control of a holding company are known as *affiliates* because they are affiliated within a holding company system.

Companies affiliated in a holding company system often distribute one another's products. For example, although banks still cannot issue—that is, accept the risk on—insurance products, an insurance company affiliate of a bank may design a product in accordance with the bank's specifications and issue a product that the bank can then sell. Such affiliations also increase the ability of insurance companies to offer a wider variety of noninsurance products, such as mutual funds.

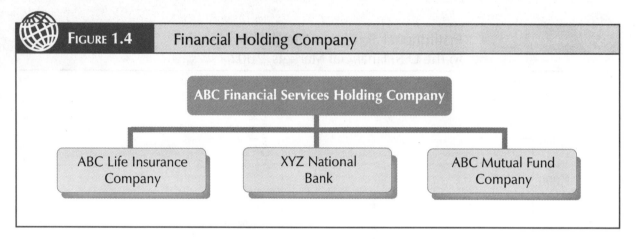

FIGURE 1.4 Financial Holding Company

ABC Financial Services Holding Company

ABC Life Insurance Company

XYZ National Bank

ABC Mutual Fund Company

## Consolidation

***Consolidation***, as the term is frequently used in the financial services industry, is the combination of financial services institutions within or across sectors. Consolidation in the financial services industry occurs primarily through mergers and acquisitions. A *merger* is a transaction wherein the assets and liabilities of two companies are combined into one company. One of the companies survives as a legal entity, and the other company ceases to exist. An *acquisition* is a transaction wherein one corporation purchases a controlling interest in another corporation, resulting in a linkage between formerly independent corporations; after the transaction, both corporations survive. Consolidation has resulted in a decreasing number of traditional financial services institutions within each sector. As the number of financial institutions has decreased, many of the remaining institutions have grown in size.

## Globalization

Today, financial services institutions operate in a global environment. Giant financial services enterprises, particularly those from Western Europe and North America, are seizing new opportunities to expand their customer bases in nations outside their countries of origin. For example, Canadian life and health insurers generated 58 percent of their premiums abroad in 2002.[3] The proportion of life insurance companies operating in the United States that are foreign-owned has climbed in recent years from 4 percent of all U.S. life insurers in 1996 to 11 percent in 2003.[4]

# Role of Government in Insurance

Governments around the world regulate insurance companies. In addition to acting as regulators, governments typically perform at least two other functions. Most governments provide social insurance programs, and most governments influence spending and savings through taxation. In performing these functions, governments affect the supply and demand for insurance in the private sector.

## Regulation of Insurance

Insurance companies protect millions of individuals against economic loss and offer them opportunities to save and invest money. Because the financial health of insurance providers is of such importance to so many people, insurers occupy a special position of public trust. As a result, the insurance industry is subject to regulation designed specifically to safeguard the public interest in insurance companies.

In most countries, the primary goals of insurance regulation are to ensure that insurance companies

- Remain *solvent*—that they are able to meet their debts and to pay policy benefits when they come due

- Conduct their businesses fairly and ethically

Insurance regulatory systems vary from country to country. In many countries, insurance regulation is centralized and under the supervision of the national government. For example, in India, authority over insurance regulation rests solely with the national Insurance Regulatory and Development Authority (IRDA). In other countries, regulation is partially decentralized, with some regulation being imposed by the national government and the remaining regulation being imposed by various jurisdictions within the country.

The United States, for example, has a *federal system* of government in which a *federal government* and a number of lower level governments, known as *state governments*, share governmental powers. As described in Insight 1.1, Canada also has a federal system of government in which powers are shared between a federal government and a number of lower level governments known as provincial governments. Although similar to the U.S. regulatory system, the Canadian insurance regulatory system provides a more prominent role for the federal government than does the U.S. insurance regulatory system.

Almost every country has adopted a constitution, which sets out the fundamental principles that determine the powers and duties of the government and the rights of the people. In a federal system such as the United States, the federal constitution is the nation's supreme law, and all other laws must be consistent with the constitution. Most states also have adopted a state constitution that serves as the state's fundamental law. In the United States and most other countries, constitutions divide governmental powers among three branches of government. Figure 1.5 identifies and describes the three branches of government.

| INSIGHT 1.1 | Canada's Insurance Regulatory System |

In Canada, insurers can be federally incorporated or provincially incorporated. The federal government and the provincial governments are jointly responsible for regulation of insurance.

### Federal Regulation

The federal *Office of the Superintendent of Financial Institutions (OSFI)* is responsible for overseeing all financial institutions in Canada, including life and health insurance companies. The OSFI regulates the solvency of federally incorporated insurers, insurers incorporated in other countries, and specified provincially incorporated insurers.

### Provincial Regulation

Insurance companies incorporated under the laws of a particular province are subject to solvency regulation and examination by the insurance department in that province, rather than by the OSFI. Provincial insurance laws also govern the market conduct of all federally incorporated *and* provincially incorporated insurers operating in that province.

Every province has established an administrative agency to enforce the province's insurance laws. Typically, this agency is known as the *Office of the Superintendent of Insurance* and operates under the direction of an individual known as the *superintendent of insurance*. Some provinces now have established an administrative agency that oversees all financial services institutions operating within the province.

The *Canadian Council of Insurance Regulators (CCIR)* is a nongovernmental committee of provincial insurance regulators that looks at emerging industry and business trends and works toward harmonizing legislation through model laws and standardized reporting requirements. As a result, provincial insurance laws are fairly uniform.

### Canadian Life and Health Insurance Compensation Corporation

The *Canadian Life and Health Insurance Compensation Corporation (CompCorp)* is a federally incorporated, nonprofit company established by the insurance industry to protect Canadian consumers against loss of benefits in the event a life or health insurance company becomes insolvent. All insurers operating in Canada are required to become members of CompCorp, which guarantees payment under covered policies up to certain specified limits.

The U.S. Constitution makes clear that all governmental powers not specifically given to the federal government are left to the state governments. One power delegated to the federal government is the authority to regulate *interstate commerce*—commerce conducted across state lines—which includes the power to regulate the insurance industry. However, the U.S. Congress has agreed to delegate its constitutional authority to regulate insurance to the states. In enacting the federal **McCarran-Ferguson Act,** or *Public Law 15,* the U.S. Congress agreed to leave insurance regulation to the states as long as Congress considered state regulation to be adequate.[5] Thus, the states have primary authority to regulate the insurance industry. Congress, however, retained the right to enact insurance legislation if it decides that state regulation is inadequate or not in the public interest, and a number of federal laws have been enacted to regulate various aspects of insurance and insurance company operations.

## State Regulation

Each state has enacted a variety of laws to regulate insurance companies, their products, and the people who sell their products. In addition, each state has established an administrative agency, typically known as the ***state***

**FIGURE 1.5** | The Three Branches of Government

The *legislative branch* consists of one or more legislative bodies, known collectively in the United States as the *legislature*, that are responsible for enacting laws to govern the applicable jurisdiction. In the United States, the federal legislature is referred to as the *Congress*. The Congress and the state legislatures are composed of two bodies, which typically are known as the Senate and the House of Representatives.

The *executive branch* consists of a number of administrative agencies or ministries that are responsible for administering, enforcing, or carrying out the jurisdiction's laws.

The *judicial branch* consists of a system of courts that are responsible for applying and interpreting the jurisdiction's laws.

*insurance department*, that is under the direction of an *insurance commissioner* or a *state superintendent of insurance*. The state insurance department is charged with making sure that insurers operating within the state comply with applicable state insurance laws and regulations.

In most respects, the various state insurance laws are similar because they are based on model laws developed by the **National Association of Insurance Commissioners (NAIC)**. The NAIC is a nongovernmental organization consisting of the insurance commissioners or superintendents of the various state insurance departments. The NAIC's primary function is to promote uniformity of state regulation by developing model bills and regulations that each state is encouraged to pass. A **model bill** is a sample law that state insurance regulators are encouraged to use as a basis for state insurance laws. We describe some specific model bills throughout this text.

As we noted earlier, insurance companies are required by law in the United States and many other countries to operate as corporations. In the United States, a business becomes a corporation by complying with the incorporation laws of one state. When the company's organizers meet the requirements for incorporation, the state issues a *certificate of incorporation* or *corporate charter* by which the business gains its legal existence as a corporation. Thereafter, the corporation must govern itself and operate in accordance with that state's laws. State laws impose requirements on matters such as the minimum number of directors a corporation must have, the duties of directors and officers, and the rights of stockholders.

Before an insurance company begins conducting business and selling insurance products within a given state, the company must obtain from the state insurance department a *certificate of authority* or *license* that grants the insurer the right to conduct an insurance business in that state. The states impose a variety of licensing requirements that are designed primarily to ensure that insurance companies are financially able to meet their obligations to pay policy benefits.

## Solvency Regulation

Each state has enacted laws designed to ensure that insurance companies operating within the state are solvent. To achieve that goal, the states impose minimum requirements on the amount of the insurer's assets, liabilities, capital, and surplus. These amounts represent components in the company's basic accounting equation, under which the company's assets must equal its liabilities and owners' equity. Insight 1.2 describes the basic accounting equation.

The states oversee the financial condition of insurance companies by reviewing an accounting report, known as the **Annual Statement**, which each insurer prepares each calendar year and files with the insurance department in each state in which it operates. The NAIC has developed an Annual Statement form that is accepted by all states so that an insurer can file the same form in all the states in which it operates.

### FAST FACT

At the end of 2003, U.S. life insurers had $3.8 trillion in assets.
**Source:** ACLI, *Life Insurers Fact Book: 2004* (Washington, D.C.: American Council of Life Insurers, 2004), 9.

---

 **INSIGHT 1.2**   |   Basic Accounting Equation

> **Basic accounting equation:**
>
> **Assets = Liabilities + Owners' equity**

■ **Assets** are all things of value owned by the company. Examples of assets include cash and investments. The states regulate the types of investments insurance companies can make to ensure that those investments are conservative and prudent. The states also impose requirements on how insurers must determine the value of their assets.

■ **Liabilities** are the company's debts and future obligations. A large portion of an insurance company's liabilities consists of the company's *policy reserves*, which represent the amount the insurer estimates it will need to pay policy benefits as they come due. The states impose requirements on the methods that insurers use to calculate the amount of their policy reserves.

■ **Owners' equity** is the difference between the amount of the company's assets and the amount of its liabilities, and it represents the owners' financial interest in the company. Owners' equity in a stock insurance company consists of the company's capital and surplus. In this context, **capital** is the amount of money invested in the company by its owners. **Surplus** is the amount by which the company's assets exceed its liabilities and capital. Because a mutual insurer does not issue stock, it has no capital, and, therefore, owners' equity in a mutual company consists only of its surplus.

In addition, state regulators conduct an on-site financial condition examination of each insurance company every three to five years. State regulators also have the discretionary authority to conduct more frequent examinations of companies that appear most likely to have financial difficulties. In such a financial condition examination, state regulators physically check the insurer's business records. The NAIC has developed an organized system of on-site examinations to coordinate this function between the states so as to avoid duplication of effort by the various states.

Relatively few insurance companies become financially unsound. When such a situation does occur, the state insurance commissioners have the authority to take certain actions. If a ***domestic insurer***—an insurer incorporated by the state—becomes financially unsound, the insurance commissioner can take steps to either rehabilitate or liquidate the company. In other words, if the company's finances can be turned around, the commissioner will try to rehabilitate it. If the company is too financially unsound, the commissioner may declare the company insolvent and act to liquidate—dissolve—the corporation. When a ***foreign insurer***—an insurer incorporated under the laws of another state—becomes financially unsound, the insurance commissioner has authority to revoke or suspend the insurer's license to operate in the state.

Finally, all states have taken steps to protect policyowners and beneficiaries of life and health insurance companies that fail. Each state has established a guaranty association composed of the life and health insurance companies operating within the state. A ***life and health guaranty association*** is an organization that operates under the supervision of the state insurance commissioner to protect policyowners, insureds, beneficiaries, and specified others against losses that result from the financial impairment or insolvency of a life or health insurer that operates in the state. The financial obligations that guaranty associations cover for insolvent insurers vary from state to state. Typically, a guaranty association provides funds to guarantee payment for certain policies up to stated dollar limits, such as those described in Insight 1.3. In some cases, a policyowner may have the option to obtain a replacement policy. To pay these obligations, the guaranty association requires all life and health insurers operating in the state to pay money into a guaranty fund.

## Regulation of Market Conduct

Each state has enacted ***market conduct laws*** that regulate how insurance companies conduct their business within the state. State insurance regulators perform periodic market conduct examinations of insurers similar to the financial examinations described in the last section. In this section, we briefly describe how the states regulate the marketing of insurance products.

## INSIGHT 1.3 | Oregon's Life and Health Insurance Guaranty Association

The Oregon Life and Health Insurance Guaranty Association is typical of state guaranty funds. When a life or health insurer authorized to conduct business in Oregon becomes insolvent—unable to pay the costs of doing business—and is liquidated by a court order, the guaranty fund pays the claims of Oregon residents according to the terms of their in-force policies issued by the insolvent insurer. The coverage limits provided by Oregon's life and health guaranty fund are as follows:

| Type of insurance | Limits of coverage |
|---|---|
| Death benefits | $300,000 |
| Life insurance cash value | $100,000 |
| Present value of annuity benefits | $100,000 |
| Health and disability benefits | $100,000 |
| Maximum per individual per insolvency | $300,000 |

**Source:** Oregon Department of Consumer & Business Services—Insurance Division, "What Happens When a Company Becomes Insolvent," 9 July 2003, http://www.cbs.state.or.us/external/ins/docs/choosing.htm#insolvent (1 June 2004).

We mentioned previously that insurance companies must be licensed by each state in which they operate. The states also require that the individuals—known as *insurance producers*—and agencies that market and sell insurance must be licensed by each state in which they conduct business. The licensing process helps ensure that insurance producers are reputable and knowledgeable about the insurance products they sell. (An example of a state insurance license application developed by the NAIC is included in the CD-ROM that accompanies the text.) To obtain a producer's license, an individual usually must

- Be sponsored for licensing by a licensed insurance company

- Complete approved educational course work and/or pass a written examination

- Provide assurance that he is of reputable character

Producers' licenses typically must be renewed each year, and many states require producers to periodically participate in continuing education courses to renew their licenses. Continuing education is intended to improve the professionalism of producers and help them keep pace with a rapidly changing industry. A state may revoke or suspend a producer's license if she engages in certain unethical practices that violate the state's insurance laws. In general, most such unethical practices involve some form of misrepresentation in which the producer deliberately makes false or misleading statements to induce a customer to purchase insurance.

Most states prohibit insurers from engaging in a variety of practices that are considered to be unfair trade practices. For example, state laws regulate the form and content of insurance advertisements to ensure that consumers are not misled about the features or limitations in advertised insurance policies.

Each state also regulates the policy forms that insurers may use within the state. A *policy form* is a standardized form that shows the terms, conditions, benefits, and ownership rights of a particular type of insurance product. An insurance company usually must file with the state insurance department a copy of each policy form it plans to use and must receive the state insurance department's approval before using the form in the state. The insurance department reviews the policy form to ensure that it contains all required policy provisions and is not unfair or deceptive in any way. Many states also impose readability requirements on insurance policies to reduce the amount of technical jargon and legal language included in those policies.

## Federal Regulation

Although the states are primarily responsible for regulating insurance companies, insurers also are subject to certain federal laws. One of the foremost areas in which federal regulation applies to insurance companies concerns the sale of investment-type insurance products. Businesses and individuals that sell securities must comply with federal securities laws, which are enforced by the federal *Securities and Exchange Commission (SEC)*. The SEC has determined that some insurance products—notably variable life insurance and variable annuities—are investment products as well as life insurance products and are subject to federal regulation. As a result, insurers that issue these variable products must comply with both federal securities laws and state insurance laws. Before selling these investment-type insurance products, a person must be a licensed insurance producer and must be registered with the *National Association of Securities Dealers (NASD)* as a registered representative in accordance with federal securities laws. To be a *registered representative*, an individual must complete a course of study and pass an examination.

A number of other federal laws, although not designed to regulate insurance, influence the operations of life and health insurance companies. The following are examples of federal laws that affect insurance operations:

- Federal consumer protection laws apply to insurance companies that engage in certain interstate activities, primarily interstate advertising. For example, the *Federal Trade Commission Act* prohibits unfair methods of competition and unfair or deceptive practices affecting commerce.[6]

- Federal laws concerning privacy affect how insurers collect and use personal information about their customers. For example, the federal *Fair Credit Reporting Act* regulates the reporting and use of consumer credit information.[7] The GLB Act, which we described earlier in the chapter, requires all financial institutions—including insurers—to develop privacy and security policies and procedures for handling nonpublic personal information about consumers.

- Federal income tax laws encourage people to invest in and employers to provide retirement savings plans. Because such tax incentives can be quite effective, the financial services industry has benefited from increased demand for private retirement savings products that are designed to comply with regulatory requirements so as to provide customers with maximum tax advantages.

- Federal laws regulate employee benefit plans. As a result, insurers must design insurance products that comply with the provisions of these laws. For example, employee benefit plans generally must comply with the terms of the *Employee Retirement Income Security Act* (*ERISA*), which we describe in Chapter 13.[8]

- Federal antiterrorism laws require insurers to implement certain measures designed to detect and prevent illegal activities used to finance terrorism. For example, under the *USA Patriot Act*, financial institutions must establish anti–money laundering programs.[9]

- Federal laws impose requirements on how public corporations are governed. The federal *Sarbanes-Oxley Act of 2002* is designed to protect investors by improving the accuracy and reliability of corporate disclosures made pursuant to the securities laws.[10]

## Social Insurance Programs

A *social insurance program* is a welfare plan that is established by law and administered by a government and that provides the population with income security. Social insurance may provide cash payments to replace income lost because of old age, disability (nonoccupational sickness or injury), death (survivor benefits), occupational injuries, and unemployment. Social insurance also may provide services such as medical care. Figure 1.6 shows the number of countries with various types of social insurance programs.

An in-depth discussion of social insurance programs is beyond the scope of this text. In later chapters, however, we describe some social insurance programs that affect insurers. For example, governments in many countries,

| FIGURE 1.6 | Social Insurance Programs by Type of Program | | | |
|---|---|---|---|---|

| Type of Program | Number of Countries | | | |
| | 1940 | 1995 | 1999 | 2002–2003 |
|---|---|---|---|---|
| Old age, disability, survivor | 33 | 158 | 167 | 174 |
| Sickness and maternity | 24 | 105 | 112 | 124 |
| Work injury | 57 | 159 | 164 | 168 |
| Unemployment | 21 | 63 | 69 | 82 |
| Family allowances | 7 | 81 | 88 | 94 |

**Source:** Social Security Administration (1995), as quoted in Harold D. Skipper, Jr., *International Risk and Insurance: An Environmental-Managerial Approach* (Boston: Irwin/McGraw-Hill, 1998), 534. Social Security Administration, *Social Security Programs Throughout the World* (Washington, DC: U.S. Government Printing Office, 2003).

including the United States, provide retirement income benefit programs and medical care programs. Insurers offer products that complement or compete with these government-provided programs.

## Taxation

Many governments use taxation as a mechanism for accomplishing social, in addition to economic, goals. Through taxation, governments can influence populations to act or refrain from acting in certain ways. For example, governments tax tobacco heavily not only to raise revenue, but also to discourage its use. Governments also offer taxpayers reductions on taxable income for contributions made to qualified charities to encourage charitable giving.

With concern growing about public retirement systems, governments are increasingly using tax policies to encourage people to invest in and employers to provide retirement savings plans. Such tax incentives can be quite effective, and they have benefited insurers and other financial services institutions because of the increased demand for private retirement savings products.

## Key Terms

life insurance policy 4
term life insurance 4
cash value life insurance 4
cash value 4
endowment insurance 4
annuity contract 4
health insurance policy 4
medical expense coverage 4
disability income coverage 4
individual insurance policy 4
group insurance policy 4
profit 3
sole proprietorship 3
partnership 3
corporation 3, 3 & 4
stock insurance company 5
mutual insurance company 5
fraternal benefit society 6
financial institution 7
financial services industry 7
life and health insurance company 7
property/casualty insurance company 7
financial intermediary 8
convergence 3 8

Gramm-Leach-Bliley (GLB) Act 8
consolidation 10
solvent 11
federal system 11
legislative branch 13
executive branch 13
judicial branch 13
McCarran-Ferguson Act 12
state insurance department 13
National Association of Insurance Commissioners (NAIC) 13
model bill 13
assets 14
liabilities 14
owners' equity 14
capital 14
surplus 14
Annual Statement 14
domestic insurer 15
foreign insurer 15
life and health guaranty association 15
market conduct laws 15
policy form 17
social insurance program 18

## Endnotes

1. This section is adapted from Mary C. Bickley, *Principles of Financial Services and Products* (Atlanta: LOMA, © 2004), 1–24. Used with permission; all rights reserved.
2. P.L. 106-102 (1999).
3. CLHIA, *Canadian Life and Health Insurance Facts,* 2003 ed. (Toronto: Canadian Life and Health Insurance Association Inc., 2003), 5.
4. ACLI, *Life Insurers Fact Book: 2004* (Washington, D.C.: American Council of Life Insurers, 2004), 5.
5. 15 U.S.C. 1011 *et seq.* (2001).
6. 15 U.S.C. 41 *et seq.* (2001).
7. 15 U.S.C. 1681 *et seq.* (2001).
8. 29 U.S.C. 1001 *et seq.* (2001).
9. P.L. 107-56 (2001).
10. P.L. 107-204 (2002).

# Introduction to Risk and Insurance

## objectives

*After reading this chapter, you should be able to*

- Distinguish between speculative risk and pure risk

- List several ways to manage financial risk

- Identify the five characteristics of insurable risks

- Define antiselection and give examples of two factors that can increase or decrease the likelihood that an individual will suffer a loss

- Define insurable interest and determine in a given situation whether the insurable interest requirement is met

All insurance provides protection against some of the financial consequences of loss. Thus, insurance meets part of individuals' and businesses' need for financial security. The insurance industry constantly designs, modifies, and updates insurance products to meet various aspects of this need. Despite these product changes, the underlying purpose of insurance products remains the same: to provide protection against the risk of financial loss. To understand insurance and how it works, you need to understand the concept of risk and which types of risk are insurable.

## The Concept of Risk

Risk exists when there is uncertainty about the future. Both individuals and businesses experience two kinds of risk—speculative risk and pure risk. *Speculative risk* involves three possible outcomes: loss, gain, or no change. For example, when you purchase shares of stock, you are speculating that the value of the stock will rise and that you will earn a profit on your investment. At the same time, you know that the value of the stock could fall and that you could lose some or all of the money you invested. Finally, you know that the value of the stock could remain the same—you might not lose money, but you might not make a profit.

*Pure risk* involves no possibility of gain; either a loss occurs or no loss occurs. An example of pure risk is the possibility that you may become disabled. If you do become disabled, you will experience a financial loss resulting from lost income and/or the costs incurred in your medical care. If, on the other hand, you never become disabled, then you will incur no loss from that risk. This possibility of financial loss without the possibility of gain—pure risk—is the only kind of risk that can be insured. The purpose of insurance is to compensate for financial loss, not to provide an opportunity for financial gain.

**Example:** Marie and Joseph Patterson are both employed full time. They have used $10,000 of their savings to purchase stock in a growing software company. They believe that the software company is strong and that their investment will soon be worth a lot more than $10,000.

**Analysis:** The Pattersons' investment in a software company is an example of speculative risk. As a result of their investment, the Pattersons may gain financially or they may lose part or all of their investment. The Pattersons are also faced with the pure risk that one or both of them could die and their family would lose the income that they now earn.

# Risk Management

We are surrounded by risks. We take risks when we travel, when we engage in recreational activities, even when we breathe. Some risks are significant; others are not. When we decide to leave an umbrella at home, we take the risk that we might get wet in a rain shower. Such a risk is insignificant. But what about the risks in the following situations?

- Ryan McGill is a 23-year-old single man who is working his way through college with part-time jobs. What if he becomes ill and requires a long hospital stay and expensive medical treatment?

- Danielle and John Peret are working parents of two school-aged children. What if either Danielle or John becomes disabled and cannot work to support the family?

- Jack and Jean Grayson own and manage a convenience store. What if a fire damages their building?

- The Widget Software Development Company's product development process depends on the genius of two employees who are computer whizzes. What happens to the company if one or both of them dies?

- Catherine Walker is an artist who supports herself by selling her artwork. What happens when she retires and her income is no longer sufficient to meet her financial needs?

In each situation, the individual, family, or business can use risk management to control the level of financial risk it faces. Risk management involves identifying and assessing the risks we face. Four risk management techniques that people and businesses can use to eliminate or reduce their exposure to financial risk are (1) avoiding the risk, (2) controlling the risk, (3) accepting the risk, and (4) transferring the risk.

## Avoiding Risk

The first, and perhaps most obvious, method of managing risk is simply to avoid risk altogether. We can avoid the risk of personal injury that may result from an airplane crash by not riding in an airplane, and we can avoid the risk of financial loss in the stock market by not investing in it. Sometimes, however, avoiding risk is not effective or practical.

## Controlling Risk

We can try to control risk by taking steps to prevent or reduce losses. For instance, Jack and Jean Grayson in one of our earlier examples could reduce the likelihood of a fire in their convenience store by banning smoking in their building and not storing boxes or papers near the building. In addition, the Graysons could install smoke detectors and a sprinkler system in their building to lessen the extent of damage likely to result from a fire. In these ways, the Graysons are attempting to control risk by reducing the likelihood of a loss and lessening the severity of a potential loss.

## Accepting Risk

A third method of managing risk is to accept, or retain, risk. Simply stated, to accept a risk is to assume all financial responsibility for that risk. Sometimes, as in the case of an insignificant risk—losing an umbrella—the financial loss is not great enough to warrant much concern. We assume the cost of replacing the umbrella ourselves. Some people consciously choose to accept more significant risks. For instance, a couple like Danielle and John Peret from one of the previous examples may decide not to purchase disability income insurance because they believe they can reduce their standard of living if one of them becomes disabled.

Individuals and businesses sometimes decide to accept total responsibility for a given financial risk rather than purchasing insurance to cover the risk. In this situation, the person or business is said to self-insure against the risk. *Self-insurance* is a risk-management technique by which a person or business accepts financial responsibility for losses associated with specific risks. For example, many employers provide a benefit plan that pays all or part of their employees' medical expenses. An employer can self-insure such a benefit plan by either setting aside money to pay employees' medical expenses or paying those expenses out of its current income.

Another option is that individuals and businesses can accept only part of a risk. For instance, an employer can partially self-insure a medical expense benefit plan by paying its employees' medical expenses up to a stated amount and buying insurance to cover all expenses in excess of that stated amount. Many employers now use self-insurance to fund their employees' health insurance plans.

## Transferring Risk

Transferring risk is a fourth method of risk management. When you transfer risk to another party, you are shifting the financial responsibility for that risk to the other party, generally in exchange for a fee. The most common way for individuals, families, and businesses to transfer risk is to purchase insurance coverage.

When an insurance company agrees to provide a person or a business with insurance coverage, the insurer issues an insurance policy. The *policy* is a written document that contains the terms of the agreement between the insurance company and the owner of the policy. The policy is a legally enforceable contract under which the insurance company agrees to pay a certain amount of money—known as the **policy benefit**, or the *policy proceeds*—when a specific loss occurs, provided that the insurer has received a specified amount of money, called the **premium**.

In general, individuals and businesses can purchase insurance policies to cover three types of risk: personal risk, property damage risk, and liability risk.

- **Personal risk** includes the risk of economic loss associated with death, poor health, and outliving one's savings. As noted in Chapter 1, life and health insurance companies issue and sell products that insure against financial losses that result from the personal risks of death, disability, illness, accident, and outliving one's savings.

- *Property damage risk* includes the risk of economic loss to your automobile, home, or personal belongings due to accident, theft, fire, or natural disaster. *Property insurance* provides a benefit if insured items are damaged or lost because of various specified perils, such as fire, theft, or accident.

- *Liability risk* includes the risk of economic loss resulting from your being held responsible for harming others or their property. For example, you can be held liable for damage you cause to another person's vehicle in an automobile accident. A business can be held liable for injury to an individual who slips and falls while walking through the business establishment. *Liability insurance* provides a benefit payable on behalf of a covered party who is legally responsible for unintentionally harming others or their property. Property insurance and liability insurance (also referred to as *property and casualty insurance*) are commonly marketed together in one policy. In the United States, insurers that issue and sell insurance policies to provide financial security from property damage risk and liability risk are known as *property/casualty insurance companies* or *property and liability insurers*. In most countries other than the United States, insurance generally is classified as either *life insurance* or *nonlife insurance*.

## FAST FACT

During 2003, people in the United States purchased $2.9 trillion in new life insurance coverage.

Source: ACLI, *Life Insurers Fact Book: 2004* (Washington, D.C.: American Council of Life Insurers, 2004), 81.

# Managing Personal Risks Through Insurance

You may wonder how an insurance company can afford to be financially responsible for the economic risks of its insureds. Insurers use a concept known as *risk pooling*. With risk pooling, individuals who face the uncertainty of a particular loss—for example, the loss of income because of a disability—transfer this risk to an insurance company. Insurance companies know that not everyone who is issued a disability income policy will suffer a disability. In reality, only a small percentage of the individuals insured by this type of policy will actually become disabled at some time during the period of insurance coverage. By collecting premiums from all individuals and businesses that wish to transfer the financial risk of disability, insurers spread the cost of the few losses that are expected to occur among all the insured persons. Insurance, then, provides protection against the risk of economic loss by applying a simple principle:

> If the economic losses that actually result from a given peril, such as disability, can be shared by large numbers of people who are all subject to the risk of such losses *and* the probability of loss is relatively small for each person, then the cost to each person will be relatively small.

## Characteristics of Insurable Risks

Insurance products are designed in accordance with some basic principles that define which risks are insurable. For a risk—a potential loss—to be considered insurable, it must have certain characteristics.

1. The loss must occur by *chance*.

2. The loss must be *definite*.

3. The loss must be *significant*.

4. The loss rate must be *predictable*.

5. The loss must *not* be *catastrophic* to the insurer.

These five basic characteristics, which are depicted in Figure 2.1, define an insurable risk and form the foundation of the business of insurance. A potential loss that does not have these characteristics generally is not considered an insurable risk.

### The Loss Must Occur by Chance

For a potential loss to be insurable, the element of chance must be present. The loss should be caused either by an unexpected event or by an event that is not intentionally caused by the person covered by the insurance. For example, people cannot generally control whether they will become seriously ill; as a result, insurers can offer medical expense insurance policies to protect against financial losses caused by the chance event that an insured person will become ill and incur medical expenses.

When this principle of loss is applied in its strictest sense to life insurance, an apparent problem arises: death is certain to occur. The *timing* of an individual's death, however, is usually out of the individual's control. Therefore, although the event being insured against—death—is a certain event rather than a chance event, the timing of that event usually occurs by chance.

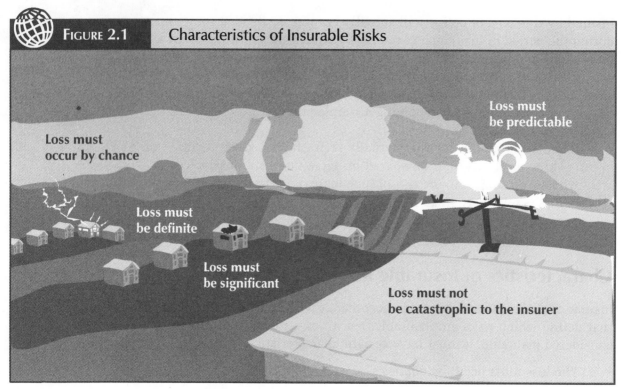

FIGURE 2.1 — Characteristics of Insurable Risks

## The Loss Must Be Definite

For most types of insurance, an insurable loss must be definite in terms of *time* and *amount*. In other words, the insurer must be able to determine *when* to pay policy benefits and *how much* those benefits should be. Death, illness, disability, and old age are generally identifiable conditions. The amount of financial loss resulting from these conditions, however, can be subject to interpretation.

One of the important terms of the contractual agreement between an insurance company and the owner of an insurance policy is the amount of policy benefit that will be payable if a covered loss occurs while the policy is in force. Depending on the way in which a policy states the amount of the policy benefit, every insurance policy can be classified as being either a contract of indemnity or a valued contract. A **contract of indemnity** is an insurance policy under which the amount of the policy benefit payable for a covered loss is based on the actual amount of financial loss that results from the loss, as determined at the time of loss. The policy states that the amount of the benefit is equal to the amount of the covered financial loss or a maximum amount stated in the contract, whichever is *less*. When the owner of such a contract submits a **claim**—a request for payment under the terms of the policy—the benefit paid by the insurance company will not be greater than the actual amount of the financial loss.

Many types of medical expense insurance policies pay a benefit based on the actual cost of a person's covered medical expenses and, as such, are contracts of indemnity. For example, assume that Bailey Smythe is insured by a policy that states the maximum amount payable to cover Bailey's medical expenses while he is hospitalized. If Bailey is hospitalized and his actual hospital expenses are less than that maximum amount, the insurer will *not* pay the stated maximum; instead, the insurer will pay a sum that is based on the actual amount of Bailey's hospital bill. Property and liability insurance policies are also contracts of indemnity.

A *valued contract* specifies the amount of the policy benefit that will be payable when a covered loss occurs, regardless of the actual amount of the loss that was incurred. Most life insurance policies state the amount of the policy benefit that will be payable if the insured person dies while the policy is in force. For example, if a woman buys a $50,000 term insurance policy on her life, the $50,000 policy benefit is listed in the policy. The amount of the policy benefit is called the policy's *face amount* or *face value* because this amount is generally listed on the face, or first, page of the policy. Some life insurance policies provide that the amount of the policy benefit may change over the life of the policy. These policies are still considered valued contracts because changes in the amount of the policy benefit are based on factors that are not directly related to the amount of the actual loss that will result from the insured's death.

## The Loss Must Be Significant

As described earlier, insignificant losses, such as the loss of an umbrella, are not normally insured. The administrative expense of paying benefits when a very small loss occurs would drive the cost for such insurance protection so high in relation to the amount of the potential loss that most people would find the protection unaffordable.

On the other hand, some losses would cause financial hardship to most people and are considered to be insurable. For example, a person injured in an accident may lose a significant amount of income if he is unable to work. Insurance coverage is available to protect against such a potential loss.

## The Loss Rate Must Be Predictable

To provide a specific type of insurance coverage, an insurer must be able to predict the probable rate of loss—the *loss rate*—that the people insured by the coverage will experience. To predict the loss rate for a given group of insureds, the insurer must predict the number and timing of covered losses that will occur in that group of insureds. An insurer predicts the loss rate for a group of insureds so that it can determine the proper premium amount to charge the owner of each policy.

No one can predict the losses that a specific person will experience. We do not know when a specific person will die, become disabled, or need hospitalization. However, insurers can predict with a fairly high degree of accuracy the number of people in a given large group who will die, become disabled, or need hospitalization during a given period of time.

These predictions of future losses are based on the concept that, even though individual events—such as the death of a particular person—occur randomly, we can use observations of past events to determine the likelihood—or *probability*—that a given event will occur in the future. An important concept that helps assure us of the accuracy of our predictions about the probability of an event occurring is the law of large numbers.

> The *law of large numbers* states that, typically, the more times we observe a particular event, the more likely it is that our observed results will approximate the "true" probability that the event will occur.

For example, if you toss a coin that has a representation of a person's head on one side, there is a 50-50 probability that the coin will land with the heads side up; this is a calculable probability. Four, or even a dozen, tosses might not give the result of an equal or approximately equal number of heads and tails—the other side of the coin—landing face up. If you tossed the coin 1,000 times, though, in approximately 50 percent of the tosses, the coin will land with the head side up; the other 50 percent of the coin tosses are likely to land on tails. The more often you toss the coin, the more likely it is that you will observe an approximately equal proportion of heads and tails and, thus, the more likely that your findings will approximate the "true" probability.

Insurance companies rely on the law of large numbers when they make predictions about the covered losses that a given group of insureds is likely to experience during a given time period. Insurance companies collect specific information about large numbers of people so they can identify the pattern of losses that those people experienced. For many years, for example, U.S. life insurance companies have recorded how many of their insureds have died and how old they were when they died. Insurance companies then compare this information with the general population records of the United States, noting the ages at which people in the general population had died.

Using these statistical records, insurance companies have been able to develop charts—called *mortality tables*—that indicate with great accuracy the number of people in a large group (100,000 people or more) who are likely to die at each age. Mortality tables display the *rates of mortality*, or incidence of death, by age, among a given group of people. Insurance companies have developed similar charts, called *morbidity tables*, which display the *rates of morbidity*, or incidence of sickness and accidents, by age, occurring among a given group of people. By using accurate mortality and morbidity tables, life and health insurers can predict the probable loss rates for given groups of insureds; insurers use those predicted loss rates to establish premium rates that will be adequate to pay claims.

## The Loss Must Not Be Catastrophic to the Insurer

A potential loss is not considered insurable if a single occurrence is likely to cause or contribute to catastrophic financial damage to the insurer. Such a loss is not insurable because the insurer could not responsibly promise to pay benefits for the loss. To prevent the possibility of catastrophic loss and ensure that losses occur independently of each other, insurers spread the risks they choose to insure. For example, a property insurer would be unwise to issue policies covering all homes within a 50-mile radius of an active volcano because one eruption of the volcano could result in more claims at one time than the insurer could pay. Instead, the insurer would also issue policies covering homes in areas not threatened by the volcano.

Alternatively, an insurer can reduce the possibility that it will suffer catastrophic losses by transferring risks to another insurer. An insurer transfers risks to another insurer by reinsuring those risks. **Reinsurance** is insurance that one insurance company—known as the **ceding company**—purchases from another insurance company—known as the **reinsurer**—to transfer risks on insurance policies that the ceding company issued. To **cede** insurance business is to obtain reinsurance on that business by transferring all or part of the risk to a reinsurer. A life insurance company typically sets a maximum amount of insurance—known as its **retention limit**—that the insurer is willing to carry at its own risk on any one life without transferring some of the risk to a reinsurer.

Some insurance companies act only as reinsurers. Other insurance companies issue policies directly to people and businesses as well as act as reinsurers. A reinsurer also sometimes cedes risks to another reinsurer in a transaction known as a **retrocession**. The reinsurance company that accepts the risk in a retrocession is known as a *retrocessionaire*. An example can help illustrate a reinsurance transaction. Note, however, that there are many different types of reinsurance transactions, and this is only one example. Figure 2.2 illustrates the example.

**Example:** The Alpha Life Insurance Company has established a retention limit of $250,000. Alpha has entered into a reinsurance agreement with the Celtic Reinsurance Company. Under the terms of the reinsurance agreement, when Alpha issues a life insurance policy with a face amount that exceeds its retention limit, the amount in excess of the retention limit is automatically ceded to Celtic. Similarly, Celtic has a retention limit of $500,000. Alpha recently issued a $1,250,000 policy to Norma Olson.

**Analysis:** As a result of the reinsurance agreement, $1,000,000 of the coverage Alpha issued Norma will be ceded to Celtic. Celtic will in turn cede $500,000 of the coverage to a retrocessionaire. If Norma dies while the policy is in force, Alpha will pay the policy benefit of $1,250,000; Celtic will reimburse Alpha for $1,000,000 of the policy benefit payable; and the retrocessionaire will reimburse Celtic for $500,000 of the policy benefit payable.

By setting a retention limit and entering into a reinsurance agreement, an insurer can issue policies that have relatively large face amounts without exposing itself to an excessive amount of risk. The owners of policies that have been reinsured generally are not aware of the reinsurance agreement between the insurer and the reinsurer. The insurance company that issued the policy collects the premiums and pays the policy benefits to the proper recipient when due.

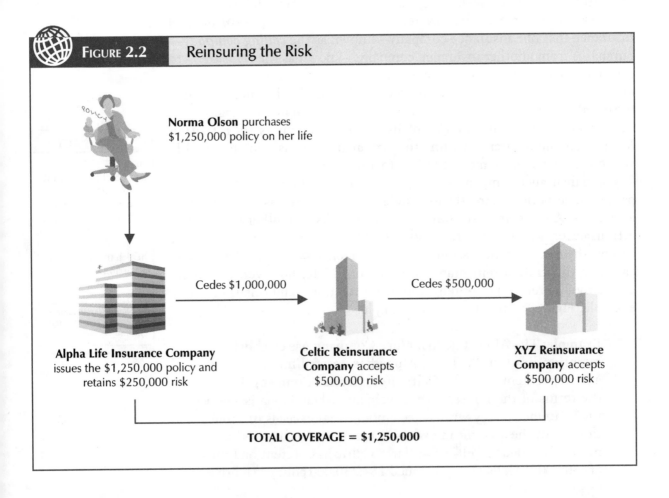

**FIGURE 2.2** — **Reinsuring the Risk**

**Norma Olson** purchases $1,250,000 policy on her life

Cedes $1,000,000

Cedes $500,000

**Alpha Life Insurance Company** issues the $1,250,000 policy and retains $250,000 risk

**Celtic Reinsurance Company** accepts $500,000 risk

**XYZ Reinsurance Company** accepts $500,000 risk

**TOTAL COVERAGE = $1,250,000**

# Insurability of Specific Risks

The five characteristics we just described are useful in identifying the general kinds of losses that are insurable and provide a helpful framework for the study of insurance principles and products. But, as you will learn, insurance is sold on a case-by-case basis, and insurers consider a number of factors when they determine whether a proposed risk is an insurable risk. Before we describe some of these factors, you need to understand the terminology we use throughout the text to describe the people who are involved in the creation and operation of an insurance policy.

The **applicant** is the person or business that applies for an insurance policy. When a policy is issued, the person or business that owns the insurance policy is known as the **policyowner**. In most cases, the applicant is also the policyowner. The **insured** is the person whose life or health is insured under the policy. Terminology varies somewhat from country to country. For example, in most of Canada the person insured by a life insurance policy is known as the *life insured*. In some countries, the term *assured* is used to refer to the person insured.

The policyowner and the insured of an individual insurance policy may be, and often are, the same person. If, for example, you apply for and are issued an insurance policy on your life, then you are both the policyowner and the insured and may be known as the *policyowner-insured*. If, however, your mother applies for and is issued a policy on your life, then she is the policyowner and you are the insured. When one person purchases an individual insurance policy on the life of another person, the policy is known as a **third-party policy**.

If the event insured against occurs while the insurance policy is in force, the insurer pays the policy benefit. Life insurance policy proceeds are usually paid to the policy's **beneficiary**—the person or party the policyowner named to receive the policy benefit. Health insurance policy benefits usually are paid either to the insured person or to the hospital, doctor, or medical care provider that provided the covered medical care services to the insured.

## Assessing the Degree of Risk

When an insurance company receives an application for insurance, the company must assess the degree of risk it will accept if it agrees to issue the policy. An insurance company cannot afford to presume that each proposed risk represents an average likelihood of loss. Not all individuals of the same sex and age have an equal likelihood of suffering a loss. Further, those individuals who believe they have a greater-than-average likelihood of loss tend to seek insurance protection to a greater extent than do those who believe they have an average or a less-than-average likelihood of loss. This tendency, which is called **antiselection**, *adverse selection*, or *selection* *against the insurer*, is a primary reason that insurers need to carefully review each application to assess properly the degree of risk the company will be assuming if it issues the requested policy. As we discuss more fully later in this text, the premium rates that an insurance company establishes are based in large part on the amount of risk the company is assuming for the policies it issues. If the insurer consistently underestimates the risks that it assumes, its premium rates will be inadequate to provide the promised benefits.

The process of identifying and classifying the degree of risk represented by a proposed insured is called **underwriting** or *selection of risks*, and the insurance company employees who are responsible for evaluating proposed risks are called **underwriters**. Underwriting consists of two primary stages: (1) identifying the risks that a proposed insured presents and (2) classifying the degree of risk that a proposed insured represents.

## Identifying Risks

Although it is not possible to predict when a specific individual will die, become injured, or suffer from an illness, insurers have identified a number of factors that can increase or decrease the likelihood that an individual will suffer a loss. The most important of these factors are *physical hazards* and *moral hazards*. A **physical hazard** is a physical characteristic that may increase the likelihood of loss. For example, a person with a history of heart attacks possesses a physical hazard that increases the likelihood that the person will die sooner than a person of the same age and sex who does not have a similar medical history. A person who is overweight has a physical characteristic that is known to contribute to health problems, and those health problems may result in the economic loss associated with higher-than-average medical expenses. Underwriters must carefully evaluate proposed insureds to detect the presence of such physical hazards.

Underwriters also must consider the effects of moral hazards on the degree of risk represented by a proposed insured. **Moral hazard** is a characteristic that exists when the reputation, financial position, or criminal record of an applicant or a proposed insured indicates that the person may act dishonestly in the insurance transaction. For example, an individual who has a confirmed record of illegal or unethical behavior is likely to behave similarly in an insurance transaction, and an insurer must carefully consider that fact when evaluating such an individual's application for insurance. The individual may be seeking insurance for financial gain rather than as protection against a financial loss. Underwriters also evaluate the moral hazards presented by individuals who provide false information on their applications for insurance. In these cases, the applicants may be trying to obtain insurance coverage that they might not otherwise be able to obtain. When underwriters evaluate applications for insurance, they take a variety of steps to identify proposed insureds who present these moral hazards.

## Classifying Risks

After identifying the risks presented by a proposed insured, the underwriter can classify the proposed insured into an appropriate risk class. A *risk class* is a grouping of insureds who represent a similar level of risk to the insurer. Classifying risks into classes enables the insurer to determine the equitable premium rate to charge for the requested coverage. People in different risk classes are charged different premium rates. Without these premium rate variations, some policyowners would be charged too much for their coverage, while others would be paying less than the actual cost of their coverage. We describe pricing in detail in Chapter 4.

To classify proposed insureds, underwriters apply general rules of risk selection, known as **underwriting guidelines**, established by the insurer. Life insurers' underwriting guidelines generally identify at least four risk classes for proposed insureds: *standard risks, preferred risks, substandard risks,* and *declined risks.*

- Proposed insureds who have a likelihood of loss that is not significantly greater than average are classified as **standard risks**, and the premium rates they are charged are called **standard premium rates**. Traditionally, most individual life and health insurance policies have been issued at standard premium rates.

- Proposed insureds who present a significantly less-than-average likelihood of loss are classified as **preferred risks**; premiums rates charged for such risks are lower-than-standard premium rates. Insurance company practices vary widely as to what qualifies a proposed insured as a preferred risk or a standard risk. As one example, some insurers categorize their standard risks into two risk classifications based on their smoking habits. Insureds who otherwise present a standard risk and are nonsmokers are classified as preferred risks and are charged less-than-standard premium rates; insureds who otherwise present a standard risk but who smoke are classified as standard risks and are charged standard premium rates. Some life insurers also have established a *super-preferred risk* classification that includes people who present an even lower level of risk than those who are classified as preferred risks.

- Those proposed insureds who have a significantly greater-than-average likelihood of loss but are still found to be insurable are classified as **substandard risks** or *special class risks*. Insurance companies use several methods to compensate for the additional risk presented by insureds who are classified as substandard risks. In individual life insurance, insurers typically charge substandard risks a higher-than-standard premium rate, called a **substandard premium rate** or *special class rate*. In individual health insurance, insurers may either charge a substandard premium rate or modify the policy in some way—such as by excluding a particular risk from coverage—to compensate for the greater risk.

- The **declined risk** category consists of those proposed insureds who are considered to present a risk that is too great for the insurer to cover. Applicants for disability income insurance coverage are also placed into the declined risk category if the insurer believes that the coverage is not needed to cover any income loss that would result from a disability.

## Insurable Interest Requirement

As noted earlier, only pure risks are insurable; insurance is intended to compensate an individual or a business for a financial loss, not to provide an opportunity for gain. At one time, people used insurance policies as a means of making wagers. For example, they purchased insurance policies on the lives of people who were completely unrelated to them and, in that way, created a possibility of financial gain for themselves if the insured people died.

The practice of purchasing insurance as a wager is now considered to be against public policy. As a result, laws in the United States and many countries require that, when an insurance policy is issued, the policyowner must have an **insurable interest** in the risk that is insured—the policyowner must be likely to suffer a genuine loss or detriment should the event insured against occur. For example, a property insurer would not sell a fire insurance policy on a particular building to a person who does not own the building because that person would not suffer an economic loss if the building were destroyed by fire. In property insurance, ownership of property is one way in which an insurable interest in the property is established.

### The Insurable Interest Requirement in Life Insurance

The presence of insurable interest must be established for every life insurance policy to ensure that the insurance contract is not formed as an illegal wagering agreement. If the insurable interest requirement is not met *when a policy is issued*, the policy is not valid. The presence of an insurable interest for life insurance usually can be found by applying the following general rule:

> An insurable interest exists when the policyowner is likely to benefit if the insured continues to live and is likely to suffer some loss or detriment if the insured dies.

Underwriters screen every application for life insurance to make sure that the insurable interest requirement imposed by law in the applicable jurisdiction will be met when the policy is issued. In other words, the insurer must determine whether the person who will be the owner of the life insurance policy—typically, the applicant for insurance—has an insurable interest in the proposed insured. If the insurer determines that the proposed policyowner does not meet the insurable interest requirement, then the insurer will not issue the policy.

In addition, each insurance company screens all applications to ensure they meet the company's own underwriting guidelines, which frequently include insurable interest requirements that go beyond the requirements imposed by law. Thus, even if the insurable interest requirement imposed by the applicable jurisdiction is met, an insurer can refuse to issue the policy if its own, more stringent insurable interest requirements are not met.

To understand how insurable interest requirements are met, we need to consider two possible situations: (1) an individual purchases insurance on her own life and (2) an individual purchases insurance on another's life. In both cases, the applicant for life insurance must name a beneficiary. Let's look at each of these situations.

All persons are considered to have an insurable interest in their own lives. A person is always considered to have more to gain by living than by dying. Therefore, an insurable interest between the policyowner and the insured is presumed when a person seeks to purchase insurance on her own life. Insurable interest laws do not require that the named beneficiary have an insurable interest in the policyowner-insured's life. In other words, the laws allow a policyowner-insured to name anyone as beneficiary.

Most insurance company underwriting guidelines, however, require that the beneficiary also must have an insurable interest in the life of the insured when a policy is issued. As a result, life insurers typically inquire into the named beneficiary's relationship to the proposed insured and may refuse to issue the coverage if the beneficiary does not possess an insurable interest in the proposed insured's life. An exception exists in the state of California, where laws now prohibit insurers from declining to issue a life insurance policy solely because the named beneficiary has no insurable interest in the proposed policyowner-insured's life.

In the case of a third-party policy, laws in many countries and in most states in the United States require only that the policyowner have an insurable interest in the insured's life when the policy is issued. Most insurance company underwriting guidelines and the laws in some states, however, require both the policyowner and the beneficiary of a third-party policy to have an insurable interest in the insured's life when the policy is issued.

Certain family relationships are assumed by law to create an insurable interest between an insured and a policyowner or beneficiary. The natural bonds of affection and financial dependence that generally exist between certain family members make this a reasonable assumption. In these cases, even if the policyowner or beneficiary has no financial interest in the insured's life, the bonds of love and affection alone are sufficient to create an insurable interest. According to laws in most jurisdictions, the insured's spouse, mother, father, child, grandparent, grandchild, brother, and sister are deemed to have an insurable interest in the life of the insured. (See Figure 2.3, which illustrates the family relationships that create an insurable interest.)

An insurable interest is *not* presumed when the policyowner or beneficiary is more distantly related to the insured than the relatives previously described or when the parties are not related by blood or marriage. In these cases, a financial interest in the continued life of the insured must be demonstrated to satisfy the insurable interest requirement. For instance, assume that Mary Mulhouse obtained a $50,000 personal loan from the Lone Star Bank of Vermont. If Mary dies before repaying the loan, the bank could lose some or all of the money it lent her. Thus, the bank has a financial and, consequently, an insurable interest in Mary's life. Similar examples of financial interest can be found in other business relationships.

The insurable interest requirement must be met before a life insurance policy will be issued. After the life insurance policy is in force, the presence or absence of insurable interest is no longer relevant. Therefore, a beneficiary need not provide evidence of insurable interest to receive the benefits of a life insurance policy.

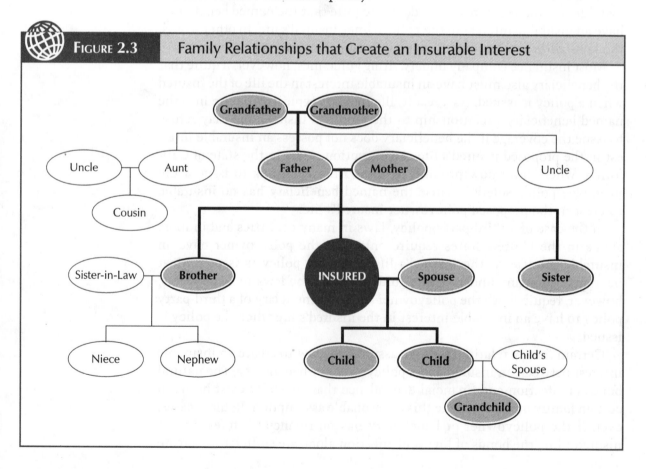

FIGURE 2.3    Family Relationships that Create an Insurable Interest

## The Insurable Interest Requirement in Health Insurance

The insurable interest requirement also must be met when a health insurance policy is issued. For health insurance purposes, the insurable interest requirement is met if the applicant can demonstrate a genuine risk of economic loss should the proposed insured require medical care or become disabled. Because of the nature of health insurance, applicants rarely seek health insurance on someone in whom they have no insurable interest. Typically, people seek health insurance for themselves and for their dependents. As a contract of indemnity, a health insurance policy provides coverage to pay for medical expenses that the insured has incurred or to replace a disabled insured's lost income. Applicants are generally considered to have an insurable interest in their own health. Additionally, for disability income insurance purposes, businesses have an insurable interest in the health of their key employees.

**Example:** Image, Inc., is a small company that contracts with other companies to conduct seminars for their management staffs. Sarah Smithers works for Image, Inc., as its primary seminar leader. Because Sarah's expertise and teaching skills are essential to the success of the business, Image, Inc., has applied for disability income coverage on Sarah.

**Analysis:** Image, Inc., would be unable to meet its scheduled seminar commitments if Sarah were ill or injured and, thus, unable to conduct seminars. As a result, Image, Inc., has a financial interest in Sarah's continued good health. This financial interest creates the necessary insurable interest for Image, Inc., to purchase disability income coverage on Sarah.

## Key Terms

speculative risk  23
pure risk  23
self-insurance  25
policy  25
policy benefit  26
premium  26
personal risk  26
contract of indemnity  28
claim  28
valued contract  29
face amount  29
probability  30
law of large numbers  30
mortality tables  30
morbidity tables  30
reinsurance  31
ceding company  31
reinsurer  31
cede  31
retention limit  31

retrocession  31
applicant  33
policyowner  33
insured  33
third-party policy  33
beneficiary  33
antiselection  33
underwriting  34
underwriter  34
physical hazard  34
moral hazard  34
risk class  35
underwriting guidelines  35
standard risk  35
standard premium rate  35
preferred risk  35
substandard risk  35
substandard premium rate  35
declined risk  36
insurable interest  36

# The Insurance Policy

## objectives

*After reading this chapter, you should be able to*

- Distinguish between a formal and an informal contract, between a bilateral and a unilateral contract, between a commutative and an aleatory contract, and between a contract of adhesion and a bargaining contract, and identify which of these types of contracts an insurance contract represents

- Define valid contract, void contract, and voidable contract, and identify the legal effect of each type of contract

- Identify the four requirements for the creation of a valid informal contract and how each of these requirements can be met in the formation of an insurance contract

- Identify the property rights that a policyowner has in the insurance policy he owns

L ife and health insurance companies market insurance products to both individuals and groups. In each case, an insurance policy is the physical evidence that an individual or organization has purchased some type of insurance coverage. As noted in Chapter 1, an *individual insurance policy* is an insurance policy that is issued to insure the life or health of a named person. Some individual policies also insure the person's immediate family or a second named person. A *group insurance policy* is a policy issued to insure the lives or health of a specific group of people. For example, most group insurance policies are purchased by employers to provide life or health insurance coverage to their employees and, sometimes, to the dependents of covered employees.

In this chapter, we describe several aspects of the insurance policy. First, we describe the policy as a contract and the requirements that the parties must meet to enter into a valid insurance contract. Then, we describe the policy as a type of property in which the policyowner gains valuable ownership rights. Unless noted otherwise, the information presented in this chapter applies to both individual and group insurance policies.

## Fundamentals of Contract Law

Before any insurance policy is purchased, the applicant for insurance and the insurance company must reach an agreement; the applicant must agree to buy the insurance coverage from the company, and the company must agree to issue that coverage. The applicant and the insurance company also must agree on the price to be paid for the coverage and the policy benefits that will be payable by the insurer. The policy describes the terms of their agreement.

An insurance policy represents a special kind of agreement known as a contract. A **contract** is a legally enforceable agreement between two or more parties. The two parties to an individual life or health insurance contract are the insurance company that issued the policy and the individual who owns the policy, known as the *policyowner*. The parties to a group insurance contract are the insurer that issued the policy and the **group policyholder**, which is the person or organization that decides what types of group insurance coverage to purchase for the group members, negotiates the terms of the insurance contract, and purchases the group insurance coverage.

The fact that a contract is legally enforceable means that the parties are bound to carry out the promises they made when entering into the contract. If a party does not carry out its promise, then that party has breached the contract. Laws provide an innocent party with remedies for losses resulting from a breach of contract. A huge body of contract law has developed over the years to define which promises are legally enforceable and what remedies are available to enforce those promises.

In Chapter 2, we described contracts of indemnity and valued contracts and noted that health insurance policies typically are contracts of indemnity and life insurance policies are valued contracts. Contracts may be categorized in several other ways, which we describe in this section. We also describe the requirements imposed by law on the formation of contracts.

## Types of Contracts

Each country has a legal system, which includes the specific laws that regulate conduct and the legal process by which those laws are enforced. Insight 3.1 describes the primary types of legal systems that exist around the world. Each legal system recognizes many types of contracts and includes rules that govern each type of contract. In this section, we identify just a few of the many types of contracts recognized by the common law system in the United States. Although differences exist in the laws of common law systems and other types of legal systems, the principles of law typically are similar.

### Formal and Informal Contracts

Contracts are either formal or informal. A ***formal contract*** is one that is enforceable because the parties to the contract met certain formalities concerning the form of the agreement. These formalities generally require that the contract be in writing and that the written document contain some form of seal in order to be enforceable. Today, only a very few types of contracts remain formal contracts. Many countries, for example, treat contracts for the sale of real property as formal contracts. We describe real property later in the chapter.

Life and health insurance contracts, like almost all contracts, are informal contracts. An ***informal contract*** is a contract that is enforceable because the parties to the contract met requirements concerning the substance of the agreement rather than requirements concerning the form of the agreement. An informal contract may be expressed in either an oral or a written fashion. Writing an agreement merely provides evidence of the contract, and oral informal contracts usually are enforceable. For example, suppose you say to your neighbor, "I will pay you $35 if you will wash my windows." If your neighbor actually washes your windows, you are legally obligated to pay him the $35 even though you did not sign a written agreement. In this situation, you made an oral informal contract with your neighbor.

**INSIGHT 3.1** | Basic Types of Legal Systems

**Common law systems** are based on the common law of England and are characterized by the fact that some laws are contained in an unwritten body of general principles and rules of law developed and followed by the courts. In a common law system, these general common law principles developed by the courts supplement the laws enacted by the legislature and, thus, form a large component of the law. Although common law rules vary from country to country, many of the rules are very similar. The following are examples of common law countries: Antigua and Barbuda, Australia, Bahamas, Barbados, Bermuda, and the United Kingdom. In addition, most provinces within Canada and most states within the United States have adopted the common law system.

**Civil law systems** are based on the Roman legal system in which the laws are codified into written codes enacted by the legislature. Thus, the laws enacted by the legislature contain the general legal principles and rules of law that apply in a civil law system. The following are examples of civil law countries: Argentina, Brazil, France, Germany, Mexico, Spain, Venezuela, and Vietnam. The Canadian province of Quebec and the U.S. state of Louisiana also are civil law jurisdictions.

**Mixed legal systems** contain elements of more than one basic type of legal system.

■ In some countries, the legal system includes elements of both the common law system and the civil law system. The legal system of the Philippines, for example, is a mixture of the common law and the civil law.

■ The legal systems in many countries have been influenced by the religion of Islam. Under an **Islamic legal system**, the law is set out in the book known as the *Koran* (or *Qur'an*), and the law of the Koran is unchanging. Singapore's legal system contains elements of the common law system and Islamic law.

■ Countries with mixed legal systems sometimes include an element of **customary laws**, which are local customs that members of a community have accepted as binding on the community's members. Customs, for example, may govern the personal affairs of individuals within a community by establishing rules for marriage, separation, divorce, and adoption. The legal system of Hong Kong is a mixture of common law and customary law. The legal system of India is a mixture of common law, customary law, and Islamic law.

**Source:** Adapted from Harriett E. Jones, *Business Law for Financial Services Professionals* (Atlanta: LOMA, © 2004), 4–7. Used with permission; all rights reserved.

In theory, life and health insurance contracts, as informal contracts, could be made in either written or oral form. In some states and some countries, laws require insurance contracts to be in writing. Life and health insurance contracts typically are expressed in written form—whether required by law or not—for two practical reasons:

- Putting the contract in writing helps prevent misunderstandings between the parties as to the terms of their agreement. Life and health insurance policies must contain a number of provisions that set forth the conditions of the contract and enable the insurance company to carry out the wishes of the policyowner. Without a written policy, legal problems are likely to arise as a result of disputes between the parties as to the terms of the agreement.

- A written contract provides a permanent record of the agreement. Life and health insurance policies are often in effect for many years. The memory of someone's oral promises made many years in the past may not be reliable, even under the best circumstances.

## Bilateral and Unilateral Contracts

As noted previously, life and health insurance contracts typically are agreements entered into by two parties—the insurance company and the individual or organization that purchased the coverage. A contract between two parties may either be unilateral or bilateral. If both parties make legally enforceable promises when they enter into a contract, the contract is *bilateral*. If only one of the parties makes legally enforceable promises when the parties enter into the contract, the contract is *unilateral*.

Suppose, for example, you contract with the Backyard Aquatics Company to have the company build a swimming pool on your property for a mutually agreed-upon price. The contractor has promised to complete the construction for that price, and you have promised to pay that amount. This contract is bilateral—both you and the contractor have made legally enforceable promises.

Life and health insurance policies, on the other hand, are unilateral contracts. The insurer promises to provide coverage in return for a stated premium. As long as premiums are paid, the insurer is legally bound by its contractual promises. The purchaser of the policy, on the other hand, does not promise to pay the premiums and cannot be compelled by law to pay the premiums. A policyowner has the right to stop paying premiums and cancel the policy at any time. Because only the insurer can be legally held to its promises, life and health insurance contracts are unilateral contracts.

## Commutative and Aleatory Contracts

Contracts may also be classified as either commutative or aleatory. A *commutative contract* is an agreement under which the parties specify in advance the values that they will exchange; moreover, the parties generally exchange items or services that they think are of relatively equal value. In our earlier example, your contract with the Backyard Aquatics Company is a commutative contract. When the contract was made, you and the contractor specified the service to be provided and the price to be exchanged for that service. In essence, you agreed that the swimming pool and the price you paid for the pool were of equal value. Most contracts fall into this like-for-like exchange category and can be classified as commutative.

In an *aleatory contract*, one party provides something of value to another party in exchange for a conditional promise. A *conditional promise* is a promise to perform a stated act *if* a specified, uncertain event occurs. If the event occurs, then the promise must be performed; if the event does not occur, the promise will not be performed. Also, under an aleatory contract, if the specified event occurs, one party may then receive something of greater value than that party gave.

Life and health insurance policies are aleatory contracts. A life insurance policy is an aleatory contract because the performance of the insurer's promise to pay the policy proceeds is contingent on the death of the insured while the policy is in force, and no one can say with certainty when the person whose life is insured will die. In fact, if a policy is allowed to terminate prior to the death of the insured, the insurer's promise to pay the policy proceeds will never be performed, even if a number of premiums have been paid. Conversely, death may occur soon after a life insurance policy is issued, and the policy benefit then becomes payable. The beneficiary would, in such a case, receive substantially more money than had been paid in premiums. Similarly, a health insurance policy is an aleatory contract under which the insurer may be liable to pay a much larger sum in benefits than it received as premiums for the policy. The insurer does not know if or when it will be liable to pay health insurance policy benefits.

## Bargaining Contracts and Contracts of Adhesion

Contracts may be further classified as either bargaining contracts or contracts of adhesion. Suppose that when you made the contract with the Backyard Aquatics Company, you had several discussions with the contractor about the contents of the contract. You asked him to specify his time schedule, the materials he would use, and the way the actual construction would be accomplished. In turn, he quoted a price for each of your requirements. You and the contractor then bargained with one another to arrive at a contract agreeable to you both. This is an example of a ***bargaining contract***, one in which both parties, as equals, set the terms and conditions of the contract.

In contrast, life and health insurance policies are contracts of adhesion. A ***contract of adhesion*** is a contract that one party prepares and that the other party must accept or reject as a whole, generally without any bargaining between the parties to the agreement. While the applicant for individual life or health insurance has choices as to some of the contract provisions, generally the applicant must accept or reject the contract as the insurance company has written it. As a result, if any policy provision is ambiguous, the courts usually interpret that provision in whatever manner would be most favorable to the policyowner or beneficiary. In other words, the terms of the contract are construed against the insurance company that drafted the contract. In contrast to individual insurance policies, group insurance agreements quite often are subject to some negotiation between the parties. Nevertheless, group insurance contracts are contracts of adhesion. Figure 3.1 lists the various types of contracts and identifies which types characterize insurance contracts.

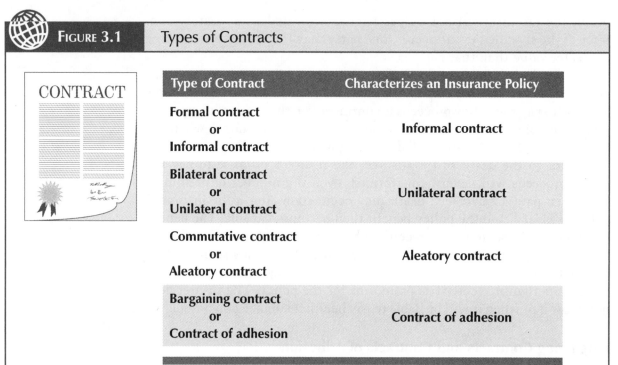

| FIGURE 3.1 | Types of Contracts |

| Type of Contract | Characterizes an Insurance Policy |
| --- | --- |
| Formal contract or Informal contract | Informal contract |
| Bilateral contract or Unilateral contract | Unilateral contract |
| Commutative contract or Aleatory contract | Aleatory contract |
| Bargaining contract or Contract of adhesion | Contract of adhesion |

## General Requirements for a Contract

The principles of contract law determine the legal status of a contract. In other words, these principles dictate whether a contract is legally enforceable and who has the right to enforce a contract. Contract law sets forth the following four general requirements that must be met for the parties to create an informal contract that is legally enforceable:

1. The parties to the contract must manifest their mutual assent to the terms of the contract.

2. The parties to the contract must have contractual capacity.

3. The parties to the contract must exchange legally adequate consideration.

4. The contract must be for a lawful purpose.

In describing the legal status of a contract, the words *valid*, *void*, and *voidable* are often used. Each of these contract terms is explained below.

- **Valid.** A ***valid contract*** is one that satisfies all legal requirements and, thus, is enforceable at law.

- **Void.** The term *void* is used in law to describe something that was never valid. A ***void contract*** is one that does not satisfy one or more of the legal requirements to create a valid contract and, thus, is never enforceable at law.

- **Voidable.** At times, one of the parties to an otherwise valid contract may have grounds to reject, or *avoid*, it. A **voidable contract** is one in which a party has the right to avoid her obligations under the contract without incurring legal liability.

In the remainder of this section, we describe the four general requirements for the formation of a valid informal contract.

## Mutual Assent

Whether a contract is made when the parties sign a written agreement or shake hands, the parties involved have agreed to something. The requirement of **mutual assent** is met when the parties reach a meeting of the minds about the terms of their agreement. For life and health insurance policies, as well as for other contracts, the parties reach this meeting of the minds through a process of *offer and acceptance* in which one party makes an offer to contract and the other party accepts that offer. For the parties to mutually assent to a contract, they must all intend to be bound by the terms of the contract. In addition, each party must clearly manifest the intent to be bound by making some outward expression of that intent.

## Contractual Capacity

For an informal contract to be binding on all parties, the parties must have **contractual capacity**—that is, they each must have the legal capacity to make a contract. To create a valid insurance contract, the insurance company must have the legal capacity to issue the policy and the applicant must have the legal capacity to purchase the policy.

### Contractual Capacity of Individuals

Every individual is presumed to have the legal capacity to enter into a valid contract. Some people, however, do not have full contractual capacity, and therefore most of the contracts they enter into are void or voidable. In most jurisdictions, most people who have limited contractual capacity either (1) are minors or (2) lack mental capacity.

A **minor** is a person who has not attained the *age of majority*—that is, the age at which a person is given by law the rights and responsibilities of an adult. Upon reaching the age of majority, a person generally has the capacity to enter into contracts. By contrast, contracts entered into by a minor are voidable by the minor. Thus, if an insurance company were to sell an insurance policy to a person who is younger than the permissible age to purchase insurance, then the company would have to provide the promised insurance protection. The minor, however, could sue to avoid the policy, and the insurance company would have to return the premiums the minor had paid on that policy. In most countries, including most states of the United States and most provinces of Canada, the age of majority is 18. Figure 3.2 lists the age of majority in some other countries.

| FIGURE 3.2 | Age of Majority in Selected Countries |

| Jurisdiction | Age of Majority |
| --- | --- |
| Argentina | 21 |
| Brazil | 18 |
| Hong Kong | 18 |
| India | 18 |
| Scotland | 16 |
| Singapore | 21 |
| Taiwan | 20 |

In many jurisdictions, the age of majority for the purpose of making life insurance contracts has been modified by law to protect insurance companies to some extent from the possibility that minors will later use their lack of legal capacity to avoid the contract. These modifications of the age of majority permit people at ages 16, 15, or even younger to purchase life and health insurance and to exercise some of a policy's ownership rights as though they were adults. In most such situations, however, the beneficiary of such a life insurance policy must be a member of the minor's immediate family.

As noted, a person's lack of mental capacity also may affect her contractual capacity. Two situations arise in which a person's mental capacity affects contractual capacity.

- A court declares a person to be insane or mentally incompetent. A contract entered into by a person who has been declared insane or incompetent is usually *void*.

- A person's mental competence is impaired, but she has not been declared insane or mentally incompetent by a court. For example, the person can be mentally impaired as a result of being drunk, drugged, or insane. Contracts entered into by someone whose mental competence is impaired are generally *voidable* by the mentally impaired person. If the person later regains mental competence, she may either reject the contract *or* require that it be carried out. The other party to the contract does not have the right to reject the contract and must carry out its terms if required to do so.

## Contractual Capacity of Organizations

As stated previously, an applicant for insurance may be either an individual or an organization that is purchasing coverage for an individual or a group. Organizations are generally presumed to have the contractual capacity of a mentally competent adult. So, an organization that has been created in accordance with the laws of the applicable jurisdiction is presumed to have contractual capacity to purchase insurance.

An insurer acquires its legal capacity to enter into an insurance contract by being licensed or authorized to do business by the proper regulatory authority. A company that is not licensed or authorized as an insurance company does not have the legal capacity to make an insurance contract. Should an unauthorized insurer issue a policy to a person who is unaware of the insurer's lack of legal capacity, the policy may be enforceable against the insurer. The legal effect of such a contract depends on the laws of the particular jurisdiction. In some jurisdictions, the contract is *void*; in other jurisdictions, the contract is *voidable* by the policyowner.

### Legally Adequate Consideration

For an informal contract to be valid, the parties to the contract must exchange **consideration**; each must give or promise something that will be of value to the other party. In addition, the consideration exchanged must be *legally adequate*. A complete description of what is considered to be legally adequate is beyond the scope of this text. In general, the courts will not concern themselves with whether the parties exchanged equal consideration; the question the courts usually focus on in such cases is whether the parties exchanged consideration that has some value to them.

The application and the **initial premium**—the first premium paid for an insurance policy—are given by the applicant as consideration for a life or health insurance contract. This consideration is given in return for the insurer's promise to pay the policy benefit if the conditions stated in the policy occur. If the initial premium is not paid, then no contract has been formed because the applicant has not provided the required consideration. **Renewal premiums**, which are premiums payable after the initial premium, are a condition for continuance of the policy and are *not* consideration for the policy.

### Lawful Purpose

No contract can be made for a purpose that is illegal or against the public interest—a contract must be made for a lawful purpose. The courts will not enforce an agreement in which one person promises to perform an illegal act, and any such contract is void. For example, unless statutes have been enacted to the contrary, gambling agreements are not enforceable at law. Also, one person cannot make a legally enforceable agreement that requires another person to do something that is in conflict with an existing law. An agreement that requires one person to kill or defraud another would not be legally enforceable.

The requirement of lawful purpose in the making of an individual life or health insurance contract is fulfilled by the presence of *insurable interest*. The primary purpose of all insurance is to protect against financial loss, not to provide a means of possible financial gain. In Chapter 2, we discussed insurable interest and its importance in insurance. The requirement that insurable interest be present at the time of application provides assurance that a life or health insurance contract is being made for the lawful purpose of providing protection against financial loss, rather than for an unlawful purpose, such as speculating on a life or profiting from ill health.

The lawful purpose requirement must be met as a condition for the *formation* of a contract. As a result, if the insurable interest requirement is not met, a valid contract was never formed and the agreement is void. Recall, however, that if the insurable interest requirement is met and the parties enter into a valid insurance contract, a continuing insurable interest is not required for the contract to remain valid.

> **Example:** When Ann Saul died, she was insured under a life insurance policy. In evaluating the death claim, the insurer discovered that the insurable interest requirement had not been met when the policy was issued.
>
> **Analysis.** The contract is void and the insurer is not required to pay the policy benefit. The insurer will likely refund all the premiums that were paid for the policy.

> **Example.** When Juan Gomez purchased an insurance policy on his life, he named his wife Lois as the beneficiary. Juan and Lois divorced several years later, but Juan did not change the policy beneficiary designation. After Juan's death, Lois filed a claim for the policy proceeds.
>
> **Analysis.** The insurable interest requirement was met when Juan purchased the policy because the named beneficiary was his wife, who had an insurable interest in Juan's life at that time. As a result, the contract is valid. Lois was no longer required to have an insurable interest in Juan's life to receive the policy proceeds following his death.

An insurable interest usually is not required in a group insurance contract because the group policyholder's interest in the contract does not induce wagering contracts as does a policyowner's interest in an individual insurance contract. The lawful purpose requirement is met in a group insurance contract when the group policyholder enters into the contract to provide benefits to covered group members.

# The Policy as Property

In addition to being governed by contract law, insurance policies are a type of property and, thus, are also subject to the principles of property law. In legal terminology, **property** is defined as a bundle of rights a person has with respect to something. In most countries including the United States, property is characterized as either real property or personal property. **Real property** is land and whatever is growing on or affixed to the land. All property other than real property is characterized as **personal property** and includes tangible goods such as clothing, furniture, and automobiles, as well as intangible property such as contractual rights. An insurance policy is *intangible personal property*—it represents intangible legal rights that have value and that can be enforced by the courts. The owner of an insurance policy—rather than the insured or the beneficiary—holds these ownership rights in an insurance policy.

**Ownership of property** is the sum of all the legal rights that exist in that property. The legal rights an owner has in property include the right to use and enjoy the property and the right to dispose of the property.

## Right to Use and Enjoy Property

The right to use and enjoy property that one owns is an inherent feature of property ownership. The owner of an insurance policy has the right to deal with the policy in a number of ways. For example, the owner of an individual life insurance policy has the right to name the policy beneficiary. The policyowner also usually has the right to change the beneficiary designation at any time while the policy is in force. In some cases, however, the policyowner may give up the right to change the beneficiary designation by making the designation irrevocable. We describe naming and changing the beneficiary of an individual life insurance policy in Chapter 9. We describe the right to name the beneficiary of a group life insurance policy in Chapter 13.

## Right to Dispose of Property

The owner of property generally has the right to dispose of the property. For example, if you own an automobile, you have the right to give it away or sell it. Similarly, the owner of an insurance policy can dispose of it. The policyowner may transfer ownership of the policy by making a gift of the policy to someone else. We describe some of these aspects of policy ownership in later chapters. For now, just remember that as property, an insurance policy consists of a bundle of ownership rights.

## Key Terms

contract
group policyholder
formal contract
informal contract
bilateral contract
unilateral contract
commutative contract
aleatory contract
conditional promise
bargaining contract
contract of adhesion
valid contract
void contract
voidable contract
mutual assent
contractual capacity
minor
consideration
initial premium
renewal premium
property
real property
personal property
ownership of property

# Part 2:
# Individual Life
# Insurance and
# Annuities

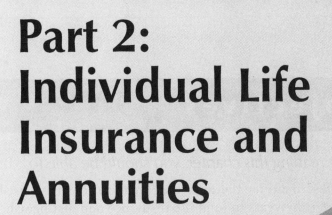

# Pricing Life Insurance

## objectives

*After reading this chapter, you should be able to*

- Describe three methods that organizations have used over the years to fund life insurance and distinguish among those methods

- Identify the three factors insurance companies use to calculate life insurance premium rates under the legal reserve system and explain how each factor affects premium rate calculations

- Explain how the level premium pricing system operates

- Identify two methods an insurer might use to change the price of a life insurance policy after it has been issued

- Define policy reserves and contingency reserves

- Calculate the insurer's net amount at risk for a given life insurance policy

For an insurer to have enough money available to pay policy benefits when they become due, the insurer determines the premium the company must charge for the specific insurance coverage provided. Insurance companies employ specialists, known as *actuaries*, who are responsible for calculating the premium rates the company charges for its products. Actuaries are trained in the mathematics of insurance and are responsible for performing all of the calculations needed to ensure that a company's products are mathematically sound. In this chapter, we describe the methods that have evolved over the years for determining life insurance premiums.

# Methods of Funding Life Insurance

The first insurers were individuals who were willing to assume someone else's risk of economic loss in return for a mutually agreed-upon price. The insurer usually issued a contract or policy that was signed at the bottom to show that the risk had been accepted. This signature under the terms of the contract is the origin of the insurance term *underwriter*. The insurer had underwritten, or accepted, the risk by placing his signature on the contract. These insurers were known as individual underwriters.

Issuing insurance at that time was a very speculative business venture. Individual underwriters had no way to predict accurately the losses they were likely to incur. Further, the underwriter had to pay all claims from his own funds. If he incurred losses that far exceeded the premiums he had received, it was possible that he might not be able to pay all claims. When organizations began to issue life insurance, they first experimented with two funding systems: the mutual benefit method and the assessment method.

## Mutual Benefit Method

Organizations known as mutual benefit societies developed an early method of obtaining money to pay death claims; they collected money *after* the death of the person who was insured. This funding method became known as the *mutual benefit method* or the *post-death assessment method*. Each member of a mutual benefit society agreed to pay an equal, specific amount of money when any other member died. Usually, the person or persons doing the administrative work for the society would receive a fee, often a small percentage of the money collected, and the rest would be paid to the insured's beneficiary. For example, assume that a society with 500 members required a $10 payment from each surviving participant when a member died. After the death of one member, the surviving 499 members would each pay $10. The total amount collected—$4,990—minus administrative fees would be paid to the deceased member's beneficiary.

Three major problems were associated with the mutual benefit method:

1. Mutual benefit societies often had problems collecting the money to pay death benefits. A society could not force its members to pay their shares and, thus, could not guarantee the amount of benefit that would be paid when a member died.

2. Unless a society constantly recruited new members, the size of the group became smaller and smaller as members died or resigned from the society. As a society's membership declined, the society either had to reduce the amount of the benefit paid following a member's death or increase the amount each surviving member was required to pay for each death.

3. As the members of a society grew older, the number of deaths increased each year. The more deaths that occurred in a given year, the more benefits the society paid; thus, each member's cost increased each year. As the cost of membership in a society increased, attracting new members became more difficult for the society. In addition, many members in good health dropped out of the society as their membership costs increased. Thus, the contributions required of the remaining members soared.

To cope with these problems, organizations developed a new form of funding life insurance benefits. This method, commonly referred to as the *assessment method*, funded life insurance benefits using pre-death assessments.

## Assessment Method

Under the **assessment method** for funding life insurance benefits, the organization that offered insurance coverage estimated its operating costs for a given period, usually one year. These operating costs included anticipated death claims and the organization's administrative expenses. The organization then divided equally among the participants in the plan the total amount of money needed to pay operating costs for the period.

> **Example.** At the beginning of a given year, a society with 500 members anticipated that 3 members would die in that year and that the society would incur $500 in administrative expenses. The society had agreed to pay a $5,000 death benefit to each member's beneficiary.
>
> **Analysis.** At the beginning of the year, each member would be assessed $31. That amount is calculated as follows:

| $15,000 | Expected death benefits payable ($5,000 × 3 deaths) |
| + $500 | Administrative expenses |
| $15,500 | Total amount needed to pay death benefits and expenses |
| ÷ 500 | Number of members |
| **$31** | **Amount required from each member** |

If the total actual cost of operations during a period was less than expected, then each participant received a refund. Alternatively, if the total operating cost was higher than expected, then the organization levied an additional assessment on each member.

Although prepayment of assessments solved the major collection problem that mutual benefit societies had faced, collection of any additional assessments was still difficult. In addition, the assessment method did not solve the problems caused by the aging of the group of insureds. As time passed, the number of deaths occurring in the group increased, and the size of each assessment then had to be increased. This higher cost deterred new members from joining, and consequently, the costs of paying death benefits had to be spread among fewer and fewer members. Finally, the assessment became so large that it was no longer affordable.

In an attempt to make an assessment plan more attractive to younger people, some organizations did charge somewhat higher assessments for older members. This approach, however, succeeded only in discouraging the healthier, older participants from continuing in the plan, and many of those participants dropped out.

## Legal Reserve System

The modern system used to price life insurance evolved from these early funding methods. Today's pricing system, known as the **legal reserve system**, is based on several premises:

- The amount of the benefit payable under a life insurance policy should be specified or calculable before the insured's death.

- The money needed to pay policy benefits should be collected in advance so that the insurer will have funds available to pay claims and expenses as they occur.

- The premium an individual pays for an insurance policy should be directly related to the amount of risk the insurance company assumes for that policy.

The legal reserve system is based on laws requiring that insurance companies establish policy reserves. In the United States as well as other countries, insurers are required to establish **policy reserves**, which are *liabilities* that represent the amount the insurer estimates it needs to pay policy benefits as they come due. Because these reserves are required by law, they are sometimes referred to as *legal reserves* or *statutory reserves*.

Remember that to keep its basic accounting equation in balance, the insurer's assets must equal its liabilities and owners' equity. If the amount of the insurer's liabilities—which includes its policy reserves—increases, then the insurer also must make a corresponding increase in the amount of its assets. The insurance company is required by law to maintain assets that are at least equal to the amount of its policy reserve liabilities. We discuss reserves in more detail later in this chapter.

# Premium Rate Calculations

Actuaries do not set the premium amount that each policyowner pays for insurance coverage. Rather, insurance company actuaries establish premium rates. A *premium rate* is a charge per unit of insurance coverage. In most cases, a coverage unit equals $1,000 of life insurance coverage. Consequently, the premium rate typically is expressed as the rate per thousand; the annual premium amount is calculated by multiplying the premium rate by the number of coverage units.

> **Example.** The annual premium rate for a $50,000 life insurance policy is expressed as $3.50 per thousand.
>
> **Analysis.** The annual premium amount for that policy would be $175, which is calculated as follows:
>
> $3.50   Premium rate = Price per unit ($1,000 of coverage)
> × 50   Number of units ($50,000 ÷ $1,000)
> **$175   Annual premium amount**

Actuaries consider many factors as they perform the calculations necessary to establish premium rates that are adequate and equitable. Premium rates must be *adequate* for the company to have enough money to pay policy benefits. Premium rates must be *equitable* so that each policyowner is charged premiums that reflect the degree of risk the insurer assumes in providing the coverage. The following factors are included in the calculation of life insurance premium rates: (1) cost of benefits, (2) investment earnings, and (3) expenses. We devote much of this chapter to discussing these factors and how they are used in determining premium rates for individual life insurance. In performing premium rate calculations, actuaries make *actuarial assumptions*, which are estimated values used in life insurance and annuity pricing, concerning each of these factors.

# Cost of Benefits

The ***cost of benefits*** for an insurance product equals all of the insurer's potential payments of benefit obligations to customers multiplied by the expected probability that each benefit will be payable. For life insurance policies, benefit obligations include the payment of policy proceeds. The probability that policy proceeds will be payable in a given year is measured by mortality statistics. ***Mortality*** is the incidence of death among a specified group of people. A ***mortality rate*** is the rate at which death occurs among a specified group of people during a specified period, typically one year. To price a life insurance product, then, an insurer must be able to predict the mortality rate for a given group of insureds.

Keep in mind that the actuaries in an insurance company are concerned with estimating the number of deaths that will occur in a given group of insureds, called a *block of insureds*, and not with predicting which individual insureds will die. Therefore, when we mention a single life insurance policy in this text, you can assume that all premium rate calculations relating to that policy are based on calculations for a *block of policies* that are like that individual policy. A ***block of policies*** is a group of policies issued to insureds who are all the same age, the same sex, and in the same risk classification. Each insurance company decides which policies are included in a block of policies when calculating premium rates. For example, an insurance company may classify into one block all term insurance policies issued to males age 35 who are nonsmokers and have no significant medical history.

In the early days of the insurance industry, few statistics were available for insurers to use to predict mortality rates. What little information insurers were able to gather included figures for the entire population, even for people who were in such poor health that they would have been considered uninsurable. Once insurers began issuing policies and paying claims, however, they began to collect data regarding insured lives. That data was more accurate for developing insurance mortality statistics because the data related only to people who insurers considered to be acceptable risks.

Today, some life insurers accumulate and share statistical information so that figures on the insurance industry's overall mortality experience may be used by all insurance companies. As we noted in Chapter 2, this information has been organized into charts, known as mortality tables, showing the mortality rates that are expected to occur at each age. The term ***expected mortality***, or *tabular mortality*, is used to mean the number of deaths that have been predicted to occur in a group of people at a given age according to a mortality table. The number of deaths that actually occur in a given group of insureds is referred to as the group's ***mortality experience***.

Mortality tables, therefore, show the mortality rates an insurer may reasonably anticipate among a particular group of insured lives at certain

**FAST FACT**

In 2003, U.S. life insurance companies had premium receipts totaling $504 billion.

**Source:** ACLI, *Life Insurers Fact Book: 2004* (Washington, D.C.: American Council of Life Insurers, 2004), 48.

ages—that is, how many people in each age group may be expected to die in a particular year. Although the mortality experience may fluctuate from group to group, the fluctuations tend to offset one another, being higher than expected for one group and lower than expected for another.

Mortality tables show that, on average, women live longer than men, as illustrated graphically in Figure 4.1. Recognizing this difference in expected life spans, most insurers price equivalent life insurance policies at a lower rate for women than for men of the same age. As Figure 4.1 also portrays, mortality rates of both males and females start high at birth and then

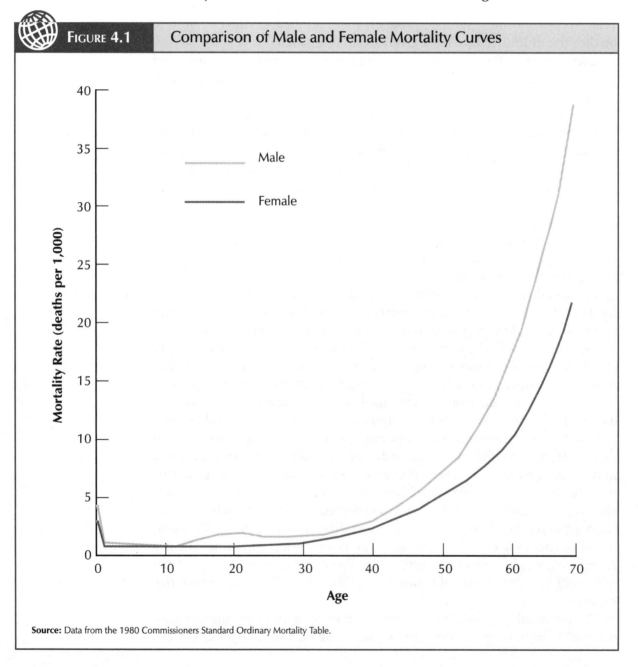

| FIGURE 4.1 | Comparison of Male and Female Mortality Curves |

**Source:** Data from the 1980 Commissioners Standard Ordinary Mortality Table.

decrease dramatically at age 1. They both then steadily decrease until about age 10, at which point they begin increasing slightly. Mortality rates of females continue this steady increase, while those of males begin to climb sharply during the teenage years, then drop again in the mid-twenties, and begin to rise again in the early thirties. Finally, the mortality rates of both males and females age 65 or over accelerate sharply with each passing year. Note that according to many mortality tables, the mortality rates of males and females are the same at age 99.

What Figure 4.1 does not display is that most mortality tables that insurers use in premium rate calculations break down the mortality rates for each sex into two additional categories: smokers and nonsmokers. In other words, mortality tables often show mortality rates for four categories of people: male nonsmokers, male smokers, female nonsmokers, and female smokers. Smoking has such a dramatic effect on mortality rates that insurance companies routinely account for that factor in the mortality tables they use to calculate life insurance premium rates.

Life insurers use mortality tables as a first step in determining the premium rate to be charged for a block of life insurance policies. The cost of benefits for a block of policies depends in part on the policy proceeds multiplied by the mortality rate. In general, the higher the mortality rate for a group of life insureds of the same age and sex, the higher the benefit cost and, consequently, the higher the premium rate. Conversely, the lower the mortality rate for a group of life insureds of the same age and sex, the lower the benefit cost and the premium rate.

The mortality rates of some groups of people, however, do not follow the pattern of standard mortality rates and are not represented in standard mortality tables. Factors such as being overweight or underweight, engaging in certain occupations or hobbies, and having various illnesses have all been studied, and results have been compiled to show how such factors affect the mortality rate at each age. When these results indicate that a particular factor increases the insured's mortality risk, an insurer may decide to charge a higher premium rate for people who possess such a risk factor. As noted in Chapter 2, people who are charged a higher than standard premium rate because they possess such risk factors are called *substandard risks,* and the premium rate charged to these people is called a *substandard premium rate.*

## Investment Earnings

The second factor that insurance companies consider when establishing life insurance premium rates is their ***investment earnings***, which is the money that insurers earn by investing premium dollars. Remember that premium dollars are the primary source of funds used to pay life insurance claims. Because most policies are in force for some time before claims become payable, the premium dollars are available for the insurer to invest.

The earnings from these investments provide additional funds that allow insurance companies to charge lower premium rates than they could if they relied on the premium amounts alone.

Insurance companies invest premium dollars in many different ways—in government and corporate bonds, mortgages, real estate, and corporate stock. In fact, insurance companies can place money in any safe investment that is likely to provide good earnings and is not prohibited by government regulation.

## How Investments Create Earnings

*Interest* is basically money that is paid for the use of money. The amount of interest that is charged for the use of money is expressed in terms of a percentage, such as 10 percent. A 10 percent interest rate indicates that a borrower must pay the lender the amount originally borrowed, plus an additional 10 percent of that amount. For example, if you were to lend your brother $1,000 for one year at an annual interest rate of 10 percent, he would owe you $1,100 at the end of the year—the $1,000 you loaned him plus $100 ($1,000 × .10 = $100). This example illustrates the payment of *simple interest*, which is interest paid on the original sum only.

When interest has been *earned* on money, but not paid, interest can accrue, or accumulate, on that unpaid interest. Paying interest on both an original principal sum and on accrued interest is called *compounding*, and the interest paid under these conditions is known as **compound interest**. For example, if you let your brother keep the $1,000 loan for an additional year without paying you the $100 of interest for the previous year, you would actually be making a second loan of $100. At a 10 percent rate of interest, you'll earn $110 interest during the second year ($1,100 × .10 = $110). Therefore, at the end of the second year, your brother will owe you a total of $1,210 ($1,100 + $110). The interest in this example was compounded annually. Interest can be compounded, however, during any selected period—a half-year, a month, or a day, for example.

Over a long period of time, compound interest has a dramatic effect on the amount of principal that has accumulated at interest. For example, if you were to save $1,000 per year for 25 years at no interest, you would have $25,000 at the end of the 25-year period. If you saved the same $1,000 per year and invested it at an interest rate of 8 percent, compounded annually, you would have more than $78,000 at the end of 25 years. (See Figure 4.2, which illustrates this example.)

For the sake of simplicity, we illustrated investment earnings in terms of an interest rate earned on loans. Any investment earnings, however, can be expressed in terms of the rate of return that the investor has earned. For example, insurance companies invest money by buying stock in other companies. While it owns stock, an insurance company will probably earn dividends on that stock. In addition, the insurer might be able to sell the

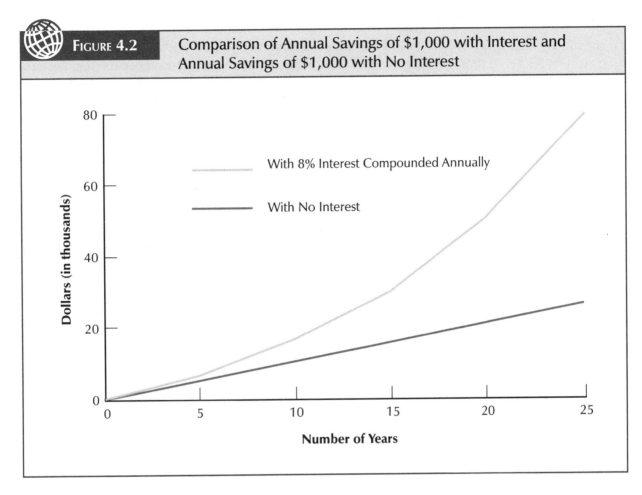

**FIGURE 4.2** Comparison of Annual Savings of $1,000 with Interest and Annual Savings of $1,000 with No Interest

stock for more than it paid for the stock. The insurer's total earnings on the stock can be expressed in terms of a percentage rate of return.

Many factors enter into the insurance company's calculations concerning the rate of return expected to be earned on its investments, and we do not go into greater detail here regarding those calculations.

## How Investment Earnings Affect Pricing

The effect of investment earnings on insurance companies and their policyowners becomes especially important in premium rate calculations. An insurer's investment earnings enable it to charge lower premium rates than would be possible if the insurer considered only the mortality risk factor. The longer a policy is in force, the greater the effect investment earnings will have on premium rate calculations. The effect of investment earnings on the cost of insurance policies that are in force for only one year is slight; by contrast, investment earnings have a substantial effect on the cost of policies that are in force for long terms or for the insured's entire lifetime.

To illustrate, assume that 1,000 men age 35 purchase insurance policies. Each policy has a face amount of $10,000, and each policy will terminate when the insured dies or reaches age 60, whichever occurs first. Because this type of policy is designed to terminate at the end of a specified term, it is a form of term life insurance. The company uses a mortality table to find the number of people in this group who can be expected to die each year during the next 25 years and the number of people who will be left alive to pay premiums each year. If the company used the 1980 CSO Table (Male) to estimate the number of deaths each year, the insurance company would find that approximately 148 of the insured people will die during the next 25 years. Therefore, the company would need a total of $1,480,000 just to provide enough money to pay for all expected claims. Using calculations that take into account both the number of people who are expected to die each year and the number of people who are expected to stay alive, the insurer can determine that if each person purchasing a policy pays a premium of approximately $62 each year, then the insurer will have enough money to pay benefits as the insureds die.

Calculating the premium this way, however, assumes that the insurance company will take the money paid as premiums, put it in a vault or some other safe place, and do nothing with it until it is needed to pay claims.

Insurance companies, however, do not treat premium dollars in this manner. Instead, companies invest the premium payments they receive. Therefore, if the insurance company in the example above projects that it can invest the money paid as premiums to earn a 5 percent rate of return each year for 25 years, then the company can reduce the annual premium charged each policyowner to about $49, yet still have enough money to pay the estimated $1,480,000 in expected claims. In this example, investment income is responsible for approximately a 21 percent reduction in the premium the insurer will charge for each policy. If the insurance company knew that it could earn a higher rate of return on investments, then the insurance company could reduce the premium amount even further.

## Expenses

A policy's **net premium** is the amount of money the insurer needs to provide the policy benefits. To calculate net premium rates, life insurers must make assumptions as to mortality rates, investment earnings, and lapse rates. The term *lapse rate* refers to the rate at which policyowners decide to drop their coverage or allow it to lapse (expire) for nonpayment of premium before the end of the premium-payment period specified in their policies. In many such situations, the insurer will not have collected enough in premiums to cover the costs of underwriting and issuing the coverage. Therefore, an insurer must add an amount to the net premium that will compensate for the costs incurred to issue policies that will be dropped or lapse.

When pricing insurance, insurers must also consider their operating costs, such as sales and commission costs, taxes, personnel salaries, and the cost of establishing and maintaining a home office, regional offices (if any), and sales offices. In addition, recordkeeping costs, including operating both manual and computer systems, are a major operating expense for insurance companies. (See Figure 4.3, which shows the portion of insurance company expenditures that is attributable to various expenses and the portion that is attributable to paying policy benefits.)

The insurance company must add an amount to the net premium to cover all of these operating costs and to provide itself with some profit. The total amount added to the net premium to cover all of the insurer's costs of doing business is called the **loading**. The net premium with the loading added is called the **gross premium**, which is the premium amount the insurer charges the policyowner to keep the policy in force.

**Net Premium + Loading = Gross Premium**

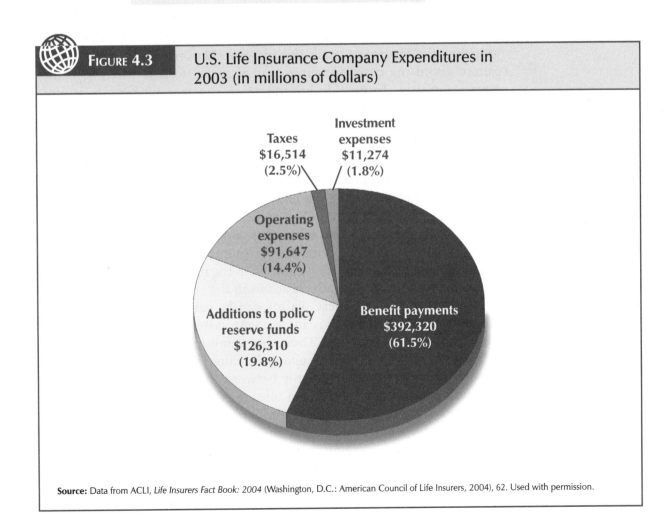

| FIGURE 4.3 | U.S. Life Insurance Company Expenditures in 2003 (in millions of dollars) |

Taxes
$16,514
(2.5%)

Investment
expenses
$11,274
(1.8%)

Operating
expenses
$91,647
(14.4%)

Additions to policy
reserve funds
$126,310
(19.8%)

Benefit payments
$392,320
(61.5%)

**Source:** Data from ACLI, *Life Insurers Fact Book: 2004* (Washington, D.C.: American Council of Life Insurers, 2004), 62. Used with permission.

We have now discussed three factors that insurers must consider in calculating the premium rate for a life insurance policy: the cost of benefits, investment earnings, and expenses. The cost of every life insurance policy must include these factors, though the manner in which insurers express a policy's cost varies depending on the type of policy. Some insurance policies, such as universal life policies, state the amount of money that the insurer needs to cover mortality and expenses and the rate of return on investments that the insurer will use to calculate the amount of the policy's premiums. We describe these policies in detail in Chapter 6. Other policies, such as term insurance and whole life insurance policies, state only the gross premium that the insurer will charge for the policy.

# The Level Premium Pricing System

The *level premium pricing system* is a life insurance pricing system that allows the purchaser to pay the same premium amount each year the policy is in force. It is used to price all types of individual life insurance policies. As we have seen, because mortality rates increase with age, the cost of providing life insurance must also increase. Unfortunately, many people cannot afford the cost of insurance in their later years when mortality rates are greater. To provide life insurance coverage for periods of more than one year at a premium rate that does *not* increase each year with the insured's age, the life insurance industry developed the level premium pricing system.

The leveling of premiums is possible because premium rates charged for level premium policies are higher than needed to pay claims and expenses that occur during the early years of those policies. In the early years, the excess premium dollars collected—those premium dollars not needed to pay claims and expenses that occur during the early years—are invested by the insurance company. As people in a group insured under a block of level premium policies grow older, the insurance company expects an increasing number of death claims from the group each year. Under the level premium system, these claims can be paid in large part with the excess premium dollars, plus investment earnings, that were collected during the early policy years. Thus, the premium rate on any one of these policies can remain level throughout the duration of the policy.

To demonstrate the relationship between the premium rate for a level premium policy and the premium rates for a series of 1-year policies, we can return to a previous example. Earlier, we described the net premium calculation for a block of $10,000 life insurance policies issued to 1,000 males age 35. The net premium for each policy was $49, payable each year during the policy's 25-year term. If each of the same 1,000 males age 35 buys a $10,000 life insurance policy that provides coverage for 1 year, instead of 25 years, the net premium charged that first year would be about $20.

This $20 net premium is less than half the $49 net premium for the level premium policy because in calculating the $20 net premium, the insurer considers the mortality rate of the group of 35-year-olds for only 1 year. If a policyowner repurchases the $10,000 policy each succeeding year, the net premium for the 1-year policy would increase each year, reaching about $43 by the time the insured reaches age 45. This amount is still less than the net premium for the level premium policy, but the price has more than doubled in the 10 years since the insureds were age 35 because the group's mortality rate increases each year. By the time the men in the insured group reach age 55, the net premium for the 1-year term policy would increase to $100, over double the net premium for the level premium policy, and by the time the insureds reach age 60, the net premium would reach $153. (See Figure 4.4, which shows the difference between the level premium amount and the premium amounts for the 1-year term policies.)

Because at the time of purchase a 1-year term insurance policy is less expensive than a similar level premium, long-term policy, a 1-year policy can provide relatively inexpensive, short-term protection. As an insured's age increases, however, so does the premium rate for a 1-year policy. The premium rate for a level premium policy, on the other hand, does not increase after the policy has been issued. Thus, the level premium system allows people to buy long-term life insurance policies that protect them at a steady cost even while their risk of death is increasing over the duration of the policy.

## Policies with Nonguaranteed Elements

We have described the elements that insurance companies must consider when pricing life insurance policies and some of the methods that insurers use to make projections regarding future experience with each pricing element. In our discussion, however, we have assumed that once each pricing element is assigned a value and the premium is set for a particular policy, the pricing process is finished. That is not always the case.

Several types of life insurance policies provide that the policy's price can change after the policy is issued. Insurance companies primarily use two methods of changing the price of a policy after it has been issued.

- The first method is to reduce the price by returning to policyowners a portion of the premium that was paid for the coverage. This premium refund is called a *policy dividend*.

- The second method consists of changing the values of the pricing factors while the policy is in force and, consequently, changing the amount charged to the policyowner for the coverage.

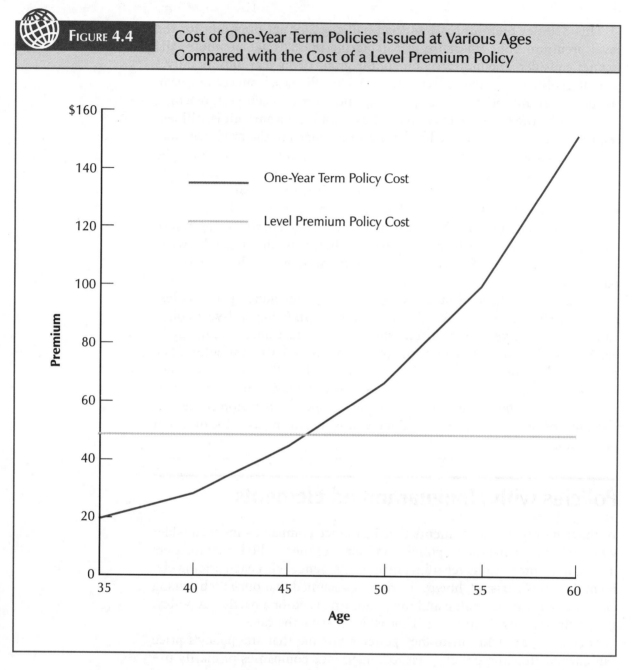

**FIGURE 4.4** Cost of One-Year Term Policies Issued at Various Ages Compared with the Cost of a Level Premium Policy

## Policy Dividends

Life insurance policies can be issued on either a participating or nonparticipating basis. A **participating policy**, sometimes referred to as a *par policy*, is one under which the policyowner shares in the insurance company's divisible surplus. A **nonparticipating policy**, also known as a *nonpar policy*, is one in which the policyowner does not share in the insurer's surplus. As noted in Chapter 1, *surplus* is the amount by which a company's assets exceed its liabilities and capital. Surplus results from a company's profitable operations. The amount of surplus available for distribution to owners of participating policies is called the ***divisible surplus***, and a policyowner's share of this divisible surplus is called a ***policy dividend***. Policy dividends are considered premium refunds, and, unlike dividends earned on shares of stock, they usually are not considered taxable income to the policyowner.

The most important concern of insurers is to make sure that enough money will be available to pay anticipated claims and expenses, as well as any additional, unexpected claims and expenses. Therefore, insurers generally are cautious when making assumptions about mortality, investment earnings, expenses, lapses, and contingencies. Actual experience in these areas is often better than anticipated. By issuing participating policies, insurance companies can return money to policyowners in the form of dividends when conditions are favorable, yet establish premium rates that are sufficient to pay promised benefits when conditions are unfavorable. Nevertheless, the insurance company must be careful that it is not too conservative in its pricing; the company wants to establish premium rates that are competitive with the rates charged by other insurance companies.

Each cost element involved in setting premium rates is a potential source of surplus. If the people insured by a company experience a more favorable mortality rate than the company expected, fewer claims will be paid. If a company earns a higher rate of return on investments than anticipated, the investment income will be greater than needed to maintain the reserves at the required levels. And if a company spends less money on expenses than was planned, additional funds will be available from the loading. An insurer that issues participating policies can distribute a portion of its surplus to the owners of those participating policies in the form of policy dividends.

A participating policy contains a policy dividend provision that gives the policyowner several choices in the way policy dividends can be used. These choices are known as *dividend options* and are discussed in Chapter 9.

Generally, the premium rates for nonparticipating policies are lower than the premium rates for equivalent participating policies because insurers issuing nonparticipating policies often use less cautious assumptions regarding mortality, investment earnings, expenses, and contingencies. However, determining in advance which type of policy—participating or nonparticipating—will ultimately be less expensive is difficult because policy dividends received by the owner of a participating policy reduce the amount of the policy's actual cost. Policy dividend amounts are not known in advance, and the policyowner is not guaranteed that policy dividends will be paid.

## Changes in Pricing Factors

Earlier we mentioned that some insurance policies specify each cost element of the policy, while others specify only the gross premium amount. Policies that list the cost elements separately usually guarantee maximum values for each cost element but specify that more favorable values will be used if the insurer believes that using the more favorable values is called for. Such a policy, for example, might guarantee that the policy's savings element will accumulate at an annual interest rate of at least 4 percent; the insurer, however, also promises to pay a higher interest rate if market conditions permit it to earn a higher than predicted rate of return on its investments. When the insurer pays interest at a rate that is higher than the guaranteed interest rate, the cost of the policy is reduced. Likewise, such policies also specify the maximum mortality charges that the insurer will assess but provide that the insurer will assess lower mortality charges if the insurance company's actual mortality experience is more favorable than was expected. The more favorable mortality charges are not guaranteed, but if applied, they reduce the policy's cost.

In most situations, policies with variable pricing factors are issued on a nonparticipating basis because their pricing structure makes declaring policy dividends unnecessary. (Remember that policy dividends are essentially premium refunds.) As with participating policies, cost comparisons among policies with varying pricing elements are difficult to make because projected favorable values are not guaranteed or known in advance. Stock insurance companies can offer both participating and nonparticipating policies. In the past, mutual insurance companies tended to offer only participating policies. Today, however, many mutuals offer both participating and nonparticipating policies. In many cases, mutual companies that want to offer nonparticipating policies (such as policies with variable pricing factors) do so by establishing a subsidiary that is organized as a stock company and offering the nonparticipating policies through that subsidiary.

# Life Insurance Reserves

Of all the terms used in the insurance industry, *reserves* is one of the most important and also one of the most easily misunderstood. In our everyday lives, we use the term *reserves* to mean something extra, something that is available in addition to our usual supply. For example, in a broad financial sense, people use the term *reserves* to refer to a fund of additional money that is available in case of some special need. In the insurance industry, however, reserves are not typically a source of money. Rather, reserves are liabilities representing the amounts of money an insurer estimates it will need to pay its future obligations.

Insurance laws impose a variety of reserve requirements on insurance companies. A discussion of all those requirements is beyond the scope of this text. Nevertheless, you should know that insurers establish a number of different types of reserve liabilities; some reserves are required by law, and others are established voluntarily by insurance companies. In this section, we describe policy reserves and contingency reserves to give you an idea of some types of reserve liabilities that insurance companies establish.

## Policy Reserves

As noted earlier, policy reserves represent the amount an insurer estimates it will need to pay policy benefits as they come due. Insurance companies must maintain assets that exceed their policy reserve liabilities so that they have the funds to pay claims when they come due; these assets must be safely invested.

Much of the regulation of the life insurance industry by governmental agencies has to do with policy reserves. To calculate the amount needed for policy reserves, for example, regulators require insurance companies to use a conservative mortality table. A **conservative mortality table** is one that shows *higher* mortality rates than the company anticipates for a particular block of policies. By using a conservative mortality table, the company is required to set aside more assets than it will probably need to pay future claims. To guarantee the safety of the assets backing policy reserves, regulators require insurers to place the funds in safe investments. Laws regarding minimum reserve amounts and investment safety are designed to protect the interests of the policyowners and beneficiaries who rely on the long-term solvency of life insurance companies.

Let's look at an example of a whole life insurance policy to illustrate the operation of the policy reserve. Under the level premium system, the insurer receives more in premiums for a block of whole life insurance policies in the early years than it needs to pay claims. The insurer must invest those excess premiums and build assets that are sufficient to back the policy reserve it has established for the block of policies. Note that the insurer must calculate policy reserves for each block of policies it has issued. Once it has established the amount of the policy reserve for a block of policies, the insurer can assign a proportionate share of that total amount to each policy.

The difference between the face amount of a policy and the policy reserve at the end of any given policy year is known as the insurance company's **net amount at risk** for the policy.

**Net Amount at Risk = Face Amount – Policy Reserve**

For example, if a $10,000 whole life insurance policy has a reserve of $3,000, then the insurance company's net amount at risk for that policy is

$7,000. If a claim should become payable on that policy, the insurer would pay $3,000 of the benefit from the assets that back the reserve on that particular policy, and it would pay $7,000—the net amount at risk—from other funds it holds. Figure 4.5 shows how a reserve for a whole life insurance policy can build up while the policy is in force. As the reserve *increases*, the net amount at risk *decreases*. In the early years of a policy, the net amount at risk is large; but by the policy's final years, the assets backing reserves can grow large enough to pay for all or almost all of the benefit due when the insured dies.

Insurers also must establish reserves for policies with far shorter durations, such as one-year term insurance policies. For purposes of establishing policy reserves for one-year term policies, the insurer assumes that it receives the total amount of premiums owed for the policies at the beginning of the year. The insurer can invest those funds until they are needed to pay claims, and thus must establish a policy reserve liability. During the policy year, the insurer pays any death claims that are incurred and thus reduces the amount of its policy reserve liability for the block of policies. At the end of the policy year when the remaining policies expire, the

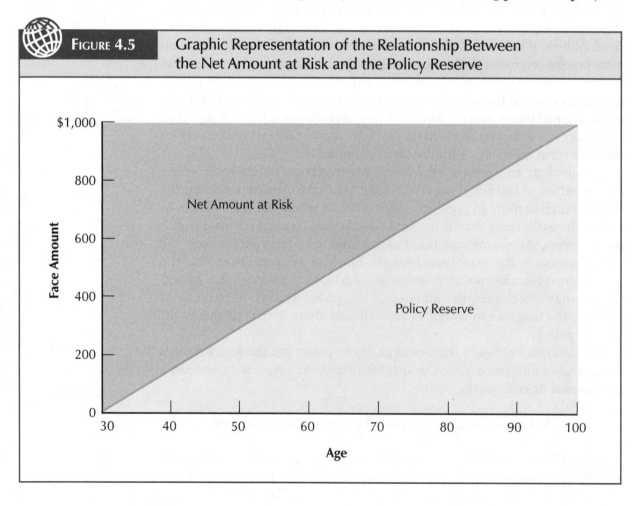

**FIGURE 4.5** Graphic Representation of the Relationship Between the Net Amount at Risk and the Policy Reserve

amount of the policy reserve is equal to zero, as no further claims will be payable under those policies.

## Contingency Reserves

As we discussed earlier, the loading sometimes includes an amount to cover unusual occurrences. Companies use these extra amounts as assets to back up **contingency reserves**, which are reserves against unusual conditions that may occur. Contingency reserves provide a safety margin in case actual experience in any area—the cost of benefits, investment earnings, or expenses—is worse than the insurer expected. Although some insurers establish contingency reserves for life insurance policies, insurers typically establish contingency reserves for health insurance policies.

# Key Terms

actuary
mutual benefit method
assessment method
legal reserve system
policy reserves
premium rate
actuarial assumptions
cost of benefits
mortality
mortality rate
block of policies
expected mortality
mortality experience
investment earnings

interest
simple interest
compound interest
net premium
loading
gross premium
level premium pricing system
participating policy
nonparticipating policy
divisible surplus
policy dividend
conservative mortality table
net amount at risk
contingency reserves

# Term Life Insurance

## objectives

*After reading this chapter, you should be able to*

- Describe the coverage provided by term life insurance policies and determine when the premium charged for term life insurance coverage may increase

- Identify three different plans of term life insurance coverage and give an example of each

- Distinguish between renewable term life insurance and convertible term life insurance

- Identify the common personal and business needs that life insurance can meet

**A**ll life insurance policies provide for the payment of a benefit upon the death of the insured while the policy is in force. Beyond that, however, the features of life insurance policies vary depending on the type of policy. As noted in Chapter 1, the three primary types of life insurance are term insurance, cash value insurance, and endowment insurance.

In this chapter, we describe term life insurance, which provides a policy benefit if the insured dies during a specified period of time. We begin the chapter by describing the characteristics of term life insurance products. Then, we describe the various plans of term life insurance and some additional features that term life insurance policies may include. Finally, we discuss some of the personal and business needs that life insurance can meet.

# Characteristics of Term Life Insurance Products

By definition, all term insurance products provide coverage for a specified period of time, called the **policy term**. The policy benefit is payable *only* if (1) the insured dies during the specified term *and* (2) the policy is in force when the insured dies. If the insured lives until the end of the specified term, the policy may give the policyowner the right to continue life insurance coverage. If the policyowner does not continue the coverage, then the policy expires and the insurer has no liability to provide further insurance coverage.

The length of the term varies considerably from policy to policy. The term may be as short as the time required to complete an airplane trip or as long as 40 years or more. Generally speaking, though, insurers seldom sell term life insurance to cover periods of less than 1 year. The term may be described as a specified number of years—1 year, 5 years, 10 years, 20 years—or it may be defined by specifying the age of the insured at the end of the term. For example, a term insurance policy that covers an insured until age 65 is referred to as *term to age 65;* the policy's coverage expires on the policy anniversary that falls either closest to, or immediately after, the insured person's 65th birthday, depending on the terms of the policy. The **policy anniversary** generally is the anniversary of the date on which coverage under the policy became effective. Both the expiration date and the policy anniversary date are usually stated on the face—or first—page of the policy.

Term life insurance protection is usually provided by an insurance policy, but it can also be provided by a rider added to a policy. A *policy rider*, which is also called an *endorsement*, is an amendment to an insurance policy that becomes a part of the insurance contract and that either expands or limits the benefits payable under the contract. A policy rider is as legally effective as any other part of the insurance contract. Riders are commonly used to provide some type of supplementary benefit or to increase the amount of the death benefit provided by a policy, although riders may also be used to limit or modify a policy's coverage. Some of the supplementary benefits—including some term insurance benefits—that are commonly provided through riders attached to life insurance policies are described in Chapter 7.

## Plans of Term Life Insurance Coverage

The amount of the benefit payable under a term life insurance policy or rider usually remains level throughout the term of the policy. Term life insurance, however, also may be purchased to provide either a benefit that *decreases* over the policy's term or a benefit that *increases* over the policy's term. Figure 5.1 shows the amounts of various plans of life insurance purchased in the United States in 2003.

| FIGURE 5.1 | Individual Purchases of Various Life Insurance Plans in the United States, 2003 | | | |
|---|---|---|---|---|
| | Number of Policies (thousands) | Percent of Total Number | Face Amount of Policies (millions) | Percent of Total Face Amount |
| **Decreasing term insurance** | 204 | 1.5% | $   57,107 | 3.3 % |
| **Level term insurance** | 6,174 | 45.7 | 1,174,554 | 67.2 |
| **Whole life and endowment insurance** | 7,132 | 52.8 | 516,034 | 29.5 |
| **Totals** | **13,510** | **100.0** | **1,747,695** | **100.0** |

**Note:** Sales of increasing term insurance are negligible.

**Source:** Data from ACLI, *Life Insurers Fact Book: 2004* (Washington, D.C.: American Council of Life Insurers, 2004), 85. Used with permission.

# Level Term Life Insurance

By far, the most common plan of term insurance is *level term life insurance*, which provides a policy benefit that remains the same over the term of the policy. For example, under a 5-year level term policy that provides $100,000 of coverage, the insurer agrees to pay $100,000 if the insured dies at any time during the 5-year period that the policy is in force. The amount of each renewal premium payable for a level term life insurance policy usually remains the same throughout the stated term of coverage.

# Decreasing Term Life Insurance

*Decreasing term life insurance* provides a policy benefit that decreases in amount over the term of coverage. The policy benefit begins as a set face amount and then decreases over the policy term according to some stated method that is described in the policy. For example, assume that the benefit during the first year of coverage of a five-year decreasing term policy is $50,000 and then decreases by $10,000 on each policy anniversary. The coverage is $40,000 for the second policy year, $30,000 for the third year, $20,000 for the fourth year, and $10,000 for the last year. At the end of the fifth policy year, the coverage expires. The amount of each renewal premium payable for a decreasing term insurance policy usually remains level throughout the policy term.

Insurance companies offer several plans of decreasing term insurance, including (1) mortgage insurance, (2) credit life insurance, and (3) family income insurance. We describe how each of these plans provides benefits to meet a specific need for insurance.

### Mortgage Insurance

*Mortgage insurance* is a plan of decreasing term insurance designed to provide a benefit amount that corresponds to the decreasing amount owed on a mortgage loan. If you have ever bought a home, you are probably aware that each payment a borrower makes on a mortgage loan consists of both principal and interest on the loan. The amount of the outstanding principal balance owed on the mortgage loan gradually decreases over the term of the mortgage, although initially the decrease is fairly slow. (See Figure 5.2 for a graphic illustration of mortgage insurance.) If the borrower purchases mortgage insurance, the amount of the policy benefit payable at any given time generally equals the amount the borrower then owes on the mortgage loan.

The term of a mortgage policy is based on the length of the mortgage, which is usually 15 or 30 years. Renewal premiums payable for mortgage insurance are generally level throughout the term.

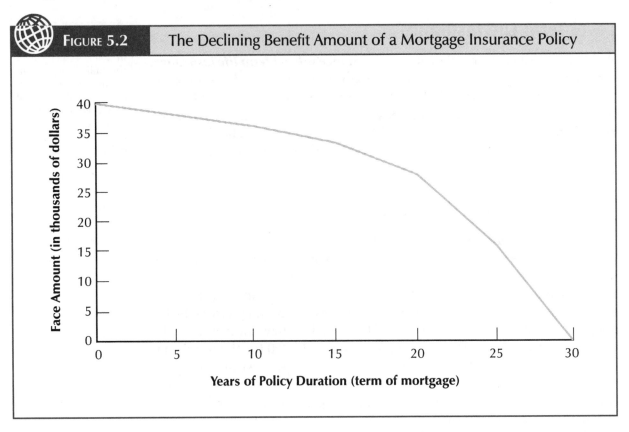

**FIGURE 5.2**    The Declining Benefit Amount of a Mortgage Insurance Policy

Often, the beneficiary of a mortgage policy uses the policy benefit to pay off the mortgage. The beneficiary, however, typically is not required to do that. In most instances, the life insurance policy is independent of the mortgage—the institution granting the mortgage is not a party to the insurance contract—and the beneficiary is not required to use the proceeds of the policy to repay the mortgage. The following example describes this situation.

**Example.** Bill Marley and his wife, Allyson, purchased a new home and obtained a 30-year mortgage from the New Home Mortgage Company. Bill decided to purchase a mortgage life insurance policy from the Star Life Insurance Company. He wanted to ensure that Allyson had funds to supplement her income so that she could afford to stay in the home if he should die before the mortgage loan was repaid. So, he named Allyson as the beneficiary. Three years later, Bill died in an accident, and Star Life paid Allyson a policy benefit of $72,150—the loan amount remaining on the mortgage. Allyson invested the policy proceeds in a mutual fund and continued to make monthly mortgage payments.

> **Analysis.** Because the contract for insurance was between Star Life and Bill Marley, Allyson was under no obligation to use the proceeds to pay the balance due on the mortgage.

A mortgage lender sometimes requires a borrower, as a condition for obtaining a mortgage loan, to purchase mortgage insurance and to name the lender as beneficiary. In this case, the borrower who purchases mortgage coverage from an insurance company is the owner of the policy, and the terms of his mortgage loan require him to maintain that coverage payable to the lender in the event of his death during the term of the mortgage. The insurance company is not a party to the mortgage loan contract, however, and its only obligation is to carry out its obligations under the mortgage insurance policy.

A variation of mortgage insurance is *joint mortgage insurance*, which provides the same benefit as a mortgage insurance policy except the joint policy insures the lives of two people. If both insureds survive until the end of the stated term, the joint mortgage policy expires. But if one of the insureds dies while the policy is in force, the insurer will pay the policy benefit to the beneficiary, who is typically the surviving insured. Note that the beneficiary is not required to use the policy benefit to pay off the mortgage. Joint mortgage insurance can meet the needs of two people who own a home together and who both must work to have enough income to make their monthly mortgage payments.

## Credit Life Insurance

*Credit life insurance* is a type of term life insurance designed to pay the balance due on a loan if the borrower dies before the loan is repaid. Like mortgage insurance, credit life insurance is usually decreasing term insurance. Unlike mortgage insurance policies, credit life insurance policies always provide that the policy benefit is payable directly to the lender, or creditor, if the insured borrower dies during the policy's term. Generally, the loan must be of a type that can be repaid in 10 years or less. Although credit life insurance is available on an individual insurance basis, most credit life insurance is sold to lending institutions as group insurance to cover the lives of the borrowers of that lender. We describe group creditor life insurance in Chapter 13.

Credit life insurance is available for automobile loans, furniture loans, and other personal loans. In addition, many credit card holders are covered by credit life insurance for the amounts they owe on their accounts; in such cases, the amount of life insurance coverage in force at any given time depends on the amount of the outstanding debt. Credit life insurance guarantees the lender that the insured's outstanding debt will be paid if the insured borrower dies before the loan is repaid. Credit life insurance also protects the insured's estate from having to pay these outstanding debts.

As with mortgage insurance, the amount of benefit payable under a credit life insurance policy is usually equal to the amount of the unpaid debt. Thus, as the amount of the loan decreases, the face amount of credit life insurance provided decreases. Premiums may be level over the duration of the loan or, in cases in which the amount of the loan varies, may increase or decrease as the amount of the outstanding loan balance—and the corresponding policy benefit—increases or decreases. Premiums for credit life insurance may be paid to the insurance company by the lender or by the insured borrower. In most cases, however, the borrower pays the credit life insurance premium to the lender, which then remits the premium to the insurer.

## Family Income Coverage

*Family income coverage* is a plan of decreasing term life insurance that provides a stated monthly income benefit amount to the insured's surviving spouse if the insured dies during the term of coverage. Monthly income benefits continue until the end of the term specified when the coverage was purchased. Family income coverage is a form of decreasing term life insurance because the longer the insured remains alive during the term of coverage, the shorter the length of time over which the insurer may be required to pay monthly income benefits; the shorter the length of the benefit payment period, the smaller the total amount of benefits the insurer will pay out.

Under some family income coverages, the insurer promises to pay the income benefit amount for at least a stated minimum number of years if the insured dies during the policy's term.

**Example:** Arnold Aceelo has purchased 10-year family income coverage that provides for a $1,000 monthly income benefit. His coverage specifies that the income benefit will be paid for at least 3 years if he dies during the 10-year term of coverage.

**Analysis:** If Arnold dies 2 years after buying the family income coverage, the insurer will pay a total of $96,000 in monthly income benefits ($1,000 × 12 months × 8 years) to Arnold's wife. If he dies 6 years after buying the coverage, the monthly income benefit will be paid for 4 years; thus, the insurer will pay Arnold's wife a total of $48,000 ($1,000 × 12 months × 4 years). If, however, Arnold dies 9 years after purchasing the coverage, then the income benefit will continue for the specified 3-year minimum, for a total of $36,000 ($1,000 × 12 months × 3 years). If he dies 11 years after purchasing the coverage, no monthly income benefit would be paid because the decreasing term insurance coverage expired 1 year before his death.

Family income coverage is most commonly purchased as a rider to a cash value life insurance policy, which we describe in the next chapter. Insurance companies sometimes also include family income coverage as a feature of a whole life policy, in which case the policy is usually called a *family income policy*. The benefit from the whole life insurance portion of the family income policy is usually paid in a lump sum following the insured's death, and the insurer then begins paying the monthly income benefits. Some family income policies, however, provide that the insurance company will pay the lump-sum benefit to the beneficiary after it has paid all the monthly income benefits. Interest on the policy proceeds that the insurer holds until the end of the monthly income benefit period may either be added to the amount of each installment payment or paid with the proceeds at the end of the installment period.

## Increasing Term Life Insurance

*Increasing term life insurance* provides a death benefit that starts at one amount and increases by some specified amount or percentage at stated intervals over the policy term. For example, an insurance company may offer coverage that starts at $100,000 and then increases by 5 percent on each policy anniversary date throughout the term of the policy. Alternatively, the face amount may increase according to increases in the cost of living, as measured by a standard index such as the Consumer Price Index (CPI).[1] The premium for increasing term insurance generally increases as the amount of coverage increases. The policyowner is usually granted the option of freezing at any time the amount of coverage provided by the increasing term life insurance. This coverage may be provided by an increasing term life insurance policy or, more commonly, as a policy rider.

# Features of Term Life Insurance Policies

Term life insurance provides only temporary protection: at the end of the stated term, the policy expires. In some cases, however, a policyowner may wish either to continue the insurance coverage for an additional term or to change the coverage to a cash value plan of insurance. Term life insurance policies often contain features that allow the policyowner to continue the life insurance coverage beyond the end of the original term. If the policy gives the policyowner the option to continue the policy's coverage for an additional policy term, then the policy is known as a *renewable term insurance policy*. If the policy gives the policyowner the right to convert the term policy to a cash value policy, then the policy is referred to as a *convertible term insurance policy*. Some policies, known as *renewable/ convertible term insurance policies*, contain both of these features.

# Renewable Term Life Insurance

Renewable term life insurance policies include a **renewal provision** that gives the policyowner the right, within specified limits, to renew the insurance coverage at the end of the specified term without submitting **evidence of insurability**—proof that the insured person continues to be an insurable risk. In other words, the insured is not required to undergo a medical examination or to provide the insurer with an updated health history. Often, all the policyowner must do to renew the policy is pay the renewal premium.

According to the provisions of nearly all renewable term insurance policies, the policyowner has the right to renew the coverage for the same term and face amount that were originally provided by the policy. For example, a 10-year, $100,000 renewable term policy usually can be renewed for another 10-year period and for $100,000 in coverage. One-year term policies and riders are usually renewable, and such coverage is called **yearly renewable term (YRT) insurance** or *annually renewable term (ART) insurance*. Most insurers also allow the policyowner to renew the policy for a *smaller* face amount and/or a *shorter* period than provided by the original contract, but not for a larger face amount and/or a longer period.

In many cases, the renewal provision places some limit on the policyowner's right to renew. The most common limitations are that (1) the coverage may be renewed only until the insured attains a stated age or (2) the coverage may be renewed only a stated maximum number of times. For example, the renewal provision of a policy may specify that the coverage is not renewable after the insured has reached age 75. Another policy may specify that the coverage is renewable no more than three times. Such restrictions exist to minimize antiselection.

When a term life insurance policy is renewed, the policy's premium rate increases. The renewal premium rate is based on the insured person's **attained age**—the age the insured has reached (attained) on the renewal date. As we described in an earlier chapter, mortality rates generally increase as people grow older. Because the insured's mortality risk has increased over the initial term of coverage, the renewal premium rate also must be increased. The renewal premium rate then remains level throughout the new term of coverage.

The renewal feature can lead to some antiselection; insureds in poor health will be more likely to renew their policies because they may not be able to obtain other life insurance. Because of this risk of antiselection, the premium for a renewable term life insurance policy is usually slightly higher than the premium for a comparable nonrenewable term life insurance policy.

**Example.** Allen Padred, age 30, just purchased a $100,000, three-year term life insurance policy on his own life. The policy's annual premium is $126. During the three-year policy term, Allen will pay $126 each year for his coverage. The policy contains a *renewal provision* that gives Allen the option to renew his policy until the policy anniversary date nearest his 65<sup>th</sup> birthday without having to submit evidence of his insurability.

**Analysis.** On the *policy anniversary* at the end of the three-year term, Allen has the right to renew his coverage. The coverage will be for the same $100,000 face amount as the original policy and for the same three-year term. The new premium amount, however, will be $145 per year to reflect Allen's *attained age* at the time of renewal. Allen will pay this higher premium each year during the three-year renewal period. At the end of the second three-year period and subsequent three-year periods until the policy anniversary date nearest his 65<sup>th</sup> birthday, Allen will again have the option to renew the policy at a premium rate based on his attained age.

## Convertible Term Life Insurance

Convertible term insurance policies contain a ***conversion privilege*** that allows the policyowner to change—convert—the term insurance policy to a cash value policy *without* providing evidence that the insured is an insurable risk. Even if the health of the person insured by a convertible term policy has deteriorated to the point that she would otherwise be uninsurable, the policyowner can obtain cash value insurance coverage on the insured because evidence of insurability is not required at the time of conversion. The premium that the policyowner is charged for the cash value policy cannot be based on any increase in the insured's mortality risk, except with regard to an increase in the insured's age.

As in the case of the renewal provision, the conversion privilege can lead to some antiselection; insureds in poor health are more likely to convert their coverage because they may not be able to obtain other life insurance. As a result, insurers usually charge a higher premium rate for a convertible term policy than they charge for a comparable nonconvertible term policy. In addition, insurers usually limit the conversion privilege in some way. For instance, some policies do not permit conversion after the insured has attained a specific age, such as 55 or 65, or after the term policy has been in force for a specified time. For example, a 10-year term policy may permit conversion only during the first 7 or 8 years of the term.

Conversion also may be limited to an amount that is only a percentage of the original face amount. For example, a 10-year term policy may permit conversion of 100 percent of the face amount only within the first 5 years of the term, and a smaller percentage, such as 50 percent of the face amount, if the policy is converted during the last 5 years of the 10-year term.

When a term insurance policy is converted to a cash value policy, the new premium rate is higher than the premium rate the policyowner paid for the term insurance policy. The increased premium rate is required because the premium charged for a cash value life insurance policy is higher than the premium charged for a comparable term insurance policy. The specific amount of the premium charged for the cash value insurance coverage provided following conversion depends on the effective date of the cash value life insurance policy. The effective date of the cash value coverage is either the date the term policy is converted to a cash value plan of insurance—known as an *attained age conversion*—or the date the convertible term policy was issued—known as an *original age conversion*.

When a term life insurance policy is converted to a cash value policy under an **attained age conversion**, the renewal premium rate is based on the insured's age when the coverage is converted.

> **Example.** John Matthews was 35 years old when he bought a five-year convertible term policy on his life. Four years later, John decided to convert the term insurance policy to a cash value life policy. The effective date of his cash value coverage is the date the conversion takes place.
>
> **Analysis.** The insurer will charge John the premium rate it currently charges insureds who are age 39—John's attained age—for a comparable cash value life insurance policy.

Some convertible term life insurance policies permit the policyowner to convert their policies by means of an **original age conversion**. When such a policy is converted, the effective date of the cash value life insurance policy is considered to be the date on which the policyowner purchased the original term insurance policy. As a result, the premium rate for the cash value policy is based on the insured's age at the time the policyowner purchased the original term insurance policy.

The renewal premium rate charged for the cash value insurance is lower under an original age conversion than under an attained age conversion because the premium rate is based on a younger age. If, in our earlier example, John Matthews had chosen an original age conversion, the renewal premium rate for the cash value insurance would be the premium rate charged for a 35-year-old male, even though John was actually 39 years old when the coverage was converted. In many cases, an insurance company will not allow an original age conversion if more than a stated number of years—such as more than five years—have elapsed since the term life insurance policy was purchased.

Under an original age conversion, the cash value insurance coverage is treated as if it had been in effect since the effective date of the convertible term policy. As a result, when a term life insurance policy is converted on an original age basis, the insurance company must establish a policy reserve equal to the reserve that would have accumulated if the policy had originally been issued as cash value life insurance. To provide the insurer with the funds to establish this reserve, the converting policyowner is required to pay all, or part, of the difference between the premiums already paid for the term insurance policy and the premiums that would have been payable had the policy been issued as a cash value life insurance policy. This payment often represents a sizable outlay of money. Consequently, attained age conversion, which does not require the policyowner to make a large cash outlay at the time of conversion, is much more common than original age conversion.

The renewal and conversion privileges are of obvious potential value to the policyowner, but they also are of value to the insurance company. Most policyowners renew or convert their term life insurance policies, not because they are in poor health, but because they want to continue their insurance protection. Therefore, insurance companies are able to keep such insurance in force without the expense of initiating new sales.

# Needs Met by Life Insurance

Life insurance provides for the payment of a benefit following the death of the insured. Such a death benefit can be used for a range of purposes. In this section, we describe some of the personal and business needs that life insurance can meet. Because all types of life insurance provide a death benefit, the needs we describe in this section can be met by any plan of life insurance. Term life insurance, however, has an advantage in that it is the least expensive plan of life insurance because it only provides protection against the financial risk of the premature death of an insured. In later chapters, we describe some of the specific uses of other types of life insurance.

## Personal Needs

People's needs for life insurance coverage vary greatly, but some of the reasons that people purchase life insurance are common to most buyers. In this section, we describe some of the typical personal needs that life insurance can meet.

## Estate Planning

When a person dies, a personal representative typically is appointed to settle the deceased person's estate. The personal representative is known as an *executor* if the person died with a valid will. The personal representative is known as an *administrator* if the person died without a valid will. The deceased's *estate* consists of all things of value—the *assets*—owned by the person when he died. These assets include cash, bank and investment accounts, real estate, and ownership interests in a business. To settle the estate, the personal representative is responsible for identifying and collecting the deceased's property, filing any required tax forms, collecting all debts owed to the deceased, and paying all outstanding debts owed by the deceased. The personal representative then distributes the remaining property to the deceased person's heirs. An individual who wants to ensure that his estate will be settled in accordance with his wishes will develop a plan—called an *estate plan*—that considers the amount of assets and debts that he is likely to have when he dies and how best to preserve those assets so that they can pass to his heirs as he desires. Life insurance is often an important component of an estate plan.

## Debts and Final Expenses

When any person dies, certain debts may become payable. Many people, for example, have debts in the form of mortgage loans, educational loans, personal loans, credit accounts, and automobile loans. In addition, some expense may be related to the death itself, such as doctor and hospital bills that are not covered by insurance, as well as funeral expenses. Many of these expenses must be paid regardless of whether the deceased worked or had any dependents. Furthermore, various taxes may be imposed on a deceased person's estate. In the United States, for example, the federal government imposes an estate tax on estates that exceed a specified value. The personal representative may have to sell assets belonging to the deceased to raise cash to pay the deceased's debts. Such a forced sale of assets can result in the assets being sold for much less than if they could be sold in a more leisurely manner. As an alternative to a forced sale of assets to raise cash, individuals can purchase insurance on their lives to provide the cash needed to pay these expenses.

## Dependents' Support

If a person who supports or helps support a family dies, the surviving dependents may face serious problems in the months immediately following the person's death. Household expenses go on; rent or mortgage payments must be made, utility bills paid, food and clothing purchased. The death may create additional expenses, such as the need to provide child care and daily household upkeep—all while family members try to cope with the emotional effects of the loss of a loved one.

Relatively few people have sufficient funds to pay their usual expenses for several months if the regular family income ceases or is reduced substantially. Life insurance can provide funds to support the family members until they obtain new methods of support or until they adjust to a lower income. In addition, the proceeds of a life insurance policy can be used to supplement the family's income. If the insured has dependents such as minor children or elderly parents, policy proceeds can be used to provide funds to support those dependents for as long as they require support and can be used to fund the education of the insured's dependents. Insight 5.1 describes some methods for determining how much life insurance an individual should purchase.

As a general rule, when the proceeds of a life insurance policy are paid in a lump sum to a named beneficiary following the death of the insured, those proceeds are not considered taxable income to the beneficiary. In other words, a policy beneficiary who receives policy death benefits is not required to pay income taxes on the policy proceeds. This favorable income tax treatment given to life insurance is designed to encourage people to provide for their dependents' financial needs.

---

 **INSIGHT 5.1**    How Much Life Insurance Is Enough?

Many formulas have been developed to help people determine how much life insurance they should purchase. One of the simplest formulas focuses on the person's current income—the amount of insurance needed is a multiple of the amount of current income. For example, the formula might recommend that people purchase at least five times their current income in life insurance. Thus, a person who earns $50,000 a year would be advised to purchase at least $250,000 of life insurance. The specific multiple amount recommended varies widely.

Another common method to establish the amount of coverage needed is to evaluate all of the person's expenses, debts, savings, and family situation. This method is much more difficult than the multiple of current income formula and requires the person to develop a comprehensive picture of his financial situation and future financial needs. For example, assume that Beth Huang is the single parent of two young children who earns $40,000 a year. Ms. Huang wants to provide for her children should she die, and she calculates that without her income it would cost at least $250,000 to support her children until they reach age 21 and are likely to be able to support themselves. Unless Ms. Huang has other sources of funds to support her children, she should consider purchasing at least $250,000 of insurance on her life. Additional needs may increase the amount of life insurance that Ms. Huang should buy.

# Business Needs

A business—or an individual who owns a business—generally purchases life insurance products for one of two reasons:

- A life insurance policy can provide funds to ensure that the business continues in the event of the death of an owner, partner, or other key person.

- A business can purchase life insurance to provide benefits for its employees.

## Business Continuation Insurance

A *business continuation insurance plan* is an insurance plan designed to enable a business owner (or owners) to provide for the business' continued operation if the owner or a key person dies. A *key person* is any person or employee whose continued participation in the business is necessary to the success of the business and whose death would cause the business a significant financial loss.

Any closely held business may need to establish a business continuation insurance plan to ensure that the business will continue if an owner or key employee dies. A *closely held business* is a sole proprietorship, a partnership, or a corporation that is owned by only a few individuals. A large corporation is not typically faced with this need for business continuation life insurance because it has the financial resources to ensure that its business continues beyond the death of any individual.

In this section, we first describe business continuation insurance plans that closely held businesses can use to fund the purchase of a deceased owner's or partner's share in the business. Then, we describe business continuation insurance plans that protect a business against the financial consequences of the death of a key person.

## Buy-Sell Agreements

Ideally, the owners of any closely held business should consider what will happen to the business if the owner, a partner, or a shareholder dies. As noted earlier, an individual's estate includes any ownership interest she had in a business. Thus, if one of the owners of a closely held business dies, the deceased owner's share of the business becomes part of her estate. For example, when the owner of a sole proprietorship dies, all of her assets—including the assets of the business—pass to her estate, and all of her liabilities—including the liabilities of the business—must be paid by the estate. Often the executor or administrator of the deceased's estate is forced to liquidate the business to provide funds to pay these liabilities. *Liquidation* is the process of selling off for cash a business' assets, such as its building, inventory, and equipment, and using that cash to pay the business' debts; any funds remaining are then distributed to the owners of the business. A forced liquidation places the surviving heirs in the position of having to take whatever price they can get for these assets at the time of the sale. The heirs often receive far less than if they had been able to wait for more acceptable offers.

A buy-sell agreement prepared in advance can alleviate many problems associated with the untimely death of a business owner. A **buy-sell agreement** is an agreement in which (1) one party agrees to purchase the financial interest that a second party has in a business following the second party's death and (2) the second party agrees to direct his estate to sell his interest in the business to the purchasing party. One or more of the parties to a buy-sell agreement often purchase life insurance to fund the buy-sell agreement. The following are some examples of how life insurance can be used to fund a buy-sell agreement:

- The owner of a sole proprietorship may enter into a buy-sell agreement with another individual, often an employee, who agrees to purchase the business at the sole proprietor's death. The individual purchases an insurance policy on the life of the sole proprietor. After the sole proprietor's death, the proceeds of the life insurance policy are paid to the individual policyowner, who can use the proceeds to purchase the business from the sole proprietor's estate.

- Although a partnership usually dissolves upon the death of a partner, the surviving partner (or partners) may create a new business. Partners often plan for the continuation of the business after the death of a partner by entering into a buy-sell agreement that sets out the terms under which a deceased partner's interest in the partnership will be purchased. The partners may purchase insurance on the lives of the other partners to fund the buy-sell agreement, or the partnership can purchase insurance on each of the partners' lives.

## Key Person Life Insurance

Another form of business continuation insurance is key person life insurance. **Key person life insurance**—or *key employee life insurance*—is insurance that a business purchases on the life of a person whose continued participation in the business is necessary to its success and whose death would cause financial loss to the business. As we described earlier in the chapter, a key person could be an owner, a partner, or an employee of the business. When a business purchases key person life insurance, the business owns, pays the premiums on, and is the beneficiary of the insurance policy. If the key person dies, the policy proceeds are paid to the business.

Many businesses depend on the continued participation of certain valuable people. The loss of a key person's expertise and services may seriously affect the firm's earnings. For example, a top salesperson or a person with important business contacts may be responsible for a large portion of the firm's income. In addition to the potential loss of a key person's services, the business must also consider the cost of training or finding a replacement for the key person. A business can provide itself with an extra layer of financial security by purchasing an insurance policy on the life of the key person. The policy proceeds can supplement the firm's earnings while it searches for and trains a replacement for the deceased employee.

Another benefit the firm can gain through the purchase of key person insurance is the enhancement of its credit position. During the period following the death of a key person, the business is likely to need additional cash flow. Sales may drop off; productivity may decline; banks, creditors, and suppliers may become uneasy and withdraw or reduce the firm's credit privileges. If, however, the firm's banks, creditors, and suppliers know that the business has protected itself by insuring the lives of its key people, they may agree to continue their business relationships with the firm on the same terms as before a key person's death.

## Life Insurance As an Employee Benefit

Many businesses purchase group life insurance policies as a way of providing benefits to their employees. Often businesses pay for all or part of these employee benefits as part of the total package under which they compensate their employees. Providing such benefits enables businesses to attract and retain qualified employees. Many employers also provide a group retirement plan for their employees. We describe these group insurance and retirement plans later in the text.

Individual insurance products also are used in some instances to provide employee benefits for selected classes of employees. Employers sometimes offer these individual benefit plans to certain employees in addition to the employee benefits that all other employees receive. By offering these additional benefits to especially valuable employees, the business can more readily attract and retain those employees.

# Key Terms

policy term
policy anniversary
policy rider
level term life insurance
decreasing term life insurance
mortgage insurance
joint mortgage insurance
credit life insurance
family income coverage
family income policy
increasing term life insurance
renewable term insurance policy
convertible term insurance policy
renewal provision
evidence of insurability

yearly renewable term
  (YRT) insurance
attained age
conversion privilege
attained age conversion
original age conversion
estate
estate plan
business continuation
  insurance plan
key person
closely held business
liquidation
buy-sell agreement
key person life insurance

# Endnote

1. An *index* provides a mathematical measure that indicates the relative changes in a specific factor—such as costs, production, or prices—at a given point in time as compared to a specific time in the past. The *Consumer Price Index (CPI)* measures the change in the price of a fixed basket of goods bought by a typical consumer; the goods included in the CPI include food, transportation, housing, utilities, clothing, and medical care.

# Cash Value Life Insurance and Endowment Insurance

## objectives

*After reading this chapter, you should be able to*

- Identify the features of whole life insurance, modified whole life insurance, and joint whole life insurance and recognize how these plans of insurance differ from one another

- Distinguish home service life insurance products from other life insurance products

- Identify which characteristics of universal life insurance are similar to characteristics of other cash value life insurance and which characteristics are unique to universal life insurance

- Distinguish among universal life, variable life, and variable universal life insurance

- Identify the characteristics of indeterminate premium life insurance and interest-sensitive whole life insurance

- Describe the characteristics of endowment insurance

I n addition to term life insurance, insurance companies offer a range of life insurance products that include a savings element, known as a cash value. Policies that have a cash value give policyowners access to cash that they can use to meet personal and business needs during insureds' lifetimes. In this chapter, we describe a variety of cash value life insurance products, ranging from traditional whole life insurance to variable universal life insurance. We also describe endowment insurance.

# Cash Value Life Insurance

Two primary characteristics distinguish cash value life insurance products from term life insurance products.

- **Cash value life insurance products offer lifetime coverage.** Term life insurance provides protection for a certain period of time and provides no benefits after that period ends. In contrast, cash value life insurance provides protection for the *entire* lifetime of the insured, so long as the policy remains in force.

- **Cash value life insurance products provide insurance coverage and contain a savings element.** Term life insurance usually provides only insurance protection. In contrast, cash value life insurance not only provides insurance protection, it also builds a cash value that functions as a savings element.

Despite these common characteristics of cash value life insurance, the various plans of cash value life insurance differ widely in their features and benefits.

## Traditional Whole Life Insurance

*Whole life insurance* provides lifetime insurance coverage at a level premium rate that does not increase as the insured ages. As we noted in Chapter 4, life insurers use the level premium pricing system so that the premium rates do not increase as the insureds' mortality rates increase. The insurance company invests the excess premium dollars it collects in the early years under the level premium pricing system and accumulates assets that are at least equal to the amount of the policy reserve liability the insurer has established for those policies. (The CD-ROM included in the back cover of the text contains a sample whole life insurance policy.)

The terminology used to describe insurance products is not consistent throughout the insurance industry. Often, two or more terms are used to identify the same product, and sometimes one term is used in several contexts. *Whole life* is perhaps the best example of an insurance term that is employed in several contexts. In one context, *whole life* refers to the broad classification of insurance products that are considered to be cash value insurance; thus, in this context, some of the newer products such as universal life insurance, variable life insurance, and adjustable life insurance are forms of whole life insurance. *Whole life* also is used to refer to a specific type of cash value insurance product. This text uses *whole life* in this last sense to refer to a specific type of cash value insurance product.

Whole life insurance policies include a table that illustrates how the policy's cash value will grow over time. Figure 6.1 provides an example of such a table of guaranteed values. If for some reason the policy does not remain in force until the insured's death, the insurer agrees to refund the cash value to the policyowner—less any surrender charges and outstanding policy loans. Because the policyowner generally has the right to surrender—or terminate—a cash value life insurance policy for its cash value during the insured's lifetime, the amount of the cash value that a policyowner is entitled to receive upon policy surrender is referred to as the **cash surrender value** or the *surrender value*. We describe the cash surrender value in detail in Chapter 8.

The size of a policy's cash value at any given time depends on a number of factors, such as the face amount of the policy, the length of time the policy has been in force, and the length of the policy's premium payment period. The reserve and the cash value of a whole life policy increase throughout the life of the policy and eventually equal the face amount of the policy. The cash value, however, does not equal the face amount until the time the insured reaches the age at the end of the mortality table used to calculate premiums for that policy. At that point, the insurer typically pays the face amount of the policy to the policyowner, even if the insured is still living.

One of the property ownership rights that a policyowner has in a whole life insurance policy is the right to receive the policy's cash value. As a result of this ownership right, the policyowner can use a policy that has accumulated a cash value as security for a loan. The policyowner can receive a loan, known as a **policy loan**, from the insurance company itself, or the policyowner can use the cash value of the policy as collateral for a loan from another financial institution. If the insured dies before a policy loan is repaid, however, the unpaid amount of the loan—plus any interest outstanding—is subtracted from the policy benefit. Policy loans are discussed in more detail in Chapter 8.

| FIGURE 6.1 | Growth of Cash Value in a $100,000 Whole Life Insurance Policy, Issued to a Male, Age 37 |

| End of Policy Year | Cash Value |
|---|---|
| 1 | —— |
| 2 | —— |
| 3 | $ 400 |
| 4 | 1,400 |
| 5 | 2,400 |
| 6 | 3,500 |
| 7 | 4,500 |
| 8 | 5,600 |
| 9 | 6,800 |
| 10 | 8,000 |
| 11 | 9,300 |
| 12 | 11,000 |
| 13 | 12,900 |
| 14 | 14,800 |
| 15 | 16,700 |
| 16 | 18,700 |
| 17 | 20,700 |
| 18 | 22,700 |
| 19 | 24,800 |
| 20 | 26,900 |
| Age 60 | 32,300 |
| Age 65 | 41,700 |

\* This table assumes premiums have been paid to the end of the policy year shown. These values do not include any dividend accumulations, paid-up additions, or policy loans.

**Source:** Adapted from Harriett E. Jones, *LOMA's Handbook of Insurance Policy Forms* (Atlanta: LOMA, © 2000), L29. Used with permission; all rights reserved.

## Premium Payment Periods

Whole life policies can be classified on the basis of the length of the policy's premium payment period. Most whole life policies are classified as either (1) continuous-premium policies or (2) limited-payment policies. The length of a policy's premium payment period directly affects both the amount of the periodic premium required for the policy and the pace at which the policy's cash value builds.

### Continuous-Premium Policies

Under a ***continuous-premium whole life policy*** (sometimes referred to as a *straight life insurance policy* or an *ordinary life insurance policy*), premiums are payable until the death of the insured. Because premiums are payable over the life of the policy, the amount of each premium payment required for a continuous-premium whole life policy is lower than the premium amount required under any other premium payment schedule for a whole life policy.

### Limited-Payment Policies

A ***limited-payment whole life policy*** is a whole life policy for which premiums are payable only until some stated period expires or until the insured's death, whichever occurs first. The policy may describe the stated period over which premiums are payable in one of two ways.

1. Premiums may be payable for a specific number of years. For example, a 20-payment whole life insurance policy is a policy for which premiums are payable for 20 years.

2. Premiums may be payable until the insured reaches a specified age. For example, a paid-up-at-age-65 whole life insurance policy provides that premiums are payable until the insured reaches the policy anniversary closest to or immediately following her 65th birthday, at which time the premium payments cease but the coverage continues. A policy that requires no further premium payments but continues to provide coverage is said to be a ***paid-up policy***.

In either case, if the insured dies before the end of the specified premium payment period, the insurer pays the death benefit to the named beneficiary and no further premiums are payable.

Limited-payment policies are designed to meet a policyowner's need for life insurance protection that continues throughout the insured's lifetime and that is funded over a limited time period. The policyowner, for example, may expect that his income will drop considerably when he retires, and yet he anticipates that he will still need life insurance coverage after retirement.

**Example.** Arabella Simpson, who has just turned 42, plans to retire at age 62, at which time her income will be reduced considerably. Arabella wishes to obtain cash value life insurance, but she is concerned that she will not be able to pay the premiums from her retirement income. She has, therefore, purchased a 20-payment whole life policy.

**Analysis.** Arabella will make her last premium payment at age 61, at which time she will have a paid-up policy that will require no further premium payments but will provide life insurance coverage for the rest of her life.

The insurer establishes the premium amounts required for a limited-payment policy so that, at the end of the premium payment period, sufficient premiums have been paid to keep the policy in force for the rest of the insured's lifetime. Because fewer annual premium payments are expected to be made for a limited-payment policy than for a comparable continuous-premium policy, the annual premium for the limited-payment policy is larger than the annual premium for an equivalent continuous-premium policy.

Likewise, cash values generally build more rapidly under limited-payment policies than they do under continuous-premium policies. Under a limited-payment policy, a cash value often is available at the end of the first policy year, whereas a cash value under a continuous-premium policy may not be available until the end of the third policy year.

## Single-Premium Policies

A *single-premium whole life policy* is a type of limited-payment policy that requires only one premium payment. The insurer uses a large part of that single premium to set up the policy's reserve. And because the cash value available on any whole life policy is related to the amount of the policy reserve—although often somewhat lower than the reserve—a sizable cash value is available immediately on any single-premium policy.

# Modified Whole Life Insurance

The traditional whole life insurance products described so far provide a constant face amount of life insurance coverage in exchange for a single premium or a series of level premiums. Some insurance companies issue whole life insurance policies under which either (1) the amount of the premium payments required changes at some point in the life of the policy or (2) the face amount of coverage changes during the life of the policy.

## Modified Premiums

A *modified-premium whole life policy* functions in the same manner as a traditional whole life policy except that the policy's annual premium changes after a specified initial period, such as 5, 10, 15, or 20 years. The initial annual premium for a modified premium whole life policy is less than the initial annual premium for a similar whole life policy issued on a level-premium basis. After the specified period, the annual premium for a modified-premium policy increases to a stated amount that is somewhat higher than the usual (nonmodified) premium would have been. This new increased annual premium is then payable as long as the policy remains in force.

The face amount of a modified-premium whole life policy remains level throughout the life of the policy. For example, a $50,000 continuous-premium whole life policy issued on the life of a 25-year-old man might call for an annual premium of $400. The annual premium for a modified-premium whole life policy for the same face amount could be $310 for the first 10 years, with the premium increasing to $600 per year thereafter for the rest of the life of the policy. (See Figure 6.2, which illustrates this example.)

The chief advantage to the policyowner of buying a modified-premium whole life policy is that he is able to purchase a larger face amount of whole life insurance than he would otherwise be able to afford. The chief disadvantage of a modified-premium whole life policy is that the cash value builds more slowly under a modified-premium policy than under a traditional whole life policy.

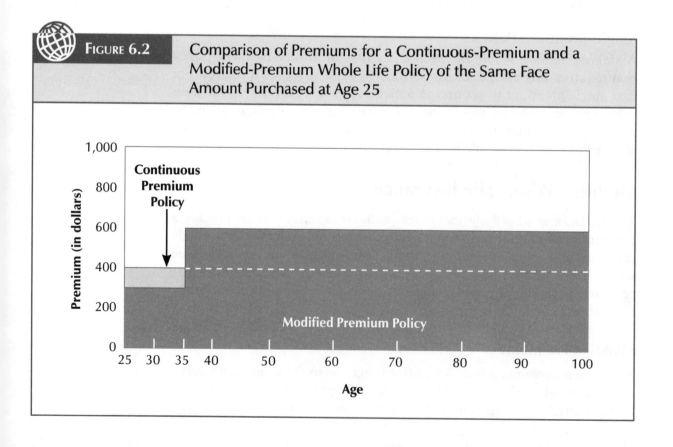

FIGURE 6.2 Comparison of Premiums for a Continuous-Premium and a Modified-Premium Whole Life Policy of the Same Face Amount Purchased at Age 25

Some insurers issue whole life policies for which premium payments are modified even more frequently. Generally known as **graded-premium policies**, these policies call for three or more levels of annual premium payment amounts, increasing at specified points in time—such as every three years—until reaching the amount to be paid as a level premium for the rest of the life of the policy. As in all modified-premium plans, the face amount of insurance remains level throughout the life of the policy.

### Modified Coverage

The second method of modifying traditional whole life insurance policies is based on the assumption that the need for large amounts of life insurance is likely to diminish as the insured grows older. For example, as a policyowner-insured grows older, she may pay off debts and mortgages, her children may leave home, and her financial obligations may decrease. If the policyowner has accumulated savings and other assets over the years, the need for life insurance may become less important. A **modified coverage policy** provides that the amount of insurance will decrease by specific percentages or amounts either when the insured reaches certain stated ages or at the end of stated time periods. For example, the face amount of a modified coverage whole life policy may begin at $100,000, decrease to $75,000 when the insured reaches age 60, decrease further to $50,000 at age 70, and then remain level for the rest of the insured's lifetime.

In anticipation of such reduced coverage at the older ages, an insurer is able, from the time of policy issue, to provide the $100,000 modified whole life policy for a lower annual premium than if the insurer were liable for the full $100,000 of coverage through the entire expected lifetime of the insured. The reason is that during the period of greatest risk of death—the period when the insured is at an advanced age—the face amount of the policy will be at its lowest level.

## Joint Whole Life Insurance

**Joint whole life insurance** has the same features and benefits as individual whole life insurance, except that it insures two lives under the same policy. Joint whole life insurance is often referred to as *first-to-die life insurance* because, upon the death of one of the insureds, the policy death benefit is paid to the surviving insured and the policy coverage ends.

Because coverage under a joint whole life policy ends once the policy death benefit is paid, the surviving insured may be left uninsured. To give the surviving insured the ability to obtain life insurance coverage, joint whole life policies usually provide a specified period—frequently 60 or 90 days—following the first insured's death within which the surviving insured may purchase an individual whole life policy of the same face amount without providing evidence of insurability. Some joint whole life policies provide the surviving insured with temporary term insurance coverage during this specified period.

## Last Survivor Life Insurance

*Last survivor life insurance*—also known as *second-to-die life insurance*—is a variation of joint whole life insurance under which the policy benefit is paid only after both people insured by the policy have died. Premiums for last survivor life insurance coverage may be payable only until the first insured dies, or premiums may be payable until the death of both insureds. In either case, a couple can obtain insurance on both of their lives for an annual premium that is usually less than the cost of either (1) two individual whole life insurance policies or (2) a joint whole life insurance policy. Last survivor life insurance was designed primarily to insure married couples who want to provide funds to pay estate taxes that may be levied after their deaths.

## Family Policies

Some insurers market a *family policy*, which is a whole life insurance policy that includes term life insurance coverage on the insured's spouse and children. The amount of term insurance coverage provided on the insured's spouse and children is a fraction—generally one-fourth or one-fifth—of the amount of the insured's whole life insurance coverage. For example, a family with three children might purchase a family policy that provides $50,000 of whole life insurance coverage on the primary insured, $12,500 of term insurance coverage on the insured's spouse (one-fourth of the amount of the coverage on the primary insured), and $10,000 of term insurance coverage for each child (one-fifth of the amount of coverage on the primary insured). Thus, a total of $92,500 of life insurance would be provided by one family policy.

Typically, the applicant for a family policy must provide evidence that all family members are insurable. Once the policy is issued, however, each child born to or adopted by the family thereafter is automatically covered by the policy, although the coverage often is not effective until the child reaches age 15 days and an additional premium may be payable for the additional coverage. However, because mortality rates are low for children older than 15 days, family policies often provide automatic coverage for additional children without imposing an additional premium charge for that coverage.

## Monthly Debit Ordinary

A *monthly debit ordinary (MDO) policy* is a whole life insurance policy that is marketed under the home service distribution system and is paid for by monthly premium payments. The *home service distribution system* is a method of selling and servicing insurance policies through commissioned sales agents, known as **home service agents**, who sell a range of products and provide specified policyowner services, including the collection of renewal premiums, within a specified geographic area. A home service agent's assigned territory is referred to as a *debit*, *agency*, or *account*. MDO policies have many of the same characteristics as traditional whole life insurance, but MDO policies tend to be sold in smaller face amounts than other whole life insurance policies.

## Pre-Need Funeral Insurance

**Pre-need funeral insurance**, or *pre-need insurance*, is whole life insurance that provides funds to pay for the insured's funeral and burial. In most cases, the policyowner and a funeral home enter into an agreement, known as an *assignment*, under which the life insurance policy benefit will be paid after the insured's death to the funeral home, which agrees to provide specified funeral services and merchandise. (We describe assignments in Chapter 10.) The face amount of the whole life insurance policy usually is designed to increase over the life of the insured so that the amount keeps pace with expected increases in the cost of providing the selected funeral services and merchandise.

Because funeral arrangements are made while the insured is living, the insured's survivors are spared from having to make these arrangements following the insured's death. Pre-need funeral insurance tends to be sold in relatively small face amounts. Some insurers market pre-need funeral insurance through funeral home employees who are licensed as insurance producers.

# A Newer Generation of Cash Value Products

During the 1970s and 1980s, the North American economy changed to such a degree that insurers, like many other financial institutions, were forced to look carefully at the products they offered. Inflation hit record highs; interest rates on savings accounts and consumer loans soared. Consumers realized that the cash values of their whole life policies were earning investment returns at rates that were much lower than the rates that savings accounts and other investment vehicles could earn. Insurers realized that much of their invested assets were earning a lower return than could be obtained through newer investments.

To address the need for insurance products that were more responsive to a changing economy, insurers began marketing a new generation of insurance products that were able to reflect current conditions in the financial marketplace. These new-generation products include universal life, adjustable life, variable life, variable universal life, interest-sensitive whole life, and indeterminate premium products.

# Universal Life Insurance

*Universal life (UL) insurance* is a form of cash value life insurance that is characterized by its flexible premiums, its flexible face amount and death benefit amount, and its unbundling of the pricing factors. All of the policies that we have described until now—both term insurance policies and whole life insurance policies—state the gross premium that the policyowner must pay to keep the policy in force. As we noted in Chapter 4, however, some policies—most notably universal life insurance policies—list each of the three pricing factors (mortality, interest, and expenses) separately. In addition, the policyowner can determine, within certain limits, the amount of the premium she wants to pay for the coverage. The larger the premium that the policyowner pays, the larger the amount of coverage that will be provided and the greater the policy's cash value will be.

In some forms of universal life policies, the cash value amount is reduced by significant expense charges, called **surrender charges**, if the policyowner chooses to surrender the policy. For these types of universal life policies, state regulators may require insurance companies to use another term, such as *account value, reserve value,* or *accumulation value,* to describe the cash value that accumulates in the policy, and a second term, either *net cash value* or *cash surrender value,* to describe the amount available to policyowners. For simplicity's sake, in this text we use the term *cash value* in connection with universal life policies.

In the following sections, we describe the distinguishing characteristics of universal life policies. In particular, we describe its flexibility—both in terms of death benefit amounts and premium amounts—and how its unbundled pricing works. We also show how a typical universal life policy operates and describe some other characteristics of the policy. Because the unbundling of the pricing structure is at the core of the operation of a universal life policy, we begin with that aspect of the policy.

## Unbundled Pricing Factors

Each of the three factors that the insurer applies to price a universal life policy is listed separately in the policy. Thus, each universal life policy specifies (1) the mortality charges that the insurer will apply, (2) the interest rate that the insurer will credit to the policy's cash value, and (3) the expense charges that the insurer will apply.

### Mortality Charges

The insurer periodically deducts a mortality charge from the universal life policy's cash value. This mortality charge is the amount needed to cover the mortality risk the insurer has assumed by issuing the policy. In other words, the mortality charge pays the cost of the life insurance coverage.

The amount of the mortality charge is based on the insured's risk classification, and the charge typically increases each year as the insured ages. Universal life policies guarantee that the mortality charge will never exceed a stated maximum amount. In addition, these policies usually provide that the mortality charge will be less than the specified maximum if the insurance company's mortality experience is more favorable than expected.

Universal life policies express the mortality charge as a charge per thousand dollars of net amount at risk. A life insurance policy's net amount at risk is the amount of the insurer's funds that would be required at any given time to pay the policy death benefit. Although the net amount at risk for most life insurance policies at any given time is equal to the policy's face value minus its reserve, the net amount at risk for a universal life insurance policy depends on whether the death benefit payable is level or varies with changes in the policy's cash value. We discuss this topic in more detail later in this section.

## Interest

A universal life insurance policy guarantees that the insurer will pay at least a stated minimum interest rate on the policy's cash value each year. The policy also provides that the insurer will pay a higher interest rate if economic and competitive conditions warrant. For example, some policies state that the interest rate paid will reflect current interest rates in the economy. Some policies state that the interest rate to be paid on the cash value will be tied to the rate paid on a standard investment, such as a specified category of U.S. government Treasury Bills. According to the terms of some universal life policies, the guaranteed interest rate is paid on cash values up to a stated amount, such as $1,000; the insurer credits any cash values greater than the stated amount with the higher current interest rate. Finally, most universal life policies provide that any portion of the cash value that is being used as security for a policy loan will earn interest at a rate that is lower than the current rate. This reduced interest rate, however, will not fall below the guaranteed minimum interest rate.

## Expenses

Each universal life insurance policy lists the expense charges that the insurance company will impose to cover the costs it incurs to administer the policy. The following expense charges may be imposed:

- A flat charge during the first policy year to cover sales and policy issue costs

- A percentage of each annual premium (such as 5 percent) to cover expenses

- A monthly administration fee

- Specific service charges for coverage changes, cash withdrawals, and policy surrenders

### Flexibility Features

A universal life insurance policy gives the policyowner a great deal of flexibility, both when he purchases the policy and over the life of the policy. When he purchases the policy, the policyowner decides, within certain limits, what the policy's face amount will be, the amount of the death benefit payable, and the amount of premiums he will pay for that coverage. The policyowner can change these choices during the life of the policy, but the insurance company must approve certain types of changes.

### Face Amount and Amount of the Death Benefit

At the time of purchasing a universal life policy, the policyowner specifies the policy's face amount and decides whether the amount of the death benefit payable will be level or will vary with changes in the policy's cash value. Under an **Option A plan** (also known as an *Option 1 plan*), the amount of the death benefit is level; the death benefit payable is always equal to the policy's face amount. Under an **Option B plan** (also known as an *Option 2 plan*), the amount of the death benefit at any given time is equal to the policy's face amount *plus* the amount of the policy's cash value. Note that the net amount at risk for an Option A plan decreases as the amount of the cash value increases. The net amount at risk for an Option B plan, however, is always equal to the policy's face amount. (See Figure 6.3, which illustrates the operation of these two plans.)

After the policy has been in force for a specified minimum time—often one year—the policyowner can request an increase or decrease in the policy's face amount. The insurer typically requires the policyowner to provide evidence of the insured's continued insurability when a proposed increase in the policy's face amount would significantly increase the policy's net amount at risk.

Before approving a decrease in a policy's face amount, the insurer must make sure that the decrease would not cause the policy to lose its status as an insurance contract and instead be classified as an investment contract. Later in this section, we describe the regulatory requirements that a policy must meet to be classified as an insurance product rather than an investment product.

### Flexible Premiums

The owner of a universal life policy can determine, within certain limits, how much to pay for the initial premium and for each renewal premium. The policyowner also has great flexibility to decide when to pay renewal premiums. The insurance company imposes maximum limits on the amounts of the initial and renewal premiums to ensure that the policy will maintain its status as an insurance product. In addition, the insurance company requires payment of at least a stated minimum initial premium. As long as the policy's cash value is large enough to pay the periodic mortality and expense charges the insurer imposes, the policy will remain in

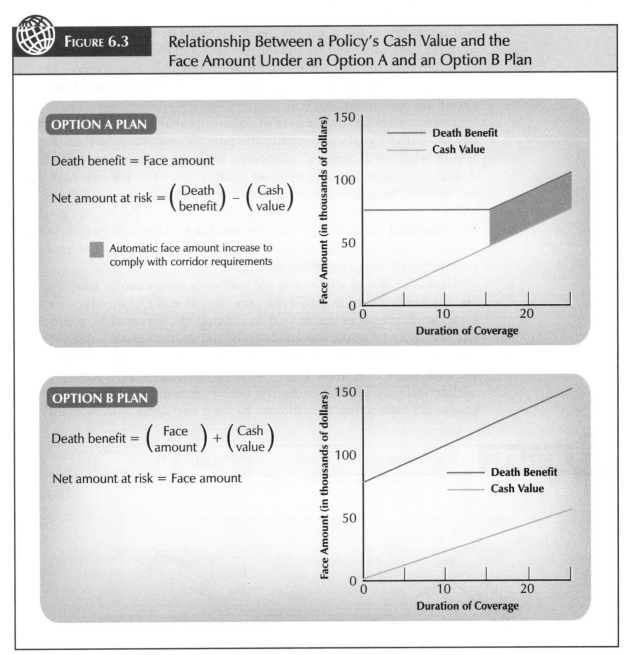

| FIGURE 6.3 | Relationship Between a Policy's Cash Value and the Face Amount Under an Option A and an Option B Plan |

**OPTION A PLAN**

Death benefit = Face amount

$$\text{Net amount at risk} = \left(\begin{array}{c}\text{Death}\\\text{benefit}\end{array}\right) - \left(\begin{array}{c}\text{Cash}\\\text{value}\end{array}\right)$$

■ Automatic face amount increase to comply with corridor requirements

**OPTION B PLAN**

$$\text{Death benefit} = \left(\begin{array}{c}\text{Face}\\\text{amount}\end{array}\right) + \left(\begin{array}{c}\text{Cash}\\\text{value}\end{array}\right)$$

Net amount at risk = Face amount

force even if the policyowner does not pay renewal premiums. If, however, the policy's cash value is insufficient to cover the periodic charges, the policy will lapse unless the policyowner pays an adequate renewal premium.

## How a Universal Life Policy Operates

When an insurer receives a universal life premium payment, it first deducts the amount of any applicable expense charges. The insurer then credits the remainder of the premium to the policy's cash value. Each month the policy remains in force, the insurer deducts the periodic mortality charges from the cash value and credits the remainder of the cash value with interest. From time to time, the insurer may deduct additional expense charges from the policy's cash value. (See Figure 6.4, which illustrates how a universal life policy operates.)

The more a policyowner pays in premiums above the amount needed to pay the policy's costs, the greater the policy's cash value will be. Regardless of when or if renewal premiums are paid, the insurer periodically deducts the mortality and expense charges from the policy's cash value and credits the cash value with interest earnings. At any time, if the cash value is not sufficient to pay those periodic charges, the insurer gives the policyowner a stated amount of time—at least 60 days—in which to pay a premium to cover those charges. If the policyowner does not make the premium payment, the policy will lapse.

The cash value of a universal life insurance policy can be used as collateral for a policy loan in much the same way that the cash value of a traditional whole life policy can be used. In addition, the universal life policyowner has the right to withdraw funds from the policy's cash value. When a policyowner withdraws funds from the cash value of a universal life policy, the cash value is reduced by the amount withdrawn plus any applicable withdrawal fees. In such cases, the policy remains in force as long as the remaining cash value is sufficient to fund the applicable mortality and

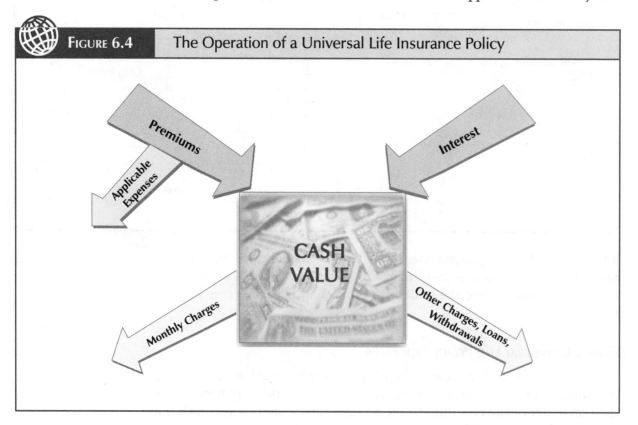

**FIGURE 6.4**    The Operation of a Universal Life Insurance Policy

expense charges. Some universal life policies also provide that the face amount of the policy will be reduced by the amount of a cash value withdrawal. We describe the policy withdrawal provision in Chapter 8.

## Effects of Regulation on Universal Life Policies

Because the operation of a universal life policy gives the policyowner the ability to pay much more in premiums than is needed to fund the cost of insurance, the amount of the policy's cash value can be much greater in relation to the face amount of the policy than is possible with a whole life insurance policy. The larger the cash value is in relation to the policy's face amount, the more a policy seems to be an investment product rather than an insurance product. U.S. federal tax laws treat life insurance products favorably. To ensure that this favorable tax treatment is available only to life insurance products, federal tax laws establish limits on the size of a life insurance policy's cash value in relation to its face amount. If the cash value exceeds the regulatory limits, then the policy is treated for tax purposes as an investment product rather than an insurance policy. In the United States, the difference between a policy's face amount and the policy's cash value required to qualify as a life insurance policy rather than an investment product is often referred to as the *Section 7702 corridor* because Internal Revenue Code Section 7702 is the section of the tax code that establishes the limits on the amount of a policy's cash value.

Insurance companies do not allow a policyowner to pay a premium amount that would result in the cash value exceeding the legislatively defined percentage of the face amount. In addition, most universal life policies provide that if the cash value exceeds the specified percentage of the face amount, then the face amount of the policy automatically is increased to an amount that will meet the legislative requirements.

## Periodic Reports

Because so many aspects of a universal life insurance policy change over the course of a year, insurers send each policyowner an annual, semiannual, or quarterly report giving the policy's current values and benefits. Generally, this report includes the following types of information:

- The amount of the death benefit payable

- The amount of the policy's cash value

- The amount of the cash surrender value, if different from the cash value

- The amount of interest earned on the cash value

- The amount of the mortality charges deducted

- The amount of the expense charges deducted

- The amount of premiums paid during the reporting period
- The amount of policy loans outstanding
- The amount of any cash value withdrawals

Figure 6.5 shows a sample universal life insurance policy annual report. Note that this sample report illustrates a policy earning interest at a rate of 7 percent. Interest rates vary over time with changes in the economy and rates being paid on such policies today tend to be lower than the illustrated rate. Nevertheless, the sample report contains the types of information that are provided to universal life insurance policyowners.

## Indeterminate Premium Life Insurance

An *indeterminate premium life insurance policy* is a type of nonparticipating whole life policy that specifies two premium rates—both a maximum guaranteed premium rate and a lower premium rate. The insurer charges the lower premium rate when the policy is issued and guarantees that rate for at least a stated period of time, such as 1 year, 2 years, 5 years, or 10 years. After that period, the insurer uses its actual mortality, interest, and expense experience to establish a new premium rate that may be higher or lower than the previous premium rate. In no case, though, will the new premium rate exceed the maximum rate guaranteed in the policy. This premium modification process continues periodically throughout the life of the policy. In general, the maximum premium rate charged is slightly higher than the rate for an equivalent nonparticipating whole life policy.

In all other respects, an indeterminate premium policy functions in the same manner as a traditional nonparticipating whole life policy. It enables insurers that issue nonparticipating policies to be more flexible in their pricing because they can change their premium rates to reflect changes in their current mortality, interest, and expense experience. Note that, to change the premium rate for an indeterminate premium policy, an insurer must change the premium rate for an entire class of policies based on the insurer's experience for that class of policies. An indeterminate premium policy is also known as a *nonguaranteed premium life insurance policy* and a *variable-premium life insurance policy*.

## Interest-Sensitive Whole Life Insurance

*Interest-sensitive whole life insurance*, which is also called *current assumption whole life insurance*, takes the concept of indeterminate premium policies one step further. In addition to varying the premium rate to reflect changing assumptions regarding the mortality, investment, and expense factors, these policies also provide that the cash value can be greater than that guaranteed if changing assumptions warrant such an increase.

| FIGURE 6.5 | Sample Annual Report for a Universal Life Insurance Policy |

**ABC Life Insurance Company**
**Universal Life**
Policy Number 000-000-00

ANNUAL NOTICE OF YOUR POLICY'S STATUS FOR YEAR
ENDING JANUARY 19, 2005

INSURED: James E. Doe
200 Spring Street
Anytown, Anystate 10000

| Date | Payments (Withdrawals) | Expense Charges | Cost of Insurance | Interest Credited | Unpaid Loans | Ending Cash Value |
|---|---|---|---|---|---|---|
| 01/19/04 | | | | | | 826.66 |
| 02/19/04 | 100.00 | 11.50 | 11.91 | — | — | 903.25 |
| 03/19/04 | 100.00 | 11.50 | 11.90 | 4.68 | — | 984.53 |
| 04/19/04 | 100.00 | 11.50 | 11.90 | 5.15 | — | 1,066.28 |
| 05/19/04 | 100.00 | 11.50 | 11.89 | 5.58 | — | 1,148.47 |
| 06/19/04 | 100.00 | 11.50 | 11.88 | 6.04 | — | 1,231.13 |
| 07/19/04 | 100.00 | 11.50 | 11.87 | 6.48 | — | 1,314.24 |
| 08/19/04 | 100.00 | 11.50 | 11.86 | 6.95 | — | 1,397.83 |
| 09/19/04 | 100.00 | 11.50 | 11.85 | 7.40 | — | 1,481.88 |
| 10/19/04 | 100.00 | 11.50 | 11.85 | 7.85 | — | 1,566.38 |
| 11/19/04 | 100.00 | 11.50 | 11.84 | 8.32 | — | 1,651.36 |
| 12/19/04 | 100.00 | 11.50 | 11.83 | 8.78 | — | 1,736.81 |
| 01/19/05 | 100.00 | 11.50 | 11.82 | 9.58 | — | 1,823.07 |
| **Totals** | **1,200.00** | **138.00** | **142.40** | **76.81** | **0** | |

| | |
|---|---|
| Death Benefit as of February 6, 2005 | 100,296.00 |
| Cash Value Balance as of January 19, 2005 | 1,823.07 |
| Interest to Be Earned, February 6, 2005 | + 10.07 |
| Total Cash Value, February 6, 2005 | 1,833.14 |
| Surrender Value as of February 6, 2005 | 1,731.98* |

*The total cash value has been reduced by the surrender charge of $101.16 to arrive at the surrender value.

The cash value currently earns 7%, except the cash value equal to any policy loan earns 6%. From February 6, 2004, to December 5, 2004, the current interest rate was 6.75%. The interest rates are effective annual interest rates.

Continued planned payments of $100 each month will provide coverage until February 6, 2057, based on guaranteed rates.

If no further payments are made, your policy will provide coverage until January 6, 2017, based on current rates, and until January 6, 2012, based on guaranteed rates.

Each policyowner usually decides whether he wants favorable changes in pricing assumptions to result in a lower premium or in a higher cash value for the policy. The policyowner also can change this decision after the policy is in force. Most interest-sensitive whole life policies state that if the policyowner does not elect an option, then the cash value increase option will apply. On the other hand, a few such policies state that changes in pricing assumptions will result in a higher face amount rather than in a lower premium or higher cash value.

If changes in the insurer's pricing assumptions result in a higher premium than the insurer charged when the policy was purchased, then the policyowner may choose to (1) lower the policy's face amount and maintain the previous level of premiums or (2) pay the higher premium and maintain the original face amount. As with an indeterminate premium policy, an interest-sensitive whole life policy guarantees that the premium rate for the coverage cannot increase above the rate guaranteed in the policy.

## Variable Life Insurance

*Variable life (VL) insurance* is a form of cash value life insurance in which premiums are fixed, but the face amount and other values may vary, reflecting the performance of the investment subaccounts selected by the policyowner. A *subaccount* is one of several alternative pools of investments to which a variable life insurance policyowner allocates the premiums she has paid and the cash values that have accumulated under her policy.

The subaccounts in which variable insurance premiums and cash values are invested are part of an insurer's *separate account*, also known as a *segregated account*, which is an investment account the insurer maintains separately from its general account to isolate and help manage the funds placed in its variable products. The *general account* is an undivided investment account in which an insurer maintains funds that support its contractual obligations to pay benefits under its guaranteed insurance products, such as whole life insurance and other nonvariable products. The funds in the general account are placed in relatively secure investments so that the insurer is assured of having funds available to pay the benefits it has guaranteed to pay policyowners.

Most variable life policies permit the policyowner to select from among several subaccounts and to change this selection at least annually. The insurer follows a different investment strategy for each subaccount. For example, some subaccounts concentrate on investing in high-growth stocks, while other subaccounts may concentrate on investing in bonds. The amount of both the policy's death benefit and cash value depend on how well the separate account investments perform. If the separate account investments perform well, then the amount of the death benefit and the cash value of the policy will increase. If the investment performance is poor, then the amount of the death benefit and the cash value will decline.

Most variable life policies guarantee that the amount of the death benefit will not fall below the amount that was initially purchased, regardless of the separate account's performance. Variable life policies, however, do not guarantee either investment earnings or a minimum cash value.

Note that the policyowner, not the insurer, assumes the investment risk of a variable life insurance policy. As a result, the U.S. Securities and Exchange Commission (SEC) has determined that variable life insurance policies are securities and, thus, are subject to federal securities regulation. Insurers that market variable life products in the United States must comply with a range of regulatory requirements governing securities in addition to complying with applicable state insurance regulatory requirements.

## Variable Universal Life Insurance

*Variable universal life (VUL) insurance*, which is also called *universal life II* and *flexible-premium variable life insurance*, combines the premium and death benefit flexibility of universal life insurance with the investment flexibility and risk of variable life insurance. Like a universal life policy, a variable universal life policy allows the policyowner to choose the premium amount and face amount. Like a variable life policy, the cash value of a variable universal life policy is placed in the separate account. The policyowner chooses from among several subaccounts and may change the chosen options at least annually. The investment returns that the insurer credits to the policy's cash value reflect the investment earnings of the subaccounts. Most insurers allow the policyowner to choose whether the policy's death benefit will remain level (an Option A account) or will vary along with changes in the investment earnings of the subaccounts (an Option B account). Like variable life policies, variable universal policies do not guarantee investment earnings or cash values. In the United States, variable universal life products are considered securities and, thus, must comply with the federal securities laws described earlier.

Figure 6.6 illustrates how variable universal life insurance products combine the features of universal life and variable life insurance products.

# Endowment Insurance

As noted in Chapter 1, *endowment insurance* provides a specified benefit amount whether the insured lives to the end of the term of coverage or dies during that term. Each endowment policy specifies a **maturity date**, which is the date on which the insurer will pay the policy's face amount to the policyowner if the insured is still living. The maturity date is reached either (1) at the end of a stated term or (2) when the insured reaches a specified age. For example, the maturity date of a 20-year endowment policy is 20 years following the policy's effective date; the maturity date of an

**FIGURE 6.6** How VUL Products Combine Features of UL and VL Products

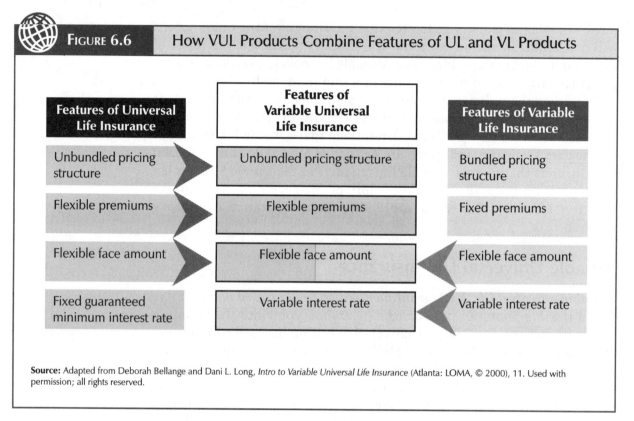

**Source:** Adapted from Deborah Bellange and Dani L. Long, *Intro to Variable Universal Life Insurance* (Atlanta: LOMA, © 2000), 11. Used with permission; all rights reserved.

---

endowment at age 65 policy is when the insured reaches age 65. If the insured dies before the maturity date, then the insurer pays the policy's face amount to the designated beneficiary. Thus, an endowment insurance policy pays a fixed benefit whether the insured *survives* to the policy's maturity date or *dies* before that maturity date.

Endowment policies share many of the features of cash value life insurance policies. For example, premiums usually are level throughout the term of an endowment policy, although a policyowner can purchase an endowment policy with a single premium or with a series of premiums over a limited period of time. Like cash value life insurance policies, endowment policies steadily build cash values. Recall that the reserve and the cash value of a whole life policy eventually equal the policy's face amount—but not until the insured reaches the age at the end of the mortality table used to calculate premiums for that policy. In contrast, the reserve and cash value of an endowment policy usually equal the policy's face amount on the policy's maturity date, which is typically much sooner than when the insured reaches the last age found in the mortality table. As a result, an endowment policy's cash value builds much more rapidly than does the cash value of a comparable whole life insurance policy.

Because endowment policies build cash values rapidly and because the cash value of an endowment policy is quite large in relationship to the face amount of the policy, endowment policies generally do not maintain the

---

## FAST FACT

During 2003, U.S. life insurers paid $528 million in matured endowment payments.

**Source:** ACLI, *Life Insurers Fact Book: 2004* (Washington, D.C.: American Council of Life Insurers, 2004), 64.

required corridor (the Section 7702 corridor) between the amount of the cash value and the face amount described earlier in connection with universal life policies. As a result, endowment policies do not receive the same favorable federal income tax treatment in the United States as do most other life insurance policies. That unfavorable tax treatment has resulted in dwindling sales of endowment insurance in the United States. Endowment insurance, however, remains a popular product in insurance markets in many other countries where tax laws treat it in a more favorable light. Insight 6.1 describes the popularity of endowment insurance in Vietnam.

**INSIGHT 6.1** | **Popularity of Endowment Insurance in Vietnam**

The life insurance industry in Vietnam came into existence in the late 1990s. As of 2003, endowment insurance is overwhelmingly the most popular type of life insurance in Vietnam, making up 94.1 percent of the market. Policies had an average face amount of US$1,420. Premiums are not tax deductible, but policy proceeds are received tax free.

**Source:** Adapted from Mary C. Bickley, *Principles of Financial Services and Products* (Atlanta: LOMA, © 2004), 110. Used with permission; all rights reserved.

# Key Terms

whole life insurance
cash surrender value
policy loan
continuous-premium
   whole life policy
limited-payment
   whole life policy
paid-up policy
single-premium
   whole life policy
modified-premium
   whole life policy
graded-premium policy
modified coverage policy
joint whole life insurance
last survivor life insurance
family policy
monthly debit ordinary
   (MDO) policy

home service distribution system
home service agent
pre-need funeral insurance
universal life (UL) insurance
surrender charges
Option A plan
Option B plan
Section 7702 corridor
indeterminate premium life
   insurance policy
interest-sensitive
   whole life insurance
variable life (VL) insurance
subaccount
separate account
general account
variable universal life (VUL)
   insurance
maturity date

# Supplemental Benefits

## objectives

*After reading this chapter, you should be able to*

- Identify three types of supplemental disability benefits that life insurance policies may provide

- Describe the characteristics of an accidental death benefit rider

- Identify three types of accelerated death benefit riders and recognize the differences among those riders

- Explain how a life insurance policy's coverage can be expanded to insure more than one individual

- Identify the two types of insurability benefit riders

Although their features vary, each type of individual life insurance provides a benefit payable upon the death of the insured. A number of other benefits, which we refer to as supplemental benefits, can be added to the various types of life insurance policies. The insurance company usually charges an additional premium amount for each supplemental benefit that is added to a policy; the additional premium charge typically ends when the supplemental benefit expires or is cancelled. Premiums paid for most supplemental benefits do not affect the cash value, if any, of the basic policy. However, as we describe, the paid-up additions option benefit allows the policyowner to obtain additional cash value.

Supplemental benefits usually are provided by adding riders to a life insurance policy, although in some situations the benefits are provided through standard policy provisions. Policy riders benefit both the policyowner and the insurer because they give both parties flexibility. When an insurance company issues a policy, it can include riders to customize a basic plan of insurance for the policyowner. If the policyowner later wants to adapt the policy to better meet his needs, the insurer can drop or add riders. Thus, the policyowner and the insurer need not enter into a new contract when the policyowner desires customized or additional coverage.

Although a variety of supplemental benefits are available, several types of supplemental benefits are fairly standard in the industry. This chapter describes the most common supplemental benefits.

# Supplemental Disability Benefits

Disability benefits generally are classified as a type of health insurance coverage because such benefits are paid to cover financial losses that result from a sickness or injury rather than those that result from the insured's death. Some disability benefits, however, can be added to the coverage provided by a life insurance policy. In this section, we describe three types of disability benefits that a life insurance policy or policy rider can provide: the waiver of premium for disability benefit, the waiver of premium for payor benefit, and the disability income benefit.

## Waiver of Premium for Disability Benefit

One of the most common supplemental benefits that may be added to nearly all individual life insurance policies is the *waiver of premium for disability (WP) benefit*. Under a WP benefit, the insurer promises to give up—to *waive*—its right to collect premiums that become due while the insured is totally disabled. Premiums that are waived under a WP benefit are actually paid by the insurance company. Therefore, if the policy is one that builds a cash value, the cash value continues to increase just as if the policyowner paid the premiums. In the case of a participating policy, the insurance company continues to pay policy dividends as if the policyowner were paying premiums.

To receive WP benefits, the policyowner must notify the insurance company in writing of a claim and must provide proof that the insured is totally disabled as defined by the WP benefit. Most WP benefits define *total disability* as the insured's inability to perform the essential acts of her own occupation or any other occupation for which she is reasonably suited by education, training, or experience. The insurance company usually reserves the right to require periodic submission of proof that the insured continues to be totally disabled. Premiums are waived throughout the life of the policy as long as the insured remains totally disabled.

The WP benefit usually contains some limitations, which are described in Figure 7.1.

As noted earlier, the WP benefit may be added to almost all types of life insurance policies, including renewable and convertible term insurance policies. If a renewable term policy's premium is being waived on a renewal date, the insurer generally renews the policy automatically in accordance with the policy's renewal provision. The insurer will continue to waive renewal premiums until either the insured is no longer totally disabled or the policy is no longer renewable.

If a convertible term insurance policy's premiums are being waived when the policy becomes convertible to whole life insurance, the policyowner usually is allowed to convert to a whole life policy, in accordance with the policy's conversion provision; the WP benefit, however, may or may not be included in the new whole life policy. If the WP benefit is included, renewal premiums continue to be waived as long as the insured is totally disabled. If the WP benefit is not included, the policyowner must resume paying renewal premiums to keep the new whole life policy in force. Some WP benefits provide that the convertible term insurance policy automatically will be converted to a whole life policy if the insured is totally disabled on the conversion date. These policies usually state that the insurer will continue to waive premiums until the recovery or death of the insured.

Because universal life insurance policies have variable premiums, the standard WP benefit usually is not offered. Instead, universal life policies may have a *waiver of costs of insurance benefit* that simply waives most of the internal costs of the policy if the insured meets the policy's definition of disability.

**Figure 7.1** | Limitations on the Waiver of Premium for Disability Benefit

- **Most WP benefits contain a three- to six-month waiting period after the insured becomes disabled before the insurer will waive the payment of premiums.** The policyowner must continue to pay premiums that come due during the waiting period, although some WP benefits provide that these premiums will be refunded should the insured still be disabled when the waiting period ends.

- **The WP benefit usually covers only disabilities that begin before the insured reaches a specified age.** Chances of disability increase significantly as an insured ages. As a result, the cost of providing the WP benefit would be quite high if it were to cover disabilities that begin after a certain age, such as age 65.

- **When an insured becomes disabled and premiums are waived, the interval at which premium payments are due cannot be changed.** This limitation prevents a policyowner from changing to a more frequent premium payment schedule. For example, if renewal premiums are payable annually, the policyowner may not change to a monthly premium payment mode. Doing so could result in some of the premiums being waived even if the disability were to end before the annual premium became due.

- **Disabilities resulting from the following causes are typically excluded from coverage:**

  - Intentionally self-inflicted injuries

  - Injuries the insured suffered while committing a crime

  - Specified health conditions, known as *pre-existing conditions*, that the insured experienced before the WP benefit became effective

  - Injuries resulting from an act of war while the insured is in military service

# Waiver of Premium for Payor Benefit

Note that the WP benefit provides a waiver of premium if the *insured* becomes totally disabled. Most individual life insurance policies are issued to a policyowner who also is the policy's insured, and the WP benefit was designed for such policies. By contrast, the waiver of premium for payor benefit was designed for third-party policies, such as juvenile insurance policies. A ***juvenile insurance policy*** is a policy that is issued on the life of a child but is owned and paid for by an adult, usually the child's parent or legal guardian. The ***waiver of premium for payor benefit*** provides that the insurance company will waive its right to collect a policy's renewal premiums if the *policyowner*—the person responsible for paying premiums—dies or becomes totally disabled.

Waiver of premium for payor benefits generally include a two-part definition of *total disability*. During the first two years of disability, the policyowner is considered totally disabled if he is unable to perform the essential acts of his own occupation. After that two-year period, the policyowner is considered totally disabled if he is unable to perform the essential acts of any occupation for which he is reasonably suited by education, training, or experience.

Because the disability or death of the policyowner triggers the waiver of premium for payor benefit, the policyowner generally must provide satisfactory evidence of his own insurability—in addition to providing evidence of the insurability of the insured—before the insurer will add this benefit to a life insurance policy. When the benefit is added to a juvenile life insurance policy, the policy or rider usually states that the insurance company will waive the premium payments only until the insured reaches a specified age, such as 18 or 21, when ownership and control of the policy typically passes to the insured. Figure 7.2 compares the features of the waiver of premium benefit and the waiver of premium for payor benefit.

# Disability Income Benefit

Another benefit that may be added to a life insurance policy is the ***disability income benefit***, which provides a monthly income benefit to the policyowner-insured if she becomes totally disabled while the policy is in force. Like WP benefits, disability income benefits typically define *total disability* as the insured's inability to perform the essential acts of her own occupation or any occupation for which she is reasonably suited by education, training, or experience.

Typically, the amount of the monthly disability income benefit is a stated dollar amount—such as $10—per $1,000 of life coverage. Life insurance coverage provided by the policy continues, and, if the insured dies before recovering from the disability, the insurer pays the policy's death benefit

---

| | |
|---|---|
| **FIGURE 7.2** | **Comparison of Waiver of Premium Benefit and Waiver of Premium for Payor Benefit** |

| **Waiver of Premium Benefit** | **Waiver of Premium for Payor Benefit** |
|---|---|
| Policy premiums are waived if the insured becomes totally disabled | Policy premiums are waived if the policyowner dies or becomes totally disabled |
| The benefit was designed for policies issued to a policyowner who also is the policy's insured | The benefit was designed for third-party policies, such as juvenile insurance policies, in which the policyowner is not the policy's insured |

---

to the named beneficiary. The disability income benefit rider also usually includes a three- to six-month waiting period before disability income benefits will begin.

> **Example.** Paxton Haynes was the policyowner-insured of a $150,000 life insurance policy that included a disability income benefit rider. The rider stated that, if Paxton became totally disabled, then the insurance company would pay him a monthly benefit of $10 per $1,000 of life insurance coverage during the period of disability; the income benefit would begin three months after the onset of a disability. While the policy was in force, Paxton became disabled as defined in the disability income benefit rider. Two years later, he died as a result of his disability.
>
> **Analysis.** Three months after he became disabled, Paxton became eligible to receive a disability income benefit of $1,500 per month.
>
> | | |
> |---:|---|
> | $10 | Monthly benefit per unit of coverage |
> | ×150 | Number of units ($150,000 ÷ $1,000) |
> | **$1,500** | **Monthly disability income benefit** |

This monthly disability income benefit was payable as long as Paxton remained disabled. Upon Paxton's death, the policy's death benefit became payable to the named beneficiary.

**FAST FACT**

In 2003, 14.6 percent of individual life insurance policies in force in the United States provided disability income benefits.

**Source:** ACLI, *Life Insurers Fact Book: 2004* (Washington, D.C.: American Council of Life Insurers, 2004), 87.

Life insurance policies that are issued with a disability income benefit generally include a WP benefit as well. In such a case, both the renewal premiums charged for the life policy and the additional premiums charged for the disability income benefit are waived during the total disability of the insured.

# Accident Benefits

Accident benefits may be added to any type of life insurance policy. The two most commonly offered accident benefits are accidental death benefits and dismemberment benefits.

## Accidental Death Benefit

An *accidental death benefit* is a supplemental life insurance policy benefit that provides a death benefit in addition to the policy's basic death benefit if the insured dies as a result of an accident. When the amount of the accidental death benefit is equal to the face amount of the life insurance policy, the benefit is often referred to as a *double indemnity benefit* because the total death benefit payable if the insured dies in an accident is double the policy's face amount. The additional sum payable if the insured dies accidentally also may be some other multiple of the policy's face amount—such as three times the face amount—or it may be an amount that is unrelated to the policy's face amount. Most accidental death benefit riders expire when the insured reaches age 65 or 70.

Generally, the accidental death benefit is payable if the insured person's death was caused, directly and independently of all other causes, by an accidental bodily injury. Determining the precise cause of an insured's death, however, can sometimes be quite difficult.

> **Example.** An insured with a history of heart problems died in an automobile accident. Her policy provides a $50,000 death benefit and includes an accidental death benefit rider that provides an accidental death benefit of $50,000.
>
> **Analysis.** If the accident itself caused the insured's death, then the $50,000 accidental death benefit is payable in addition to the policy's $50,000 basic death benefit. On the other hand, the insured may have died from a heart attack while driving, causing her to lose control of the automobile. If so, then her death did not result from an accident, and only the policy's $50,000 basic death benefit is payable to the named beneficiary.

Accidental death benefit provisions usually contain several exclusions and limitations. For example, the provision typically states that the insurance company will not be required to pay the accidental death benefit if the insured's death results from certain stated causes, including the following:

- Self-inflicted injuries (suicide)

- War-related accidents

- Accidents resulting from aviation activities if, during the flight, the insured acted in any capacity other than as a passenger

- Accidents resulting from the insured's committing a crime

Some accidental death benefit provisions contain a limitation that relates to the time span between the insured's death and the accident that caused the death. This time span is usually stated as 3 months or 90 days, though some provisions specify a longer period. The insured's death must occur within the stated time after the accident for the accidental death benefit to be payable. This limitation is included because of the difficulty that can arise in determining the cause of an insured's death. When the insured obviously died as the result of an accident, many insurance companies will disregard the stated time limit and pay the accidental death benefit. Now medical science often can prolong life functions almost indefinitely, sometimes extending the life of an accident victim who in the past would have died shortly after the accident. Further, some states prohibit insurers from including a limitation concerning time span in accidental death benefit riders.

Keep in mind that these exclusions and limitations relate only to the accidental death benefit. With few exceptions, which are described later in this text, the basic death benefit provided by the life insurance policy is payable regardless of the cause of the insured's death.

## Dismemberment Benefit

When an accidental death benefit provides an additional benefit for dismemberment, it is called an *accidental death and dismemberment (AD&D) benefit*. AD&D benefits generally specify that the insurer will pay a stated benefit amount if an accident causes the insured to lose any two limbs or sight in both eyes. The amount of the dismemberment benefit usually is equal to the amount of the accidental death benefit. In many cases, however, a smaller amount—such as one-half the amount of the accidental death benefit—will be payable if the insured loses one limb or sight in one eye as the result of an accident. The loss of a limb may be defined either as the actual physical loss of the limb or as the loss of the use of the limb. Usually, AD&D benefits state that the insurer will not pay both accidental death benefits and dismemberment benefits for injuries suffered in the same accident.

# Accelerated Death Benefits

An **accelerated death benefit**, also known as a *living benefit*, provides that a policyowner-insured may elect to receive all or part of the policy's death benefit before his death if certain conditions are met. The payment of an accelerated death benefit reduces the death benefit that will be paid to the beneficiary at the insured's death by the amount of the living benefit that was paid to the policyowner-insured. These benefits continue to gain popularity for several reasons. First, the segment of the population composed of the elderly is growing. These individuals frequently suffer from illnesses that require medical care. Second, the cost of health care continues to increase. Third, medical advances tend to postpone death and prolong the need for medical care.

In an effort to keep administrative costs down, life insurers generally offer accelerated death benefit coverage only on policies with large face amounts, such as $100,000 or $250,000 and above. Some insurers also require that before they pay any accelerated death benefit, the beneficiary must sign a release acknowledging that the policy's death benefit will be reduced by the amount paid to the policyowner-insured under the accelerated death benefit provision. Also, if the policyowner has assigned the policy, then the assignee must sign such a release. (We describe assignments in Chapter 9.)

The specific amount of accelerated death benefits that are payable under a policy and the circumstances that trigger such payments depend on the wording of the benefit provision or rider. In this section, we describe three commonly offered types of accelerated death benefits: the terminal illness benefit, the dread disease benefit, and the long-term care benefit.

## Terminal Illness Benefit

The most common type of accelerated death benefit is the terminal illness benefit. The **terminal illness (TI) benefit** is a benefit under which the insurer pays a portion of the policy's death benefit to a policyowner-insured who suffers from a terminal illness and has a physician-certified life expectancy of 12 months or less. A statement by an attending physician establishes evidence of the terminal condition and certifies that the insured is likely to die within the time period specified in the rider.

The amount of the TI benefit that is payable varies from insurer to insurer. Some policies permit payment of the full face amount prior to the insured's death. Generally, however, the maximum TI benefit payable is a stated percentage—usually between 25 and 75 percent—of the policy's face amount up to a specified maximum dollar limit such as $250,000. The benefit usually is paid in a lump sum to the policyowner. The remainder of the death benefit is paid to the beneficiary following the insured's death. Figure 7.3 provides some examples of how insureds have used the funds they received in the form of accelerated death benefits.

---

**FIGURE 7.3** | Using Accelerated Death Benefits

The following are a few examples of how an insured might use money received as accelerated death benefits:

■ Payment of his medical expenses

■ Payment of his outstanding debts and living expenses

■ Payment of home health care costs

■ Payment of travel expenses for himself and/or his family

---

Unlike other supplemental benefits for which insurers impose an additional premium charge, the terminal illness benefit typically is paid for by an administrative charge that the insurer assesses when a policyowner-insured elects to exercise the TI benefit.

## Dread Disease Benefit

A **dread disease (DD) benefit**, also known as a *critical illness benefit*, is an accelerated death benefit under which the insurer agrees to pay a portion of the policy's face amount to the policyowner if the insured suffers from one of a number of specified diseases. The remainder of the death benefit is paid to the beneficiary following the insured's death.

An insured becomes eligible for DD benefits when he has certain diseases or undergoes certain medical procedures specified in the rider. These specified diseases or medical procedures are known as the *insurable events* and usually include

- Life-threatening cancer
- Acquired immune deficiency syndrome (AIDS)
- End-stage renal (kidney) failure
- Myocardial infarction (heart attack)
- Stroke
- Coronary bypass surgery

Some DD benefits also include vital organ transplants and Alzheimer's disease as insurable events.

Although the accelerated death benefit usually is paid in a lump sum, some insurers pay the benefit in monthly installments over a period of 6 to 12 months. Most insurers provide DD coverage only to insureds who are under the age of 70 and only to insureds who have no serious health problems, and some insurers do not make payments for multiple or recurring events.

The DD benefit may offer a waiver of premium option under which the insurer agrees to waive all renewal premiums payable for the life insurance policy after the accelerated death benefit is paid. Sometimes the waiver of premium option applies only to premiums payable while the insured remains disabled; if the insured recovers, then subsequent renewal premiums are not waived.

Another form of dread disease coverage can be purchased as supplemental medical expense coverage. We describe such dread disease coverage in Chapter 15.

## Long-Term Care Insurance Benefit

A *long-term care (LTC) insurance benefit* is an accelerated death benefit under which the insurer agrees to pay a monthly benefit to a policyowner if the insured requires constant care for a medical condition. The types of care given and medical condition required to qualify for the LTC benefit are specified in the LTC policy provision or rider. Premiums generally are waived on both the long-term care benefit and the basic life insurance policy during the period that the insured receives LTC benefits.

The amount of each monthly LTC benefit payment generally is equal to a stated percentage of the policy's death benefit. For example, the benefit may state that 2 percent of the policy's death benefit will be paid each month if the insured requires nursing home care and 1 percent of the death benefit will be paid each month if the insured requires home health care. The insurer usually pays monthly benefits until a specified percentage of the policy's basic death benefit has been paid out. This percentage typically falls between 50 and 100 percent of the policy's face amount. Any remaining death benefit is paid to the beneficiary after the insured's death.

Most LTC benefits impose a 90-day waiting period before accelerated death benefits are payable; no benefits are payable until 90 days following the date on which the insured becomes eligible for benefits. According to the terms of some LTC benefits, however, coverage must be in force for a given period of time, usually one year or more, before the insured will qualify for LTC benefits.

## Benefits for Additional Insureds

Term insurance riders can be added to most cash value life insurance policies to increase the amount of the benefit payable if the insured dies while the coverage is in force. In addition, various riders can be added to life insurance policies to provide benefits if someone other than the policy's insured dies. These riders take several forms, but the most common are the spouse and children's insurance rider, the children's insurance rider, and the second insured rider.

## Spouse and Children's Insurance Rider

A *spouse and children's insurance rider* is a supplemental life insurance policy benefit that provides term life insurance coverage on the insured's spouse and children. The coverage provided by such a rider typically is sold on the basis of coverage units. Usually, each coverage unit of a spouse and children's insurance rider provides $5,000 of term insurance coverage on the spouse and $1,000 of term insurance coverage on each child. Most insurance companies do not offer more than 5 or 10 coverage units.

The premium for the children's coverage is a specified, flat amount that does not change with the number of children in the family. In other words, the insurer charges the same premium for a family with one child as it charges for a family with six children. Therefore, the insurer does not have to revise the premium for a spouse and children's insurance rider if additional children are born or adopted into the family after the coverage is purchased. Those additional children are covered automatically at no extra premium charge, although the coverage typically does not take effect until the child reaches age 15 days.

**Example.** Wallace Groom purchased a $100,000 whole life insurance policy. He also purchased 10 coverage units under a spouse and children's insurance rider to cover his wife, Elizabeth, his 16-year-old daughter, Felicity, and his 6-year-old son, Fred.

**Analysis.** The following coverages are provided under Wallace's spouse and children's insurance rider:

> $50,000 of term insurance coverage on Elizabeth
>
> $10,000 of term insurance coverage on Felicity
>
> $10,000 of term insurance coverage on Fred

If Wallace and Elizabeth have more children, the rider automatically will provide $10,000 of term insurance coverage on each additional child at no extra premium charge.

The term insurance coverage on each child expires when that child reaches a stated age, typically 21 or 25. Such riders, however, usually include a conversion privilege that allows the child to convert his term insurance coverage to an individual life insurance policy. For example, the rider may permit each child to convert up to five times the amount of his term insurance coverage to an individual cash value insurance policy without providing evidence of his insurability.

## Children's Insurance Rider

A **children's insurance rider** is a supplemental life insurance policy benefit that provides term life insurance coverage on the insured's children. Insurers developed this form of coverage largely in recognition of the growing number of single-parent households The rider operates in the same fashion as does a spouse and children's insurance rider, except that no spousal coverage is included. The premium charged for each coverage unit is a stated amount, regardless of the number of children covered, the ages of those children, or the age and sex of the insured parent. For example, a single mother of three children could purchase a children's insurance rider for the same amount that would be charged to a single father of two children.

## Second Insured Rider

A **second insured rider**, also called an *optional insured rider* or an *additional insured rider*, is a supplemental life insurance policy benefit that provides term insurance coverage on the life of a person other than the policy's insured. The person insured under the rider is known as the *second insured* and may be the spouse of the insured, another relative, or an unrelated person, such as a business partner of the insured. The amount of coverage a second insured rider provides usually is not related to the amount of coverage the basic policy provides. The premium rate charged for the second insured rider is based on the risk characteristics of the second insured, not on the risk characteristics of the person insured under the basic policy.

# Insurability Benefits

Insurers offer two types of supplemental benefits that allow policyowners to purchase additional insurance without the insured providing evidence of insurability at the time of purchase. These benefits are the guaranteed insurability benefit and the paid-up additions option benefit.

## Guaranteed Insurability Benefit

The **guaranteed insurability (GI) benefit**—sometimes referred to as a *guaranteed insurability option (GIO)*—is a supplemental life insurance policy benefit that gives the policyowner the right to purchase additional insurance of the same type as the basic life insurance policy—for an additional premium amount—on specified option dates during the life of the policy without supplying evidence of the insured's insurability. Thus, the GI rider guarantees that the policyowner will be able to purchase additional life insurance even though the insured may no longer be in good health.

Typically, the amount of coverage the policyowner may purchase on an option date is limited to the policy's face amount or to an amount specified in the GI rider, whichever is less. For example, a GI rider attached to a $50,000 whole life policy may give the owner the right to purchase an additional $10,000 of whole life insurance coverage on each of certain stated dates. The GI rider also may permit the purchase of additional life insurance coverage when certain events occur, such as when the insured marries or at the birth of a child. Most GI riders, however, limit the benefit by permitting the policyowner to exercise the GI option only until the insured reaches age 40.

Although the right to purchase the additional coverage is automatic, the actual purchase is not. A policyowner who desires the extra coverage must take positive action to purchase the new coverage. Most GI riders specify that if the policyowner does not exercise the option on one of the specified dates, that option is lost forever, though the policyowner is permitted to exercise the next option when it comes due.

Some GI riders provide automatic temporary term insurance coverage for the period during which the policyowner has the right to exercise her option to purchase additional insurance coverage. This term insurance coverage usually lasts 60 to 90 days and is designed to protect the beneficiary in cases in which the policyowner is delayed in taking the necessary action to exercise the option.

If the life insurance policy also includes a WP rider and the insured is disabled at the time an option to purchase additional insurance goes into effect, then the insurance company automatically issues the additional life insurance coverage. The insurance company also waives the payment of renewal premiums for all of a policy's coverages to which the WP rider applies until the recovery or death of the insured.

## Paid-Up Additions Option Benefit

The **paid-up additions option benefit** is a supplemental life insurance policy benefit that allows the owner of a whole life insurance policy to purchase single-premium paid-up additions to the policy on stated dates in the future without providing evidence of the insured's insurability. For example, many paid-up additions option riders allow the policyowner to purchase paid-up additional whole life insurance on each policy anniversary. Because the additions are whole life insurance, the paid-up additions also have their own cash values.

Premiums for the paid-up additions are based on the net single premium rate for the coverage at the insured's age at the time the paid-up additions are purchased. Typically, the premium that a policyowner can apply to purchase the paid-up additions must fall between the minimums and maximums established in the rider. Most riders state that if the policyowner does not exercise the purchase option for a stated number of years, then the rider will terminate. At that time, the paid-up additions already purchased remain in force, but the policyowner can no longer exercise the option to purchase new paid-up additions.

## Key Terms

waiver of premium for disability (WP) benefit
juvenile insurance policy
waiver of premium for payor benefit
disability income benefit
accidental death benefit
double indemnity benefit
accidental death and dismemberment (AD&D) benefit
accelerated death benefit

terminal illness (TI) benefit
dread disease (DD) benefit
long-term care (LTC) insurance benefit
spouse and children's insurance rider
children's insurance rider
second insured rider
guaranteed insurability (GI) benefit
paid-up additions option benefit

# Individual Life Insurance Policy Provisions

## objectives

*After reading this chapter, you should be able to*

- Identify the documents that make up the entire contract between the owner of a life insurance policy and the insurer

- Recognize situations in which an insurer has the right to avoid a life insurance contract

- Apply the terms of the standard grace period provision to determine in a given situation whether a life insurance policy has lapsed for nonpayment of premium

- Identify situations in which a life insurance policy can be reinstated and the conditions the policyowner must meet to reinstate the policy

- Determine the action an insurer likely will take if it discovers a misstatement of the age or sex of the person insured by a life insurance policy

- Identify the types of policies that contain a policy loan provision and the types that contain a policy withdrawal provision

- Identify and describe the nonforfeiture options typically included in cash value life insurance policies

- Identify the exclusions that insurers sometimes include in individual life insurance policies

As noted in Chapter 3, an insurance policy is a contract between an insurance company and the policyowner. The provisions included in the written policy set forth the terms of the parties' agreement, including the rights and obligations of the parties. Many of these provisions are standard in principle—though not in exact wording—throughout the life insurance industry worldwide. In this chapter, we describe many of the provisions that typically are included in individual life insurance policies. We first describe provisions that are found in all types of individual life insurance policies. Then we describe provisions that are unique to cash value life insurance policies. Later chapters describe other basic life insurance policy provisions—the policy dividends provision and the settlement options provision.

# Standard Policy Provisions

All types of individual life insurance policies include provisions that describe the operation and effect of the policies as legally binding contracts. Although the specific wording varies from policy to policy and from insurer to insurer, all types of individual life insurance policies include the provisions we describe in this section: the free-look provision, entire contract provision, incontestability provision, grace period provision, reinstatement provision, and misstatement of age or sex provision. As described in Insight 8.1, the provisions included in policies and the wording of those provisions often are subject to regulatory requirements.

## Free-Look Provision

Individual life insurance policies generally include a *free-look provision* or *free-examination provision* that gives the policyowner a stated period of time—usually ten days—after the policy is delivered in which to examine the policy. During the free-look period, the policyowner has the right to cancel the policy and receive a full refund of the initial premium payment. Insurance coverage is in effect throughout the free-look period or until the policyowner rejects the policy, if sooner.

> **Example.** Yoko Matsuto applied for an individual insurance policy on her life and paid the initial premium. The insurer issued the policy and delivered it to Yoko. Two days later, Yoko changed her mind about purchasing the policy. Before she could contact the insurer to cancel the policy, Yoko was killed.

**Analysis.** During the ten-day free-look period, Yoko had the right to cancel the policy and receive a full premium refund. However, because the policy was in force when Yoko died, the insurer is obligated to pay the policy death benefit to the named beneficiary.

## Entire Contract Provision

The ***entire contract provision*** defines the documents that constitute the contract between the insurance company and the policyowner. By limiting the terms of the contract to the specified written documents, the entire contract provision prevents oral statements from affecting the terms of the policy and prevents controversies from developing regarding the terms of the contractual agreement.

The specific wording of the entire contract provision varies depending on whether the policy is a closed contract or an open contract. A ***closed contract*** is a contract for which only those terms and conditions that are printed in—or attached to—the contract are considered to be part of the contract. The entire contract provision in these policies states that the entire contract consists of the policy, any attached riders, and the attached copy of the application for insurance. The provision ensures that

### INSIGHT 8.1  Regulation of Policy Provisions

Insurers in the United States must comply with a range of regulatory requirements that govern the contents of the policies they issue. Most states have enacted laws that spell out the required wording of standard provisions that insurers must include in individual life insurance policies. Insurers, however, have the right to include provisions that are more favorable to policyowners than those required by law. Before issuing or delivering an individual insurance policy in a given state, an insurer generally must submit the policy form to the state insurance department and must receive departmental approval of the form.

Canada's provincial governments also regulate life insurance policy provisions and require that policies contain certain provisions, including a grace period provision and a reinstatement provision. Unlike U.S. insurance laws, however, Canada's provincial insurance laws directly grant certain rights to life insurance policyowners and beneficiaries and impose certain obligations on insurers. When such rights are granted by law, the rights exist regardless of whether they are included in a life insurance policy. For example, insurance laws in most provinces specify the documents that constitute a life insurance contract. The legally specified documents constitute the life insurance contract even if the policy itself does not include an entire contract provision. In addition, if a policy has an entire contract provision that conflicts with the applicable provincial insurance law, then the provincial insurance law governs which documents form the contract. Although insurers are not required to include provisions spelling out these statutory rights and obligations, insurers routinely include such provisions in their life insurance policies, and policies issued in Canada and the United States generally contain the same basic provisions.

policyowners have access to all of the terms of the contractual agreement. With the exception of policies issued by fraternal insurers, all individual life insurance policies issued in the United States are closed contracts.

An *open contract* is a contract that identifies the documents that constitute the contract between the parties, but the enumerated documents are not all attached to the contract. Fraternal insurers typically issue life insurance policies as open contracts, which state that the entire contract consists of the policy and any attached riders; the fraternal society's charter, constitution, and bylaws; the attached policyowner's application for membership in the society; and the attached declaration of insurability, if any, signed by the applicant. When a fraternal insurer issues a policy, it does not attach a copy of the fraternal's charter, constitution, and bylaws to the policy. Fraternal insurers are permitted to use open contracts because membership in the fraternal society is a requirement for purchasing insurance through the society. When a person becomes a member of a fraternal society, he receives a copy of the society's charter, constitution, and bylaws, and, thus, has the opportunity to examine these documents.

In addition to defining the documents that make up the contract, the entire contract provision usually states that (1) only specified individuals—such as certain officers of the insurer—can change the contract, (2) no change is effective unless made in writing, and (3) no change will be made unless the policyowner agrees to it in writing.

## Incontestability Provision

As noted in Chapter 3, when a contract is voidable, one party to the contract has the right to avoid his obligations under the contract without incurring legal liability to the other party. In other words, the party has the right to avoid, or reject, an otherwise enforceable contract. The rules of contract law give an insurer the right to avoid an otherwise enforceable insurance contract if the applicant misrepresented material facts in the application for insurance. State insurance laws, however, limit the time within which an insurer has such a right. As a result, life insurance policies contain an *incontestability provision* that describes the time limit within which the insurer has the right to avoid the contract on the ground of material misrepresentation in the application. In this section, we describe material misrepresentations and the operation of the incontestability provision.

### Material Misrepresentation

Applications for life insurance policies contain questions designed to provide the insurance company with relevant information so that it can decide whether the proposed insured is an insurable risk. According to the rules of contract law, statements made by the parties when they enter into a contract can be classified as either warranties or representations. A *warranty* is a statement that will invalidate the contract if the statement is not literally true. In contrast, a **representation** is a statement that will invalidate the contract if the statement is not substantially true. Statements made in an application for insurance are considered to be representations rather than warranties.

> **Example.** Dominique Ravel purchased an insurance policy on her life, stating on her application that she had visited the doctor for an infected toe on her left foot. In fact, she had visited the doctor for an infected toe on her right foot.
>
> **Analysis.** The statement in Dominique's application is not literally true. However, statements made in an application for life insurance are representations, not warranties. As a result, even though the statement is not literally true, it does not automatically invalidate the contract as long as it is substantially true.

A false or misleading statement in an application for insurance is known as a **misrepresentation**. Some statements contained in the application are more important to the insurer's decision to issue a policy than are other statements. A misrepresentation that would affect the insurance company's evaluation of the proposed insured is called a **material misrepresentation**. A misrepresentation is considered material when, if the truth had been known, the insurer would not have issued the policy or would have issued the policy on a different basis, such as for a higher premium or for a lower face amount. A misrepresentation in an application for life insurance gives the insurer grounds to avoid the contract only if it was a material misrepresentation. Some examples will help to illustrate the types of misrepresentations that are considered to be material misrepresentations.

> **Example.** Indira Patel's application for life insurance contained the statement that she had visited a doctor on July 10, when the actual date of the visit was July 9.
>
> **Analysis.** The insurer's decision as to whether Indira is an insurable risk will not change based on the misstatement as to the date of the doctor visit. This misrepresentation, therefore, is not a material misrepresentation and cannot be used by the insurance company to avoid the contract.

> **Example.** Anthony Abernathy's application for life insurance contained the statement that he had visited a doctor on July 10 for a regular physical examination when, in fact, the reason for the visit was that he was being treated for heart disease.

**Analysis.** The purpose of a proposed insured's visit with a doctor may be very relevant to the insurance company's evaluation of the application for insurance. To evaluate his application properly, the insurance company needed to know that Anthony suffered from heart disease. As a result, the misrepresentation about the purpose of the doctor visit is a material misrepresentation if the insurance company would have made a different decision about issuing the life insurance policy had it known the truth.

## Operation of Incontestability Provision

If an insurer discovers a material misrepresentation in an application for life insurance when it is evaluating the application, the insurer probably will decide not to issue the policy. What happens if the insurance company issues a life insurance policy and later discovers a material misrepresentation in the application? In such a case, the terms of the policy's incontestability provision usually govern whether the insurance company can avoid the contract. A typical incontestability provision included in life insurance policies issued in the United States reads as follows:

> **Incontestability.** We will not contest this policy after it has been in force during the lifetime of the insured for two years from the date of issue.

The provision limits the period during which the insurer has the right to avoid the contract to two years from the date the policy was issued. This two-year contestable period is the maximum period permitted by law in most states. A period shorter than two years is permitted because that would be more favorable to the policyowner, and some policies do include a one-year contestable period.

As a general rule, after a policy's contestable period has ended, the insurer cannot avoid the contract. Laws in most states, however, contain an exception—an insurer may contest a policy at any time if the application for insurance contained a fraudulent misrepresentation. A *fraudulent misrepresentation* is a misrepresentation that was made with the intent to induce the other party to enter into a contract and that did induce the innocent party to enter into the contract. In reality, insurers seldom exercise their right to avoid a life insurance contract on the basis of a fraudulent misrepresentation because they usually are unable to obtain sufficient evidence to prove the misrepresentation was fraudulent.

Including the phrase *during the lifetime of the insured* is important because, in effect, this phrase makes the policy contestable forever if the person whose life is insured dies during the stated contestable period. As a result, the insurance company will have the opportunity to investigate for material misrepresentation when a death claim arises within the contestable period of a life insurance policy. If the phrase *during the lifetime of the insured* were not included and the insured died during the contestable period, the beneficiary could possibly delay making a death claim until after the contestable period expired. The insurer might then be prevented from contesting the policy and, thus, would be required to pay the death claim even if the application contained a material misrepresentation.

In the United States, an insurer has the right to use a material misrepresentation in the application as the basis for avoiding a life insurance contract only if a copy of the application for insurance was attached to the policy the insurer issued and delivered to the applicant. In other words, the application for insurance is not considered a part of the contract unless it is attached to the policy when the policy is issued. Fraternal insurers meet the requirement that the application be attached by attaching to the policy a copy of the policyowner's application for membership in the fraternal society and the declaration of insurability, if any, signed by the applicant for insurance.

The purpose of the incontestability provision is to assure policyowners and beneficiaries that after the contestable period has ended, the insurer cannot avoid the policy on the basis of a material misrepresentation in the application for insurance. The provision allows the beneficiary to know with certainty that if all required premiums are paid and the policy has been in force for at least the stated period, the insurer will pay the policy proceeds following the insured's death.

> **Example.** In the previous example, Anthony Abernathy did not disclose the true reason for his visit to the doctor. Anthony died five years after the policy was issued. In evaluating the death claim, the insurer discovered this material misrepresentation.
>
> **Analysis.** Because the policy's contestable period had expired by the time the insurer discovered the misrepresentation, the insurer does not have the right to contest the validity of the contract. As a result, the insurer must pay the policy proceeds to the named beneficiary.

The insurance laws regarding the contestability of a life insurance policy may be somewhat different in other countries than they are in the United States. Insight 8.2 describes the incontestability provision typically used in Canada.

**INSIGHT 8.2** | Incontestability Provision in Canada

A typical incontestability provision included in life insurance policies issued in Canada reads as follows:

> **Incontestability.** In the absence of fraud, we will not contest this policy after it has been in force during the lifetime of the insured for two years from when the policy takes effect or two years from the date it has been reinstated, if later.

As in the United States, provincial insurance laws limit to a maximum period of two years after the policy becomes effective the time during which the insurer may avoid a life insurance contract on the ground of material misrepresentation.

Provincial insurance laws state that the application for insurance is a part of the contract. As a result, even if a copy of the application is not attached to the policy when it is issued, the insurer has the right to contest the contract's validity based on material misrepresentations contained in that application.

## Grace Period Provision

The **grace period provision** specifies a length of time following each renewal premium due date within which the premium may be paid without loss of coverage. The specified time, known as the **grace period**, typically is 30 or 31 days, and the policy remains in force throughout that period. If the insured dies during the grace period, then the insurer will pay the policy proceeds to the named beneficiary. The insurer, however, usually deducts the amount of any unpaid renewal premium from the amount of the policy proceeds.

If a renewal premium is not paid by the end of the grace period, the policy is said to **lapse**. Some insurers, however, do not consider a policy as having lapsed if that policy has a cash value; the owner of a policy that provides a cash value has the right to continue the coverage under a nonforfeiture option. We describe nonforfeiture benefits later in the chapter. This text, in keeping with general usage, uses the terms *lapse* or *lapsed* in connection with any policy on which a renewal premium has not been paid by the end of the grace period.

**FAST FACT**

The lapse rate of individual life insurance policies in the United States decreased from 9.3 percent in 1995 to 7.7 percent in 2003.

**Source:** ACLI, *Life Insurers Fact Book: 2004* (Washington, D.C.: American Council of Life Insurers, 2004), 86.

> **Example.** Michael Etheridge was the policyowner-insured of a $100,000 term life insurance policy. The policy's annual renewal premium was due on March 21 of each year. His policy contained a typical grace period provision. Michael died on April 10, 1998, without having paid the renewal premium then due.
>
> **Analysis.** Because Michael died during his policy's grace period, the insurer was liable to pay the policy proceeds to the named beneficiary, but it may deduct the amount of the unpaid renewal premium from those proceeds.

**Example.** Assume that Michael Etheridge died on June 15, 1998, without having paid the renewal premium due on March 21, 1998.

**Analysis.** The insurer would not be obligated to pay the policy benefit to the named beneficiary because the policy lapsed for nonpayment of premium on April 21, 1998—following the expiration of the policy's grace period.

Some life insurance policies, such as universal life insurance policies, do not require scheduled premium payments. The grace period provision contained in a universal life policy is applied when the cash value is insufficient to meet the policy's monthly mortality and expense charges. Depending on the wording of the grace period provision, the grace period for such a policy will begin on either (1) the date on which the cash value is insufficient to cover the policy's entire monthly mortality and expense charges, in which case the grace period will continue for 61 or 62 days after that date, or (2) the date on which the cash value is zero, in which case the grace period will continue for 30 or 31 days after that date. The grace period provision in these policies also states that at least 30 or 31 days before the coverage expires, the insurance company will notify the policyowner that the cash value is insufficient to meet the policy charges and that the coverage will terminate if the policyowner does not make a premium payment that is large enough to cover those charges. If the person whose life is insured dies during the policy's grace period, then the insurer will pay the policy death benefit, but it will deduct from those proceeds the amount required to pay the overdue mortality and expense charges.

**Example.** Felicia Wagner is the policyowner-insured of a universal life insurance policy. Felicia has not made a premium payment in several years, during which time the insurer has used the policy's cash value to pay the monthly mortality and expense charges. Currently, the policy's remaining cash value is insufficient to cover the mortality and expense charges that are payable.

**Analysis.** The insurer will send Felicia a notice that her policy will continue under the grace period provision for 61 days, by which time she must make a premium payment sufficient to cover the overdue mortality and expense charges to keep the policy from lapsing. If Felicia should die during the 61-day grace period, the insurer will pay the policy death benefit, less the amount of any overdue mortality and expense charges, to the named beneficiary.

# Reinstatement Provision

Individual life insurance policies typically include a **reinstatement provision** which describes the conditions that the policyowner must meet to reinstate a policy. **Reinstatement** is the process by which a life insurance company puts back into force a life insurance policy that either has (1) been terminated because of nonpayment of renewal premiums or (2) been continued under the extended term or reduced paid-up insurance nonforfeiture option. (We describe these nonforfeiture options later in the chapter.) Most insurers do not permit reinstatement if the policyowner has surrendered the policy for its cash surrender value. When an insurer reinstates a policy, the original policy is again in effect; the insurer does not issue a new policy.

To reinstate a life insurance policy, the policyowner must fulfill the conditions stated in the policy's reinstatement provisions. The following conditions typically must be met to reinstate a policy:

- The policyowner must complete a reinstatement application within the time frame stated in the reinstatement provision. (See Figure 8.1, which shows a sample reinstatement application.)

- The policyowner must provide the insurance company with satisfactory evidence of the insured's continued insurability.

- The policyowner must pay a specified amount of money; the amount required depends on the type of policy being reinstated. We describe this amount later in this section of the chapter.

- The policyowner may be required to either pay any outstanding policy loan or have the policy loan reinstated with the policy.

Perhaps the most significant of these conditions concerns the required evidence of insurability. This condition is necessary to help prevent antiselection. If no evidence of insurability were required, those people who were unable to obtain insurance elsewhere because of poor health or other factors would be more likely to apply for reinstatement than would those who were in good health.

How much and what kind of evidence of insurability is necessary depends on the circumstances of each individual policy and on the practices of each insurer. If a policy has been out of force for a very short time and the insurer has no reason to suspect a problem, it may accept a simple statement from the insured certifying that he is in good health. In fact, if reinstatement is requested and overdue premiums are paid only a month or so after the expiration of the grace period, many insurers will reinstate the policy without requiring evidence of insurability. Insurance companies, however, may require a medical examination or other evidence of insurability if (1) the grace period expired longer than a month before the

| FIGURE 8.1 | Sample Reinstatement Application |

## Application for Reinstatement of Life Insurance

**ABC LIFE INSURANCE COMPANY**
**100 Ordinary Avenue, New York, New York 00000**

**Note:** This form can be used only within the 6 months after the date in Section A.

### SECTION A

The Insurer specified above is requested to reinstate Policy No. _____ 200 000 000 _____
including any loan agreement. The first unpaid premium was due on _____ April 1 _____ ,
20 _05_ and the total sum required (including any interest) to reinstate is $ _____ 116.32 _____ .
(Please enclose your check for this amount.)

### SECTION B

1. INSURED?

| _____ John _____ | _____ | _____ Doe _____ |
| First Name | Middle Initial | Last Name |

2. DATE OF BIRTH?          Mo. __7__  Day __1__  Yr. __1958__

3. Since the date in Section A, has the insured or any other person who was covered under
   the policy (in Section A):

|  | Yes | No |
|---|---|---|
| (a) been in a hospital or other medical facility or been unable to be actively at work or to attend school? | ☐ | ☒ |
| (b) consulted with, or intend to consult with, a physician for any illness or for symptoms of undiagnosed origin? | ☐ | ☒ |

   (Do not include colds, minor virus infections, minor injuries, or normal
   pregnancy.)
   If "Yes" to either 3(a) or 3(b), this application may not be used. Contact your
   ABC agent or our local office for further assistance.

### THOSE WHO SIGN THIS APPLICATION AGREE THAT:

1. Reinstatement will not take effect until (a) the Insurer approves the application, and (b) the sum
   required by the Insurer with respect to this application is paid during the lifetime of all persons to
   be covered under the reinstated policy.

2. All of the statements in this application are correctly recorded and are complete and true to the
   best of the knowledge and belief of those who made them.

3. No agent has any right to accept risks, make or change contracts, or give up any of ABC's rights or
   requirements.

Date at _____ Any town, Any state _____
(City or town, and state or province)

on _____ July 1 _____ , 20 _05_

Countersigned by _____
(Lic. resident agent, if required
by statute or regulation)

Signature of
Insured _____

Signature of Owner if other
than Insured _____

Spouse or Other Required
Signature, if any _____

reinstatement request, (2) the insurer has any reason to suspect that a health or other problem may be present, and/or (3) the face amount of the policy is large.

The specific amount of money required to reinstate a policy depends on the type of policy. For a fixed-premium policy, such as a whole life policy, the policyowner must pay all back premiums plus interest on those premiums. The insurer charges interest at the rate specified in the reinstatement provision. Payment of back premiums with interest is needed to bring the policy reserve to the same level as the reserve for a similar policy that has been kept in force without a lapse in premium payments.

For a flexible-premium policy, such as a universal life policy, the policyowner must pay an amount sufficient to cover the policy's mortality and expense charges for at least two months. In addition, some such policies require that the policyowner pay mortality and expense charges for the period between the date of lapse and the date of reinstatement.

Because reinstating a life insurance policy may require the policyowner to pay a sizable sum of money, each policyowner must decide whether reinstating the original policy or purchasing a new policy is more advantageous. One advantage to reinstating a fixed-premium policy is that the premium rate for the original policy is based on the insured's age at the time the policy was purchased. A comparable new policy usually calls for a higher premium rate because the new policy's premium rate is based on the age the insured has attained. Another advantage of reinstatement is that the original policy's cash value is also reinstated. A new policy may take two or three years to begin building a cash value. In addition, the original policy may contain certain provisions that are more liberal than the provisions in policies that the insurer is currently issuing. For example, the interest rate for a policy loan on the original policy may be lower than the interest rate that will be charged for a policy loan under a new policy.

Another important point about reinstatement is that typically a new contestable period begins on the date on which the policy is reinstated. During this new contestable period, the company may avoid a reinstated policy only on the basis of material misrepresentations made in the application for reinstatement. The insurer may not avoid the policy on the basis of material misrepresentations made in the original application unless the original contestable period has not yet expired.

For term life insurance policies that have lapsed for nonpayment of premiums, some insurance companies have adopted a practice known as **redating**. Under this practice, the insurance company agrees to reinstate a term insurance policy that has lapsed and to redate the policy. In other words, the insurer changes the policy date to the date on which the policy is reinstated. As a result, the premium rate charged for the redated policy will be based on the insured's attained age and will be higher than the premium rate charged for the original policy. However, the policyowner is able to reinstate the policy without having to repay all back premiums and interest. The requirements for redating are that the policyowner request the reinstatement within the time frame stated in the policy's reinstatement provision and provide evidence of the insured's continued insurability.

## Misstatement of Age or Sex Provision

An insurer or a policyowner may discover that the age or sex of the insured is incorrect as stated in the life insurance policy. Because the age and sex of the insured are significant factors in determining the amount of the premium charged for a policy, a misstatement of the insured's age or sex is a significant error. Most life insurance policies include a *misstatement of age or sex provision* that describes the action the insurer will take to adjust the amount of the policy benefit in the event that the age or sex of the insured is incorrectly stated. This provision in a life insurance policy states that if the age or sex of the insured is misstated and the misstatement resulted in an incorrect premium amount for the amount of insurance purchased, then the insurer will adjust the face amount of the policy to the amount the premium actually paid would have purchased if the insured's age or sex had been stated correctly.

Insurers adjust the face amount of the policy when they discover a misstatement of age or sex *after* the death of the insured. If the misstatement is discovered *before* the death of the insured, however, the insurer may give the policyowner the option to pay—or receive as a refund—any premium amount difference caused by the misstatement instead of having the insurer adjust the policy's face amount.

Note that when an insurance company adjusts the amount of the benefit payable under a life insurance policy because of a misstatement of age or sex, the insurer is enforcing the misstatement of age or sex provision. Such an action by an insurance company is not a contest of the validity of the contract and, thus, is not prohibited by the policy's incontestability provision.

> **Example.** While processing a death claim, the insurance company discovered that when Lamar Caspar applied for insurance on his life, he mistakenly listed his age as 25, when in fact he was age 30.
>
> **Analysis.** The insurer will reduce the policy's face amount to the amount that the premiums paid would have purchased for Lamar at age 30.

> **Example.** While processing a death claim, the insurance company discovered that when Leeanne Bouvier applied for insurance on her mother's life, she mistakenly stated that her mother was age 60, when in fact she was then 55 years old.

**Analysis.** When it calculates the amount of policy proceeds payable, the insurer will increase the face amount of the policy to the amount that the premiums paid would have purchased for Leeanne's mother at age 55.

# Provisions Unique to Cash Value Policies

Cash value life insurance policies typically contain several provisions in addition to those described in the previous section. The provisions that are unique to cash value life insurance policies relate to policy loans and withdrawals and to nonforfeiture options.

## Policy Loans and Policy Withdrawals

Cash value life insurance policies typically grant the policyowner the right to borrow money from the insurer by using the cash value of the policy as security for the loan. The *policy loan provision* grants the owner of a life insurance policy the right to take out a loan for an amount that does not exceed the policy's cash value less one year's interest on the loan. A policy loan is actually an advance payment of part of the amount that the insurer eventually must pay out under the policy.

A policy loan differs from a commercial loan in two respects. First, the policyowner is not legally obligated to repay a policy loan. The policyowner, however, may repay any part or all of the loan at any time. If a policy loan has not been repaid when the insured dies, the insurer deducts the amount of the unpaid loan from the policy benefit that is payable. In contrast, a commercial loan creates a debtor-creditor relationship between the borrower and the lender. The borrower is legally obligated to repay a commercial loan.

> | FAST FACT |
> At the end of 2003, U.S. life insurer loans to policyowners against their policies' cash values totaled $105 billion.
>
> **Source:** ACLI, *Life Insurers Fact Book: 2004* (Washington, D.C.: American Council of Life Insurers, 2004), 28.

**Example.** At the time of his death, Joseph Mangano was insured by a $50,000 whole life insurance policy. The policy had an unpaid policy loan in the amount of $2,000.

**Analysis.** The insurance company will deduct the amount of the unpaid policy loan from the policy proceeds. As a result, the named beneficiary will receive $48,000 ($50,000 − $2,000).

A policy loan also differs from a commercial loan in that the insurance company does not perform a credit check on a policyowner who requests a policy loan. The policyowner's request is evaluated only in terms of the amount of the net cash value available. The laws in most states permit companies to defer granting policy loans, except for loans made for the purpose of paying premiums, for a specified period, usually up to six months.

This deferral option, which insurers rarely enforce, is intended to protect insurers from suffering significant financial losses if large numbers of policyowners request policy loans.

Insurers charge interest on each policy loan, and interest usually is charged annually. Although policy loan interest may be paid at any time, the policyowner is not required to pay the interest. Any interest charges that are unpaid become part of the policy loan. Therefore, when we speak of the amount of the policy loan outstanding, that amount includes any unpaid interest that has accrued on the loan. If the amount of a policy loan plus unpaid interest increases to the point at which the total indebtedness is greater than the amount of the policy's cash value, then the policy terminates without further value. The insurer must notify the policyowner at least 30 days in advance of such a policy termination.

In the past, the interest rate that insurers charged on policy loans was guaranteed in each policy. Currently, many policies state that the policy loan interest rate will vary—that is, the interest rate that is charged may change from year to year according to current economic conditions. Many policies that include a varying loan interest rate specify that the rate charged will not exceed a stated maximum rate.

Universal life insurance policies typically include a policy withdrawal provision and a policy loan provision. A **policy withdrawal provision**, which is often called a *partial surrender provision*, permits the policyowner to reduce the amount in the policy's cash value by withdrawing up to the amount of the cash value in cash. Insurers do not charge interest on policy withdrawals; the amount in the cash value is simply reduced by the amount of the withdrawal. Many policies impose a charge for each withdrawal and limit the number of withdrawals allowed within each one-year period.

## Nonforfeiture Provision

The **nonforfeiture provision** sets forth the options available to the owner of a cash value policy if the policy lapses or if the policyowner decides to surrender—or terminate—the policy. Most nonforfeiture provisions give the policyowner the right to select from among several nonforfeiture options if a premium is unpaid when the grace period expires. These nonforfeiture options include the cash payment nonforfeiture option, two continued insurance coverage options—reduced paid-up insurance and extended term insurance—and the automatic premium loan option. Most policies include an **automatic nonforfeiture benefit**, which is a specific nonforfeiture benefit that becomes effective automatically when a renewal premium for a cash value life insurance policy is not paid by the end of the grace period *and* the policyowner has not elected another nonforfeiture option. The most typical automatic nonforfeiture benefit is the extended term insurance benefit.

## Cash Payment Nonforfeiture Option

The *cash payment nonforfeiture option* states that a policyowner who discontinues premium payments can elect to surrender the policy and receive the policy's cash surrender value in a lump-sum payment. Following the surrender of a policy, all coverage under the policy terminates.

Cash value policies include a chart that lists cash surrender values at various times, and these policies describe the method used to compute those values. Laws in most states require that these cash surrender values meet or exceed the amount that would be provided based on a formula stated in the laws. This formula takes into account the type and plan of insurance, the age of the policy, and the length of the policy's premium payment period. In most cases, applying this formula requires that the policy provide a cash surrender value by the end of the second or third policy year. Insurance companies often issue policies that provide a cash surrender value sooner than required by law and that provide a larger cash surrender value than that required by law.

The amount of cash value actually available to a policyowner upon surrender of a policy may not be the exact cash surrender value amount described in the policy. Paid-up additions, dividend accumulations, advance premium payments, and policy loans will result in additions to and subtractions from the cash surrender value. (We describe dividend accumulations and advance premium payments in Chapter 10.) The amount the policyowner will actually receive after such adjustments have been made is called the *net cash surrender value*. Because paid-up additions also build cash values, the cash values of such additions also are added to the amount the policyowner can collect upon surrender of the policy.

> **FAST FACT**
>
> During 2003, U.S. life insurers paid $35 billion in cash surrender values on life insurance policies that were voluntarily terminated.
>
> **Source:** ACLI, *Life Insurers Fact Book: 2004* (Washington, D.C.: American Council of Life Insurers, 2004), 63.

**Example.** Lise Andrew wants to surrender her whole life insurance policy for its net cash surrender value. The cash value amount shown in her policy is $5,000, and the cash value of the paid-up additions Lise has purchased is $150. Lise also has accumulated $250 in policy dividends, has made an advance premium payment of $200, and has an outstanding policy loan plus interest of $1,000.

**Analysis.** The net cash surrender value payable to Lise is $4,600, calculated as follows:

| | |
|---|---|
| $5,000 | Cash value amount listed in policy |
| + 150 | Cash value of paid-up additions |
| + 250 | Amount of policy dividend accumulations |
| + 200 | Amount of advance premium payment |
| –1,000 | Policy loan, plus interest, outstanding |
| **$4,600** | **Net cash surrender value** |

When a policyowner withdraws the net cash surrender value, the policy—and all coverage under the policy—terminates. At the time of the withdrawal, the policyowner usually surrenders the policy—that is, returns it to the insurer.

Insurers have the legal right to defer payment of any policy's cash surrender value for a period of up to six months after the owner of the policy requests payment. A few jurisdictions, however, have shortened this maximum deferral period. The insurance company's right to defer payment is designed to protect the insurer's cash reserves should a rush of surrenders occur over a short period of time. Insurers have rarely enforced this right to defer payment.

## Continued Insurance Coverage Nonforfeiture Options

Many policies that build a cash value provide the insured with the option of discontinuing premium payments and continuing insurance coverage as either reduced paid-up insurance or extended term insurance.

### Reduced Paid-Up Insurance

Under the *reduced paid-up insurance nonforfeiture option*, the policy's net cash surrender value is used as a net single premium to purchase paid-up life insurance of the same plan as the original policy. The premium charged for the paid-up insurance is based on the age the insured has attained when the option goes into effect. The amount of paid-up insurance that can be purchased under this option is smaller than the face value of the original policy—thus the name *reduced* paid-up insurance.

Policies that include this option contain a chart listing the amount of reduced paid-up insurance that is available each year for the first 20 years the policy is in force. The amount of reduced paid-up insurance listed for each year is based on the cash value listed in the policy for that year. The actual amount of reduced paid-up insurance available might be higher or lower than the amount listed, depending on the size of the net cash surrender value. If the net cash surrender value is larger than the listed cash value amount, as might be the case if the policy includes paid-up additions, then the amount of reduced paid-up insurance available is greater than the reduced paid-up amount listed in the chart.

If a policy loan is outstanding, the net cash surrender value is lower than that listed in the chart because the insurer subtracts the amount of the outstanding loan from the listed cash value; as a result, the amount of reduced paid-up insurance available is less than the amount listed in the policy. The policyowner, however, may ask the insurer to use the actual cash value without deducting the outstanding loan amount to purchase the reduced paid-up insurance. In that case, the policy loan remains in effect and the insurer continues to charge interest on the loan. If the loan is not repaid before the insured dies, the loan amount is deducted from the amount payable at the insured's death. By continuing the loan, however, the policyowner can purchase a larger amount of paid-up life insurance because the net cash surrender value is not reduced by the amount of the policy loan.

The insurance purchased under the reduced paid-up insurance option has the same duration as the original policy. Thus, if the original policy was a whole life policy, then the reduced paid-up coverage remains in force throughout the insured's lifetime. If the original policy was an endowment at age 65 policy, then the coverage remains in force until the insured attains age 65.

Note that the premium amount charged by the insurer for this coverage is based on net premium rates; that is, the insurer does not add an amount to the net premium to cover expenses. As a result, buying insurance in this manner is usually less expensive than taking the policy's value in cash and purchasing another paid-up insurance policy. The coverage issued under this option continues to have and to build a cash value, and the policyowner continues to have the rights available to the owner of any life insurance policy, including the right to surrender the policy for its cash value and the right to receive dividends if the original policy was issued on a participating basis. Any supplemental benefits that were available on the original policy, such as accidental death benefits, are usually *not* available when the policy is continued as reduced paid-up insurance. (See Figure 8.2, which illustrates the amount of paid-up insurance that might be available to a male applicant 40 years of age under two traditional whole life policies.)

### Extended Term Insurance

Under the ***extended term insurance nonforfeiture option***, the insurance company uses the policy's net cash surrender value to purchase term insurance for the full coverage amount provided under the original policy for as long a term as the net cash surrender value can provide. The length of the term depends on the amount of the coverage, the amount of the net cash surrender value, the sex of the insured, and the insured's attained age when the policyowner exercises the extended term option.

**FIGURE 8.2  Illustrative Reduced Paid-Up Insurance Amounts (Male, 40 Years of Age)**

| Type of Policy | Paid-Up Insurance per $1,000 of Face Amount at End of Policy Year | | |
| --- | --- | --- | --- |
| | 5 | 10 | 20 |
| Continuous-premium whole life policy | $178 | $368 | $ 613 |
| 20-payment whole life policy | 283 | 557 | 1,000 |

To calculate the amount and term of the extended term insurance, the insurer first determines the amount of the policy's net cash surrender value that is available to pay the premium for the coverage. The insurer then calculates the amount of extended term insurance available under this option. Generally, the amount of extended term insurance available is the amount of insurance that would have been payable under the original policy. Recall, however, that amounts such as paid-up additions, dividend accumulations, and policy loans result in additions to and subtractions from the face amount of insurance provided by a policy. Because the amount payable under the policy would be reduced by the amount of any indebtedness, such as a policy loan, and would be increased by the face amount of any paid-up additions, these reductions and increases typically also are made when the insurer calculates the amount of coverage available under the extended term insurance option. Otherwise, the insurer would, in effect, be granting a greater or lesser amount of actual coverage than the amount that was in effect before the policyowner exercised the nonforfeiture option. The following example illustrates how the amount of extended term insurance available is typically calculated.

| $10,000 | Face value of policy |
| + 200 | Face value of paid-up additions |
| − 1,000 | Policy loan outstanding |
| **$9,200** | **Amount of term insurance available** |

| $2,500 | Listed cash value |
| + 50 | Cash value of paid-up additions |
| − 1,000 | Policy loan outstanding |
| **$1,550** | **Net cash surrender value** |

Thus, the insurer would use the $1,550 net cash surrender value as a net single premium to purchase $9,200 of term life insurance for as long a period as that $1,550 would purchase.

In contrast, some insurers take a different approach to calculating the amount of extended term insurance available when a policy loan is outstanding. These insurers account for the existence of a policy loan by reducing the amount of the net cash surrender value by the amount of the policy loan but do not reduce the face amount of coverage. The following example illustrates how these insurers would calculate the amount of extended term insurance available.

| $10,000 | Face value of policy |
| + 200 | Face value of paid-up additions |
| **$10,200** | **Amount of term insurance available** |

> $2,500  Listed cash value
> + 50  Cash value of paid-up additions
> −1,000  Policy loan outstanding
> **$1,550  Net cash surrender value**
>
> Thus, the insurer would use the $1,550 net cash surrender value as a net single premium to purchase $10,200 of term life insurance for as long a period as that $1,550 would purchase.

According to the terms of most policies, a policyowner who has elected the extended term nonforfeiture option can no longer exercise the policy loan privilege or receive policy dividends. The policyowner, however, does have the right to cancel the extended term insurance and surrender the policy for its remaining cash value. As with the reduced paid-up option, any supplementary benefits that were available under the original policy usually are not available when the policy is placed under the extended term insurance option.

A life insurance policy that includes the extended term insurance option contains a chart showing the length of time the original face value of the policy will be continued in force under the extended term option for each of the first 20 policy years. Figure 8.3 shows a sample table of guaranteed values for a whole life policy, including the duration of extended term insurance available at the end of specified policy years.

Because of the way in which they operate, universal life insurance policies typically do not include an extended term insurance nonforfeiture option. Recall that the insurer periodically deducts mortality and expense charges from the policy's cash value. Thus, even if the owner of a universal life policy pays no premium, the policy continues in force until the cash value is exhausted by the routine monthly deductions.

## Automatic Premium Loan Option

Under the ***automatic premium loan (APL) option***, the insurer will automatically pay an overdue premium for the policyowner by making a loan against the policy's cash value as long as the cash value equals or exceeds the amount of the premium due. The use of the automatic premium loan keeps the original policy in force for the full amount of coverage, including all supplemental benefits. An automatic premium loan provision is required by law in a few states, and it is widely used in policies issued in most other states.

Universal life insurance policies usually do not include an automatic premium loan provision because a similar benefit is already provided in these policies as part of their monthly cash value deduction mechanism.

| FIGURE 8.3 | Sample Table of Guaranteed Nonforfeiture Values |
|---|---|

### Table of Guaranteed Values*

Plan: Whole Life
Face Amount: $50,000
Age of Insured at Issue: 35

| End of Policy Year | Cash Value | Paid-Up Insurance | or | Extended Insurance Years | Extended Insurance Days | End of Policy Year |
|---|---|---|---|---|---|---|
| 1 | — | — | | — | — | 1 |
| 2 | — | — | | — | — | 2 |
| 3 | $ 150 | $ 750 | | 0 | 336 | 3 |
| 4 | 600 | 2,750 | | 3 | 101 | 4 |
| 5 | 1,050 | 4,600 | | 5 | 55 | 5 |
| 6 | 1,550 | 6,550 | | 6 | 311 | 6 |
| 7 | 2,000 | 8,100 | | 8 | 23 | 7 |
| 8 | 2,550 | 9,950 | | 9 | 132 | 8 |
| 9 | 3,050 | 11,450 | | 10 | 85 | 9 |
| 10 | 3,600 | 13,000 | | 11 | 9 | 10 |
| 11 | 4,200 | 14,600 | | 11 | 270 | 11 |
| 12 | 5,050 | 16,900 | | 12 | 305 | 12 |
| 13 | 5,900 | 19,050 | | 13 | 257 | 13 |
| 14 | 6,800 | 21,150 | | 14 | 169 | 14 |
| 15 | 7,700 | 23,150 | | 15 | 13 | 15 |
| 16 | 8,650 | 25,050 | | 15 | 192 | 16 |
| 17 | 9,550 | 26,700 | | 15 | 296 | 17 |
| 18 | 10,550 | 28,500 | | 16 | 51 | 18 |
| 19 | 11,500 | 30,000 | | 16 | 113 | 19 |
| 20 | 12,500 | 31,550 | | 16 | 170 | 20 |
| Age 60 | 16,800 | 36,100 | | 15 | 186 | Age 60 |
| Age 65 | 21,450 | 39,750 | | 14 | 9 | Age 65 |

* This table assumes premiums have been paid to the end of the policy year shown. These values do not include any dividend accumulations, paid-up additions, or policy loans.

# Life Insurance Policy Exclusions

Life insurance policies sometimes contain **exclusions**—provisions that describe circumstances under which the insurer will not pay the policy proceeds following the death of the insured. For example, policies issued during periods of war or threats of war in the past sometimes included a *war exclusion clause*, which stated that the insurer would not pay the policy proceeds if the insured's death was connected with war. Currently, U.S. insurers rarely include a war exclusion provision in policies they issue. Similarly, in the early years of air travel, life insurance policies often included an *aviation exclusion provision*, which stated that the insurer would not pay the policy proceeds if the insured's death resulted from aviation-related activities. Today, this type of policy exclusion is primarily applied only to activities connected with military or experimental aircraft. Some insurers, however, include an aviation exclusion in policies that insure pilots and crew members flying privately owned aircraft.

An exclusion still typically included in individual life insurance policies is the **suicide exclusion provision** that governs the payment of policy proceeds if the insured dies as a result of suicide. Insurance companies try to protect themselves against the possibility of antiselection by excluding suicide as a covered risk for a specified period—usually two years—following the date the policy is issued. The general opinion is that this exclusion period is sufficient to protect against situations in which a person purchases insurance with the knowledge that the insured plans to commit suicide. A sample suicide exclusion provision follows.

> **Suicide Exclusion.** Suicide of the insured, while sane or insane, within two years of the date of issue, is not covered by this policy. In that event, this policy will end and the only amount payable will be the premiums paid to us, less any loan.

Note that in the event the insured's death from suicide occurs during the two-year exclusion period, the insurance company is not liable to pay the policy's death benefit. The insurer, however, will return the premiums paid for the policy less the amount of any unpaid policy loan. The suicide exclusion provision in some policies states that the insurer will pay the larger of (1) the policy's cash surrender value or (2) the premiums paid for the policy if the insured commits suicide during the suicide exclusion period.

# Key Terms

free-look provision
entire contract provision
closed contract
open contract
incontestability provision
warranty
representation
misrepresentation
material misrepresentation
fraudulent misrepresentation
grace period provision
grace period
lapse
reinstatement provision
reinstatement
redating
misstatement of age or sex provision
policy loan provision
policy withdrawal provision
nonforfeiture provision
automatic nonforfeiture benefit
cash payment nonforfeiture option
net cash surrender value
reduced paid-up insurance nonforfeiture option
extended term insurance nonforfeiture option
automatic premium loan (APL) option
exclusion
suicide exclusion provision

# Life Insurance Policy Ownership Rights

## objectives

*After reading this chapter, you should be able to*

- Distinguish between primary and contingent beneficiaries and between revocable and irrevocable beneficiaries

- Identify the person in a given situation who is entitled to receive the proceeds of a life insurance policy following the insured's death

- Describe restrictions imposed on beneficiary changes and the procedures followed to effect a change in beneficiary

- Recognize the premium payment modes that insurers typically offer on individual life insurance policies

- Identify the policy dividend options that most commonly are included in participating life insurance policies and describe the characteristics of each option

- Identify the settlement options that typically are included in life insurance policies and describe the features of each option

- Identify the methods by which ownership of a life insurance policy can be transferred

A s described in Chapter 3, an insurance policy is property that represents intangible legal rights that have value and that can be enforced by the courts. When a life insurance policy is issued, the policy's ownership rights vest in the policyowner. Most of these ownership rights are spelled out in the policy, and some ownership rights vary depending on the type of policy. In this chapter, we describe these ownership rights. We begin by describing the policyowner's right to name the beneficiary who will receive the policy proceeds following the insured's death. Next, we describe the policyowner's rights concerning premium payments, policy dividends, and settlement options. We also describe how the owner of a policy can transfer her ownership rights to another party.

# Naming the Beneficiary

The beneficiary of a life insurance policy may be a named individual, the executor of an estate, a trustee, a corporation, a charitable organization, or any other entity. A policyowner also can designate a group of persons as beneficiary. A beneficiary designation that identifies a certain group of persons, rather than naming each person, is called a **class designation**. The beneficiary designation "my children" is an example of a class designation.

In Chapter 2, we described the insurable interest requirement that helps prevent an insurance contract from being purchased as an illegal wagering agreement. Because the insurable interest requirement must be met to form a valid life insurance contract, insurance companies routinely review the beneficiary designations contained in applications for life insurance to determine whether the insurable interest requirement has been met. Insurance companies do not, however, review later changes in the beneficiary designation because the insurable interest requirement applies only at the time of policy issue.

## Primary and Contingent Beneficiaries

The **primary beneficiary**, or *first beneficiary*, is the party designated to receive the policy proceeds following the death of the insured. If more than one party is named as primary beneficiary, the policyowner may indicate how the proceeds are to be divided among the parties. If the policyowner does not make such an indication, then the insurer divides the proceeds evenly among the primary beneficiaries who survived the insured. Note that, to receive policy proceeds, the primary beneficiary must survive the insured; the beneficiary's estate has no claim to the policy proceeds if the beneficiary dies before the insured.

**Example.** At the time of her death, Val Lundy owned an insurance policy on her life. Val's three brothers were named as the policy beneficiaries, and all three brothers survived Val.

**Analysis.** Unless Val had indicated otherwise, the policy proceeds will be divided equally among the three beneficiaries.

The policyowner also may designate a contingent beneficiary who will receive the policy proceeds if the primary beneficiary should die before the insured. A *contingent beneficiary*, sometimes referred to as a *secondary beneficiary* or *successor beneficiary*, can receive the policy proceeds only if all designated primary beneficiaries have predeceased the insured. The policyowner can name any number of contingent beneficiaries and may decide how the proceeds are to be divided among the contingent beneficiaries. The designation of contingent beneficiaries can be especially important in cases in which the primary beneficiary dies and the policyowner is unable to designate a new beneficiary before the policy becomes payable. The following examples illustrate the rights of primary and contingent beneficiaries to receive the policy proceeds.

**Example.** Ira Shulman owned a $50,000 insurance policy on his life. He named his wife, Myrna, as primary beneficiary and his sons, Abe and Jacob, as equal contingent beneficiaries. Ira was survived by his wife and both sons.

**Analysis.** The $50,000 policy proceeds are payable to the primary beneficiary, Myrna.

**Example.** Ira Shulman named his wife, Myrna, as primary beneficiary and his sons, Abe and Jacob, as equal contingent beneficiaries. Both Myrna and Abe died several years before Ira died.

**Analysis.** As the sole surviving contingent beneficiary, Jacob is entitled to receive the $50,000 policy proceeds.

**Example.** Ira Shulman named his sons, Abe and Jacob, as equal primary beneficiaries and his wife, Myrna, as contingent beneficiary. Jacob died several years before Ira, who was survived by Abe and Myrna.

**Analysis.** As the sole surviving primary beneficiary, Abe is entitled to receive the $50,000 policy proceeds.

Insurers usually prefer that policyowners name at least a primary and a contingent beneficiary, and most insurers permit the designation of additional levels of contingent beneficiaries. Naming additional levels of contingent beneficiaries helps the policyowner to be certain that the proceeds will be paid to the desired party. Contingent beneficiaries at any given level typically have a right to the policy proceeds only if all beneficiaries in the preceding levels have predeceased the insured. Keep in mind, however, that the disposition of policy proceeds in any given case depends on the specific wording of the beneficiary designation.

## No Surviving Beneficiary

If no beneficiary has been named or none of the named beneficiaries is living when the insured dies, then the policy proceeds typically are paid to the policyowner, if the policyowner is living. If the policyowner is deceased, then the proceeds are paid to the policyowner's estate.

> **Example.** When Pearl Windsor died, she owned an insurance policy on her life. Pearl's husband was the primary beneficiary and her two children were contingent beneficiaries. No named beneficiary survived Pearl.
>
> **Analysis.** Because no named beneficiary survived the insured, the policy proceeds are paid to the policyowner's—in this case, Pearl's—estate.

Alternatively, some policies contain a **preference beneficiary clause**, or *succession beneficiary clause*, which states that if the policyowner does not name a beneficiary, then the insurer will pay the policy proceeds in a stated order of preference. For example, a preference beneficiary clause might list the following order: the spouse of the insured, if living; then the children of the insured, if living; then the parents of the insured, if living. If no living recipients are available from that list, then the proceeds would be paid to the estate of the insured. The preference beneficiary clause is found more often in group life insurance and monthly debit ordinary insurance policies than in other types of individual life insurance policies.

## Facility-of-Payment Clause

Certain types of policies, generally those with small face amounts, allow the insurance company to pay some part of the proceeds to someone other than the named beneficiary. Group life, monthly debit ordinary life, and a few individual whole life insurance policies contain a **facility-of-payment clause** that permits the insurance company to pay all or part of the policy proceeds either to a relative of the insured or to anyone who has a valid claim to those proceeds. The amounts paid under this clause usually are small and are intended to reimburse an individual who has incurred funeral expenses or final medical expenses on behalf of the insured. This clause is very important in cases in which a party other than the named beneficiary has assumed these expenses on behalf of the insured and either (1) the named beneficiary is a minor or (2) the named beneficiary is dead and the policyowner's estate has become the beneficiary of the policy.

> **Example.** For several months before his death, Clyde Dozier was cared for by his brother, Dwayne, who paid some of Clyde's final medical expenses. Clyde was the policyowner-insured of a life insurance policy that contained a facility-of-payment clause. The policy proceeds were payable to Clyde's estate.
>
> **Analysis.** In accordance with the terms of the facility-of-payment clause, the insurer will be able to pay some part of the policy proceeds to Dwayne as reimbursement for the medical expenses he incurred on Clyde's behalf. Any remaining policy proceeds will be paid to Clyde's estate.

## Changing the Beneficiary

Life insurance policies usually give the policyowner the right to change the beneficiary designation as many times as she desires over the life of the policy. This right to change the beneficiary designation is known as the **right of revocation**. A beneficiary designation is said to be *revocable* if the policyowner has the unrestricted right to change the designation during the life of the insured. Most insurers refer to any beneficiary so designated as a **revocable beneficiary**. If the policyowner has the right to change the beneficiary designation only after obtaining the beneficiary's consent, then the designation is said to be *irrevocable*. Insurers refer to any beneficiary so designated as an **irrevocable beneficiary**.

### Revocable Beneficiary

The vast majority of designated beneficiaries of life insurance policies are revocable beneficiaries. A revocable beneficiary generally has neither a legal interest in the proceeds nor any involvement with the policy until the insured person dies. During the insured's lifetime, the revocable beneficiary has no rights to any policy values and cannot prohibit the policyowner from exercising any policy ownership rights, including the right to change the beneficiary. Thus, during the insured's lifetime, a revocable beneficiary's interest in the life insurance policy is said to be a "mere expectancy" of receiving the policy proceeds.

## Irrevocable Beneficiary

A policyowner may at any time designate a beneficiary as an irrevocable beneficiary. After making such a designation, the policyowner gives up the right to change the beneficiary designation unless the irrevocable beneficiary consents to such a change. An irrevocable beneficiary has a vested interest in the proceeds of the life insurance policy even during the lifetime of the insured. A *vested interest* is a property right that has taken effect and cannot be altered or changed without the consent of the person who owns the right.

Because an irrevocable beneficiary has a vested interest in the policy proceeds, most insurers do not permit the policyowner who has designated an irrevocable beneficiary to exercise all of his ownership rights in the contract without that irrevocable beneficiary's consent. For example, the policyowner cannot obtain a policy loan, surrender the policy for cash, or assign ownership of the policy to another party without the consent of the irrevocable beneficiary. (Assignments are discussed later in this chapter.)

Under certain circumstances, a policyowner may be able to name a new beneficiary, even if the original beneficiary designation is irrevocable. Commonly, if the policyowner wishes to make a change, the policyowner must obtain the irrevocable beneficiary's written consent to the change of beneficiary. In addition, most life insurance policies contain a provision stating that the rights of any beneficiary, including an irrevocable beneficiary, will terminate if the beneficiary should die before the insured dies. This provision prevents the automatic payment of the proceeds to the estate of the irrevocable beneficiary and permits the policyowner to designate a new beneficiary following the death of an irrevocable beneficiary.

> **Example.** When Omar Mikulsky purchased an insurance policy on his life, he named his sister Shari as the irrevocable beneficiary. Several years later, Omar married and wanted to change the beneficiary designation to his wife. At that time, however, Shari was terminally ill and unable to provide a written consent to the beneficiary change.
>
> **Analysis.** Without the consent of the irrevocable beneficiary—or a person who qualifies to represent her—Omar cannot change the policy's beneficiary designation. If Shari dies, Omar can then change the beneficiary designation.

As a general rule, a beneficiary designation is revocable unless the policyowner voluntarily gives up the right to change the beneficiary and makes the designation irrevocable. In some jurisdictions around the world, however, laws limit a policyowner's right to change a beneficiary designation. Insight 9.1 describes a few situations in which a policyowner's right to change a life insurance policy's beneficiary designation is limited by law.

## INSIGHT 9.1 Legislative Limitations on Beneficiary Changes

In some jurisdictions, laws have been enacted to protect spousal rights to life insurance policy proceeds. In the Canadian province of Quebec, for example, if the owner of a life insurance policy designates her spouse as the beneficiary, then that designation is considered by law to be an irrevocable designation *unless* the policyowner specifically reserves the right to change the beneficiary.

Laws in community-property states in the United States also protect spousal rights in some cases. A *community-property state* is one in which, by law, each spouse is entitled to an equal share of the income earned by the other and, under most circumstances, to an equal share of the property acquired by the other during the period of their marriage. In the community-property states (Arizona, California, Idaho, Louisiana, Nevada, New Mexico, Texas, Washington, and Wisconsin), an insurance policy is property that is classified as community property if it was bought during the marriage with community funds. A spouse who is named as the revocable beneficiary of a policy that is commu-

nity property has certain vested rights in the policy.

For example, assume that a husband used community funds to purchase a policy on his life, which thus became community property. When he purchased the policy, he named his wife as the revocable beneficiary. Shortly before his death, the husband changed the beneficiary designation without obtaining his wife's consent. A court is likely to find that the wife has a right to half of the policy proceeds because the policy was community property in which she had an equal ownership share.

## Beneficiary Change Procedure

If a policyowner has retained the right to change the beneficiary, the procedure to make such a change is straightforward and relatively simple. Each life insurance policy specifies the change of beneficiary procedure required. A sample change of beneficiary provision follows:

> While the Insured is living, you can change a beneficiary in a notice you sign which gives us the facts that we need. When we record a change, it will take effect as of the date you signed the notice, subject to any payment we made or action we took before recording the change.

Note that a beneficiary change can be made only during the insured's lifetime. Once the insured dies, the named beneficiary has a vested interest in the policy proceeds, and the policyowner cannot deprive the beneficiary of that interest.

The most important procedural point in a change of beneficiary is a written notification to the insurer of the change. Most insurance companies require only that the policyowner notify the company in writing of the change of beneficiary for the change to be effective. This method of changing the beneficiary is called the ***recording method***. Some insurers also may require that a change of beneficiary request be signed by disinterested witnesses or that the documents requesting the change be authenticated by a notary public. A *notary public* is a public officer who is authorized to certify and authenticate certain types of documents. (See Figure 9.1, which shows a sample change of beneficiary form.)

Older policies that have been in force for many years may contain a change of beneficiary procedure known as the endorsement method. An **endorsement** is a document that is attached to a policy and is a part of the policy contract. Under the **endorsement method**, the name of the new beneficiary must be added to the policy itself for the beneficiary change to be effective. The endorsement method is rarely used today for beneficiary changes, although it was a common procedure in the past.

# Premium Payments

Most individual life insurance policies give the policyowner several rights concerning premium payments, including the right to choose the premium payment mode (frequency) and the right to choose from among several premium payment methods.

## Mode of Premium Payment

When a policyowner is required to pay periodic renewal premiums to keep the policy's coverage in force, the policyowner and insurer must agree on how often those premiums will be paid. A policy's **premium payment mode** is the frequency at which renewal premiums are payable. Each insurance company determines which premium payment modes it will make available to its policyowners. Most insurers offer to accept renewal premiums for individual life insurance policies on an annual, semiannual, quarterly, or monthly basis. The applicant selects one of these premium payment modes when he completes the application for insurance. Typically, the policyowner also may change the mode of premium payment after the policy has taken effect.

To keep their administrative costs down, insurers often require scheduled renewal premium payments to be at least equal to a stated minimum amount. The policyowner may not select a premium payment mode that results in a premium less than that required minimum amount. For example, the insurance company may require a minimum monthly premium payment of at least $20 for a policyowner to choose a monthly premium payment mode. If the monthly premium amount were less than that minimum, then the policyowner would be required to choose a less frequent mode of payment, such as quarterly or semiannually.

| FIGURE 9.1 | Sample Change of Beneficiary Form |
|---|---|

## Change of Beneficiary

*(Read the provisions printed below before completing this form. Please print or type.)*

**ABC LIFE INSURANCE COMPANY** is requested to make the following changes of beneficiary. Indicate how many policies to be changed _____ .

Policy (or Policies) Numbered _____

on the life of _____ the Insured

| First Name & Middle Initial | Last Name |
|---|---|

### Request for Change of Beneficiary

Change the beneficiary designation of the above numbered policy (or policies) to (give Full Name, Residence Address, and Relationship to Insured):

First Beneficiary _____

Second Beneficiary _____

Third Beneficiary _____

I understand and agree that:

1. The Provisions Relating to Beneficiary Designation printed below are made a part of the above beneficiary designation and a part of the above numbered policy (or policies).
2. When countersigned for ABC Life, this change of beneficiary will take effect as of the date this request was signed, subject to any payment made or other action taken by the Company before recording the change. When this change takes effect, it will terminate any existing settlement agreement or election of an optional method of payment, and any existing beneficiary designation.
3. Every beneficiary named above, including a spouse, is revocable unless this designation provides that such beneficiary is irrevocable.

Date _____ , 20 ____      _____

Signature(s) of person(s) with right to change beneficiary (and any other required signature)

### For ABC LIFE USE ONLY: Recording of Beneficiary Change Request

Countersigned for ABC Life by _____ on _____ , 20 ___

☐ Change(s) Recorded and Copy(ies) Returned to be Retained with Policy(ies)

☐ Change(s) Recorded and Copy(ies) Attached as Endorsement on Policy(ies)

Returned to: _____ By _____ on _____ , 20 ___

### Provisions Relating to Beneficiary Designation

**Naming of Beneficiary and Death of Beneficiary:** Unless otherwise provided in the policy, or in the beneficiary designation above, the following provisions shall apply:

1. Beneficiaries (or payees) may be classed as first, second, and so on. The stated shares of life insurance or death benefit proceeds will be paid to any first beneficiaries who survive the Insured. If no first beneficiaries survive, payment will be made to any surviving second beneficiaries, and so on. Surviving beneficiaries in the same class will have an equal share in the proceeds, or in any periodic income payments payable from these proceeds, unless the shares are otherwise stated.
2. If no beneficiary for a stated share of any life insurance or death benefit proceeds survives the Insured, the right to those proceeds will pass to the Owner. If the Owner was the Insured, the right to those proceeds will pass to the Insured's estate. If any beneficiary dies at the same time as the Insured, or if the policy so provides, within 15 days after the Insured but before proof of the Insured's death is received by the Company, the proceeds will be paid as though that beneficiary died first.

**Change of Beneficiary:** Even if there is anything in the policy (or policies) that states otherwise, the person having the right to change a beneficiary can do so while the Insured is living by using this signed notice furnishing the necessary information to the Company without submitting the policy to the Company for endorsement. A copy of this form will be returned to the Owner to be kept with the policy after the change has been recorded. When the Company records the change, it will take effect as of the date this notice was signed, subject to any payment made or other action taken by the Company before recording.

# Method of Premium Payment

Individual insurance policies usually state that renewal premiums are payable at the insurer's home office or an authorized branch office. A policyowner, however, does not need to visit an insurance company office to pay each premium. Although renewal premiums for policies may be paid in person, policyowners usually pay premiums by mail, by automatic payment techniques, or through payroll deduction. In most cases, policyowners do not pay renewal premiums to an insurance producer because life insurance producers generally are authorized to accept only initial premiums. One exception, as noted in Chapter 6, is that home service agents generally are authorized to accept renewal premium payments.

## Payment by Mail

A policyowner who chooses to pay renewal premiums by mail receives a premium notice from the insurance company before each premium due date. In most cases, the policyowner returns a portion of the notice along with the premium payment.

A policyowner usually may pay the renewal premium in cash, by money order, or by check. As a result of federal money laundering laws in the United States, however, many insurers now discourage policyowners from paying premiums in cash, and many insurers limit the amount they will accept in the form of a money order. Many insurers will accept a charge against a policyowner's credit card as a means of paying the premium. If the premium is not paid in cash, however, the insurer's acceptance of the premium is contingent on its actual collection of the money. In other words, if a policyowner pays a premium by check and the check is not honored by the policyowner's bank because of insufficient funds, then the premium payment was not made. When a required renewal premium is paid by a check that is not honored, the policy will lapse if the policyowner does not pay the required premium within the policy's grace period.

> **Example.** A quarterly premium payment was due on April 8 on Sidney Bullock's life insurance policy, which contained a 31-day grace period. Sidney mailed a check to the insurance company on May 4 for the full amount of the premium due. The insurer received the check on May 7, but Sidney's bank refused to honor the check because his bank account did not have enough funds to cover the amount of the check.
>
> **Analysis.** Because the insurance company received the check on May 7, the premium was received within the policy's grace period. However, the check was not honored by Sidney's bank. As a result, the renewal premium was not paid within the policy's grace period, and Sidney's policy will lapse.

### Automatic Payment Techniques

Many policyowners choose to pay renewal premiums through an automatic payment technique. Policyowners who choose an automatic payment method do not receive renewal premium notices and do not regularly mail premium payments to the insurance company. Instead, these policyowners arrange to have renewal premiums paid automatically. The most common automatic premium payment techniques include the electronic funds transfer method and the payroll deduction method.

Most insurance companies today permit premiums to be paid by the *electronic funds transfer (EFT) method* under which policyowners authorize their banks to pay premiums automatically on premium due dates. When this method is used, funds to pay premiums are automatically transferred from the bank to the insurer. No paper checks are generated, and notice of the transaction simply appears on the policyowner's bank statement.

Sometimes, insurers permit premiums to be paid by payroll deductions, which require the cooperation of the policyowner's employer. Under the *payroll deduction method*, the employer deducts insurance premiums directly from an employee's paycheck. Generally, several employees must use the payroll deduction method and have policies with the same insurance company for the employer to institute such a system. The employer usually sends the insurer a single check for the total amount of premiums due on all such policies.

Automatic premium payment methods have produced two important results. They have (1) reduced insurance companies' administrative expenses for policies with monthly and quarterly premium payment modes and (2) reduced the instances in which policyowners forget to pay renewal premiums. Therefore, when policyowners choose one of these automatic payment methods, most insurance companies forgo or reduce the extra charges that would otherwise be added for semiannual, quarterly, or monthly premium payment modes. In addition, some companies offer monthly and quarterly premium payment modes only to those policyowners who have chosen an automatic payment technique.

# Policy Dividend Options

We noted in Chapter 4 that a participating policy gives the policyowner the right to share in the insurer's divisible surplus through the receipt of policy dividends. Although dividends are not guaranteed, most insurers periodically pay dividends on their participating life insurance policies that are expected to remain in force over a long term. Any policy dividend declared for a policy is payable on the policy's anniversary date, and the terms of many life insurance policies state that the policy must be in force for two years before any policy dividends will be payable.

The amount payable as policy dividends is determined annually by an insurance company's board of directors, which must act in accordance with any applicable statutory requirements. The amount of any policy dividend that is paid primarily reflects (1) the insurance company's actual mortality, interest, and expense experience during the year; (2) the plan of insurance; (3) the policy's premium amount; and (4) the length of time the policy has been in force. Generally, dividend amounts increase substantially with the age of the policy.

**FAST FACT**

During 2003, U.S. life insurers paid over $15 billion in policy dividends.

**Source:** ACLI, *Life Insurers Fact Book: 2004* (Washington, D.C.: American Council of Life Insurers, 2004), 64.

The owner of a participating life insurance policy may receive policy dividends in a number of different ways, called **dividend options**. Most insurance companies include five dividend options in their participating life insurance policies: (1) the cash dividend option, (2) the premium reduction option, (3) the accumulation at interest option, (4) the paid-up additional insurance option, and (5) the additional term insurance option. The applicant for a participating policy usually selects a dividend option when she completes the policy application. Over the life of a participating policy, the policyowner may change the dividend option at any time, though a change to the additional term insurance option is subject to certain restrictions. Each participating life insurance policy also specifies an **automatic dividend option**, which is the dividend option that the insurer will apply if the policyowner for some reason does not choose an option. Most policies specify the paid-up additional insurance option as the automatic dividend option.

## Cash Dividend Option

Under the **cash dividend option**, the insurance company sends the policyowner a check in the amount of the policy dividend that was declared. Some policies also provide that if the policyowner does not cash the dividend check within a stated period, such as one year, then the insurer will apply the amount of the dividend under another option, such as the paid-up additions option.

## Premium Reduction Option

Under the **premium reduction dividend option**, the insurer applies policy dividends toward the payment of renewal premiums. Unless a policy has been in force for many years, the annual policy dividend usually is not large enough to pay an entire annual renewal premium. If a policyowner is paying premiums more often than annually, the dividend may cover one or more of the installments. The insurer notifies the policyowner of the amount of the policy dividend and bills the policyowner for the difference, if any, between the premium amount due and the amount of the policy dividend.

## Accumulation at Interest Option

Participating life insurance policies usually contain an **accumulation at interest dividend option** under which the policy dividends are left on deposit with the insurer to accumulate at interest. During the life of the policy, the policyowner typically has the right to withdraw part or all of these dividends and accumulated interest at any time. If the policyowner surrenders the policy, the insurer will pay the policyowner both the accumulated value of the policy dividends and the policy's cash surrender value. Any policy dividends that are on deposit with the insurer when the insured dies usually are payable to the named beneficiary rather than to the policyowner.

## Paid-Up Additional Insurance Option

Under the **paid-up additional insurance dividend option**, the insurer uses any declared policy dividend as a net single premium to purchase paid-up additional insurance on the insured's life; the paid-up additional insurance is issued on the same plan as the basic policy and in whatever face amount the dividend can provide at the insured's attained age. Because the premium charged for paid-up additions does not include an amount to cover the insurer's expenses, the cost of paid-up additions is less than the cost of comparable coverage provided by a new life insurance policy.

If the policy is one that builds cash values, then the paid-up additions purchased with policy dividends also build cash values, and the policyowner has the right to surrender those additions for their cash value at any time while the policy is in force. Although the face amount of the paid-up additions purchased each year under this option may be relatively small, over the life of a policy, the total additional insurance available can be substantial.

Figure 9.2 illustrates how the paid-up additional insurance option increases the total death benefit payable under a policy. In this illustration, the insured was 40 years old when he purchased a $100,000 participating whole life insurance policy and selected the paid-up additional insurance option. After the policy had been in force for two years, the insurer declared a dividend of $5 for his policy. The insurer automatically applied the $5 dividend to purchase a paid-up whole life addition of $16, the amount of paid-up whole life insurance that the $5 net single premium would purchase at the insured's attained age. As a result, the total death benefit payable under the policy increased to $100,016. The next year, the insurer used the $21 policy dividend to purchase another paid-up whole life addition—this time for $65—and the total death benefit payable under the policy increased to $100,081. As you can see from the illustration in Figure 9.2, when the insured reached age 65, the total amount of paid-up

| FIGURE 9.2 | Illustration of Paid-Up Additional Insurance Option |

| Insured's Age | Dividend Declared | Paid-Up Dividend Additions Current Year | Total Paid-Up Dividend Additions to Date | Total Death Benefit |
|---|---|---|---|---|
| 40 | $ 0 | $ 0 | $ 0 | $100,000 |
| 42 | 5 | 16 | 16 | 100,016 |
| 43 | 21 | 65 | 81 | 100,081 |
| — | — | — | — | — |
| 50 | 229 | 598 | 1,905 | 101,905 |
| — | — | — | — | — |
| 60 | 1,664 | 3,342 | 22,280 | 122,280 |
| — | — | — | — | — |
| 65 | 2,771 | 5,042 | 49,357 | 149,357 |

additions purchased with policy dividends totaled $49,357, thus increasing the total death benefit payable under the policy to $149,357.

## Additional Term Insurance Option

Under the **additional term insurance dividend option**, the insurer uses each policy dividend as a net single premium to purchase one-year term insurance on the insured's life. Often called the *fifth dividend option*, the additional term insurance option is not offered by as many insurance companies as are the other dividend options.

The policyowner's right to purchase one-year term insurance under this option is limited in some respects. First, the maximum amount of one-year term insurance that can be purchased each year is often limited to the amount of the policy's cash value. Second, before a policyowner is permitted to change from another dividend option to the additional term insurance option, insurers usually require evidence of the insured's insurability. This requirement is designed to prevent antiselection because a policyowner is more likely to change to this dividend option if the insured is in poor health rather than to apply dividends to purchase the more expensive paid-up additions. In contrast, insurers usually allow a policyowner to change to the paid-up additional insurance option without providing evidence of the insurability of the insured.

If the annual policy dividend is larger than the premium required to purchase the amount of one-year term insurance permitted—generally the cash value of the policy—then the insurer applies the remaining amount under one of the other dividend options.

Figure 9.3 illustrates how the additional term insurance dividend option increases the amount of a policy's death benefit. Note that this is the same policy we illustrated in Figure 9.2. In this example, any dividends not needed to purchase additional term insurance are used to purchase paid-up additions. On the policy's anniversary date after the second policy year (insured age 42), the insurer paid a policy dividend of $5. The insurer used $3 of that amount to purchase one-year term insurance equal to the policy's cash value ($1,400). The $2 remaining of the policy dividend was used to purchase paid-up additions; in this case, the insurer was able to purchase additions of $9. As a result, the total death benefit available during the policy's third year was $101,409—the $100,000 face amount *plus* the $1,400 of one-year term insurance *plus* the $9 paid-up addition. The $1,400 in one-year term coverage expired at the end of the policy year, but the $9 paid-up

| FIGURE 9.3 | Illustration of Additional Term Insurance Dividend Option | | | | | | |
|---|---|---|---|---|---|---|---|
| (1) | (2) | (3) | (4) | (5) (Column 2– Column 4) | (6) | (7) ($100,000+ Column 3+ Column 6) | (8) ($100,000+ Column 6) |
| Age of Insured | Dividend Declared | Amount of One-Year Term Available (Cash Value of Policy) | Cost of One-Year Term Insurance | Remaining Dividend | Total Amount of Paid-Up Additions Purchased to Date | Total Death Benefit (Beginning of Year) | Total Death Benefit (End of Year) |
| 40 | $ 0 | $ 0 | $ 0 | $ 0 | $ 0 | $100,000 | $100,000 |
| 42 | 5 | 1,400 | 3 | 2 | 9 | 101,409 | 100,009 |
| 43 | 21 | 2,829 | 5 | 16 | 81 | 102,910 | 100,081 |
| — | — | — | — | — | — | — | — |
| 50 | 229 | 13,100 | 35 | 194 | 1,539 | 114,639 | 101,539 |
| — | — | — | — | — | — | — | — |
| 60 | 1,664 | 32,800 | 218 | 1,446 | 18,903 | 151,703 | 118,903 |
| — | — | — | — | — | — | — | — |
| 65 | 2,771 | 42,800 | 479 | 2,292 | 36,138 | 178,938 | 136,138 |

addition remained in force. On the next policy anniversary, the insurer paid a policy dividend of $21, which it used to purchase one-year term insurance in the amount of the policy's cash value; any dividends remaining were used to purchase paid-up additions. As in our earlier illustration, the amount of paid-up insurance purchased with the excess dividends builds gradually, but it does not build as rapidly as it does when the total amount of the policy dividend each year is used to purchase paid-up additions.

## Settlement Options

In most cases, the proceeds of a life insurance policy are paid in a lump sum following the insured's death. Typically, the insurer pays the lump sum directly to the beneficiary in the form of a check. Alternatively, many insurance companies deposit the policy proceeds into an interest-bearing checking account that the insurer establishes in the beneficiary's name. Depositing the proceeds into such an account constitutes a lump-sum settlement because the beneficiary has immediate and complete access to the total amount of the policy proceeds. The insurer periodically pays interest at a specified rate on all funds that it holds in such an account. Interest is often paid monthly at current market rates. The insurer provides the beneficiary with checks that the beneficiary can use as he wishes to withdraw the account funds. For example, the beneficiary can withdraw the entire amount deposited into the account by writing one check, or he can write any number of checks. Once the beneficiary has withdrawn all of the funds, the insurer closes the account.

In addition to lump-sum settlements of policy proceeds, insurance companies provide several alternative methods of receiving the proceeds of a life insurance policy. These alternative methods are called **settlement options** or *optional modes of settlement*, and insurers that provide such options include a settlement options provision in their life insurance policies. The **settlement options provision** grants a policyowner or a beneficiary several choices as to how the insurance company will distribute the proceeds of a life insurance policy.

The policyowner may select one of the optional modes of settlement at the time of application or at any time while the policy is in force. The policyowner also has the right to change to another settlement option at any time during the insured's lifetime.

A policyowner who selects a settlement option for the beneficiary may choose to make the settlement mode *irrevocable*, in which case the beneficiary will not be able to change to another option when the policy proceeds become payable. If the selected settlement option is not irrevocable, then the mode is considered to be *revocable* and the beneficiary has the right to select another settlement option when the proceeds become payable. Further, if the policyowner has not chosen a settlement mode when the policy proceeds become payable, then the beneficiary has the right to choose a settlement option.

The person or party who is to receive the policy proceeds under a settlement option is referred to as the *payee*. The party who elects an optional mode of settlement—either the policyowner or the beneficiary—also has the right to designate a **contingent payee**, or *successor payee*, who will receive any proceeds still payable at the time of the payee's death.

Insurers commonly offer four optional modes of settlement in their individual life insurance policies. These settlement options are the interest option, the fixed-period option, the fixed-amount option, and the life income option.

## Interest Option

The **interest option** is a settlement option under which the insurance company invests the policy proceeds and periodically pays interest on those proceeds to the payee. The policy usually guarantees that the insurer will pay at least a stated minimum interest rate, but the insurer may pay a higher rate if that rate is consistent with the company's investment earnings.

Generally, the insurance company pays interest on the proceeds annually, unless the payee requests more frequent payments. A payee may request a more frequent payment schedule only if the amount of the proceeds being held is large enough to generate interest installments of at least a specified amount during each selected period. For example, a policy's settlement provision may state that a payee can request monthly interest installments only if the policy proceeds would earn at least $50 a month in interest. If the amount of each payment would fall below the specified minimum, then the administrative costs the insurer incurs in making monthly payments would be too high. Therefore, the insurer would require the payee to select a less frequent payment schedule—annually or quarterly, for example.

Occasionally, the payee prefers for the insurance company to invest the policy proceeds and to allow the interest earned to accumulate rather than to be paid to the payee. For example, if the payee is a minor, companies often agree to hold the accumulated interest until the minor reaches the age of majority. Insurance companies, however, generally do not allow the interest to be left on deposit indefinitely.

An insurance company will not hold policy proceeds under the interest option indefinitely. The maximum length of time a company will hold policy proceeds at interest is usually the lifetime of the payee or 30 years, whichever is longer. If the payee dies before receiving payment and the 30-year period has expired, the insurer pays the policy proceeds in a lump sum to the contingent payee. If the payee dies before the 30-year period has expired, then the contingent payee may have the insurance company continue to hold the policy proceeds under the interest option until the original 30-year period ends; at the end of the original 30-year period, the insurer will pay the policy proceeds to the contingent payee in a lump sum.

The payee generally has the right to withdraw all or part of the policy proceeds at any time or to place all of the proceeds—including any interest that the insurer is holding—under another settlement option. Sometimes, however, the payee's withdrawal privilege is limited. When the policyowner selects the interest option, he may choose to give the payee a restricted or an unrestricted withdrawal privilege. A restricted withdrawal privilege usually limits the amount of the policy proceeds that the payee may withdraw. Often, however, the policyowner specifies the interest option as the mode of settlement so that the payee will have the time to make a rational decision on which method of settlement will be most suitable for him. In such cases, an unrestricted withdrawal privilege usually is included in the option, and the payee may at any time choose to withdraw all the proceeds in a lump sum or to place all the proceeds under another settlement option.

## Fixed-Period Option

The *fixed-period option* is a settlement option under which the insurance company agrees to pay policy proceeds in equal installments to the payee for a specified period of time. Each payment will consist partly of the policy proceeds being held by the company and partly of the interest earned on the proceeds. As with the interest option, the policy states the minimum guaranteed interest rate that will be earned on the proceeds and states that the rate may be higher if the company's investment returns are better than expected.

The amount of each installment paid under the fixed-period option depends primarily on the amount of the policy proceeds, the interest rate, and the length of the payment period that the policyowner or beneficiary chooses. Installments may be paid annually or more frequently—even monthly if the amount of each installment is large enough to meet the company's minimum requirements. Policies usually contain a chart that shows, for selected payment periods, the guaranteed amount of monthly payments that will be made per $1,000 of net policy proceeds.

> **Example.** When she died, Jocelyn Schiller owned a $100,000 insurance policy on her life. She had named her son Randy as sole beneficiary and had selected the fixed-period settlement option. The policy stated that the insurer would pay interest of at least 4 percent and contained the following chart—based on

a 4 percent interest rate—listing the amount of each installment payment that would be payable under the fixed-period option:

| Fixed Period (Number of Years) | Minimum Monthly Payment per $1,000 of Proceeds |
|:---:|:---:|
| 1 | $85.12 |
| 2 | 43.39 |
| 3 | 29.49 |
| 4 | 22.55 |
| 5 | 18.38 |

Jocelyn specified that the insurer should make the benefit installment payments over a four-year period.

**Analysis.** According to the terms of the policy, the insurer guarantees that it will pay Randy $2,255 each month over the four-year period.

$22.55    Minimum monthly payment per unit
× 100    Number of units ($100,000 ÷ 1,000)
**$2,255**    **Minimum monthly benefit amount**

The amount of the monthly payment may be larger than $2,255 if the insurance company earns a more profitable rate of return than that guaranteed by the policy.

If the policyowner has not designated the fixed-period option as irrevocable, many policies permit the payee to cancel the option at any time and to collect all of the remaining policy proceeds and unpaid interest in a lump sum. The payee, however, usually does not have the right to withdraw only a part of the funds during the payment period. Such a partial withdrawal would reduce the amount of the remaining funds and would require the insurer to recalculate the entire schedule of benefit payments.

The fixed-period option is designed to provide the payee with a temporary income for a specified period of time—for example, while children are dependent or while a payee is receiving education or training to become employed. This option also is widely used to provide the payee with income until another anticipated income source, such as a pension, begins.

## Fixed-Amount Option

The *fixed-amount option* is a settlement option under which the insurance company pays equal installments of a stated amount until the policy proceeds, plus the interest earned, are exhausted. As with the fixed-period option, the fixed-amount option states the minimum guaranteed interest rate that the insurer will pay on the policy proceeds it holds. The number of installments that the insurer will pay depends on the amount of the policy proceeds, the interest rate, and the fixed amount selected. The larger the amount of the proceeds, the longer the period for which the insurer will make installment payments of the fixed amount. If the payee dies before the proceeds plus interest are exhausted, the insurer pays the total amount of remaining proceeds to the contingent payee.

The payee receiving the policy proceeds under the fixed-amount settlement option generally has the right to withdraw part or all of the remaining policy proceeds at any time. If the payee makes a partial withdrawal, then the insurer will continue making installment payments of the selected amount but will reduce the number of installments it pays. In many cases, the payee also has the right to increase or decrease the amount of each installment payment. Increasing the amount of each payment means that the proceeds will be exhausted more rapidly and fewer payments will be made. Alternatively, reducing the amount of each installment means that the proceeds will be paid over a longer time.

The fixed-amount option is useful when the policyowner or beneficiary wants to be sure that adequate income will be available, even if for only a short time. For instance, the beneficiary may have the capacity to earn an adequate income but may have reasons to postpone employment.

## Life Income Option

The *life income option* is a settlement option under which the insurance company agrees to pay the policy proceeds in periodic installments over the payee's lifetime. As we have seen, both the fixed-amount and fixed-period options provide installment payments for only a limited time. Therefore, the policyowner or beneficiary who chooses one of those options must be certain that providing a temporary income is the best way to distribute the policy proceeds. If other sources of income are not likely to be available in the future, then the payee may be better served by a permanent income provided through the life income option, even though this method of settlement typically results in smaller installment payments than would be available under the fixed-amount or fixed-period options.

Under the life income option, the insurance company agrees to use the policy proceeds as a net single premium to purchase a life annuity for the payee. Recall that an *annuity* is a series of periodic payments. A *life annuity* is an annuity that provides periodic benefit payments for *at least* the lifetime of a named individual. In other words, the payee is entitled to receive annuity benefit payments throughout his lifetime. As we describe in Chapter 11, insurance companies offer several types of life annuity policies. Therefore, insurance companies also give the policyowner or beneficiary who chooses the life income option the right to select from among several types of life annuities. Settlement option provisions most commonly include the following life income options.

- The **straight life income option** under which the policy proceeds are used to purchase a *straight life annuity*

- The **life income with period certain option** under which the policy proceeds are used to purchase a *life income annuity with period certain*

- The **refund life income option** under which the policy proceeds are used to purchase a *life income with refund annuity*

- The **joint and survivorship life income option** under which the policy proceeds are used to purchase a *joint and survivor annuity*

The various types of life annuities we have mentioned are defined in Figure 9.4 and are described in more detail in Chapter 11.

The settlement options provision also guarantees that each periodic annuity benefit payment will be at least as large as a stated amount. Policies typically contain charts that list the amount of the guaranteed minimum benefit payments that will be available under each of the life income options. If the insurer's annuity rates in effect at the time of settlement would result in larger payment amounts, then the insurer typically provides the larger amounts, rather than the guaranteed amounts.

---

 **FIGURE 9.4**  **Types of Annuities**

| **Straight life annuity** | An annuity that guarantees the payment of periodic annuity benefits throughout the lifetime of the annuitant. |
| --- | --- |
| **Life income annuity with period certain** | A life annuity that guarantees the payment of periodic annuity benefits throughout the annuitant's life *and* guarantees that the payments will be made for at least a certain period, even if the annuitant dies before the end of that period. |
| **Life income with refund annuity** | A life annuity that guarantees the payment of periodic annuity benefits throughout the lifetime of the annuitant *and* guarantees that at least the purchase price of the annuity will be paid in benefits. |
| **Joint and survivor annuity** | A life annuity that guarantees the payment of periodic annuity benefits to two or more individuals, continuing until both or all of the individuals die. |

# Transfer of Policy Ownership

If the owner of a life insurance policy has contractual capacity, then she has the right to transfer ownership of some or all of her rights in the policy. An ownership transfer, however, is not accomplished by simply handing someone the policy. The two ways in which a policyowner may transfer ownership rights are by assignment and by endorsement.

## Transfer of Ownership by Assignment

An *assignment* is an agreement under which one party transfers some or all of his ownership rights in a particular property to another party. The property owner who makes an assignment is known as the *assignor*; the party to whom the property rights are transferred is known as the *assignee*.

The right to assign any property, including a life insurance policy, is subject to some restrictions. To make a valid assignment of an insurance policy, the policyowner must have contractual capacity. As a result, if the policyowner is a minor or, for some other reason, lacks contractual capacity, any attempt by the policyowner to assign the policy is invalid.

Another restriction is that the assignment of a life insurance policy may not infringe on the vested rights, if any, of a beneficiary. If the policy's beneficiary has been named irrevocably, then the beneficiary has a vested right to the policy proceeds. An assignment made without such a beneficiary's consent is invalid. Note that when the beneficiary is a revocable beneficiary, the policyowner has an unlimited right to assign the policy.

The final restriction is that an assignment that is made for illegal purposes, such as speculating on a life or committing fraud, is invalid. *Fraud* is an act by which someone intentionally deceives another party and induces that other party to part with something of value or to give up a legal right.

### Assignment Provision

Because the right to assign any property is granted by law, insurers are not required to give a policyowner notice of his right to assign a life insurance policy. Most life insurance policies, however, do include an assignment provision. The *assignment provision* describes the roles of the insurer and the policyowner when the policy is assigned. An example of a life insurance policy's assignment provision follows.

> **Assignment.** While the insured is living, you can assign this policy or any interest in it. As owner, you still have the rights of ownership that have not been assigned. We must have a copy of any assignment. We will not be responsible for the validity of an assignment. An assignment will be subject to any payment we make or other action we take before we record it.

The insurance company is not obligated to act in accordance with the terms of an assignment unless it has received written notice of the assignment. Because the assignee wants to protect her own interests, the assignee typically assumes responsibility for notifying the insurance company, in writing, of the assignment.

An assignment is an agreement between the assignee and the assignor. The insurance company is not a party to the agreement. Therefore, the policy's assignment provision states that the insurer is not responsible for the validity of any assignment. When an insurance company receives written notice of an assignment, the company presumes that the assignment is valid. The insurance company, however, has no control over the validity of the assignment and usually cannot be held liable for having acted in accordance with an assignment that is later determined to be invalid. However, if the insurer was aware of circumstances that should have made the insurer question the assignment's validity—for example, if the insurer was aware that the policyowner had been declared mentally incompetent—then the insurer may be held liable for acting in accordance with the assignment.

> **Example.** Jim Pipcinski was the policyowner-insured of a life insurance policy issued by the Ace Life Insurance Company. When Jim died, Ace's policy records indicated that the policy had been assigned to the Cargill Bank. As a result, Ace paid the policy proceeds to Cargill. Later, a court determined that the assignment to Cargill was invalid.
>
> **Analysis.** Whether Ace will be liable to pay the policy proceeds again will depend on whether Ace was aware of any facts that should have made it question the validity of the assignment. If Ace had no such knowledge, then it will not be required to pay the policy proceeds again.

## Types of Assignment

An assignment may take one of two forms: an absolute assignment or a collateral assignment. Whether an assignment is absolute or collateral depends on whether the assignee has received complete ownership of the policy or only certain specified ownership rights in the policy.

### Absolute Assignment

An *absolute assignment* of a life insurance policy is an assignment under which a policyowner transfers all of his policy ownership rights to the assignee. The policyowner-assignor has no further rights under the contract, and the assignee becomes the policyowner. If a policyowner absolutely assigns a policy without receiving any payment in exchange, he is considered to have made a gift of the policy to the assignee. For example, parents who purchase insurance on their child's life often transfer ownership of the policy—as a gift—to the child when she reaches the age of majority. By contrast, if financial compensation is involved, the absolute assignment is considered to be the equivalent of a sale of the policy. For example, a business organization that owns an insurance policy on the life of a key person may sell the policy to the key person in exchange for the policy's cash value when that key person leaves employment. Such a transfer of the policy's ownership typically is accomplished by means of an absolute assignment.

In most situations, such as those mentioned above, an absolute assignment is made to the person insured by the policy. In most places, however, a policy can be absolutely assigned to anyone, regardless of whether the assignee has an insurable interest in the life of the insured. Figure 9.5 illustrates an absolute assignment form.

## Collateral Assignment

A *collateral assignment* of a life insurance policy is a temporary assignment of the monetary value of a life insurance policy as collateral—or security—for a loan. For example, if a person takes out a personal loan from a bank, that person may collaterally assign a life insurance policy to the bank as security for the loan. A collateral assignment differs from an absolute assignment in three general respects.

1. **The collateral assignee's rights are limited to those ownership rights that directly concern the monetary value of the policy.** The policyowner retains all ownership rights that do not affect the policy's value. For example, the right to name the policy beneficiary and the right to select a dividend payment option remain with the policyowner. The policyowner-assignor, however, is not permitted to take out a policy loan or surrender the policy for its cash surrender value while a collateral assignment is in effect unless the assignee consents. This limitation is imposed to protect the assignee's right to the policy's value because a policy loan and a policy surrender both diminish that value.

2. **The collateral assignee has a vested right to the policy's monetary values, but that right is limited.** The assignee's rights to the policy's values are limited to the amount of the assignor's indebtedness to the assignee. Consequently, if the policy proceeds become payable, the assignee is entitled to receive only the amount of the indebtedness; any remaining amount must be paid to the policy's beneficiary. Note also that the assignee can receive this amount only in a lump sum and cannot select a settlement option.

3. **The collateral assignee's rights to the policy values are temporary.** If the assignor repays the amount owed to the collateral assignee, the assignment terminates, and all of the policy's ownership rights revert to the policyowner. Once the loan is repaid, the policyowner usually secures from the assignee a release of the assignee's claim to the policy proceeds. The policyowner then forwards that release to the insurance company to notify the company that the assignment is no longer in effect.

| FIGURE 9.5 | Absolute Assignment Form |

---

## Absolute Assignment

Policy # _____    Life of _____

The undersigned hereby assigns and transfers without any exception, limitation, or reservation whatsoever to _____ [Name and address of each assignee] all (his, her, its, their) assignable benefits, interest, property, and rights in the policy described above.

The nature and effect of this assignment shall be as indicated in the following expressions of intent and purpose, namely

- This assignment is ☐ for a valuable consideration ☐ without a valuable consideration.

- If two or more assignees are named above, their interests under this assignment shall be as indicated in the line before which an "X" is inserted below.

  ☐ Joint owners with right of survivorship between them

  ☐ Common owners with no right of survivorship between them

  ☐ Life interest, use, and enjoyment in _____ [Name of life owner] with absolute control and power of disposition in such assignee during his or her lifetime; remainder interest in other assignee(s). If there are two or more assignees entitled to receive remainder interests, such interests shall be of the nature indicated in the line before which an "X" is inserted below:

  ☐ Joint owners with right of survivorship between them

  ☐ Common owners with no right of survivorship between them

- This assignment cancels and rescinds any reversionary provision in favor of the assignor or his estate, whether contained in the policy or in any writing or provision pertaining to the policy.

- This assignment does not affect or change the beneficiary designation or settlement presently contained in the policy assigned. Proceeds payable on death will be paid in accordance with such designation or settlement unless same be hereafter changed by the assignee(s), when the right to make such change exists under the policy.

---

**Source:** Adapted from Jane Lightcap Brown and Kristen L. Falk, *Insurance Administration*, 2nd ed. (Atlanta: LOMA, © 2002), 387. Used with permission; all rights reserved.

## Problems Resulting from Assignment

Some problems may arise when a policyowner assigns his life insurance policy. The most common problem occurs when the insurer is not notified in writing of an assignment. An insurance company pays the proceeds of a policy to the recipient who appears entitled to those proceeds according to the company's records. If the company has not been notified of an assignment, then it pays the proceeds to the person the policyowner named to receive those proceeds—the beneficiary of the life insurance policy or the payee of annuity benefits. The assignee might then attempt to collect the proceeds. If the insurer had not been notified of the assignment before it paid the proceeds to the beneficiary, then the insurer would be protected from also having to pay the proceeds to the assignee.

> **Example.** Isabel Mahoney collaterally assigned the insurance policy she owned on her life as security for a loan. When Isabel died, the insurance company had not been notified of the assignment, and, thus, it paid the policy proceeds to the named beneficiary. The assignee later claimed the policy proceeds.
>
> **Analysis.** Because the insurer was not notified of the assignment before it paid the policy death benefit, it has no liability to pay the proceeds again to the assignee.

## Transfer of Ownership by Endorsement

Many life insurance policies issued today specify a simple, direct method of transferring all the policy's ownership rights. Under this method, known as the *endorsement method*, policy ownership is completely transferred without requiring the policyowner to enter into a separate assignment agreement. The endorsement method is commonly used when a policy is given as a gift. For example, a parent may give a child ownership of a policy on the child's life when the child reaches age 21.

The right to change the policy's owner is generally spelled out in the policy. A typical change of ownership provision follows.

> **Change of ownership.** You can change the owner of this policy, from yourself to a new owner, in a notice you sign, which gives us the facts that we need. When this change takes effect, all rights of ownership in this policy will pass to the new owner.
>
> When we record a change of owner or successor owner, these changes will take effect as of the date you signed the notice, subject to any payment we made or action we took before recording these changes. We may require that these changes be endorsed in the policy. Changing the owner or naming a new successor owner cancels any prior choice of successor owner, but does not change the beneficiary.

According to this policy provision, to change the ownership of the policy, the policyowner must notify the insurer, in writing, of the change. When the insurance company makes note of the ownership change in its records, the change becomes effective as of the date the policyowner signed the written notification. For example, assume that on December 10, a policyowner signed and mailed to the insurer a written notice giving ownership of his life insurance policy to his daughter. The insurer received the written notice on December 14 and noted the change in its records on that day. As a result, the ownership change would be considered effective on December 10.

Note, however, that the change of ownership provision gives the insurer the right to require that the ownership change be endorsed in the policy. In such a case, the policyowner must send the policy to the insurance company, and the insurer will add to the policy an endorsement that states the name of the new owner. In some situations, the policy cannot be submitted to the company for the ownership change to be endorsed in the policy. For example, after an unfriendly divorce, a spouse who is the revocable beneficiary may have the policy and refuse to give it to the policyowner. In such situations, the general rule of law is that if the policyowner has taken all reasonable steps to submit the policy and if the insurance company has received written notice to change the ownership of the policy, then the requested change of ownership will be effective.

The transfer of ownership provision usually states that the insurance company is not responsible for any payments it made to the owner of record before it received written notice of an ownership change and recorded that change. This provision protects the insurance company from the new owner's contesting the insurer's actions if a loan were granted or benefit payments were made between the date the policyowner signed the notification and the date the insurance company recorded the change.

# Key Terms

class designation
primary beneficiary
contingent beneficiary
preference beneficiary clause
facility-of-payment clause
right of revocation
revocable beneficiary
irrevocable beneficiary
vested interest
community-property state
recording method
endorsement
endorsement method
premium payment mode
electronic funds transfer (EFT) method
payroll deduction method
dividend options
automatic dividend option
cash dividend option
premium reduction dividend option
accumulation at interest dividend option
paid-up additional insurance dividend option
additional term insurance dividend option
settlement options
settlement options provision
payee
contingent payee
interest option
fixed-period option
fixed-amount option
life income option
life annuity
straight life income option
life income with period certain option
refund life income option
joint and survivorship life income option
assignment
assignor
assignee
fraud
assignment provision
absolute assignment
collateral assignment

# Paying Life Insurance Policy Proceeds

## objectives

*After reading this chapter, you should be able to*

- Identify the steps that claim examiners follow to evaluate life insurance claims

- Recognize the general rule stated in a simultaneous death act and explain how that rule is affected if a policy contains a survivorship clause

- Describe the purpose of the legal remedy of interpleader

- Calculate the proceeds payable under a given life insurance policy following the death of the insured

- Describe why an insurer may deny a death claim when the insured person has disappeared

- Recognize how laws in various jurisdictions define a *wrongful killing* that disqualifies the beneficiary of a life insurance policy from receiving the policy proceeds

To effectively manage the payment of claims, insurance companies establish standard procedures that their employees follow when processing life insurance claims. These standard procedures are designed to strike a balance between the beneficiary's right to prompt settlement of his claim and the insurance company's need to evaluate each claim's validity. Not only does the beneficiary have the right to expect prompt settlement, but the laws of many countries require the prompt settlement of claims. On the other hand, the payment of fraudulent or mistaken claims can result in significant losses to insurance companies and increases in insurance costs. Insurers have a responsibility to their owners and policyowners to take reasonable steps to avoid paying invalid claims. The insurance company also must be certain that it pays policy proceeds to the proper beneficiary, or the insurer could be faced with a valid second claim to those proceeds.

In this chapter, we describe the procedures that insurers typically follow to process routine life insurance policy claims. We also describe some special claim situations insurers sometimes face in determining who is entitled to receive life insurance policy proceeds.

## Processing Life Insurance Claims

The claim examination process begins when a claimant to life insurance policy proceeds notifies the insurance company that the insured has died. Typically, the person who claims life insurance policy proceeds following the insured's death is the policy's primary beneficiary. When an insurer is notified of an insured's death, the insurer typically provides the claimant with a claim form on which the claimant provides the information the insurer needs to begin processing the claim. (See Figure 10.1, which shows a sample claim form.)

In addition to completing the claim form, the claimant must furnish the insurer with proof of his claim. In other words, the claimant must provide the insurer with proof that the person insured by the policy has died. The documents that life insurers accept as proof of a loss vary somewhat from country to country. In the United States, most insurers require claimants to submit an official death certificate as proof that the insured has died. A death certificate is a legal document signed by a government official who has the authority to issue death certificates. Some insurers will accept an *Attending Physician's Statement* (*APS*), which is a document reporting the care given by a physician who has treated a person. Insurers in other jurisdictions may require claimants to submit more extensive information, or they may accept other forms of documentation as proof of a claim. For example, most insurance companies in Canada

| FIGURE 10.1 | Sample Claim Form |

## ABC Life Insurance Company
### 100 Ordinary Avenue, New York, N.Y. 00000

**Please see proof of death requirements on reverse side before completing this form.**

Policies under which claim is made by the undersigned:

| Numbers | Numbers | Numbers |
|---|---|---|
| _____ | _____ | _____ |
| _____ | _____ | _____ |
| _____ | _____ | _____ |

1.  a.  Deceased's name in full _____
    b.  Residence _____
    c.  Occupation _____

2.  Date of birth _____     Place of birth _____

3.  a.  Date of death _____     Place of death _____
    b.  Cause of death _____
    c.  Duration of illness _____

4.  Names and addresses of Attending Physicians

    Name                                      Address

    _____          _____
    _____          _____

5.  a.  What is your relationship to the deceased? _____
    b.  Do you claim this insurance as beneficiary? _____
    c.  If you are not the beneficiary, in what capacity are you making this claim? _____

NOTE: If you are a beneficiary designated to receive policy proceeds in a single sum and wish to have information regarding any optional methods of settlement which may be available to you, please consult your ABC agent or the Office through which you are submitting this statement.

Claimant's
Signature _____          Age _____

Address _____
                    (Street)

_____
                    (City)

Date _____          _____
                    (State)

accept an official death certificate, an Attending Physician's Statement, a coroner's certificate of death, or a hospital's certificate of death as proof of an insured's death.

When an insurer receives a claim form and proof of loss documentation, the insurer begins to evaluate the claim. The insurance company employee who is responsible for carrying out the claim examination process generally is known as a ***claim examiner***, *claim approver*, *claim analyst*, or *claim specialist*. In processing and paying a claim, the claim examiner (1) determines the status of the policy, (2) verifies the identity of the insured, (3) verifies that the loss insured against has occurred, (4) verifies that the loss is covered by the policy, (5) determines who is entitled to receive the policy proceeds, and (6) calculates the amount of the benefit that is payable. We describe each of these steps in the claim examination process.

## Determine the Status of the Policy

Before paying a claim, the claim examiner must ensure that the policy was in force when the insured died. Thus, the claim examiner must verify that the policy had not lapsed for nonpayment of premium before the insured's death. In addition, the claim examiner must ensure that the policy did not terminate for any other reason before the insured's death. For example, a term life insurance policy may have reached the end of its term and expired. If, for any reason, coverage was not in force when the insured died, then the insurer is not liable to pay the policy proceeds.

## Verify the Identity of the Insured

The claim examiner compares the insured's identification in the claim form and in the proof of loss document with the identifying information contained in the insurer's policy records to confirm that the person who died was the person insured by the policy. This step protects the insurance company against fraudulent and mistaken claims.

A claim is considered to be a ***fraudulent claim*** when the claimant intentionally attempts to collect policy proceeds by providing false information to the insurer. For example, if the person insured by a policy is still living and the beneficiary submits a false death certificate to collect the policy proceeds, the beneficiary is committing fraud. Laws in many countries prohibit the filing of a fraudulent claim and impose both criminal and civil penalties on anyone who files such a claim. Insight 10.1 describes some of the differences between criminal laws and civil laws.

A claim is considered to be a ***mistaken claim*** when a claimant makes an honest mistake in presenting a claim to the insurer. The beneficiary might, for example, mistakenly believe that the policy insured the deceased person

**FAST FACT**

During 2003, U.S. life insurers paid $51 billion to beneficiaries following the deaths of insureds. Of that total, $32 billion was paid under individual life insurance policies.

**Source:** ACLI, Life *Insurers Fact Book: 2004* (Washington, D.C.: American Council of Life Insurers, 2004), 62.

**INSIGHT 10.1**    Criminal Laws and Civil Laws

Laws in most countries can be categorized as either criminal laws or civil laws. *Criminal laws* are laws that define certain acts as crimes and provide a specific punishment for each crime. When a person is charged with a crime, the government is the party that prosecutes its case in a court proceeding against the individual. An individual who is convicted of a crime may be subject to a variety of penalties that range from the imposition of fines to imprisonment.

*Civil laws* are laws that are concerned with private—that is, nongovernmental—rights and remedies. For example, a dispute between an insurer and a claimant to insurance policy proceeds is a civil dispute. Although most civil disputes are settled by the parties involved, some disputes cannot be resolved by the parties. Governments typically establish a system for resolving such disputes within their jurisdictions. In the United States, the parties generally turn to the courts for a resolution.

A person's actions may violate both criminal and civil laws. For example, assume that Harold Green violated a traffic law and, thus, caused an automobile accident in which several people were injured. Mr. Green's violation of the law may lead to both a criminal proceeding and a civil proceeding against Mr. Green. In the criminal proceeding, the government would prosecute Mr. Green for violating the traffic laws. Although a criminal proceeding might result in Mr. Green's being punished by the government by imprisonment or the imposition of fines, it would not provide remedies for the individuals Mr. Green injured. A civil proceeding would provide a forum for the injured victims to seek relief from Mr. Green for the injuries they suffered as a result of Mr. Green's actions. The most typical remedy available to the injured party in a civil action is *damages*, which consists of monetary compensation that is recovered by the injured party from the party whose wrongful conduct caused the injured party's loss or injury.

---

when it actually insured someone else. The long-term nature of a life insurance policy sometimes accounts for a misidentification of the insured. A policy may have been issued decades before the claim was submitted. The applicant, the insurance producer, and others involved in issuing the policy might have died, moved away, or otherwise become unavailable. The policy may have been issued before the beneficiary was born, and policyowners often change a beneficiary designation while a policy is in force. As a result, the beneficiary, who may be unfamiliar with the policy's terms, could mistakenly submit a claim.

The claim examiner also must compare the insured's sex and date of birth as shown on the insurer's policy records to the sex and date of birth or age at death as stated on the death certificate and the claim form. If the information provided contains any discrepancies, then the claim examiner may ask the claimant to provide additional documents. For example, the claimant might be required to provide the insurer with the insured's birth certificate as proof of age. If the insured's age or sex were misstated in the insurer's records, the examiner must account for that discrepancy when she calculates the amount of the death benefit that is payable.

## Verify That a Loss Occurred

The claim examiner must examine the proof of loss document provided by the claimant to verify that the insured has died. In most cases, the death certificate or other proof of loss document submitted by the claimant provides all of the information the claim examiner needs to verify the loss. Later in the chapter, we describe situations in which the claimant is unable to provide proof of loss because the insured has disappeared.

## Verify That the Loss Is Covered

The claim examiner must review the terms of the insurance policy to determine whether the insured's death is a covered loss and whether the policy contains any exclusions that might affect her decision about paying the claim. As we have noted, life insurance policies often contain provisions that limit the insurer's liability if the insured dies as a result of specified causes. The most common of these exclusions is the suicide exclusion provision. If the cause of the insured's death is excluded from coverage, then the insurer is not liable to pay the policy death benefit. Policies that contain such an exclusion typically provide that if the insured dies as a result of the excluded cause, then the insurer's liability is limited to returning the premiums paid for the policy. Some policies limit the insurer's liability to the amount of the policy's cash surrender value.

> **Example.** Shondra Gillespie was insured by a life insurance policy that contained a two-year suicide exclusion period and that provided an accidental death benefit. Shondra died as the result of a fall from a fourth-floor window several months after the policy was issued.
>
> **Analysis.** The claim examiner must determine why Shondra fell. If the fall was the result of an accident, then the insurer is liable to pay both the basic death benefit and the accidental death benefit. If Shondra committed suicide, however, then the insurer's liability is limited to the amount of premiums paid for the policy because Shondra died as a result of suicide during the policy's suicide exclusion period.

## Identify the Proper Payee

After the claim examiner has determined that the claim is valid, she must identify the person who is entitled to receive the policy proceeds. Notice that the sample claim form shown in Figure 10.1 contains several questions that request information about the claimant. Although the claimant typically is the beneficiary of the policy, the claimant might claim the policy proceeds as the assignee of a collateral assignment or as the personal representative of the insured's estate.

In any case, the claim examiner reviews the company's policy records to determine who is entitled to the policy proceeds. If a collateral assignment was in effect when the insured died, then the assignee is entitled to all or a portion of the policy proceeds. If no assignment was in effect and the primary beneficiary survived the insured, then proceeds are payable to the primary beneficiary. (See Figure 10.2 for an illustration of how the claim examiner determines who is entitled to policy proceeds.) If the primary beneficiary predeceased the insured, then proceeds are payable to the contingent beneficiary. If no named beneficiary survives the insured, then proceeds typically are payable to the policyowner; if the policyowner was also the person insured by the policy, then proceeds are payable to the policyowner-insured's estate.

In the vast majority of claims, the claim examiner is able to determine quickly who is entitled to policy proceeds. Sometimes, however, the claim examiner must investigate the claim further to determine the proper recipient of policy proceeds. We describe three such situations that require further investigation by the claim examiner: common disasters, short-term survivorship, and conflicting claimants.

## Common Disasters

Sometimes, the insured and the beneficiary die in the same accident, but no proof is available to show that one person survived the other. This situation is referred to as a *common disaster* because the accident or disaster was *common* to more than one person. The claim examiner must investigate because the beneficiary is entitled to the policy proceeds only if she survived the insured. If the beneficiary survived the insured but died before the insurer pays the policy proceeds, then those proceeds are generally payable to the beneficiary's estate, unless the policy provides otherwise.

If no proof exists as to whether the insured died before the beneficiary died, how can the claim examiner determine who should receive the policy proceeds? Many jurisdictions have enacted a **simultaneous death act** that governs how insurance companies are to evaluate common disaster situations. A typical simultaneous death act states the following general rule:

> If the insured and the beneficiary die at the same time or under circumstances that make it impossible to determine which of them died first, the insured is deemed to have survived the beneficiary, and policy proceeds are payable as if the insured outlived the beneficiary, unless the policy provides otherwise.

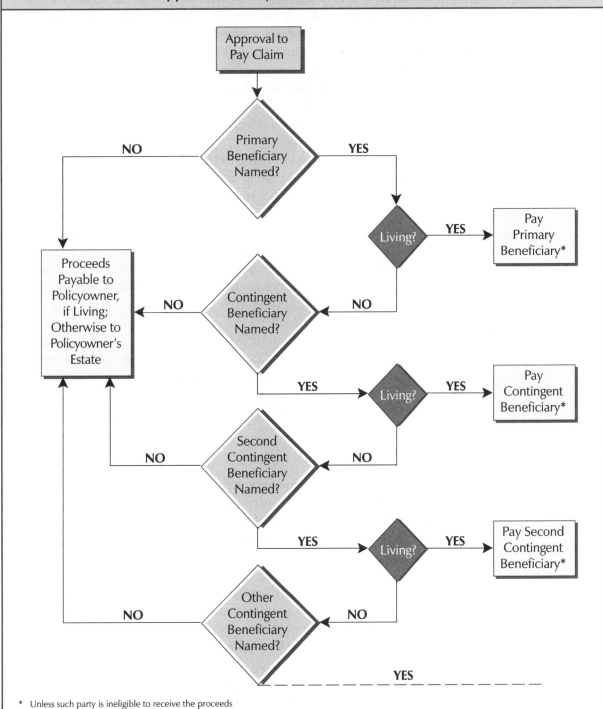

FIGURE 10.2 | Primary Steps in Determining the Correct Beneficiary of Life Insurance Policy Proceeds After the Claim Has Been Approved for Payment

* Unless such party is ineligible to receive the proceeds

Let's look at an example to illustrate how this general rule of law affects the payment of life insurance policy proceeds.

**Example.** Duffy Drago and his wife, Ally, died in an airplane crash, and the evidence did not show which of them died first. Duffy was insured under a policy that he owned; Ally was the primary beneficiary and Duffy's mother was the contingent beneficiary. Ally was insured under a policy that she owned; Duffy was the primary beneficiary, and Ally's father was the contingent beneficiary. Although Ally's father survived her, Duffy's mother died several years before the crash.

**Analysis.** Because no evidence exists as to the order in which Duffy and Ally died, we must apply the general rule stated in the simultaneous death act to each policy.

- **Duffy's policy.** The insured, Duffy, is deemed to have survived the primary beneficiary, Ally. Thus, the policy proceeds are payable to the contingent beneficiary, if she survived the insured. Because Duffy's mother predeceased him, the policy proceeds are payable to Duffy's estate.

- **Ally's policy.** The insured, Ally, is deemed to have survived the primary beneficiary, Duffy. Thus, the policy proceeds are payable to the contingent beneficiary, if he survived the insured. Because Ally's father survived her, the policy proceeds are payable to him.

## Short-Term Survivorship

A simultaneous death act does not affect how policy proceeds are paid in cases in which the beneficiary survives the insured. If the beneficiary survives the insured by any length of time—even if only for a few minutes—the right to receive the policy proceeds generally vests in the beneficiary when the insured dies. That means that if the beneficiary survives the insured but dies before receiving the policy proceeds, then the proceeds are payable to the beneficiary's estate. The policyowner, however, may prefer that the proceeds be paid to someone other than the beneficiary's heirs if the beneficiary survives the insured by only a short time.

Some life insurance policies include a survivorship clause that deals with this potential problem. A *survivorship clause* states that the beneficiary must survive the insured by a specified period, usually 30 or 60 days, to be entitled to receive the policy proceeds. If the beneficiary survives the insured by the stated time, then the beneficiary's right to the policy proceeds vests. If the beneficiary does not survive the stated time, then the policy proceeds are paid as if the beneficiary predeceased the insured. As a result of the survivorship clause, the policy proceeds are more likely to be distributed as the policyowner had intended.

> **Example.** When she died, Maddie Brady was insured under a policy that included a survivorship clause requiring the beneficiary to survive the insured by 30 days. Her husband, Patrick, was the policy's primary beneficiary, and her mother was the contingent beneficiary. Maddie and Patrick died as the result of an automobile accident. Maddie died within a few minutes of the accident, and Patrick died two hours later.
>
> **Analysis.** Because the beneficiary survived the insured, the simultaneous death act does not govern this situation. Therefore, we must look at the terms of the policy, which includes a survivorship clause. Because Patrick died only two hours after Maddie died, he did not survive her by the required 30 days and the proceeds are payable as if he died before Maddie. Thus, the proceeds are payable to the contingent beneficiary, Maddie's mother.

## Conflicting Claimants

In most cases, policy proceeds are payable to the primary beneficiary, who is the only person who claims those proceeds. Even if several people claim the proceeds of a policy, the insurance company and the various claimants usually are able to agree on how the proceeds should be paid. But what does the insurer do if it receives several claims and cannot determine from its policy records who is entitled to the proceeds? If the insurer pays the proceeds to one claimant, it could later be required to pay the proceeds a second time if the other claimant in fact had a better claim to the proceeds.

> **Example.** Both Sylvia Smith and Jack Jones submitted a claim for the proceeds of an insurance policy on the life of Bobby Smith. The insurance company decided that Sylvia was the proper beneficiary and paid the proceeds to her. Jack filed a lawsuit against the insurance company seeking to recover the policy proceeds. The court found that Jack was entitled to the policy proceeds.
>
> **Analysis.** The court verdict in favor of Jack means that the insurance company must pay the policy proceeds to him. Because Sylvia probably will not agree to refund the policy proceeds to the insurer, the insurer will have paid the proceeds twice.

Laws in many countries provide a remedy to insurance companies that are faced with conflicting claims to policy proceeds. In the United States, when an insurance company cannot determine the correct beneficiary for the policy proceeds, or fears that a court might disagree with its opinion as to the correct beneficiary, the company may use the remedy of interpleader. *Interpleader* is a procedure under which an insurance company that cannot determine which claimant is entitled to receive policy proceeds may pay such proceeds to a court and ask the court to decide the proper recipient. If the case involves conflicting claimants, the court will hold the policy proceeds and release the insurance company from the court proceedings, thus releasing the insurer from any further liability. The court then examines the evidence, determines who is entitled to the proceeds, and pays those proceeds to that claimant. Insight 10.2 describes similar procedures that are available to insurers in Canada.

## Calculate the Amount of the Benefit Payable

Before paying a claim, the claim examiner must calculate the amount of policy proceeds payable. For most individual life insurance policies, the claim examiner calculates the amount of proceeds payable following the insured's death by adding together a number of items and deducting certain other items. The claim examiner first adds together the following items:

- The amount of the **basic death benefit payable.** In most cases, the basic death benefit is the policy's face amount. If the policy was in

**INSIGHT 10.2** — Canadian Procedures that Protect Insurers When Conflicting Claims Are Made

When paying a life insurance policy claim, the insurer wants to be sure that its liability for the claim is legally discharged and that it will not be liable to pay the claim again. In some cases, an insurer knows that it is liable to pay a claim but cannot obtain a valid discharge of its liability. Examples include situations in which the insurer has received two or more competing claims to the policy proceeds or the insurer is unable to locate the person who is entitled to payment. The insurance laws in Canada provide procedures whereby an insurer in such a case can obtain a valid discharge.

In most Canadian provinces, the insurance company's remedy in such a case is to pay the policy proceeds into court. The court then discharges the insurer from further liability for the claim, examines the evidence, decides who is the proper recipient, and pays the proceeds to that claimant. Notice that this procedure, referred to as *payment into court*, is very similar to the U.S. remedy of interpleader.

In the province of Quebec, when several people claim insurance proceeds, the insurer can be discharged from further liability by paying the policy proceeds to the provincial Minister of Finance. The Minister holds the proceeds until a court decides which claimant is entitled to them or until the interested parties agree among themselves who is to receive them.

force under the reduced paid-up insurance nonforfeiture option when the insured died, then the amount of the basic death benefit payable is less than the face amount. In addition, the policy's face amount must be adjusted up or down if the insured's age or sex was misstated.

- The amount of any **accidental death benefits payable**.

- The amount of any **declared but unpaid policy dividends**.

- The amount of any **accumulated policy dividends**, including interest, left on deposit with the insurer.

- The face amount of any **paid-up additions**.

- The amount of any **unearned premiums paid in advance**. Policyowners sometimes pay premiums before those premiums are due. A policyowner, for example, might pay two annual premiums when he purchases a policy. If the insured dies shortly before the second annual premium is payable, the insurer usually would refund the amount of the second year's premium because the insurer had not earned that premium.

After totaling the amount of the foregoing items, the claim examiner must subtract the following items from that total:

- The amount of any **outstanding policy loans.**

- The amount of any **premium due and unpaid** at the time of the insured's death. This item appears when the insured dies during the policy's grace period before the premium due has been paid.

The result of this calculation is the total benefit amount payable. The insurer pays this total amount in a lump sum or according to the terms of a settlement option selected by the policyowner or beneficiary.

**Example.** When Jeff Nguyen died, he was insured under a $100,000 life insurance policy. At that time, $420 in accumulated policy dividends were on deposit with the insurer, and Jeff had an outstanding policy loan of $1,635.

**Analysis.** The total policy benefit that the insurer was liable to pay the policy beneficiary was $98,785. That amount was calculated as follows.

| | |
|---|---|
| $100,000 | Face amount of policy |
| + 420 | Accumulated policy dividends |
| − 1,635 | Outstanding policy loan |
| **$98,785** | **Total policy benefit payable** |

# Special Claim Situations

By following its routine claim examination procedures, an insurance company can establish the validity of most claims and ensure that it pays the proper amount to the correct party. Sometimes, however, the claim examiner must investigate a claim further. We already have described some special claim situations that arise if the policy contains an exclusion, such as a suicide exclusion provision. Claim examiners also pay special attention to death claims that occur during a policy's contestable period and claims that involve an accidental death benefit or the insured's disappearance. Claims in which the beneficiary was responsible in some way for the insured's death also require special consideration.

## Policy Contests

As described in Chapter 8, if the application for a life insurance policy contains a material misrepresentation, then the insurer has the right to avoid the insurance contract during its contestable period. If the policy's contestable period has not yet expired when the insurer receives a death claim, the claim examiner considers whether there is any reason to suspect that the application for the policy contains a material misrepresentation.

> **Example.** Cherie Tanner's application for life insurance indicated that she was in good health. Six months after the policy was issued, Cherie died as the result of cancer.
>
> **Analysis.** The policy's contestable period has not ended. Thus, the claim examiner will investigate further to determine whether Cherie had been treated for cancer before the policy was issued and failed to disclose that fact.

If the claim examiner can gather enough evidence to prove the charge of material misrepresentation in the application for insurance, the insurer usually denies liability to pay the policy proceeds and refunds the premiums paid for the policy. Typically, the claim department consults with the company's legal representatives before contesting a policy on the ground of material misrepresentation.

## Accidental Death Benefit Claims

When an insurer receives a claim for a policy's basic death benefit and an accidental death benefit, the claim examiner evaluates the claim to determine whether the cause of the insured's death meets the policy's definition of "accidental." To determine the cause of an insured's death, the claim examiner may ask the claimant to provide additional proof of loss documents. Insurers sometimes request an Attending Physician's Statement from the physician who treated the insured prior to his death. Insurers also sometimes ask the claimant to provide an autopsy report. Insurers typically request these additional proof of loss documents only in cases in which (1) unusual circumstances surround the insured's death so that the claim examiner has reason to doubt the stated cause of death, (2) the policy provides additional benefits such as an accidental death benefit, or (3) the insured dies during the policy's contestable period.

If an insurer determines that the insured's death was not accidental as defined in the policy, then it pays the policy's basic death benefit but denies the claim for accidental death benefits.

> **Example.** Hilda Fallon was insured under a $100,000 life insurance policy that contained a typical accidental death benefit rider. Hilda died as a result of suicide five years after the policy was issued.
>
> **Analysis.** When Hilda died, the policy's suicide exclusion period had expired. Thus, the insurer was liable to pay the policy's $100,000 death benefit to the named beneficiary. However, Hilda's death from suicide was not accidental, and, thus, the insurer was not liable to pay the policy's accidental death benefit.

## Disappearance of the Insured

Sometimes a beneficiary files a claim for life insurance policy proceeds following the disappearance of the insured. In such situations, the claimant cannot provide the insurer with a death certificate or other document that proves the insured is dead. Without sufficient proof of an insured's death, the insurer cannot pay the policy proceeds. The claimant in such a case has the right to ask a court to declare the insured dead. If the insured disappeared under circumstances that make it likely he is dead, a court may be willing to find that the insured is dead. If, however, the insured disappeared without explanation, courts typically find that the insured is dead or presumed dead only if the following conditions are met:

- The insured must have been missing for a specified time—seven years in most jurisdictions.

- The insured's absence is unexplained.

- A reasonable search for the insured has taken place.

- No one has had communication with the insured since his disappearance.

Upon receiving a court order stating that the insured is dead or presumed dead, the insurer can pay the policy proceeds to the proper beneficiary if the policy was in force on the date of the insured's presumed death. As a result, when an insured disappears, the policyowner, beneficiary, or other interested party must continue to pay the policy's renewal premiums as they come due until the court issues an order that the insured is dead or presumed dead. The court sometimes states in its order the date on which the insured is deemed to have died. If the court establishes such a date, then the insurer refunds all premiums paid after that date. Often, however, the court order does not state the date of the insured's death; in those cases, the insured is deemed to have died on the date of the court order. If the policy lapsed for nonpayment of premium before the court order, the insurer has no liability to pay the policy proceeds.

## Beneficiary Wrongfully Kills the Insured

Another special situation that the claim examiner occasionally faces occurs when the person who claims the proceeds of a life insurance policy is responsible for the death of the insured. Permitting someone to profit from wrongful acts is not in the public interest. As a result, laws in many countries disqualify the beneficiary from receiving the policy proceeds if the beneficiary wrongfully killed the insured.

Laws vary somewhat from jurisdiction to jurisdiction as to what constitutes a wrongful killing that would disqualify a beneficiary. As a general rule, a beneficiary who is convicted in a criminal court proceeding of intentionally killing the insured is disqualified from receiving life insurance policy proceeds. In many jurisdictions, a beneficiary who is convicted of a lesser criminal offense—such as manslaughter—also is disqualified from receiving policy proceeds. As described in Insight 10.3, a beneficiary's attempt to kill an insured affects the beneficiary's rights to policy proceeds in some jurisdictions.

The fact that a beneficiary is not charged with a crime or is not convicted in a criminal proceeding of wrongfully killing the insured does not mean that the beneficiary is automatically entitled to receive the policy proceeds. Without regard to the outcome of a criminal court proceeding, a civil court can determine that the beneficiary wrongfully killed the insured and is disqualified from receiving the policy proceeds. Typically, a civil court proceeding in this type of case is begun by the beneficiary following the insurance company's determination that the beneficiary is disqualified because she wrongfully killed the insured. Remember that an insurer has a fiduciary obligation to pay only valid claims. If the insurer determines that a beneficiary wrongfully killed the insured, it has a duty to all of its policyowners and beneficiaries to deny the claim.

**INSIGHT 10.3** | **Quebec's Laws Governing a Beneficiary's or Policyowner's Attempt to Kill the Insured**

 Laws in the Canadian province of Quebec impose relatively severe penalties when a life insurance policy beneficiary or policyowner attempts to kill the insured—even if that attempt is unsuccessful. When a beneficiary attempts to kill the insured, the beneficiary designation is revoked, and the beneficiary is prohibited from ever collecting the policy proceeds. If the owner of a life insurance policy attempts—even if unsuccessfully—to kill the insured, then the life insurance contract is void.

In most cases in which a beneficiary is disqualified from receiving policy proceeds, the life insurance contract is valid and the insurer is liable to pay the policy proceeds to someone, such as the contingent beneficiary. If, however, it is proven that the policy was purchased with the intention to profit from the insured's death, then the life insurance contract is void because the lawful purpose requirement was not met when the contract was created.

# Key Terms

Attending Physician's Statement (APS)
claim examiner
fraudulent claim
criminal laws
civil laws
damages
mistaken claim
simultaneous death act
survivorship clause
interpleader
payment into court

# Annuities and Individual Retirement Arrangements

**objectives**

*After reading this chapter, you should be able to*

- Define the term *annuity contract*

- Distinguish between immediate and deferred annuity contracts, single-premium and flexible-premium annuity contracts, and fixed and variable annuity contracts

- Explain important contractual provisions of an individual annuity

- Identify and distinguish among the types of payout options available under annuity contracts

- List the factors that affect the value of an annuity's periodic income payments and describe the effect of each factor

- List and explain the fees and charges typically paid by annuity contract owners

- Distinguish between a traditional IRA and a Roth IRA

In this chapter, our focus shifts from life insurance policies to annuities and individual retirement arrangements marketed by insurance companies. Annuities often are described as the flip side of life insurance because certain annuities can protect against the financial risk of outliving one's financial resources, whereas life insurance protects against the financial risk of premature death.

In the most general terms, an **annuity** is a series of periodic payments. Most of us make and receive such periodic payments. For example, your monthly rent or mortgage payments constitute an annuity, and salaries paid on a regular, periodic basis are annuities. As noted in Chapter 1, an *annuity contract* is a legally enforceable agreement under which an insurer gives a named person the right to receive a series of periodic income payments in exchange for a premium or a series of premiums. In this text, we use the terms *annuity* and *annuity contract* interchangeably to refer to annuity contracts.

In some countries, such as Argentina, companies that issue life insurance policies and annuity contracts must be different legal entities. In the United States, annuities are considered to be life insurance products, and only life insurance companies are permitted to issue annuities. Thus, annuities must comply with state insurance laws and regulations. Although only insurers may issue annuities, many types of financial institutions, including depository institutions and broker-dealers, may market and distribute annuities.

We begin this chapter by describing some general features of annuities. Then we describe various individual annuity products that insurance companies have designed to help individuals accumulate and/or distribute funds, typical annuity contract provisions, and the financial design of annuity contracts. We also describe the taxation of qualified and nonqualified annuity contracts. We conclude the chapter with a discussion of individual retirement arrangements.

## Introduction to Annuities

As we described in Chapter 3, a contract is a legally enforceable agreement that consists of a promise or set of promises. The terms of an annuity contract govern the rights and duties of the contracting parties. The parties to an annuity contract are (1) the insurer that issued the contract and (2) the person or business, known as the **contract owner**, that owns and exercises all rights and privileges of the annuity contract. As with a life insurance policy, the insurer issues a written agreement to the contract owner; the written agreement contains all of the terms of the contract entered into by the parties.

**FAST FACT**

During 2003, life insurance companies in the United States received $289 billion in annuity premiums.

**Source:** ACLI, *Life Insurers Fact Book: 2004* (Washington, D.C.: American Council of Life Insurers, 2004), 93.

Insurers sell annuities on both an individual and a group basis. Thus, the contract owner can be either an individual or an organization that purchases the annuity on behalf of a group of individuals. For now, we describe only individual annuities; we discuss group annuities in Chapter 14 when we describe group retirement plans.

As part of the contractual agreement between the parties to an annuity, the contract owner pays a single premium or a series of premiums to the insurer. Premiums that insurers receive for annuities generally are referred to as *annuity considerations*. The insurer pools the money it has received from a large group of contract owners, and it invests those pooled funds. The insurer uses the pooled funds and investment earnings on those funds to make periodic income payments as they come due.

The annuity contract specifies the **annuitant**, the person whose lifetime is used to determine the amount of benefits payable under the contract. The **payee** is the person or entity named to receive the periodic income payments under an annuity contract. In most cases, the contract owner, the annuitant, and the payee are the same person.

The date on which the insurer begins to make the periodic income payments is known as the **annuity date** or the *income date*. The period during which the insurer makes periodic income payments is known as the **payout period** or *liquidation period*. An **annuity period** is the time span between each of the payments in the series of periodic income payments. The annuity period is typically either one month or one year; other options, such as quarterly or semiannual payments, are also available. For example, an annuity contract that provides for a series of annual income payments has an annuity period of one year and is referred to as an *annual annuity*. An annuity contract that provides for a series of monthly income payments has an annuity period of one month and is referred to as a *monthly annuity*.

Every annuity contract includes a **payout options provision** that lists and describes each of the payout options from which the contract owner may select. **Payout options**, also known as *settlement options*, are the choices a contract owner has as to how the insurer will distribute annuity benefits during the payout period. Later in the chapter, we describe some of the payout options typically available under an annuity contract.

## Types of Annuity Contracts

As noted earlier, annuity contracts may be issued either as individual or group contracts. Annuity contracts can be categorized in a number of other ways, including according to

- When periodic income payments begin

- How often premiums are paid

- How annuity premiums are invested

As we explain in this chapter, all of the categories overlap one another. Figure 11.1 illustrates major classifications of annuities.

## Immediate and Deferred Annuities

An annuity can be classified as either an immediate annuity or a deferred annuity, depending on when the insurer is to begin making periodic income payments. An *immediate annuity* provides periodic income payments that generally are scheduled to begin one annuity period after the date the contract is issued. Thus, an immediate annuity is used to distribute funds as a periodic income over a specified period of time. The owner of an immediate annuity selects the date on which periodic income payments are to begin and selects a payout option.

A *deferred annuity* is an annuity under which periodic income payments are scheduled to begin more than one annuity period after the date on which the annuity was purchased. The period between the contract owner's purchase of a deferred annuity and the beginning of the payout period is known as the *accumulation period*. During a deferred annuity's accumulation period, the insurer invests the premiums paid by the contract owner and the annuity builds an accumulation value. A deferred annuity's *accumulation value* is equal to the amount paid for the annuity, *plus* interest earned, *less* the amount of any withdrawals and fees. The manner in which the policy provides for investment earnings on the

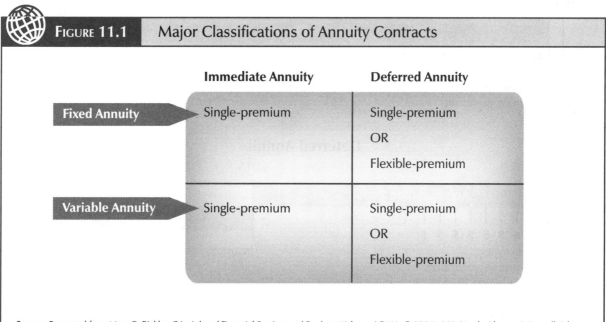

**FIGURE 11.1** | Major Classifications of Annuity Contracts

|  | Immediate Annuity | Deferred Annuity |
|---|---|---|
| **Fixed Annuity** | Single-premium | Single-premium OR Flexible-premium |
| **Variable Annuity** | Single-premium | Single-premium OR Flexible-premium |

accumulation value depends on whether the deferred annuity is a fixed annuity or a variable annuity. We describe these distinctions later in the chapter.

$$\begin{pmatrix} \text{Accumulation} \\ \text{value of a deferred} \\ \text{annuity} \end{pmatrix} = \begin{pmatrix} \text{Net amount} \\ \text{paid for} \\ \text{annuity} \end{pmatrix} + \begin{pmatrix} \text{Interest} \end{pmatrix} - \begin{pmatrix} \text{Withdrawals} \end{pmatrix}$$

People often purchase deferred annuities during their working years in anticipation of the need for retirement income later in their lives. In addition to being a vehicle for accumulating savings, a deferred annuity gives the contract owner the right to receive periodic income payments at some time in the future. Exercising the right to receive periodic income payments from a deferred annuity is known as ***annuitization***. Figure 11.2 illustrates the difference between an immediate annuity and a deferred annuity.

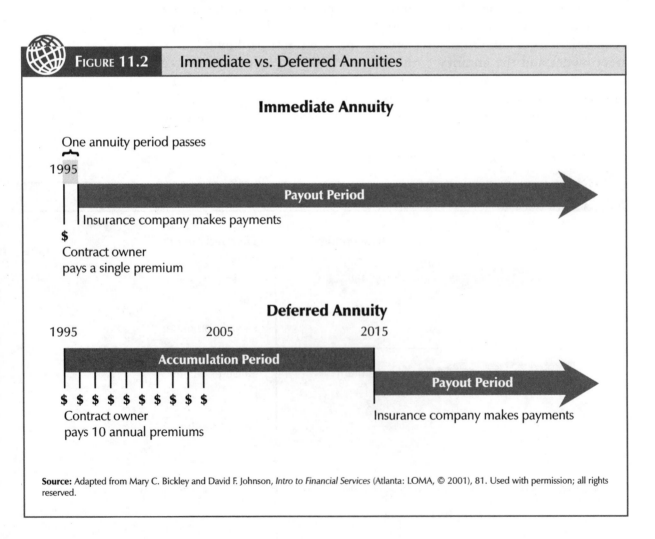

**FIGURE 11.2** | Immediate vs. Deferred Annuities

**Immediate Annuity**

One annuity period passes

1995

Payout Period

Insurance company makes payments

$
Contract owner
pays a single premium

**Deferred Annuity**

1995            2005            2015

Accumulation Period

Payout Period

$ $ $ $ $ $ $ $ $
Contract owner
pays 10 annual premiums

Insurance company makes payments

# Single-Premium and Flexible-Premium Annuities

Annuity contracts can be categorized as either a single-premium annuity or a flexible-premium annuity according to how often premiums are paid. A *single-premium annuity* is an annuity that is purchased by the payment of a single, lump-sum amount. Periodic income payments under a single-premium annuity may begin shortly after the premium is paid or may begin many years after the premium is paid. All immediate annuities are single-premium annuities.

Under a *flexible-premium annuity*, the contract owner pays premiums on a periodic basis over a stated period of time; the amount of each premium payment, however, can vary between a set minimum amount and a set maximum amount. For example, the policy might allow the contract owner to pay any premium amount between $250 and $10,000 each year. The contract owner also can choose not to pay any premium in a given year; the only requirement is that any premium amount paid each year must fall within the stated minimum and maximum.

Despite the many potential varieties of annuities, three configurations of annuity features are particularly common: the single-premium immediate annuity, the single-premium deferred annuity, and the flexible-premium deferred annuity. These types of annuities are described in Figure 11.3.

# Fixed and Variable Annuities

People who purchase annuities have different purposes in mind for the funds they place in an annuity. Annuity contract owners also have different capacities for assuming a financial risk when they place money in their annuities. Thus, many insurers offer two general options to annuity purchasers: (1) the insurer will guarantee to pay at least a stated interest rate on the annuity funds it holds or (2) the insurer will pay interest at a rate that is not guaranteed; instead, the interest rate will vary according to the earnings of certain investments held by the insurer.

### Fixed Annuities

A *fixed annuity* is an annuity contract under which the insurer guarantees that (1) the contract's accumulation value will experience no loss of principal and will earn at least a minimum guaranteed interest rate and (2) the periodic income payments will not fall below a stated minimum amount. Most fixed annuities specify that once the insurer begins making periodic income payments, the amount of each payment will not change. A few fixed annuities, however, specify that periodic income payments may increase if the insurer's investment earnings exceed those the insurer expected when it calculated the benefit amount.

| FIGURE 11.3 | Popular Types of Annuities |

A *single-premium immediate annuity (SPIA) contract* is an immediate annuity that is purchased with a lump-sum premium payment on the date the contract is issued.

> **Example:** Roger Draper, age 65, is using his retirement savings of $75,000 to purchase an immediate annuity that will provide monthly income payments beginning one month after he purchases the contract.

A *single-premium deferred annuity (SPDA) contract* is a deferred annuity that is purchased with a lump-sum premium payment on the date the contract is issued. Under an SPDA, the insurer holds the single-premium payment at interest until a date specified by the contract owner as the date on which periodic income payments are to begin. During the first contract year of an SPDA, most insurers will accept additional premiums, known as *window premiums.*

> **Example:** Belinda Argus, age 45, is changing jobs and is using a lump-sum distribution she received from a retirement plan as a single premium to purchase a deferred annuity. She has requested that periodic income payments begin when she retires at age 65. Thus, the accumulation period of her annuity contract is scheduled to be 20 years.

Under a *flexible-premium deferred annuity (FPDA) contract*, the contract owner typically must pay an initial premium of some minimum amount and then may make additional payments at any future times, usually subject to some smaller minimum amount. The contract owner may choose not to pay any premium in a given year. The only requirement is that any premium amount paid must meet the stated minimum.

> **Example:** Maria Montoya purchased a deferred annuity with planned monthly premiums of $100. She paid an initial premium of $1,000 and paid $100 per month for three months before experiencing a financial emergency. Six months later, after resolving the financial emergency, Ms. Montoya began making premium payments of $150 per month.

**Source:** Adapted from Mary C. Bickley, *Principles of Financial Services and Products* (Atlanta: LOMA, © 2004), 266. Used with permission; all rights reserved.

If the fixed annuity is an *immediate annuity*, then the amount of the periodic income payments is known when the insurer issues the annuity contract. The purchaser pays a single premium amount, and the insurer calculates the periodic income payment amount that will be provided by that premium amount.

If the fixed annuity is a *deferred annuity*, then the annuity contract includes a chart of annuity values, similar to that shown in Figure 11.4. This chart lists the amount of the periodic income payment that is guaranteed for each $1,000 of accumulation value. According to the chart in our figure, for example, if the annuity's accumulation value on the maturity date is $20,000 and the annuitant is age 40, then the insurer will pay the annuitant $82.60 per month (20 × $4.13 = $82.60) for the remainder of the annuitant's life. Note, however, that the amounts listed in the policy are the minimum guaranteed periodic income payment amounts. These are the payment amounts that the insurer is comfortable guaranteeing when it issues a fixed annuity. At the annuity date, the insurer reevaluates its investment experience and the current investment climate; if the investment climate is more favorable than expected, then the insurer may pay a larger amount per $1,000 of accumulation value than the annuity guaranteed.

**FIGURE 11.4  Guaranteed Values of a Fixed Annuity**

| Age* | Payments for Life Only | Payments Guaranteed for 10 Years | 15 Years | 20 Years |
|---|---|---|---|---|
| 40 | $4.13 | $4.12 | $4.11 | $4.09 |
| 45 | 4.36 | 4.34 | 4.32 | 4.28 |
| 50 | 4.65 | 4.62 | 4.58 | 4.52 |
| 55 | 5.05 | 4.99 | 4.91 | 4.81 |
| 60 | 5.56 | 5.45 | 5.32 | 5.14 |
| 65 | 6.27 | 6.07 | 5.82 | 5.48 |
| 70 | 7.33 | 6.89 | 6.38 | 5.76 |
| 75 and over | 8.95 | 7.89 | 6.87 | 5.92 |

Minimum Monthly Income Payment for Each $1,000 of Accumulation Value

* Age on birthday preceding the due date of the first payment.

A fixed deferred annuity contract also describes the manner in which the insurer will credit investment earnings to the annuity's accumulation value. When the annuity is purchased, the insurer typically guarantees that the accumulation value will be credited with a stated interest rate for at least a stated time, usually from one to five years. Such an annuity also specifies that, after that initial time, the interest rate credited will not fall below a stated rate, such as 3 percent. The actual interest rate that the insurer will apply after the initial period, however, may be greater than the guaranteed rate if the insurer's investment earnings justify the higher rate. Often, the contract specifies that the interest rate that will be credited will be tied either to a published index or, more commonly, to the insurer's overall investment results. An *index* is a statistical measurement system that tracks the performance of a group of similar investments.

When an insurer provides interest rate guarantees in an annuity contract, the insurer agrees to assume the investment risk of the contract. The insurer places the funds in relatively secure investments, such as bonds and preferred stocks, as part of its general account. If the insurer's general account performs well, the insurer can pay interest rates that are higher than the rates guaranteed in its contracts while still achieving profits from the general account. The insurer, however, takes the risk that if its investments perform poorly and its investment returns are less than the minimums guaranteed in its contracts, then the insurer will lose money.

Hybrid types of annuity products, such as equity-indexed annuities (EIAs) and market value adjusted (MVA) annuities have been introduced into the fixed annuity market. Figure 11.5 describes these hybrid annuities.

## Variable Annuities

A *variable annuity* is an annuity under which the amount of the accumulation value and the amount of the periodic income payments fluctuate in accordance with the performance of one or more specified investment funds. Because the insurer makes no guarantees regarding the principal, interest rate, or the amount of periodic income payments, the insurer retains no risk under the contract. Instead, the contract owner bears all the investment risk, benefiting from all gains that result from profitable investments and incurring all losses from unprofitable investments. Because of this investment risk transfer, federal laws in the United States treat variable annuities as securities that must comply with federal securities laws.

### Subaccounts

The mechanism that allows this investment risk transfer from the insurer to the purchaser is the separate account. As we described in Chapter 6, a separate account is an investment account maintained separately from the insurer's general account to isolate and help manage the funds placed in variable insurance products, such as variable life insurance and variable annuities. The insurer's separate account includes a number of subaccounts,

### FIGURE 11.5 — Hybrid Annuities

**Equity-Indexed Annuities**

An **equity-indexed annuity (EIA)** is a type of annuity that offers certain principal and earnings guarantees, but also offers the possibility of additional earnings by linking the contract to a published index. EIAs typically are classified as fixed annuities because of the guarantees they offer. However, like variable annuities, EIAs offer the potential for higher returns depending on investment performance.

**Market Value Adjusted Annuities**

A **market value adjusted (MVA) annuity**, also known as a *modified guaranteed annuity*, is an annuity that offers multiple guarantee periods and multiple fixed interest rates. Rather than being "locked in" with fixed earnings for the life of the contract, contract owners can move or withdraw premium deposits at certain times stipulated in the contract to take advantage of prevailing market interest rates.

To be issued as fixed annuities in the United States, EIAs and MVA annuities must meet certain regulatory requirements. Those EIAs and MVA annuities that do not meet regulatory requirements are considered variable products, which must be registered as securities.

**Source:** Adapted from Mary C. Bickley, *Principles of Financial Services and Products* (Atlanta: LOMA, © 2004), 269. Used with permission; all rights reserved.

---

which are alternative investment funds within an insurer's separate account. The owner of a variable annuity may allocate premiums among a choice of subaccounts and has the right to (1) transfer money among subaccounts, (2) change the percentage of money allocated to specific subaccounts, and (3) change the subaccounts in which future premiums are invested. Insight 11.1 describes variable annuity subaccounts.

Typically, variable annuities offer a wide variety of variable subaccounts. In addition, contract owners usually can place a portion of premiums in a *fixed subaccount*, which is a subaccount that guarantees payment of a fixed rate of interest for a specified period of time. Unlike money invested in variable subaccounts, money invested in a fixed subaccount is held in the insurer's general account.

## Accumulation Units

A variable deferred annuity contract owner's premium payments purchase *accumulation units*, which represent ownership shares in selected subaccounts of the separate account held during the accumulation period. The number of accumulation units that a given premium will purchase depends on the value of the investments in the subaccount when the premium is paid. Thus, if the value of the investments held in a subaccount is low, the value of each accumulation unit also is low; as a result, more accumulation units can be purchased for a given amount of premium than when the investment value of the subaccount is high.

**INSIGHT 11.1** | Variable Annuity Subaccounts

At the time a variable annuity contract owner purchases her annuity, she must select at least one subaccount in which to invest her premiums. If the contract owner chooses more than one subaccount, she must specify what percentage of premiums she wishes to invest in each subaccount. The insurer will distribute the initial premium payment and any additional premiums to the specified subaccounts in the percentages indicated. For example, suppose that Trisha Hart chooses to invest her premium payments in four subaccounts as follows:

> **20 percent to Subaccount A**
>
> **10 percent to Subaccount B**
>
> **50 percent to Subaccount C**
>
> **20 percent to Subaccount D**

If Ms. Hart makes an initial premium payment of $5,000, the insurer will invest $1,000 in Subaccount A, $500 in Subaccount B, $2,500 in Subaccount C, and $1,000 in Subaccount D. During the accumulation period, a variable annuity's accumulation value will fluctuate directly with the investment performance of the chosen subaccounts.

**Source:** Adapted from Mary C. Bickley, *Principles of Financial Services and Products* (Atlanta: LOMA, © 2004), 270. Used with permission; all rights reserved.

**Example.** Will Howard purchased a variable deferred annuity and selected Subaccount A as the investment vehicle for his annuity. Over a three-month period, the value of an accumulation unit in Subaccount A was as follows:

January — $2.00

February — $3.00

March — $2.50

Will paid a premium of $600 in each of those three months.

**Analysis.** In January, the $600 premium purchased 300 accumulation units ($600 ÷ $2.00 = 300). In February, the $600 premium purchased 200 accumulation units ($600 ÷ $3.00 = 200). In March, the $600 premium purchased 240 accumulation units ($600 ÷ $2.50 = 240). Over the three-month period, the $1,800 that Will paid in premiums was sufficient to purchase a total of 740 accumulation units (300 + 200 + 240).

As a contract owner pays premiums throughout the accumulation period, his total number of accumulation units gradually increases. The value of a contract owner's investment in a variable annuity subaccount depends on both the number of accumulation units held and the current value of an accumulation unit. Insight 11.2 illustrates how changes in the value of an accumulation unit affect the value of a contract owner's investment in a variable annuity subaccount.

In Insight 11.2, the number of accumulation units remains constant, but the value of the subaccount fluctuates. This fluctuation results from changes in the value of an accumulation unit, which in turn results from changes in the market value of the underlying investments. Through the valuation mechanism, market performance affects the value of the contract owner's investment in a variable annuity. Keep in mind that increasing or decreasing the number of accumulation units held in a variable subaccount also can change the value of the contract owner's investment.

## Annuity Units

At the beginning of the payout period, the variable annuity contract owner typically has the option of receiving periodic income payments that

- Are fixed in amount from a fixed subaccount

- Fluctuate to directly reflect the investment experience of specified variable subaccounts

- Are based on the results of some combination of fixed and variable subaccounts, so that a portion of the periodic income payments would be stable and another portion would fluctuate

---

**INSIGHT 11.2    Calculating Subaccount Values during the Accumulation Period**

In the table below, the value of 100 accumulation units in a variable annuity subaccount is equal to $600 when the current value of an accumulation unit is $6.00. If the value of an accumulation unit drops to $4.00, the value of the annuity investment will drop to $400. However, if the value of an accumulation unit rises to $8.00, then the value of the annuity investment will increase to $800.

| Date | Number of Accumulation Units | Accumulation Unit Value | Subaccount Value |
|------|------------------------------|-------------------------|------------------|
| January 2005 | 100 | $6.00 | $600 |
| January 2006 | 100 | $4.00 | $400 |
| January 2007 | 100 | $8.00 | $800 |

**Source:** Adapted from Mary C. Bickley, *Principles of Financial Services and Products* (Atlanta: LOMA, © 2004), 271. Used with permission; all rights reserved.

If the contract owner selects the variable payout option, the insurer pays to the payee a series of payments that vary throughout the payout period. Under this option, the value of the annuity remains in the separate account. When the contract is annuitized, the annuity's accumulation units are used to purchase annuity units. **Annuity units** are shares in the subaccounts of an insurer's separate account that determine the size of future periodic income payments under a variable annuity contract after the contract has been annuitized. The calculation of the number of annuity units that can be purchased for each dollar applied depends on a number of factors, including the current value of the accumulation units, the current value of the annuity units, the length of the annuity period (for example, monthly or annually), and the payout option elected. Further, the amount of periodic income payments varies over the payout period depending on the then current value of an annuity unit. For an individual variable annuity contract owner, then, the periodic income payment amount he will receive depends on the total number of annuity units he has purchased and the current value of each annuity unit when the benefit is paid.

The insurer must periodically recalculate the value of an annuity unit based on the investment experience of the subaccount. The insurer then recalculates the amount of the periodic income payment by multiplying the total number of annuity units times the then current value of an annuity unit. Note that, for all single life and most joint life payout options (which we discuss in the next section), the total number of annuity units remains the same throughout the payout period; the value of an annuity unit varies depending on the investment experience of the subaccount. Thus, the amount of the periodic income payment changes as the value of the subaccount changes. If the subaccount's value increases, then the income payment increases; if the subaccount's value declines, then the income payment decreases correspondingly.

# The Annuity Contract

Many of the provisions that typically are included in individual life insurance policies also are included in individual annuity contracts. The following provisions generally are included in all types of individual annuity contracts:

- An *entire contract provision*, which states that the entire contract consists of the annuity contract, the application if it is attached to the contract, and any attached riders. The provision is basically the same as that included in individual life insurance policies except that the application for an annuity contract is not necessarily required to be included as part of the annuity contract.

- A *free-look provision* or *free-examination provision*, which gives the contract owner a stated period of time—usually ten days—after the contract is delivered in which to examine the policy. During the free-look period, the contract owner has the right to cancel the contract and receive a full refund of all premiums paid. The provision is basically the same as that included in individual life insurance policies.

- An *incontestability provision*, which typically states that, after the contract becomes effective, the insurer may not contest the validity of the contract. This provision is much more restrictive to the insurer than its counterpart provision in life insurance policies. Annuity contracts that include certain supplementary benefits—such as a waiver of premium for disability—limit the time, typically to a maximum of two years, during which the insurer may contest the validity of the coverage provided by the supplementary benefit based on a material misrepresentation in the application.

- A *misstatement of age or sex provision*, which states that if the annuitant's age or sex was misstated in the application, then the annuity benefits payable will be those that the premiums paid would have purchased for the correct age or sex.

- An *assignment provision*, which is like the assignment provision included in individual life insurance policies in that it describes the roles of the insurer and the contract owner when the contract is assigned. Unlike individual life policies, individual annuity contracts generally state that if the contract is part of specified types of qualified retirement plans, then the contract may not be sold, assigned, transferred, or pledged as collateral for a loan or for any other purpose to any other person.[1] This prohibition against the assignment of specified types of qualified retirement plan contracts is required by U.S. federal tax laws, and, thus, such contracts are not assignable. We describe qualified retirement plans in Chapter 14.

Like participating individual life insurance policies, participating individual annuity contracts must include a *dividends provision*, which describes the contract owner's right to share in the insurer's divisible surplus, if any, and the dividend payment options available to the contract owner. Most participating annuity contracts state that the insurance company does not expect to pay policy dividends. Instead, insurers usually increase the interest rate they pay on participating annuities above the minimum rate guaranteed in the contracts and, thus, they allow the owners of participating annuities to share in the insurers' gains.

## Deferred Annuity Contract Provisions

Deferred annuity contracts generally include a number of provisions that govern the rights of the contract owner during the annuity's accumulation period. For example, the **withdrawal provision** gives the contract owner the right to withdraw all or a portion of the annuity's accumulation value during the accumulation period. Most contracts allow the contract owner to withdraw a stated percentage of the annuity's accumulation value each year without charge. If the contract owner withdraws more than that stated percentage in one year, then the insurer generally imposes a **withdrawal charge**. Withdrawals of less than a stated minimum amount typically are not permitted. A withdrawal permanently reduces the annuity's accumulation value.

Throughout the accumulation period, the contract owner also has the right to surrender the annuity for its **surrender value**—the accumulation value *less* any surrender charges included in the policy. A **surrender charge** is a fee typically imposed if the annuity contract is surrendered within a stated number of years after it was purchased. An insurer usually imposes a surrender charge during the early years of an annuity contract as a way to recoup the costs it incurred in issuing the contract. The amount of any surrender charge that is imposed usually declines over time.

$$\left( \begin{array}{c} \text{Surrender value of a} \\ \text{deferred annuity} \end{array} \right) = \left( \begin{array}{c} \text{Accumulation} \\ \text{value} \end{array} \right) - \left( \begin{array}{c} \text{Surrender} \\ \text{charge} \end{array} \right)$$

By contrast, insurers usually do not impose surrender charges when the accumulation value of a deferred annuity is paid as a death benefit. Deferred annuity contracts usually provide a **death benefit**, also known as a *survivor benefit*, which is a benefit that equals at least the amount of the annuity's accumulation value and that is to be paid to a beneficiary designated by the contract owner if the contract owner dies before periodic income payments begin.

## Guaranteed Benefits

Some people are reluctant to deposit funds into a variable annuity because they fear losing their money as a result of market fluctuations. Insurers have responded to such concerns by adding enhanced benefits to variable annuity contracts. A variable annuity contract may contain none, some, or all of these features. The following are the most common of these enhanced benefits:

- The **guaranteed minimum accumulation benefit (GMAB)** is a variable annuity contract feature that guarantees a return of premiums paid if the contract remains in force for a specified period of time.

- The *guaranteed minimum withdrawal benefit* (*GMWB*) is a variable annuity contract feature that guarantees that up to a certain percentage of the amount paid into the contract will be available for withdrawals annually, even if subaccount investments perform poorly.

- The *guaranteed minimum death benefit* (*GMDB*) is a variable annuity contract feature that guarantees that if the contract owner dies before periodic income payments begin, the beneficiary will receive at least the amount that was paid into the contract, less any withdrawals, even if poor investment performance causes the contract's accumulation value to be less than the premiums paid.

- The *guaranteed minimum income benefit* (*GMIB*) is a variable annuity contract feature that guarantees that variable periodic income payments will not fall below a certain amount—usually a specified percentage of the first periodic income payment—even if investments drop in value as a result of poor performance.

Because these guarantees increase risk for the insurer, insurers usually charge contract owners extra for these benefits.

## Payout Options

When a deferred annuity reaches the payout period, all provisions relating to the policy's accumulation value—including the withdrawal provision and the death benefit provision—become inoperable. At that time, the contract owner may elect to have the accumulation value distributed in a single payment, known as a lump-sum distribution. Alternatively, the contract owner may select a payout option, and the terms of the payout option provision then govern the parties' rights and obligations under the contract. In the case of an immediate annuity, the applicant chooses the payout option when he applies for the annuity. An annuity in the payout period is commonly called a *payout annuity*. In this section, we describe the typical annuity payout options.

Because some annuity contract owners want the security of knowing that they can get to their money in case of an emergency, some insurers have added a commutation right to payout options. A *commutation right* permits the owner of a payout annuity to withdraw all or part of the contract's remaining periodic income payments in a lump sum. However, if a contract owner chooses to exercise the commutation right, the withdrawal will reduce the amount of any future periodic income payments.

### Period Certain Annuity

An annuity can be purchased to provide periodic payments over a period of time that is unrelated to the lifetime of an annuitant. A *period certain*

**FAST FACT**

U.S. life insurance companies paid $31 billion in individual annuity contract benefit payments during 2003.

**Source:** ACLI, *Life Insurers Fact Book: 2004* (Washington, D.C.: American Council of Life Insurers, 2004), 95.

*annuity*, also known as an *annuity certain*, is an annuity that is payable for a stated period of time, regardless of whether the annuitant lives or dies. The stated period over which the insurer will make periodic income payments is called the *period certain*. At the end of the period certain, periodic income payments cease. The period certain annuity is useful when a person needs an income for a specified period of time. A period certain annuity also might be purchased to provide income during a specified period until some other source of income, such as a pension, becomes payable.

> **Example.** Midori Hayakawa is a 50-year-old office manager who plans to retire at age 60. She will not begin receiving pension benefits from her employer-sponsored pension plan until she reaches age 65. Thus, she wants to purchase an annuity that will provide her with periodic income payments during the 5-year period following her retirement before she begins receiving her pension benefits.
>
> **Analysis.** Midori wants to begin receiving annuity benefit payments in 10 years, when she retires at age 60. Thus, she should purchase a 10-year deferred annuity. Midori wants to receive periodic income payments only until she begins to receive her pension benefits. Thus, she should elect a payout option under which annuity benefits are paid as a 5-year period certain annuity.

## Fixed-Amount Annuity

A *fixed-amount annuity* guarantees the payment of periodic income payments of a specified minimum dollar amount for as long a period as the annuity's accumulation value will provide, regardless of whether the annuitant lives or dies. Once the total accumulation value has been paid out, periodic income payments end and the insurer has no further liability under the annuity contract.

## Life Annuity

As noted in Chapter 9, a *life annuity* is an annuity that provides periodic income payments for *at least* the lifetime of the named annuitant. Life annuities take a variety of forms. The most basic form of life annuity is the *straight life annuity*, which provides periodic income payments for only as long as the annuitant lives. Upon the death of the annuitant, the insurer has no further liability under the annuity contract. Because of the uncertainty of when an annuitant will die, the purchaser of a straight life annuity runs the risk that she may pay a great deal more in premiums than she will receive in periodic income payments. Many people are unwilling to accept such a risk, and thus they purchase life annuities that contain more guarantees than are contained in a straight life annuity.

A *joint and survivor annuity* provides periodic income payments to two or more annuitants, and those payments continue until both or all of the annuitants die. The terms of a joint and survivor annuity contract determine whether the amount of each periodic income payment remains the same after the death of one of the annuitants. For example, the annuity might provide that the amount of the periodic income payments will remain the same until the last annuitant dies, or the annuity might provide that the amount of the periodic income payments will be reduced by a stated amount, such as 50 percent, following the death of the first annuitant. Of course, the premium amount required to fund the annuity will vary, depending on the amount of benefits that are to be paid out—the larger the expected amount of periodic income payments, the larger the premium required to pay for the annuity.

A *life annuity with period certain* guarantees that the insurer will make periodic income payments throughout the annuitant's life and guarantees that the payments will be made for at least a certain period, even if the annuitant dies before the end of that period. The contract owner selects the guaranteed period, which is often 5 or 10 years, and—assuming the annuitant is the payee—names a contingent payee. If the annuitant dies before the period certain has expired, then the contingent payee becomes entitled to receive the periodic income payments throughout the remainder of the period certain. If the annuitant dies after the expiration of the period certain, periodic income payments cease.

> **Example.** Jameel Stegall purchased a life annuity with a 10-year period certain. He named himself as the annuitant and the payee. He named his wife, Alma, as contingent payee. Jameel died 7 years after periodic income payments began.
>
> **Analysis.** Alma will receive the periodic income payments throughout the remainder of the 10-year period certain—for 3 years. After the expiration of the 10-year period certain, no more benefit payments will be made. Had Jameel lived 15 years after periodic income payments began, he would have received payments throughout his life, and Alma would have received no payments after his death.

The *life with refund annuity*, also known as a *refund annuity*, provides periodic income payments throughout the lifetime of the annuitant and guarantees that at least the purchase price of the annuity will be paid out. This guarantee means that if the annuitant dies before the total of the periodic income payments made equals the purchase price, a refund will be made to a contingent payee designated by the contract owner. The amount of the refund is equal to the difference between the purchase price of the annuity and the amount that has been paid out in benefits.

**Example.** Anwar Lake paid a single premium of $120,000 for a refund annuity that would provide an annuity benefit of $10,000 per year during his lifetime. He named his wife, Maria, as the contingent payee. Anwar died 7 years after benefit payments began; at the time of his death, he had received periodic income payments totaling $70,000.

**Analysis.** Maria will be entitled to a refund of $50,000, which is the difference between the $120,000 purchase price and the $70,000 paid in periodic income payments during Anwar's lifetime. Had Anwar lived for 15 years after periodic payments began, he would have received more in benefits than he paid for the annuity (15 years × $10,000 per year = $150,000). In that case, Maria would not have received a refund payment following Anwar's death.

# Financial Design of Annuities

An annuity contract owner pays a premium or premiums to the insurer, which invests the premiums from a large group of contract owners and uses the premiums and investment earnings to provide the benefits promised under the annuity contract. In this section, we discuss the factors that affect the amount of periodic income payments, and we explain annuity fees and charges.

## Factors Affecting Amount of Periodic Income Payments

An insurer uses a combination of factors to calculate the amount of the benefits that it will pay under an annuity contract. Every calculation of contract values, however, is based on the following basic mathematical principle:

> A sum of money, known as the *principal*, that is invested for a certain *period of time* at a stated *rate of interest* can be paid out in a series of periodic income payments over a stated *period of time*.

This mathematical principle contains four variables:

1. **The amount of the principal invested.** Premiums increase principal. Withdrawals and surrenders decrease principal.

2. **The time over which the principal grows at interest.** For annuity contracts, this time period is the accumulation period. The pattern of premium payments over time affects the length of time that the principal earns interest. The longer the time period, the larger the interest earnings will be.

3. **The interest rate that represents investment earnings.** Some annuity contracts earn interest at a stated rate. Other contracts, however, earn investment income that may not carry a stated interest rate. In all cases, however, an interest rate can be used to represent the investment earnings.

4. **The number and timing of periodic income payments.** The number of periodic income payments is determined by the frequency of payments and the total length of the payout period. For all types of life annuities, the number and timing of periodic income payments also depends on mortality experience. The longer the annuitant is expected to live, all other factors being equal, the smaller the periodic income payments will be. Similarly, the shorter the time period the annuitant is expected to live, all other factors being equal, the larger the periodic income payments will be. Insight 11.3 describes annuity mortality rates.

## INSIGHT 11.3   Annuity Mortality Rates

As noted in the text, the length of the payout period of a life annuity is linked to the length of the annuitant's lifetime. Mortality studies have provided insurers with information on how many persons in a given group of people of the same age and gender are expected to be alive at the end of any given year. *Annuity mortality rates*—the mortality rates experienced by persons purchasing life annuities— are not identical to the mortality rates experienced by persons insured by life insurance policies. In general, annuitants as a group live longer than do individuals who purchase life insurance.

Because annuity benefits are payable while the annuitant continues to live, a life annuity protects against the personal risk of outliving one's financial resources. Thus, those people who are in good health and who anticipate a long life are more interested in purchasing life annuities than are those people who are in poor health. This form of antiselection is the opposite of the form of antiselection found in life insurance, where those people who are in poor health or who have some other reason to expect a shorter-than-normal lifespan are more interested in purchasing life insurance than are those people who

are in good health. Also, in contrast to the operation of life insurance premium rates, life annuity premium rates decrease as mortality rates increase. In other words, the higher the mortality rate for a group of annuitants, the lower the premium rate that the insurer will charge for those annuities. As a result of these facts, if insurers used life insurance mortality tables to calculate premium rates for life annuities, then the premiums they collected would be inadequate to provide the lifetime annuity benefits promised. Thus, insurers have developed annuity mortality tables to use in calculating premium rates for life annuities.

Figure 11.6 summarizes the relationships among the important factors that affect periodic income payments.

## Annuity Fees and Charges

Although our discussion to this point has greatly simplified the financial design of annuities, it is accurate to the extent that it considers investment earnings and funding the amount of periodic income payments. Insurers also must incorporate their expenses into the financial designs of annuities, and they do so using one or more of the following fees and charges:

- A *front-end load* is an amount charged to the contract owner at the time she pays for the annuity. The front-end load compensates the insurer for sales commissions and other expenses associated with acquiring the business. For example, assume that an individual purchases a fixed deferred annuity for $50,000 and that the annuity has a front-end load of 2.5 percent of the premium. The amount of the front-end load is $1,250 (2.5 percent × $50,000). Thus, the insurer deducts the $1,250 from the amount paid and invests the remainder of $48,750 in the purchaser's accumulation account.

- A *back-end load*, also known as a *surrender charge*, is an amount charged to the contract owner when she withdraws money from the product. In variable annuities, a back-end load is known as a

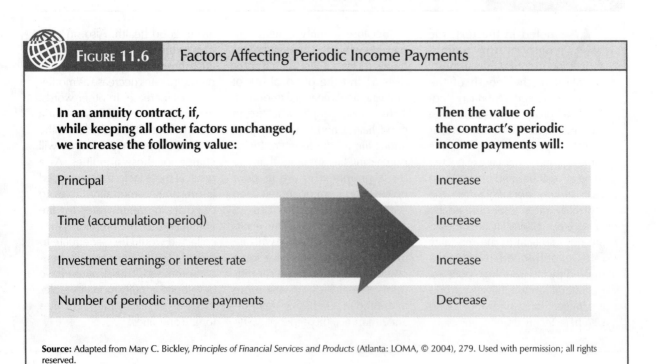

**FIGURE 11.6** | Factors Affecting Periodic Income Payments

| In an annuity contract, if, while keeping all other factors unchanged, we increase the following value: | Then the value of the contract's periodic income payments will: |
| --- | --- |
| Principal | Increase |
| Time (accumulation period) | Increase |
| Investment earnings or interest rate | Increase |
| Number of periodic income payments | Decrease |

**Source:** Adapted from Mary C. Bickley, *Principles of Financial Services and Products* (Atlanta: LOMA, © 2004), 279. Used with permission; all rights reserved.

*contingent deferred sales charge (CDSC)*. The back-end load/CDSC is expressed as a percentage of the withdrawal and typically decreases over time. Eventually the contract owner can withdraw funds with no load being incurred.

- A *periodic fee*, also known as a *maintenance fee*, is an amount payable at predetermined intervals—for example, every year or every month. A periodic fee typically compensates the insurer for its administrative expenses. The fee can be either a flat amount or a percentage of the accumulation value.

- Insurers also might impose a *service fee*, which is a one-time fee charged for specific services.

Contracts typically do not impose both a front-end load and a back-end load, as both loads are charged to offset commission costs.

Variable annuities charge the following additional fees:

- A *mortality and expense risk (M&E) charge* to cover three guarantees, which are the contract's benefits: (1) Any guaranteed death benefit payable to a designated beneficiary; (2) the fixed payout options, which guarantee that a certain amount will be paid for the life of the annuitant; and (3) the guarantee that contract expenses will increase no more than the maximums stated in the contract. The M&E charge generally is expressed as a percentage of the accumulation value.

- An *investment management fee* to cover professional investment management services. This fee usually is expressed as a percentage of the accumulation value.

## Taxation of Annuities

As illustrated in Figure 11.7, annuities are an increasingly popular product in the United States, and annuities now represent the largest portion of the premium receipts of U.S. life insurance companies. The popularity of annuities to U.S. consumers is in part the result of favorable federal income tax treatment, which typically includes tax deferral of investment earnings. In other words, the investment income that the contract owner is earning on his premium payments generally is not subject to taxation until the investment income is actually paid out by the insurer to the named recipient.

The taxation of an annuity varies depending on whether the annuity is a qualified annuity or a nonqualified annuity.

- A *qualified annuity* is an annuity contract purchased to fund or distribute funds from a qualified plan. A *qualified plan* technically is a

**FIGURE 11.7** Premium Receipts of U.S. Life Insurance Companies

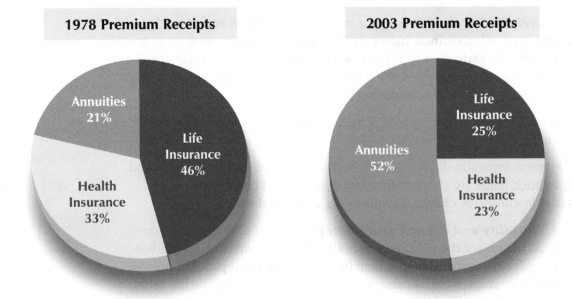

**1978 Premium Receipts**

Annuities 21%
Life Insurance 46%
Health Insurance 33%

**2003 Premium Receipts**

Life Insurance 25%
Annuities 52%
Health Insurance 23%

**Source:** Data from ACLI, *Life Insurers Fact Book: 2004* (Washington, D.C.: American Council of Life Insurers, 2004), 49. ACLI, *Life Insurers Fact Book: 2003* (Washington, D.C.: American Council of Life Insurers, 2003), 53. Used with permission.

retirement plan that receives favorable income tax treatment by meeting the requirements imposed by federal tax laws and the Employee Retirement Income Security Act (ERISA). However, a broader, less formal usage of *qualified plan* includes other tax-advantaged savings plans such as IRAs, which we describe in the next section.

- A ***nonqualified annuity*** is an annuity that is not part of a qualified plan.

Under current U.S. federal tax laws, qualified annuities are taxed in accordance with the tax laws that apply to the qualified plan that the annuities fund. In contrast, all nonqualified annuities are treated the same for purposes of U.S. federal income taxes. Premiums are not tax deductible, but investment earnings are tax deferred. Thus, each periodic income payment received under a nonqualified annuity is considered to consist of the following two parts:

1. One portion of each payment is considered a return of premiums, which is not taxable because the purchaser has already paid income taxes on that amount.

2. The remainder of each payment is considered taxable investment income because the purchaser has never paid income taxes on the contract's investment earnings.

By contrast, tax laws in many countries, including Canada, do not provide this favorable treatment for annuities. In these countries, investment earnings from an annuity generally are taxable as income throughout the life of the annuity unless the annuity is used to fund a qualified retirement plan.

# Individual Retirement Arrangements

The governments of many countries have enacted laws that provide federal income tax advantages to certain individuals who deposit funds into specified types of retirement savings plans. These laws are designed to encourage taxpayers to establish savings plans for their retirement. In this section, we describe individual retirement arrangements in the United States. Insight 11.4 describes individual retirement savings plans in Canada. Many individuals also participate in group retirement plans established by their employers. We describe these group retirement plans in Chapter 14.

**FAST FACT**

During 2002, Canadians paid over $9 billion in premiums for individual annuity contracts.

**Source:** CLHIA, *Canadian Life and Health Insurance Facts*, 2003 ed. (Toronto: Canadian Life and Health Insurance Association Inc., 2003), 10.

 **INSIGHT 11.4** Canadian Individual Retirement Savings Plans

In Canada, any gainfully employed person, including a person who is covered by an employer-sponsored registered pension plan, may establish a qualified retirement account known as a **registered retirement savings plan (RRSP)**. A person who establishes an account that qualifies as an RRSP can deduct from his gross taxable income the amount of his annual contribution to the RRSP, which is generally a stated percentage of his annual earned income, subject to a stated maximum amount. The permitted contribution amount varies depending on whether the person is also covered by a registered pension plan, which is a pension plan that receives favorable tax treatment. A person who is not covered by a registered pension plan may deduct a larger contribution amount than can an individual who does participate in a registered pension plan.

The investment income earned on the funds in an RRSP is not taxed until the funds are withdrawn. Individuals who establish RRSP accounts must begin withdrawing the accumulated funds by the time they reach age 69.

**Source:** Adapted from Mary C. Bickley, *Principles of Financial Services and Products* (Atlanta: LOMA, © 2004), 290. Used with permission; all rights reserved.

An *individual retirement arrangement (IRA)* is a retirement savings plan that allows a person with taxable compensation to deposit a stated amount of that compensation into a savings arrangement that meets certain requirements specified in the federal tax laws and, thus, receives favorable federal income tax treatment. An IRA may take one of two forms:

1. An *individual retirement account* is a trust or custodial account created in the United States for the exclusive benefit of an individual and his beneficiaries. The trustee or custodian must be a bank, investment company, stock brokerage, or similar organization. A *custodial account* is an account set up at a depository institution or other financial institution for a minor or other person who lacks legal capacity.

2. An *individual retirement annuity* is an individual annuity issued by an insurance company.

The financial services industry uses the acronym *IRA* to refer to individual retirement arrangements as a whole, as well as to individual retirement accounts and individual retirement annuities. To avoid confusion in terminology, we use the acronym *IRA* to refer to both types of individual retirement arrangements. When individual differences exist, we distinguish between an individual retirement account and an individual retirement annuity.

The sponsoring financial institution handles the administrative aspects of an individual retirement savings plan. For example, the insurance company that issues an individual retirement annuity ensures that the annuity meets the legislative requirements to qualify as an individual retirement arrangement and obtains approval from the Internal Revenue Service (IRS) that the plan qualifies. The insurer invests the funds deposited into the individual retirement annuity and manages the account. Individual retirement annuity funds may be placed in any of several types of investments, such as stocks, bonds, or real estate.

The tax treatment of an IRA varies depending on whether it is a traditional IRA or a Roth IRA.

## Traditional IRA

A *traditional IRA*, also known as a *regular IRA*, is an IRA in which contributions may be deductible and investment earnings are tax deferred until the funds are withdrawn. In other words, the amounts that an individual contributes to a traditional IRA—up to a stated maximum—usually are deductible from her gross income in the year in which those funds were contributed to the IRA. Thus, a taxpayer who meets specific criteria can reduce her current taxable income by making a contribution to a traditional IRA. She can defer the payment of federal income taxes until she withdraws the funds from the IRA during retirement, when the withdrawals presumably will be taxed at a lower rate than the tax rate she would have paid on those amounts during her working years. In addition, the investment earnings on a traditional IRA generally are not taxed until the funds are withdrawn.

The following is a summary of the current federal tax treatment of a traditional IRA:

1.  Anyone who is less than age 70½ and who has taxable compensation may contribute up to a certain maximum amount or 100 percent of his taxable compensation, whichever is less, per year into a traditional IRA. The maximum amount that can be contributed by persons under age 50 is $4,000 in years 2005 through 2007 and $5,000 in 2008 through 2010. The maximum amount that can be contributed by persons 50 and older is $4,500 in 2005, $5,000 in 2006 and 2007, and $6,000 in 2008 through 2010.

2.  Certain individuals may deduct traditional IRA contributions from their current taxable income. However, if a person or his spouse was an active participant in a qualified employer-sponsored retirement plan at any time during the year for which contributions were made, the deduction may be reduced or eliminated depending on the person's income level and tax filing status.

3.  Taxation of investment earnings is deferred until funds are withdrawn. With only a few exceptions, however, penalties are imposed on withdrawals made before the taxpayer attains age 59½.[2]

4.  A taxpayer must begin making annual withdrawals of at least a specified minimum amount by April 1 of the calendar year after he reaches age 70½; after that time, he may not make additional contributions to his IRA.

**Example.** Devon Smithby, who is not married, worked for a small printing company that did not provide a pension plan for its employees. For 10 years, beginning when he was 56, Devon deposited $2,000 a year into a traditional IRA. At age 73, Devon retired from the printing company and began making monthly withdrawals from his IRA.

**Analysis.** Devon did not have to pay income taxes on the money he deposited into his IRA at the time of his investment. He was required to pay taxes on both the principal and the investment earnings when he withdrew the money from the IRA. Devon also had to pay a penalty because he did not begin making withdrawals from his IRA by April 1 of the calendar year after he turned 70½.

## Roth IRA

A **Roth IRA** is an IRA that provides for nondeductible contributions annually, but tax-free qualified withdrawals. In other words, contributions are not taxed when they are withdrawn because they were taxed previously. In addition, all investment earnings accumulate on a tax-free basis, rather than on a tax-deferred basis as occurs with a traditional IRA, and such earnings are also distributed on a tax-free basis provided they qualify. To qualify for tax-free withdrawals of the investment earnings, the taxpayer must (1) have held the Roth IRA for at least five years and (2) be over age 59½ or be a qualified first-time homebuyer. Just as with a traditional IRA, federal tax laws impose limits on the amount of contributions a taxpayer may make to a Roth IRA. Unlike traditional IRAs, Roth IRAs are not subject to minimum distribution requirements.

## Key Terms

annuity
contract owner
annuitant
payee
annuity date
payout period
annuity period
payout options provision
payout options
immediate annuity
deferred annuity
accumulation period
accumulation value
annuitization
single-premium annuity
flexible-premium annuity
single-premium immediate
   annuity (SPIA) contract
single-premium deferred
   annuity (SPDA) contract
window premiums
flexible-premium deferred
   annuity (FPDA) contract
fixed annuity
index
equity-indexed annuity (EIA)
market value adjusted
   (MVA) annuity

variable annuity
fixed subaccount
accumulation unit
annuity unit
withdrawal provision
withdrawal charge
surrender value
surrender charge
death benefit
guaranteed minimum
   accumulation benefit (GMAB)
guaranteed minimum
   withdrawal benefit (GMWB)
guaranteed minimum death
   benefit (GMDB)
guaranteed minimum income
   benefit (GMIB)
payout annuity
commutation right
period certain annuity
period certain
fixed-amount annuity
straight life annuity
joint and survivor annuity
life annuity with period certain
life with refund annuity
annuity mortality rates
front-end load

back-end load
periodic fee
service fee
mortality and expense
  risk (M&E) charge
investment management fee
qualified annuity
qualified plan
nonqualified annuity

registered retirement
  savings plan (RRSP)
individual retirement
  arrangement (IRA)
individual retirement account
custodial account
individual retirement annuity
traditional IRA
Roth IRA

---

# Endnotes

1. One exception to this rule is that a tax-sheltered annuity may be used as collateral for a loan from the insurer that issued the annuity. A *tax-sheltered annuity* is a special type of qualified retirement plan that specified employers may establish for their employees.

2. As of 1998, taxpayers younger than 59½ may make penalty-free withdrawals from a regular IRA to pay qualified higher education expenses or to buy a first home.

# Part 3:
# Group Insurance

# Principles of Group Insurance

## objectives

*After reading this chapter, you should be able to*

- Identify the parties to a group insurance contract

- Contrast group underwriting with individual underwriting and identify the most important group underwriting considerations

- Distinguish between contributory and noncontributory group insurance plans

- Describe the operation of the probationary period and the actively-at-work requirement

- Identify situations in which a group member's coverage terminates while the group policy remains in force

- Distinguish among manual rating, experience rating, and blended rating

- Contrast insurer-administered plans with self-administered plans

I n previous chapters, we focused on individual life insurance. In this chapter, we turn our attention to group insurance, and we concentrate on those aspects of group insurance that are common to both group life and group health insurance. We begin by describing the group insurance contract. Then we explain group insurance underwriting. We also describe some of the provisions that are found in group insurance policies, the process that insurance companies use to set group premium rates, and the manner in which group insurance policies are administered. We cover specific group insurance products in later chapters.

## Group Insurance Contracts

Although individual insurance and group insurance are similar in many ways, these insurance products also differ in many ways. The most obvious difference is that, rather than insuring one person or one family, a group insurance plan insures a number of people under a single insurance contract, called a ***master group insurance contract***.

The parties to a master group insurance contract are the insurance company and the *group policyholder*, which is the person or organization that decides what types of group insurance coverage to purchase for the group members, negotiates the terms of the group insurance contract with the insurer, and purchases the group insurance coverage. The term *policyholder* is used rather than the term *policyowner* because the group policyholder does not have the same ownership rights in the group insurance policy that a policyowner has in an individual insurance policy. Instead, some of these rights are granted to the insured group members. For example, each group member insured under a group life insurance policy has the right to name the beneficiary who will receive the benefit payable upon that group member's death. By contrast, an individual life insurance policy grants that right to the policyowner, rather than to the insured.

When an insurance company and a group policyholder enter into a master group insurance contract, the insurer issues a policy that contains the terms of the contractual agreement. An important term found in every group insurance policy is a description of the individuals who are covered by the policy. In the United States, the individuals covered by a group insurance policy are referred to as the ***group insureds***, and we use that term in this text. Terminology varies from country to country. In Canada, for example, an individual insured under a group life insurance policy is referred to as a *group life insured*; an individual insured under a group health insurance policy is known as a *group person insured*.

The policyholder usually is responsible for handling some of the administrative aspects of the group insurance plan. For example, the policyholder typically is responsible for enrolling new group members in the plan. The group policyholder also is responsible for making all premium payments to the insurer, although the policy may require that the insured group members contribute some or all of that premium amount. If insured group members are not required to contribute any part of the premium for the coverage, then the group insurance plan is a *noncontributory plan*. If the group members must contribute some or all of the premium to be covered under the group insurance policy, then the plan is a *contributory plan*. A contributory group insurance policy covering employees typically requires the covered employees to pay their portion of the premium through payroll deduction.

## Formation of the Contract

As we described in Chapter 3, an insurance contract is an informal contract that must be formed in accordance with the rules of contract law. Thus, to form a valid group insurance contract, the policyholder and the insurer must

- Mutually agree to the contract's terms
- Both have contractual capacity
- Exchange legally adequate consideration
- Form the contract for a lawful purpose

The parties to a group insurance contract meet the first three of these requirements in much the same manner as do the parties to an individual insurance contract. However, the last requirement—the lawful purpose requirement—is met somewhat differently. Recall that the lawful purpose requirement is met for an individual insurance contract by the presence of insurable interest. Insurance laws typically exclude group life and health insurance contracts from the insurable interest requirement because the group policyholder's interest in the contract does not induce wagering as does an insured's interest in an individual insurance contract. The lawful purpose requirement is met for a group insurance contract because the policyholder enters into the contract to provide a benefit to covered group members.

## Certificates of Insurance

Insured group members are not parties to the master group insurance contract, do not participate in the formation of the contract, and do not receive individual copies of the contract. However, insured group members have certain rights under the contract. Insurance laws typically require the insurer to provide the group policyholder with written descriptions of the group insurance plan; the group policyholder then delivers a written description to each group insured. This document, known as the ***certificate of insurance***, describes (1) the coverage that the group insurance contract provides and (2) the group insured's rights under the contract. As a result, an insured group member often is referred to as a ***certificate holder***. Many policyholders describe the group insurance coverage in a special benefit booklet. In such cases, the benefit booklet contains the information that would be included in a certificate, and the benefit booklet serves as the group insurance certificate.

# Group Insurance Underwriting

**FAST FACT**

At the end of 2003, 43 percent of all life insurance in force in the United States was group life insurance.

Source: ACLI, *Life Insurers Fact Book: 2004* (Washington, D.C.: American Council of Life Insurers, 2004), 88.

One of the areas in which group insurance differs significantly from individual insurance is in the area of underwriting. Individual life and health insurance underwriting requires that the proposed insured *individual* meet the insurer's underwriting requirements. In contrast, group insurance underwriting generally focuses on the characteristics of the *group* and, with the exception of very small groups, usually does not require each proposed group insured to provide individual evidence of insurability. Nevertheless, the goal of group underwriting is the same as the goal of individual underwriting—to determine whether a group of people presents an average risk and whether the group's loss experience will be predictable and acceptable to the insurer. When evaluating a group, the group underwriter also seeks to prevent antiselection and to ensure that the administrative costs involved in providing the insurance are as low as possible. Finally, the group underwriter must assign the group a risk classification and determine the appropriate premium rates to charge for the group insurance.

Each insurance company establishes its own underwriting guidelines that define the types of group insurance coverage it will provide and the types of groups it will insure. In every case, however, the group underwriter considers specific characteristics of a group when evaluating whether the group is an acceptable risk. These risk characteristics include the reason for the group's existence, the size of the group, the flow of new members into the group, the stability of the group, the required percentage of eligible group members who must participate in the plan, the way in which benefit levels will be determined, and the activities of the group. We describe each of these risk characteristics to give you an overview of the types of characteristics that the group underwriter must consider. In any given situation, however, the group underwriter may need to consider a variety of other characteristics of the group.

## Reason for the Group's Existence

Group underwriting guidelines usually require that for a group to be eligible for coverage, the group must have been formed for a reason other than obtaining insurance. The likelihood of antiselection in a group formed solely to obtain group insurance coverage would be very great because people who think they would not qualify for individual insurance would be more likely to join such a group than would individuals who can obtain individual insurance. The groups that are eligible for coverage usually can be placed into one of the following categories:

- A **single-employer group** consists of the employees of a single employer. The policyholder is either the employer or the trustees of a trust created by the employer. Insight 12.1 describes trusts and their role in providing group insurance coverage. Most group insurance policies insure the employees of a single employer.

- A **labor union group** consists of workers who are members of a *labor union*, which is an association that promotes the welfare, interests, and rights of its members. Typically, the group insurance policy is issued to the trustees of a trust established to purchase insurance for union members.

 **INSIGHT 12.1** | Trusts and Their Uses in Providing Group Insurance

A *trust* is a fiduciary relationship in which one or more persons, known as the *trustees*, hold legal title to property—known as the *trust fund*—for the benefit of another person, known as the *trust beneficiary*. A *fiduciary* is a person who holds a position of special trust. Thus, when a group insurance contract is issued to the trustees of a trust, the trustees own the policy and have a fiduciary obligation to carry out the terms of the policy for the benefit of the group insureds.

Group insurance policies often are issued to the trustees of a trust that is established for the purpose of providing group insurance coverage to a group of people. In the United States, for example, the federal *Taft-Hartley Act* prohibits employers from making premium contributions on behalf of employees who belong to a labor union covered by a group insurance contract *unless* the contract is issued to a trust established for the purpose of purchasing insurance for union members. As a result of the Taft-Hartley Act, policies insuring labor union groups in the United States usually are issued to the trustees of a trust fund, and labor union groups are often referred to as *Taft-Hartley trusts*. Labor union groups also are sometimes referred to as *negotiated trusteeships* because they are created by an agreement negotiated between one or more labor unions and the employers of union members.

- A **multiple-employer group** consists of the employees of (1) two or more employers in the same industry, (2) two or more labor unions, or (3) one or more employers *and* one or more labor unions. Typically, the group policy is issued to the trustees of a trust established by the employers and/or labor unions.

- An **association group** consists of individuals who share a common bond. For example, group members may work in a specific industry or may share a common characteristic, such as individuals who are alumni of a specific college. An association group is eligible for group insurance only if it was formed for a purpose other than obtaining group insurance. The group policyholder is either the association or the trustees of a trust established for the benefit of members of one or more associations. Figure 12.1 describes some of the types of association groups that are eligible for group insurance coverage.

- A **debtor-creditor group** consists of persons who have borrowed funds from a lending institution, such as a bank. The creditor is the group policyholder. Both life insurance and disability income coverages are issued to this type of group. Life insurance coverage issued to debtor-creditor groups is usually called *group creditor life insurance* or *creditor group insurance*. (This and other group life coverages are discussed in the next chapter.)

- A **credit union group** consists of the members of one or more *credit unions*, which are cooperative associations that pool the savings of their members and use those funds to make loans to members. The group policy usually is issued to the credit union or to the trustees of a trust created by one or more credit unions.

- A **discretionary group** consists of the members of any other type of group that qualifies for group insurance coverage according to applicable state insurance laws.

Because most group insurance policies insure a group of employees, this text concentrates on employer-employee group insurance policies. We sometimes refer to the group policyholder as the *employer* and to the group insureds as the *employees*.

Underwriting guidelines vary somewhat for each of the preceding types of groups. For example, group underwriting guidelines typically require the employer in an employer-employee group insurance plan to pay at least a portion of the group insurance premium. This requirement, which is imposed by law in most states in the United States, gives the employer a financial interest in the operation of the plan. By contrast, other group policyholders usually are not required to pay a portion of the group insurance premium.

| FIGURE 12.1 | Types of Association Groups |

■ **Trade association.** An association of firms that operate in a specific industry.

■ **Association of individuals.** An association of individuals who share a common bond other than the common purpose of obtaining insurance. The following types of associations of individuals are typically eligible for group life and health insurance:

- **Professional association.** An association of individuals who share a common occupation, such as an association of medical doctors, attorneys, or engineers.

- **Public employee association.** An association of individuals employed by a state, county, or city government or by a state or local school board.

- **Common interest association.** An association of individuals who share a common status or a common interest. Examples include associations of retired persons, participants in a specific sport, or alumni of a specific college.

Some underwriting guidelines are more stringent for some types of groups than for other types of groups. For example, antiselection by individual group members is much more likely to occur in association groups in which group membership is voluntary than in employer-employee groups. As a result, insurance companies often impose more stringent underwriting requirements on association groups than on employer-employee groups. An insurer might be willing to issue an employer-employee group insurance policy to a group with as few as 10 members, but it might refuse to issue an association group policy covering fewer than 50 association members.

## Size of the Group

Recall that one of the underwriter's goals is to predict the loss rate that the group will experience. The size of the group has a strong impact on the underwriter's ability to predict the group's probable loss rate. In general, the larger the group, the more likely that the group will experience a loss rate that approximates the predicted loss rate. When group insurance plans were first introduced, only groups with at least 50 members were eligible for coverage. This requirement enabled the group underwriting process to function successfully and, consequently, to enable insurers to issue coverage without requiring evidence of insurability from the group's members.

Minimum size requirements prevented many small groups from obtaining group insurance coverage. Over the years, insurers began relaxing the requirements. Currently, a substantial number of the group life insurance policies in force cover groups with fewer than 10 members.

As group size requirements were relaxed, underwriters also needed to modify the group underwriting process because that process functions best only when applied to large groups. The extent of modification needed depends on the group's size. For very small groups, such as groups with fewer than 15 members, group underwriting guidelines often require each individual member of the group to submit satisfactory evidence of insurability. When calculating the anticipated loss rate of a slightly larger group, such as a group with between 15 and 50 members, the underwriter often pools several groups that are of the same approximate size and are in the same business sector. By considering the expected experience of a number of small groups, the underwriter can expect the experience of those small groups taken as a whole to approximate the experience of a single large group.

Although such modifications in the group underwriting process have enabled insurers to issue coverage to all group sizes, not all insurers participate in the small group market. Many insurers establish their own minimum group size requirements and do not offer insurance to groups with fewer than the required minimum number of members.

## Flow of New Members into the Group

Another important group underwriting requirement is that a sufficient number of new members must enter the group periodically. Young, new members are needed (1) to replace those who leave the group and, consequently, to keep the group size stable and (2) to keep the age distribution of the group stable. If a group did not add young, new members for a number of years, then the increasing age of the group's original members would adversely affect the group's age distribution, and the group's loss rate and premium rate would increase as a result. But if young, new members are continually joining the group, the age distribution of the group should remain more stable, as should the expected loss rate. Of course, the term *young* is relative; to a group composed entirely of retired people, a new group member who is 65 would be considered young and would help keep the group's age distribution stable.

## Stability of the Group

Despite the generally favorable results of changes in group membership, the insurance company also must be able to expect that the group will remain a group for a reasonable length of time and that the composition of the group will remain relatively stable. Otherwise, the costs of administering the plan would become prohibitively high. Therefore, underwriters avoid issuing coverage to groups that anticipate experiencing excessive changes in group membership. For example, a group of seasonal or temporary workers generally would not be considered an insurable group.

## Participation Levels

Group insurance underwriting requirements set limits as to the minimum percentage of eligible group members who must be covered by a group insurance plan for the insurance company to provide the coverage. Note that these requirements relate to participation by *eligible group members*. Each group insurance policy defines which group members are eligible for coverage. We describe these eligibility requirements later in the chapter.

Minimum participation requirements are designed to guard against the effects of antiselection and to avoid discrimination. The specific participation requirement that is imposed usually depends on whether the group insurance plan is a noncontributory plan or a contributory plan.

Typically, a noncontributory plan must cover all eligible employees; to do otherwise would be discriminatory. Therefore, 100 percent participation is required in noncontributory plans. By contrast, insurers do not require 100 percent participation in contributory plans. An employer may not require employees to participate in a contributory group insurance plan, and some group members probably will decide not to enroll in the plan. To minimize antiselection, however, most insurers require that at least 75 percent of the eligible employees in a contributory group insurance plan participate in the plan. A higher percentage of employees may participate in the plan, but a percentage of participation lower than 75 percent will cause the group to lose its eligibility for coverage. Without this requirement, the insurance company could not rely on the group underwriting process because an unusually large percentage of group members might be individuals who were uninsurable on an individual basis.

## Determination of Benefit Levels

The group policyholder typically works with the insurer to establish a fair and nondiscriminatory method to determine the benefit levels—that is, the types and amounts of coverage—offered to the group insureds. Some group insurance plans, for example, offer the same benefit amount to all group members. A more common method is to vary the benefit amount according to specific objective criteria, such as salary, occupation, or length of employment.

After the method of determining benefit levels is determined, a description of the method is incorporated into the master group insurance contract.

Thus, the group insureds are not permitted to select their coverage amounts individually. This step is necessary to avoid antiselection. Otherwise, those group members who are in poor health and unable to secure individual insurance would probably select larger benefit amounts than healthy members would select.

Some group policies allow covered group members to select additional coverages from a schedule of optional coverages. In most such situations, the group insurer minimizes the effects of antiselection by (1) limiting the optional coverages that the group plan can offer and (2) retaining the right to reject an insured group member's election of the optional coverage if the benefit levels of such optional coverages are high and the insured group member cannot provide satisfactory evidence of insurability.

**FAST FACT**

During 2003, U.S. life insurers paid $18 billion in death benefits to group life insurance policy beneficiaries.

**Source:** ACLI, *Life Insurers Fact Book: 2004* (Washington, D.C.: American Council of Life Insurers, 2004), 62.

## Activities of the Group

A group is assigned a risk classification—standard, substandard, or declined—based on the group's normal activities. If the group's activities are not expected to contribute to a greater-than-average loss rate among its members, then the group is classified as a standard risk. Most employer-employee and association groups qualify as standard risks.

If a group's activities are expected to lead to a higher-than-average loss rate among its members, then the group is classified as a substandard risk and is charged a higher premium rate than is a group classified as a standard risk. For example, a group consisting of coal miners may be classified as a substandard risk because of the hazards involved in mining.

If the group's normal activities are extremely dangerous, some insurance companies will decline the group for coverage. For example, many insurers would decline to issue group life insurance coverage to a group consisting entirely of race car drivers.

The extent to which a group's activities affect that group's risk classification depends on the type of coverage provided by the group insurance policy. Activities that significantly affect a group's *morbidity* risk often have little effect on the group's *mortality* risk. Consequently, a group that is assigned a substandard health insurance rating might be assigned a standard rating for a life insurance policy.

# Group Insurance Policy Provisions

Certain provisions are included in every group insurance policy, whether it provides life or health insurance coverage. These standard policy provisions define which group members are eligible for group insurance coverage, identify the policy's grace period, establish when the policy and a group member's coverage become incontestable, and govern when the group insurance policy terminates and when a group insured's coverage terminates.

# Eligibility Requirements

As we noted earlier in the chapter, each group policy describes who is eligible for coverage under the policy. Group insurance policies are permitted by law to define eligible employees as those employees in a specified class or those in specified classes. These classes must be defined by requirements that are related to conditions of employment, such as salary, occupation, or length of employment. For example, most group insurance policies state that an employee must work full-time to be eligible for coverage; thus, part-time workers are excluded from the class of eligible employees.

Some group insurance policies provide coverage both for eligible group members and for the dependents of covered group members. Group insureds who are covered as dependents typically do not have the same rights as do group insureds who are covered as members of the insured group, such as the employees who are covered by an employer-employee group policy. For example, a covered dependent typically does not have the right to name the beneficiary of his coverage; instead, the policy usually specifies that the beneficiary of any dependent group life coverage is the insured group member. Further, if dependent coverage is optional, then the insured group members—not their dependents—have the right to elect or reject that coverage. Because of such differences in the rights of group insureds, we use the term *insured group members* to refer to the individuals who are covered as members of the insured group to distinguish those insureds from other group insureds who are not members of the insured group.

Provisions in many group insurance policies contain requirements that new group members must meet to be eligible for coverage. The most common of these eligibility provisions are the actively-at-work provision and the probationary period. An ***actively-at-work provision*** requires that to be eligible for coverage, an employee must be actively at work—rather than ill or on leave—on the day the insurance coverage is to take effect. If the employee is not actively at work on the day the coverage is to take effect, then the employee is not covered by the group insurance policy until she returns to work.

A ***probationary period*** is the length of time—typically, from one to six months—that a new group member must wait before becoming eligible to enroll in the group insurance plan. A probationary period requirement can reduce a plan's administrative costs when new employees work for only a short period before terminating their employment. Under a noncontributory group insurance plan, a new employee who has met all other eligibility requirements is automatically covered at the end of the probationary period. By contrast, if the plan is contributory, then the probationary period is typically followed by an eligibility period.

The ***eligibility period***, which is also called the *enrollment period*, usually extends for 31 days and is the time during which a new group member may first enroll for group insurance coverage. As part of the enrollment process, the employee must sign a written authorization allowing the employer to make payroll deductions from her salary to cover the amount of her premium contributions; contributory group insurance coverage will not become effective until the employee completes such an authorization. An employee who declines coverage when she first becomes eligible for that coverage or who drops out of the plan ordinarily must submit satisfactory evidence of insurability before she is allowed to join the plan at a later date.

> **Example.** Felipe and Conchita Romero recently relocated to a different city and will soon begin working at new jobs. They both will be eligible for coverage under group life insurance policies provided by their employers. Both policies provide similar coverage, and both include a 30-day probationary period. The primary difference is that Felipe's coverage is noncontributory, whereas Conchita's coverage is contributory. They want to determine when their group insurance coverages will become effective.
>
> **Analysis.** Felipe's noncontributory coverage will automatically become effective on the first day following the end of the 30-day probationary period. Because Conchita's coverage is contributory, her 30-day probationary period will be followed by an eligibility period. At any time during the eligibility period, she may enroll for the coverage and sign a written authorization allowing her employer to deduct her group insurance premium contributions from her salary. Thus, once the 30-day probationary period is over, Conchita's coverage will become effective as soon as she signs the authorization within the eligibility period.

## Grace Period Provision

Group life and health insurance policies typically contain a 31-day grace period provision. As in the case of an individual insurance policy, the insurance coverage provided by a group insurance policy remains in force during the grace period. If the group policyholder does not pay the premium by the end of this period, the group policy will terminate. Unlike the grace period provision in an individual insurance policy, the grace period provision in a group insurance policy specifies that if the policy terminates for nonpayment of premiums, then the group policyholder is legally obligated to pay the premium for the coverage provided during the grace period.

## Incontestability Provision

Group insurance policies include an incontestability provision that limits the period during which the insurance company may use statements in the group insurance application to contest the validity of the master group insurance contract. Generally, the incontestability provision in a group insurance policy limits the period during which the insurer may contest the contract to two years from the date of issue. Material misrepresentation occurs much less frequently in group insurance applications than in individual insurance applications. As a result, insurance companies rarely contest the validity of group insurance contracts.

The incontestability provision also allows an insurance company to contest an individual group member's coverage without contesting the validity of the master group contract itself. Individuals insured under a group insurance policy usually are not required to provide evidence of insurability to be eligible for group coverage. Sometimes, however, group insureds are required to provide such evidence. If a group insured makes material misrepresentations about his insurability in a written application, then the incontestability provision allows the insurer to contest the group insured's coverage on the ground of material misrepresentation in the application. The period during which the insurer has the right to contest the validity of a group insured's coverage usually is one or two years after the date of that group insured's application.

> **Example.** Joey Matsuoko was required to fill out a medical questionnaire to be eligible for group medical expense coverage. In completing the questionnaire, Joey made material misrepresentations about his health. Several months later, Joey filed a claim for medical expense benefits. While investigating the claim, the insurance company discovered Joey's material misrepresentations. The group policy contained a two-year contestable period.
>
> **Analysis.** The insurer discovered the material misrepresentations within two years after Joey's coverage became effective. As a result, the insurer had the right to contest the validity of Joey's coverage on the basis of those material misrepresentations. The validity of the master group insurance contract was not affected by Joey's material misrepresentations.

## Termination Provisions

As we have described, the coverage an individual insurance policy provides is effective as long as the individual insurance policy is in force;

coverage terminates when the individual policy terminates. Similarly, under many types of group insurance contracts, a group member's coverage terminates when the master group policy terminates. However, a group insured's coverage also may terminate even though the group insurance policy remains in effect. The following sections describe group insurance policy provisions that govern (1) when the group insurance policy terminates and (2) when a group insured's coverage terminates.

## Termination of the Group Insurance Policy

According to the terms of most group insurance policies, the group policyholder may terminate the policy at any time by notifying the insurer in writing that it has decided to terminate the policy. For example, if the group policyholder is able to obtain comparable coverage from another insurance company at a lower premium, then the policyholder is likely to switch carriers rather than renew the more expensive policy.

If certain conditions are met, the insurance company also has the right to terminate the group insurance policy on any premium due date. The terms of the policy state the conditions that must be met for the insurer to terminate the policy. Recall, for example, that group insurers often establish participation requirements; if the group's participation level falls below the required minimum, the insurance company has the right to terminate the policy. To terminate the policy, the insurer must provide the group policyholder with advance written notification that the policy will terminate on a specified renewal premium due date.

## Termination of a Group Insured's Coverage

Group insurance policies contain provisions that describe when a group insured's coverage terminates. Most group insurance policies provide that a group insured's coverage terminates if the group insured (1) ceases to be a member of a class of persons eligible for coverage, (2) terminates her employment or group membership, or (3) fails to make a required contribution to the premium.

# Group Insurance Premiums

The group policyholder is responsible for paying the premiums to the insurance company, though group members must contribute to that premium payment if the group insurance plan is a contributory plan. In the following sections, we discuss how the insurer establishes the premium rates to charge for a group's coverage, how specific premium amounts are calculated, and how excess premiums can be refunded.

# Premium Rates

Insurance companies typically establish group insurance premium rates on a case-by-case basis; that is, an insurer evaluates each group and establishes a premium rate that will be adequate to pay the group's claims and will be equitable to the policyholder. To establish premium rates that meet these criteria, the insurer must determine what costs it will incur in (1) providing the benefits promised by the group insurance policy and (2) administering the group insurance plan.

Unlike individual insurance premium rates, the premium rate for a group insurance policy usually is recalculated every year that the policy remains in force. The insurer generally guarantees the group's premium rate for only one year and may change the premium rate at the beginning of each policy year or on any premium due date; it may not, however, change the premium rate more than once in any 12-month period.

Next, we describe how insurers use manual rating, experience rating, and blended rating to establish the initial premium rate to charge a group and to calculate in succeeding years the renewal premium rates that the group will be charged.

## Manual Rating

*Manual rating* is a method insurers use to calculate group insurance premium rates without considering the particular group's prior claims and expense experience. Rather, the insurance company uses its own past experience to estimate the group's expected claims and expense experience. However, an insurer may use industry studies on mortality and expenses when the insurer has limited data on a new product or market or wants to evaluate its own data.

Insurance companies typically use manual rating to set the initial premium rates to charge groups that have not previously been insured and to set both initial premium rates and renewal premium rates for small groups. In both cases, the groups have no prior claims or expense experience on which the insurer can rely to set the premium rate. The claims experience of a small group generally is unreliable because the group is not large enough for the insurer to determine whether the group's prior experience is a result of chance or actually reflects the group's average experience.

## Experience Rating

*Experience rating* is a method of setting group insurance premium rates under which the insurer considers the particular group's prior claims and expense experience. Insurance companies typically use experience rating to set renewal premium rates for large groups. In many cases, insurers also use experience rating to set the initial premium rate to charge a large group that is currently insured by another insurance company. In such a case, the insurer is able to obtain information about the group's prior experience.

## Blended Rating

Some groups are too small for an insurer to rely fully on experience rating, yet they are large enough for the insurer to consider their claims and expense experience to be significant. In such situations, the insurer uses **blended rating**—a method that uses a combination of experience rating and manual rating to set the group's premium rate. The larger the group is, the more credibility the insurer can assign to the group's own experience and the less the insurer relies on manual rating.

## Additional Premium Rate Considerations

Setting a group's premium rate is often a complicated process. In addition to determining whether or to what extent a group's own experience can be used, an insurer also must consider a number of other factors when setting premium rates. For example, the insurer must consider the benefits provided by the group plan. In addition, the amount of administrative expense an insurer incurs in connection with group insurance coverage varies widely from one group to another and depends, to a great extent, on how much of the plan's administration the policyholder will handle. We discuss group insurance administration later in this chapter. For now, keep in mind that many factors enter into an insurer's premium rate calculations. In later chapters, as we describe the benefits that group life and health insurance policies provide, we note how specific coverage factors affect a group's premium rate.

# Premium Amounts

Group insurance premiums typically are payable monthly. As we have described, the insurance company establishes the premium rate for a group insurance policy at the beginning of each policy year. That premium rate typically is calculated on the basis of a stated benefit unit. For example, the premium rate for group life insurance is usually based on a benefit unit of $1,000. In other words, the premium rate is stated as a rate per $1,000 of death benefit provided by the group life insurance policy.

Although the *premium rate* is generally guaranteed for one year, the *premium amount* payable each month varies, depending on the amount of insurance in force that month. A group life insurance policy, for example, requires a monthly premium amount that is equal to the premium rate per $1,000 of coverage multiplied by the number of benefit units ($1,000 of coverage) in force that month. Thus, if an employer hires several new employees one month, the premium amount the employer pays to the insurer will increase; the premium rate per $1,000 of coverage, though, does not change during the year.

**Example.** The Weaver Company provides $25,000 of noncontributory group life insurance coverage for each of its full-time employees. The current monthly premium rate for this coverage is $.35 per $1,000 of coverage. In January, Weaver had 10 full-time employees. In March, Weaver hired 2 new full-time employees, who became eligible for group life insurance coverage in April. Calculate the premium amounts payable each month from January through April.

**Analysis.** In January, February, and March, Weaver provided $25,000 of group life insurance coverage to 10 employees. Thus, the premium amount payable in each of those three months was $87.50.

| | |
|---|---|
| $25,000 | Coverage per employee |
| × 10 | Number of employees |
| **$250,000** | **Total group coverage** |
| | |
| $0.35 | Monthly premium rate |
| × 250 | Number of coverage units ($250,000 ÷ $1,000) |
| **$87.50** | **Monthly premium payment** |

In April, Weaver provided $25,000 of group life insurance coverage to 12 employees. Thus, the premium amount payable in April was $105.

| | |
|---|---|
| $25,000 | Coverage per employee |
| × 12 | Number of employees |
| **$300,000** | **Total group coverage** |
| | |
| $.35 | Monthly premium rate |
| × 300 | Number of coverage units ($300,000 ÷ $1,000) |
| **$105** | **Monthly premium payment** |

## Premium Refunds

At the end of each policy year, a portion of the group insurance premiums paid during the year may be refunded to the group policyholder. Group insurance premium refunds are similar to the policy dividends provided for participating individual life insurance policies and are usually called *dividends* by those companies that also issue individual participating policies. Companies that do not issue participating policies generally call these premium refunds *experience refunds*.

The insurer determines the amount of a premium refund on the basis of its evaluation of the group's claim and expense experience. If the group is large enough, the evaluation is based on that group's experience alone. If the group is small, the evaluation is based on a blend of the experiences of that group and of similar small groups. If the group incurred fewer claims or if the insurer incurred lower administrative expenses than anticipated when the insurer established the group's premium rate, then the insurer refunds a portion of the premium paid for the coverage.

All premium refunds are payable to the group policyholder, even if the plan is contributory. If the amount of the refund to the policyholder of a contributory plan is greater than the portion of the group premium that was paid out of the policyholder's funds, then the excess must be used for the benefit of the individual participants in the plan. For example, when an employer receives a premium refund that is larger than the amount the employer paid out of its own funds, the employer may apply the excess refund to pay a portion of the employees' contributions during the next year or to pay for additional benefits for covered employees.

# Group Plan Administration

Group insurance enables a number of people to be insured at a cost that is relatively low compared to the cost of individual insurance. Insurers are able to provide relatively low-cost group coverage because of the expense savings inherent in the operation of group insurance policies. These savings result from the fact that the expenses an insurer incurs in administering a group insurance policy are much lower than those incurred in administering individual policies. Of course, the cost of administering one group insurance policy is usually higher than the cost of administering one individual policy; but, the cost of administering one group insurance policy covering 50 people is lower than the cost of administering 50 individual policies. For example, underwriting and policy issue costs are generally lower for group insurance because the insurer usually underwrites the group as a whole rather than each individual member, and it issues a master policy rather than many individual policies. In addition, sales costs are much lower for one group policy than for a number of individual policies. Expenses are also lower because the group policyholder often handles many of the clerical duties that the insurer must perform for each individual policy.

The administration of a group insurance plan is primarily a matter of recordkeeping. For example, some of the necessary records for a group life insurance plan include the name of each plan participant, the amount of insurance on each participant, and the name of each beneficiary. If the insurance company maintains these records, the plan is an **insurer-administered plan**. If the group policyholder keeps the records, the plan is a **self-administered plan**. In either case, the insurer receives monthly reports regarding the composition of the group and any changes in the group.

# Key Terms

master group insurance contract
group insured
noncontributory plan
contributory plan
certificate of insurance
certificate holder
trust
trustee
trust fund
trust beneficiary
fiduciary
actively-at-work provision
probationary period
eligibility period
manual rating
experience rating
blended rating
insurer-administered plan
self-administered plan

# Group Life Insurance

## objectives

*After reading this chapter, you should be able to*

- Describe how group life insurance is regulated in the United States

- Describe the purpose and operation of benefit schedules in group life insurance policies

- Identify the party who designates the beneficiary of a group insured's life insurance coverage

- Describe a group insured's conversion rights when the insured's group life insurance coverage terminates

- Contrast the operation of the misstatement of age provision included in individual life insurance policies and that provision included in group life insurance policies

- Identify the features of group term insurance plans, group accidental death and dismemberment plans, group permanent plans, and group creditor life insurance plans

I n terms of coverage amounts, group life insurance is the fastest growing line of life insurance in North America. In 1950, group life insurance accounted for about 20 percent of the total amount of life insurance coverage in force. During the 1970s alone, however, the amount of group life insurance in force in the United States tripled. In 2003, group life insurance accounted for over 42 percent of the total amount of life insurance in force in the United States. In Canada, group life insurance is approaching 50 percent of the total amount of life insurance in force.[1] Figure 13.1 illustrates the growth of group life insurance coverage in the United States.

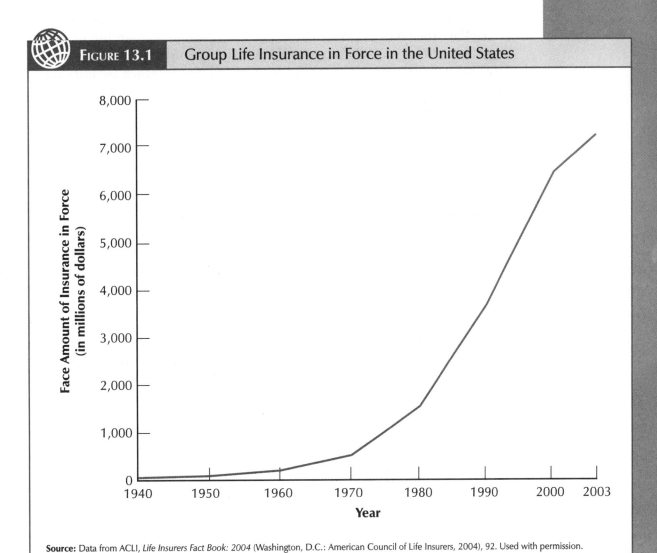

**FIGURE 13.1** Group Life Insurance in Force in the United States

**Source:** Data from ACLI, *Life Insurers Fact Book: 2004* (Washington, D.C.: American Council of Life Insurers, 2004), 92. Used with permission.

We begin our discussion of group life insurance by describing how group life insurance is regulated and some of the provisions that typically are included in group life insurance policies. Then we describe the types of group life insurance policies that are available. Finally, we describe how group creditor life insurance policies differ from other forms of group life insurance.

# Regulation of Group Life Insurance

Because it is an insurance product, group life insurance is subject to the same types of insurance laws and regulations that regulate individual life insurance products. As noted in Chapter 1, in the United States, the states have primary authority to regulate the insurance industry. Thus, the states regulate the content and operation of individual and group life insurance policies. Most states have enacted laws based on the National Association of Insurance Commissioners (NAIC) *Group Life Insurance Definition and Group Life Insurance Standard Provisions Model Act* (*Group Life Insurance Model Act*), and, thus, state regulation of group life insurance is fairly uniform.

Because group life insurance often is provided by employers as an employee benefit, group life insurance also is governed by laws that relate to employer-employee relations. Many countries have enacted laws designed to ensure that all employees are treated equally in the workplace. Employment laws typically prohibit discrimination regarding hiring, advancement, wages, and other terms and conditions of employment. Terms and conditions of employment include employer-sponsored plans that provide employee benefits, such as group insurance plans; consequently, employers must ensure that employee benefit plans comply with these laws.

Many jurisdictions also have enacted laws specifically designed to regulate group insurance plans. In the United States, a number of federal laws directly regulate group insurance plans. For example, the federal *Age Discrimination in Employment Act* (*ADEA*) protects older workers from being discriminated against because of their age.[2] The ADEA prohibits employers with 20 or more employees from discriminating on the basis of age against individuals who are age 40 and older. Because the cost of providing group insurance benefits to older workers is greater than the cost of providing the same benefits to younger workers, employers sometimes reduce the level of benefits provided to older workers. The ADEA permits employers to reduce the level of certain group insurance benefits—including life insurance benefits—for older workers, as long as the employer's premium contributions for those benefits at least equal its contributions for the benefits provided to younger workers. Retired workers are not protected by the ADEA, which does not require employers to provide post-retirement life insurance coverage to their employees.

Another federal law, the **Americans with Disabilities Act (ADA)**, requires that disabled employees of certain employers have equal access to the life and health insurance coverages that are available to other employees.[3] The ADA allows coverage benefit limitations but prohibits the denial or limitation of benefits based solely on the fact that a person has a disability.

Most employer-employee group life and health insurance plans in the United States must comply with the federal **Employee Retirement Income Security Act (ERISA)**, which was designed to ensure that certain minimum plan requirements are contained in employee welfare benefit plans.[4] ERISA defines a **welfare benefit plan** as any plan or program that an employer establishes to provide specified benefits to plan participants and their beneficiaries. Figure 13.2 lists the benefits that subject a welfare benefit plan to ERISA's requirements. ERISA also contains detailed provisions that regulate employer-sponsored retirement plans. We describe how ERISA regulates group retirement plans in Chapter 14.

---

 **FIGURE 13.2**    Employee Benefits that Subject a Welfare Benefit Plan to ERISA

- Medical, surgical, or hospital care benefits

- Sickness, accident, disability, death, or unemployment benefits

- Vacation benefits

   - Day-care benefits

   - Scholarship funds

   - Prepaid legal services

   - Apprenticeship or training programs

   - Certain benefits, which include severance benefits and housing benefits, described in the Labor Management Relations Act*

*The Labor Management Relations Act, also known as the Taft-Hartley Act, is a federal law that regulates labor relations of enterprises engaged in interstate commerce. 29 U.S.C. 141 *et seq.* (2002).

# Group Life Insurance Policy Provisions

In Chapter 12, we described some of the features of a typical group insurance policy. Group life and health insurance policies, for example, typically include provisions that concern eligibility requirements, grace periods, incontestability, and the conditions under which the policy terminates and under which a group insured's coverage terminates. A number of other provisions typically are included in group life insurance policies, and many of these provisions are very similar to provisions found in individual life insurance policies. In this section, we describe some additional provisions that typically are included in group life insurance policies. These provisions relate to (1) benefit amounts, (2) beneficiary designation, (3) conversion, (4) misstatement of age, and (5) settlement options.

## Benefit Amounts

Every group life insurance policy identifies the amount—or the method the insurer uses to determine the amount—of each group insured's life insurance coverage. Group life insurance policies cannot describe coverage amounts on an individual basis, because such a provision would violate group underwriting guidelines that seek to prevent antiselection. Instead, coverage amounts must be established using an objective factor, such as job classification or salary level.

Group life insurance policies typically include a schedule, known as a ***benefit schedule***, that defines the amount of life insurance the policy provides for each group insured. Several types of group life insurance benefit schedules are common in employer-employee plans. One type of benefit schedule bases the amount of coverage on a specified formula. For example, the amount of coverage provided for each employee covered by the group life insurance plan is often a specified multiple of the employee's salary. Alternatively, the benefit schedule may provide a standard amount of coverage for every employee. Still other benefit schedules specify an amount of coverage that varies depending on the employee's job classification. For example, the amount of coverage provided may vary depending on whether the employee is a senior executive, a manager, or a nonmanagement employee. Figure 13.3 provides some illustrations of the types of benefit schedules that may be included in group life insurance policies.

If a group life insurance policy provides coverage for dependents, then the policy includes a separate benefit schedule that defines the amount of coverage provided for each covered dependent. Such a benefit schedule may specify that a flat amount of coverage is provided for all covered dependents, or the benefit schedule may specify one amount for the group member's spouse and a lower amount of coverage for each covered dependent child. Insurance company requirements and the laws of some jurisdictions require that the amount of coverage provided on the dependents

**FIGURE 13.3** | Examples of Group Life Insurance Policy Benefit Schedules

| Benefit Schedule Based on Annual Salary | |
| --- | --- |
| **Salary** | **Amount of Life Insurance** |
| Less than $60,000 | 1 × salary |
| $60,000 to $100,000 | 2 × salary |
| Over $100,000 | 3 × salary |

| Benefit Schedule Based on Standard Amount | |
| --- | --- |
| **Salary** | **Amount of Life Insurance** |
| Any | $50,000 per group insured |

| Benefit Schedule Based on Job Classification | |
| --- | --- |
| **Job Classification** | **Amount of Life Insurance** |
| Nonmanagement personnel | $30,000 |
| Supervisors | $50,000 |
| Managers | $100,000 |
| Officers | $200,000 |

of an insured group member be less than the amount provided for the group member.

## Beneficiary Designation

Under the terms of a group life insurance policy—*unless* it is a creditor group life policy—each insured group member has the right to name a beneficiary who will receive the insurance benefit that is payable when that group insured dies. (We describe creditor group life policies later in the chapter.) The insured group member, rather than the group policyholder, must make this beneficiary designation, and the insured group member has the right to change the beneficiary designation. If the policy provides for dependent coverage, then the insured group member also has the right to designate the beneficiary of such coverage; alternatively, the group policy may specify that the insured group member is automatically designated as the beneficiary of any coverage provided on the group member's dependents.

**Example.** Chuck O'Sullivan is employed by the Dane Company, which purchased a group life insurance policy to insure its employees and their dependents. The group policy provides $100,000 of life insurance coverage on Chuck and $25,000 of life insurance coverage on both Chuck's wife and his son.

**Analysis.** According to the requirements of most insurance companies, Chuck has the right to name the beneficiary who is entitled to receive any group life insurance benefits following his own death. In addition, Chuck will be the named beneficiary who is entitled to receive any benefits payable following the death of his wife and son, or Chuck will have the right to name someone else as the beneficiary entitled to receive those benefits.

The beneficiary designation rules and restrictions that apply to individual life insurance beneficiary designations also apply to group life insurance beneficiary designations. The only other restriction on the insured group member's right to name the beneficiary is that he may *not* name the group policyholder as beneficiary *unless* the plan is a group creditor life plan.

As we noted in Chapter 9, group life insurance policies sometimes include a preference beneficiary clause, which states that if the policyowner does not name a beneficiary, then the insurer will pay the policy proceeds in a stated order of preference. Additionally, some group life insurance policies include a facility-of-payment clause, which permits the insurance company to pay all or part of the policy proceeds either to a relative of the insured or to anyone who has a valid claim to those proceeds. Laws in some states limit the amount that may be paid under a facility-of-payment clause to a maximum of $2,000; any remaining policy proceeds must be paid to the designated beneficiary or to the estate of the group insured.

## Conversion Privilege

Group life insurance policies typically include a conversion privilege. The *conversion privilege* allows a group insured whose coverage terminates for certain reasons to convert her group insurance coverage to an individual policy of insurance, without presenting evidence of her insurability.

The rights of a group insured to convert her group life insurance coverage vary depending on the reason for the termination of that coverage. Two general situations arise in which a group insured's group life insurance coverage terminates: (1) the group insured ceases to be eligible for coverage—she terminates employment, leaves the group, or ceases to be a member of an eligible class—or (2) the group life insurance policy terminates. We describe the group insured's conversion privilege in each of these situations as required by the NAIC Group Life Insurance Model Act.

## Insured's Eligibility for Group Insurance Terminates

When a group insured's coverage terminates because he terminates employment or ceases to be a member of an eligible class, the NAIC Group Life Insurance Model Act requires that he be given the right to purchase individual life insurance without providing evidence of insurability. To exercise the conversion privilege, the group insured must complete an application for an individual life insurance policy and pay the first premium within 31 days after his group coverage terminates.

In general, the group insured is allowed to purchase any type of individual life insurance policy that the insurer is then issuing, but the amount of coverage the group insured may purchase is limited. Some group life insurance policies allow the group insured to convert up to the amount of insurance he received under the group policy. According to the Group Life Insurance Model Act, a group life insurance policy shall provide that the face amount of the individual policy cannot exceed the difference between (1) the amount of the group insured's coverage under the original group life policy and (2) the amount of group coverage for which the insured will become entitled within the 31-day conversion period.

> **Example.** Amin Bhutta, age 35, terminated his employment with the Maroon Company and immediately began working for the Jade Company. Under Maroon's group life insurance policy, Amin had group life coverage of $100,000. Jade's group life insurance policy will provide him with $60,000 of life insurance coverage. Amin would like to convert his Maroon group life insurance to an individual plan.
>
> **Analysis.** The terms of Maroon's group life insurance policy determine the maximum amount of group life coverage that Amin will be allowed to convert to an individual life insurance policy without providing evidence of insurability. According to the Group Life Insurance Model Act, the Maroon policy may limit this amount to a maximum of $40,000, which is the difference between the amount of coverage Amin had under the Maroon policy and the amount he will become entitled to receive under the Jade policy.

The premium rate the insured is charged for the individual life insurance policy is the standard premium rate that the insurance company charges an insured of the group insured's sex and attained age for the type of individual policy that the group insured is purchasing.

## Group Life Insurance Policy Terminates

According to the NAIC Group Life Insurance Model Act, each group insured must be granted the right to convert her group insurance coverage to individual coverage if the group life insurance policy terminates and the group insured was covered under the policy for at least five years before the termination of the policy. In such a situation, each insured group member is given a 31-day conversion period during which she may purchase an individual policy without submitting evidence of insurability. The maximum amount of coverage each group member can purchase is equal to the lesser of either (1) $10,000 or (2) the amount of coverage in force under the group plan minus the amount of group coverage for which the insured becomes entitled within 31 days of the policy's termination.

> **Example.** Jocelyn Carver, Alexandra Shire, and Sam Melendez were employed by the Troup Company when it went out of business, and all were insured under Troup's employer-employee group life policy when that policy terminated. Jocelyn and Alexandra both had been insured for 10 years and had $20,000 of coverage; Sam's $20,000 coverage had been effective for 2 years. Alexandra and Sam obtained new jobs within 2 weeks and became eligible for $15,000 of group life insurance coverage. Jocelyn decided to leave the work force and return to school.
>
> **Analysis.** Sam is not eligible to convert his group life insurance coverage because he was not covered by Troup's plan for at least 5 years. By contrast, Jocelyn and Alexandra had been insured under Troup's group life insurance policy for at least 5 years when it terminated; thus, they have the right to purchase individual life insurance without providing evidence of insurability. Jocelyn may purchase up to $10,000 of individual coverage because she is not entitled to be insured under a new group life insurance policy. Alexandra may purchase up to $5,000 of individual coverage—the difference between the amount of her coverage under Troup's policy ($20,000) and the amount of group coverage to which she became entitled under her new employer's policy ($15,000).

## Extension of Death Benefit

The NAIC Group Life Insurance Model Act requires group life insurance policies to contain a provision that, in effect, extends coverage on a group insured during the 31-day conversion period, even if the group insured does not exercise his conversion privilege. If the group insured dies during the 31-day conversion period and has not been issued an individual policy, then the insurer must pay a death benefit. The death benefit payable is the largest amount that the insurer would have issued as an individual policy to the group insured. Thus, if any individual described in the previous two examples died during the 31-day conversion period without being issued an individual policy, the insurer would be liable to pay a death benefit equal to the amount of insurance the individual was entitled to convert to individual coverage.

## Misstatement of Age

As noted in Chapter 8, the misstatement of age and sex provision included in individual life insurance policies specifies that the insurer will adjust the amount of the death benefit payable to reflect a misstatement of the insured's age or sex. By contrast, the amount of the benefit payable following a group insured's death is specified in the group life insurance policy's benefit schedule. As a result, the misstatement of age provision in most group life insurance policies specifies that if the amount of the premium required for the plan is incorrect as the result of a misstatement of a group member's age, then the insurer will retroactively adjust the amount of the premium required for the coverage to reflect the group insured's correct age. The amount of the death benefit payable remains unaffected. Because group life insurance is rated on a unisex basis, such policies typically do not include a misstatement of sex provision.

## Settlement Options

When a person insured under a group life insurance policy dies, the beneficiary of the group insured's coverage usually receives the death benefit in a lump sum. Sometimes settlement options also are available. If so, the group life insurance policy gives the group insured and/or the beneficiary the right to choose a settlement option. All of the usual settlement options described in Chapter 9 are generally made available. However, for a group insured or beneficiary to select the life income option, the death benefit payable usually must be at least a stated minimum amount.

---

# Group Life Insurance Plans

The majority of all group life insurance policies are yearly renewable term (YRT) insurance plans. Group accidental death and dismemberment plans are also commonly issued, either as separate plans or in addition to other group life insurance coverage. Some group cash value life insurance plans are issued, but these plans are rare and typically provide coverage only for group members who have retired. As we describe these various types of group life insurance plans, we describe some aspects of how these plans are treated for income tax purposes.

# Group Term Life Insurance

The YRT insurance coverage under group life insurance policies is similar to YRT coverage under individual policies. Evidence of insurability is not required from the group insureds each year when the coverage is renewed. These term policies do not build cash values, and the insurer has the right to change the premium rate each year.

When employers pay the premiums to provide their employees with group term insurance, the employees receive a financial benefit. In the United States, with specific exceptions, an employee can receive up to $50,000 of noncontributory group term insurance coverage without incurring an income tax liability. However, an employee must pay federal income taxes on the employer's cost of providing group term life insurance over $50,000. The cost of this coverage, which is not the same as the premium paid by the employer, is determined by reference to a government table.

> **Example.** Laurel Martin and Erik Stein are employed by the Atrium Corporation and are enrolled in Atrium's noncontributory group term insurance plan. Laurel has $75,000 of coverage, and Erik has $45,000 of coverage.
>
> **Analysis.** Laurel and Erik are each entitled to receive $50,000 of noncontributory group term insurance coverage without incurring an income tax liability. Erik has $45,000 of coverage, so he is not required to pay income tax on this benefit. Laurel, however, has $75,000 of coverage, and she must pay income tax on the employer's cost to provide her with the additional $25,000 of coverage.

Group YRT insurance is sometimes used to fund other employee benefit plans that supplement the benefits provided by a group life insurance plan. For example, an employer may establish a **survivor income plan**, which is an employee benefit plan that provides periodic income payments to specified dependents who survive a covered group member. Survivor income benefits typically are funded by group YRT insurance. In other words, when a group insured dies, the proceeds of his YRT insurance pay the benefits promised to his surviving dependents under the survivor income plan.

Most survivor income plans provide monthly installment payments that are based on the amount of the group insured's salary prior to his death and on the number of his surviving dependents. For example, the plan may state that the monthly survivor income benefit payable equals (1) 20 percent of the insured's monthly salary if the insured is survived by only a spouse or only dependent children or (2) 30 percent of the insured's monthly salary if the insured is survived by both a spouse and at least one dependent child. The benefits paid to a surviving spouse usually continue until the earlier of (1) a specified time after the spouse remarries or (2) the spouse reaching age 65. The benefit paid on behalf of a surviving unmarried child usually continues until the child reaches age 19, unless the child is a full-time student, in which case the benefit is paid until the child is no longer a full-time student or until the child reaches age 23, whichever occurs first.

The premiums paid by an employer for survivor income coverage are treated for federal income tax purposes in the manner we described earlier with respect to other group term life coverage. Thus, the amount of coverage necessary to provide the specified income benefits must be calculated. If this coverage amount, along with any other group term benefit amount, exceeds $50,000, then the employee must pay income tax on the employer's cost of providing the excess coverage.

## Accidental Death and Dismemberment Insurance

Accidental death and dismemberment (AD&D) benefits may be included as part of a group life or group health policy, or they may be issued under a separate group insurance policy. The low cost of AD&D benefits makes them an attractive addition to group insurance plans, especially to employer-employee group plans. When the accidental death benefit is added to a group term life insurance plan, the accidental death benefit amount usually is equal to the amount of the death benefit provided under the basic group term insurance plan. For example, assume that a group insured has $50,000 of basic group life insurance coverage and a $50,000 AD&D benefit. If the group insured dies as the result of an accident, the beneficiary would be entitled to receive $100,000.

Many AD&D plans also provide an additional travel accident benefit that covers only accidents occurring while the employee is traveling for the employer. In other words, an employee may die as the result of an accident that occurs while he is traveling. If the accident occurs while the employee is on vacation, his beneficiary will receive benefits under the AD&D coverage only; if the accident occurs while the employee is on a business trip, his beneficiary will receive benefits under the AD&D coverage plus an additional benefit because he was traveling for the employer.

> **Example.** Daisy Fitzpatrick is covered under the group insurance plan provided by the Sycamore Company. Sycamore's policy provides $100,000 of group term life insurance, $50,000 of group accidental death and dismemberment insurance, and $25,000 of business travel accident insurance.

**Analysis.** If Daisy dies in an accident while she is traveling on business for Sycamore, then her beneficiary will be entitled to receive $175,000 in benefits ($100,000 + $50,000 + $25,000). If Daisy dies in an accident while she is on vacation, then her beneficiary will be entitled to receive $150,000 in benefits ($100,000 + $50,000).

Accidental death and dismemberment policies are also often part of the group life insurance plans purchased by travel groups, automobile clubs, or transportation companies, such as railroads and airlines.

**FAST FACT**

During 2003, U.S. life insurers received $25 billion in group life insurance premiums.

**Source:** ACLI, *Life Insurers Fact Book: 2004* (Washington, D.C.: American Council of Life Insurers, 2004), 47.

## Group Cash Value Life Insurance

Group plans that provide cash value life insurance are less popular than group term insurance plans primarily because they do not receive the favorable income tax treatment that group term life insurance plans receive. Nevertheless, group cash value life insurance plans sometimes are used by employers to help their employees purchase life insurance coverage that will continue after retirement, when their group term insurance coverage typically ends. In most situations, group cash value life insurance is offered as a *supplemental coverage*, which means that group members are offered the coverage on an optional basis as an addition to their group term life insurance coverage. Covered employees usually are required to pay a significant portion of the premium for such supplemental coverages. Therefore, participation levels in group cash value life insurance plans generally are much lower than are the participation levels that insurers require under other contributory group insurance plans.

The specific characteristics of group cash value life insurance coverage vary from plan to plan. The three most commonly offered group cash value life insurance plans are (1) group paid-up plans, (2) level premium whole life plans, and (3) group universal life plans. Some employers offer their employees a group variable universal life insurance plan.

### Group Paid-Up Plans

Group life insurance purchased under a group paid-up plan combines paid-up whole life insurance with decreasing amounts of term insurance. These plans are contributory plans under which

- The employee's premium contribution is used as a net single premium to purchase paid-up whole life insurance

- The employer's premium contribution is used to purchase the amount of group term insurance required to bring the employee's total coverage up to a predetermined amount

The total amount of paid-up insurance on each participating employee increases each year, and the amount of group term insurance that the employer must purchase for participating employees decreases each year.

The premium paid by the employer for the term portion of the coverage is eligible for the same favorable income tax treatment that group YRT premiums receive. Although the employee receives no tax benefits in connection with the premiums used to purchase cash value life insurance, that insurance is in force for the employee's lifetime and stays in force after the employee retires or leaves the group.

## Level Premium Whole Life Plans

Some insurance companies make level premium whole life insurance available on a group basis. Level premium coverage usually is written on a limited-payment whole life plan, such as whole life paid-up at age 65. Because these policies build cash values, employers often use them to provide retirement income benefits for employees.

If the group whole life insurance plan is noncontributory, then the employee's rights in the policy's values usually are not vested. As a result, if the employee leaves the group, then his coverage under the group plan terminates and any accumulated cash value belongs to the employer. If the group plan is contributory, then the employee has a vested right in the policy up to the amount of the employee's premium contributions.

## Group Universal Life Plans

Shortly after individual universal life insurance plans were introduced, group insurers began offering group universal life plans. Employers can use these plans to help employees establish life insurance coverage that will continue after the employees retire.

In many ways, group universal life plans function much more like individual insurance policies than like group insurance policies. Under most group universal life plans, an insured group member chooses the amount of premium she wishes to pay; the employer usually does not pay any portion of the premium. In turn, the amount of the policy's cash value depends on the premium amount the group insured pays. Group members can use these products as savings vehicles in the same manner that individual universal life policyowners can.

Group underwriting principles may be used, although if the available coverage amounts are high, as they often are, group members may be required to provide some evidence of insurability to be eligible for the coverage. Group members also can change their coverage amounts, although increases in coverage amounts may require evidence of insurability.

If the group is large enough, the mortality charges assessed under a typical group universal life policy are based on the group's own claims experience. The expense charges for group universal life plans often are lower than comparable charges for individual plans because the group policy-holder handles some of the administrative aspects of the plan.

Group universal life plans differ from most other group life insurance plans in that under a group universal life plan, an individual has *portable coverage*, which means that an insured employee who leaves the group can continue his coverage under the group plan. In most other types of group life insurance plans, an individual who leaves the group and wishes to retain the coverage can do so only by converting her group insurance coverage to an individual insurance policy.

### Group Variable Universal Life Plans

Group variable universal life insurance plans are similar to group universal life insurance plans. However, as with individual variable universal life insurance, the participants are given a choice of different options for investing their cash value.

## Group Creditor Life Insurance

*Group creditor life insurance* is insurance issued to a creditor, such as a bank, to insure the lives of the creditor's current and future debtors. Unlike other group life insurance policies, group creditor life policies designate the policyholder—the creditor—as the beneficiary to receive the benefit payable when a group insured dies. At any given time, the amount of insurance on each group insured is equal to the amount of the outstanding debt that person owes to the policyholder-creditor. In some jurisdictions, the amount of insurance as well as the duration of a covered loan may be subject to maximum limits, regardless of the amount of the debt.

The premium for group creditor life insurance coverage usually is paid by the debtor, although it may be paid entirely by the creditor or shared by the creditor and the debtor. Laws in many jurisdictions impose limits on the premiums that debtors may be charged for such coverage. For example, most states set a maximum premium rate that debtors may be charged. This maximum usually is expressed in terms of a stated maximum premium amount per $1,000 of insurance coverage. If the debtor is required to pay a portion of the premium, he must be given the right to refuse to purchase the group creditor coverage. Note that the terms of a credit transaction may require the debtor to secure the loan with some form of insurance coverage. The creditor, however, may not require the debtor to purchase such coverage from the creditor as a condition of obtaining credit. In other words, the debtor may be required to purchase coverage but has the right to purchase that coverage from any source he chooses.

**Fast Fact**

In 2003, more than $153 billion of group creditor life insurance was in force in the United States.

**Source:** ACLI, *Life Insurers Fact Book: 2004* (Washington, D.C.: American Council of Life Insurers, 2004), 89.

# Key Terms

Age Discrimination in Employment Act (ADEA)
Americans with Disabilities Act (ADA)
Employee Retirement Income Security Act (ERISA)
welfare benefit plan
benefit schedule
conversion privilege
survivor income plan
portable coverage
group creditor life insurance

# Endnotes

1. ACLI, *Life Insurers Fact Book: 2004* (Washington, D.C.: American Council of Life Insurers, 2004), 88; CLHIA, *Canadian Life and Health Insurance Facts*, 2003 ed. (Toronto: Canadian Life and Health Insurance Association Inc., 2003), 1.
2. 29 U.S.C. 621-34 (2001).
3. 29 U.S.C. 12101-213 (2001).
4. 29 U.S.C. 1001 *et seq.* (2001).

# Group Savings and Retirement Plans

## objectives

*After reading this chapter, you should be able to*

- Identify the types of requirements that are imposed by law on qualified employer-sponsored retirement plans

- Explain the tax advantages of certain retirement plans

- Identify and describe the four broad types of employer-sponsored retirement plans

- Distinguish among SEP, SIMPLE, and Keogh plans

- Identify the types of provisions that a plan document must contain

- List and describe the various employer-sponsored retirement plan funding vehicles that U.S. life insurance companies provide

- Describe the features of the U.S. Social Security system and Canada's Old Age Security Act

I n Chapter 11, we described individual annuity products and noted that individuals often purchase such products to provide themselves with an income after they retire. Individual annuities are not the only source of retirement income, however. Often, people receive retirement income from various government programs and from private retirement plans—group retirement plans sponsored by employers and unions. Life insurance companies are involved in the funding and administration of many private retirement plans.

Just as group life and health insurance plans provided as employee benefits are subject to government regulation, so are many private retirement plans. In turn, those private retirement plans that meet various government requirements are granted special income tax benefits. When establishing a retirement plan, employers and unions usually want to ensure that the plan qualifies for favorable income tax treatment. To meet this customer need, life insurance companies design their group retirement products to meet applicable regulatory requirements.

In this chapter, we first examine the various government regulations that apply to group retirement plans and the benefits gained by meeting such requirements. We then describe the types of group retirement plans that are available and how insurance companies are involved in the funding and administration of these retirement plans. We conclude the chapter by describing government-sponsored retirement plans.

# Regulation of Retirement Plans

To encourage employers and unions to establish private retirement plans, income tax laws contain incentives that provide economic benefits to both the **plan sponsors**—the employers and unions that establish plans—and the **plan participants**—the employees and union members who are covered by the plans. As noted in Chapter 11, a U.S. retirement plan that receives favorable income tax treatment by meeting the requirements imposed by U.S. federal tax law and the Employee Retirement Income Security Act (ERISA) is known as a *qualified plan*. In Canada, a retirement plan that meets the legal requirements to receive favorable income tax treatment is referred to as a **registered plan**.

The majority of retirement plan legislation in the United States is provided by ERISA, which we described in Chapter 13. ERISA establishes standards that all qualified retirement plans must meet. Following are some of the requirements that ERISA imposes on qualified retirement plans:

- Nondiscrimination requirements prohibit a qualified retirement plan from discriminating in favor of highly paid employees.

- A retirement plan must contain specified minimum *vesting* requirements that define when a plan participant is entitled to receive partial or full benefits under the plan even if he terminates employment prior to retirement. In all cases, a participant's right to receive benefits funded by his own contributions vests immediately in the participant; those contributions belong to the participant. ERISA imposes time limits within which a plan participant's right to receive benefits funded by employer contributions must vest.

- A variety of requirements are imposed on the investment of plan assets to ensure the safety of those assets. For example, plan assets typically must be held and invested by either an insurance company or the trustee of a trust.

- The plan sponsor is required to report certain information about the plan's provisions to governmental agencies and to plan participants.

- Individuals who administer the plan and hold plan assets are deemed to be fiduciaries, and they must comply with various statutory guidelines in carrying out their duties. Above all, fiduciaries must carry out their duties by acting solely for the benefit of plan participants.

ERISA also amended the federal tax laws as those laws apply to qualified retirement plans. Although tax laws tend to be amended fairly frequently, we can make the following generalizations about the federal income tax treatment of contributions to and earnings from a qualified retirement plan:

- Within stated limits, the contributions that an employer makes to a qualified plan are considered a business expense and are deductible from the employer's current taxable income.

- The contributions an employer makes to a qualified plan on behalf of a plan participant are *not* considered current taxable income to the participant. Instead, a plan participant's payment of income taxes on the employer's contributions is deferred until she actually receives benefits from the plan.

- Depending on the plan, a participant can make tax-deductible contributions, nondeductible contributions, or a combination of both. If a participant has made nondeductible contributions to a qualified plan, the portion of the payments representing that part of the principal is not taxed again when the participant receives benefit payments. However, when she receives benefit payments, a participant pays income tax on the value of any deductible amounts contributed to the plan.

- The investment earnings on plan contributions—whether the contributions are made by the employer or the employee—are allowed to accrue on a tax-deferred basis. As in the case of employer contributions, plan participants pay income taxes on these investment earnings only when they actually receive benefits from the plan.

Some retirement plans are contributory plans that require employees to make contributions to fund the plan. In the United States, employees generally are not able to deduct from their taxable income the amount of their contributions to an employer-sponsored retirement plan. For this reason, many retirement plans in the United States are noncontributory plans that do not require employee contributions. There are exceptions to these rules, however, and we describe some of those exceptions later in the chapter.

# Types of Retirement Plans

The specific provisions of any given retirement plan govern the operation of the plan. We can identify four general types of qualified employer-sponsored retirement plans: (1) pension plans, (2) savings plans, (3) profit sharing plans, and (4) stock bonus plans. The distinctions among these types of plans are important because the statutory requirements imposed on retirement plans vary somewhat depending on the type of plan. Keep in mind, however, that these statutory requirements are complex, and our discussion is intended to provide only a general overview.

## Pension Plans

The term *pension plan* can have a variety of meanings, depending on the context in which it is used. For purposes of our classification system, a ***pension plan*** is an agreement under which an employer establishes a plan to provide its employees with a ***pension***—a lifetime monthly income benefit that begins at retirement. The employer obligates itself to fund, in advance, at least a portion of the pension plan's promised benefits each year. Although pension plans typically provide other types of benefits to covered employees, the primary goal of a pension plan is to provide plan participants with periodic retirement income benefits in the form of a life annuity. In Canada, a pension plan that meets the requirements to qualify for favorable tax treatment is known as a ***registered pension plan (RPP)***. Insight 14.1 describes such registered pension plans.

> ### FAST FACT
>
> In 2002, just over 51 percent of all workers in the United States were participants in a pension plan.
>
> **Source:** U.S. Bureau of Labor Statistics, *Current Population Survey*, March 2003 (Washington, D.C.: Bureau of Labor Statistics, 2003).

## Savings Plans

A ***savings plan*** is a retirement plan to which a plan sponsor may make contributions on behalf of a plan participant if the participant makes

**INSIGHT 14.1** | Canadian Registered Pension Plans

To qualify for favorable federal tax treatment, a retirement income plan must be approved by and registered with the Canada Revenue Agency, which is the federal department that is responsible for Canadian tax, trade, and border administration. The registration requirements vary depending on the type of plan. As a general rule, requirements are similar to the requirements that ERISA imposes on qualified retirement plans in the United States. The following are some of the general types of requirements that a pension plan must meet to qualify for registration:

- The plan must contain specified minimum vesting requirements.

- Plan benefits must be *portable*, which means that benefits can be moved from one registered plan to another.

- Plan assets must be invested in accordance with specified standards.

Those pension plans that meet the requirements for registration with the Canada Revenue Agency are eligible to receive the following tax benefits:

- Employer contributions, within specified limits, are deductible from the employer's current taxable income.

- Employer contributions are not included in the employee's current taxable income.

- Within specified limits, employee contributions are deductible from the employee's current taxable income. An individual taxpayer may contribute to a variety of registered retirement plans and, subject to an overall maximum contribution limit, may deduct the amounts of those contributions from his taxable income.

- Investment earnings are allowed to accrue tax-free until participants receive plan benefits.

contributions to the plan. An account is established for each plan participant, and all contributions made on behalf of a participant are credited to that account and are invested in accordance with the terms of the plan document. The amount of an employee's contributions to a savings plan are subject to statutory limitations; the amount of an employer's contribution usually is equal to the amount contributed by the employee or is a percentage of that amount, subject to a specified maximum. For example, the plan document often specifies that an employee may contribute a percentage of his salary to the plan, subject to specified minimums and maximums, and that the employer matches that contribution up to a stated maximum percentage of the employee's salary.

CHAPTER 14: GROUP SAVINGS AND RETIREMENT PLANS

**Example.** The Compton Company sponsors a savings plan that allows full-time employees to participate by contributing from 1 to 10 percent of their monthly salaries. Compton will match any employee contribution up to a maximum of 3 percent of the employee's salary. Irene Kowalsky, Wilbur Jensen, and Lorie Chen are all full-time employees. During the month of April, Irene made no plan contribution; Wilbur contributed 2 percent of his $2,000 monthly salary, and Lorie contributed 10 percent of her $3,000 monthly salary.

**Analysis.** Wilbur's 2 percent contribution ($40) will be credited to his account, and Compton will make a matching contribution of $40. Lorie's 10 percent contribution ($300) will be credited to her account, and Compton will make a matching contribution of 3 percent of Lorie's $3,000 monthly salary ($90). Because Irene made no contribution to the plan, Compton will make no contribution on her behalf.

Employee contributions to most types of savings plans are not tax deductible. To provide an incentive to employees to participate in such plans, tax laws in the United States allow employees to contribute to a special type of savings plan, known as a ***401(k) plan***, on a pre-tax basis. In other words, when an employee contributes to a 401(k) plan, the amount of her contribution is not included in her current gross taxable income. Instead, the employee will be taxed when she withdraws funds from her 401(k) plan. To participate in a 401(k) plan, an employee must enter into a salary reduction arrangement that permits the employer to deduct the amount of the employee's plan contribution from her salary.

**Example.** Chad Green has become eligible to participate in a savings plan. His friend, Iris Major, has become eligible to participate in a 401(k) plan. Chad and Iris earn the same salary—$30,000 a year—and they have each decided to contribute $2,000 a year to the plan.

**Analysis.** Iris can contribute to her 401(k) plan on a pre-tax basis. As a result, her $2,000 plan contribution reduces the amount of her gross taxable income to $28,000. Chad's contribution to a savings plan has no effect on the amount of his gross taxable income, which remains at $30,000.

Insight 14.2 describes a group RRSP, which is a popular savings plan found in Canada.

---

**INSIGHT 14.2** | Canadian Group Registered Retirement Savings Plans

A s we noted in Chapter 11, an individual who wishes to establish a retirement savings program in Canada can purchase a registered retirement savings plan (RRSP) and, within stated limits, can deduct the amount of his annual plan contributions from his taxable income for federal income tax purposes. Many employers in Canada sponsor group RRSPs to help their employees save for retirement. A **group RRSP** is an employer-sponsored registered retirement savings plan in which an account is established for each participating employee. Employ-

ees and employers are permitted to make plan contributions within specified limits, and any employer contributions are treated as if they were made by the employee. As a result, all funds deposited into an individual's account are immediately vested with the employee, and for income tax purposes the employee can deduct the amount of all contributions— employee and employer—from his current taxable income.

---

**FAST FACT**

In 2002, Canadians paid more than $11 billion in group annuity premiums.

**Source:** CLHIA, *Canadian Life and Health Insurance Facts*, 2003 ed. (Toronto: Canadian Life and Health Insurance Association Inc., 2003), 10.

## Profit Sharing Plans

A **profit sharing plan** is a retirement savings plan that is funded primarily by cash contributions payable from the employer's profits. Because employer contributions to such plans are based on company profits, and profits can fluctuate, the amount of contributions varies from year to year. If conditions warrant, the employer may not make any contribution in some years. Although a profit sharing plan accumulates retirement assets on behalf of plan participants, the plan does not promise to provide monthly retirement income benefits.

Employers are permitted some latitude with respect to the amount of their plan contributions. Nevertheless, U.S. federal laws impose conditions that qualified profit sharing plans must meet. Qualification rules require that employer contributions (1) must be substantial and recurring and (2) cannot unduly benefit highly paid employees. Although most profit sharing plans are noncontributory plans, some plans in the United States allow employee contributions.

## Stock Bonus Plans

A **stock bonus plan** is a retirement plan into which a corporate plan sponsor makes contributions on behalf of plan participants in the form of the corporation's stock. A *stock option plan* is regarded as a type of stock bonus plan. Contributions to a stock bonus plan are not dependent upon corporate profits. The value of the stock shares, however, fluctuate. Stock bonus plans accumulate retirement assets on behalf of participants, but do not promise to provide a monthly retirement income.

# Retirement Plans for Small Businesses and the Self-Employed

Small employers, including self-employed individuals, often find the costs associated with setting up a retirement plan to be prohibitive. In the United States, several additional types of retirement plans can be established by small employers; such retirement plans are eligible for tax advantages, but they do not have to comply with ERISA to the extent that most large private retirement plans must comply. A self-employed individual is considered both the employer and the employee under these plans, which include simplified employee pensions, savings incentive match plans for employees, and Keogh plans.

## Simplified Employee Pensions

A *simplified employee pension* (*SEP*) is a written plan that allows an employer to make contributions to an individual retirement arrangement (IRA) for each participating employee, although the employer is not required to contribute each year. To participate in the plan, an employee must have an IRA into which the employer deposits its contributions. Note that it is the employee—not the employer—who owns the IRA. Because the employee owns the SEP IRA, the employee is immediately vested in all amounts that are deposited into the IRA. Contributions to a SEP in 2004 could not exceed the lesser of (1) 25 percent of the employee's compensation up to $205,000 or (2) $41,000. This dollar limit is subject to cost-of-living adjustments after that year.

Although employers can no longer establish SEP plans that allow for employee pre-tax contributions, employers and employees may still make pre-tax contributions to existing plans established before 1997. The employer's contributions to SEP IRAs are tax deductible as a business expense from the employer's taxable income, subject to the legislatively defined maximums. The amount of an employer's contributions generally is not taxable to the plan participants. A self-employed person can deduct from his taxable income contributions made to his own plan. Earnings on all contributions are tax deferred. Withdrawals are allowed without penalty only after age 59½, and withdrawals of contributions and investment earnings are taxable as income.

## Savings Incentive Match Plans for Employees

Small business owners and self-employed persons may choose to establish a savings incentive match plan for employees (SIMPLE) IRA or a savings incentive match plan for employees (SIMPLE) 401(k). A *savings incentive match plan for employees (SIMPLE) IRA* is a written salary reduction agreement between an employer with 100 or fewer employees and its employees; the agreement allows eligible employees (including self-employed individuals) to choose to

- Reduce compensation by a certain percentage each pay period and

- Have the employer contribute the amount of the salary reduction to a SIMPLE IRA on the employee's behalf

Contributions are subject to legislatively established maximum amounts. In addition, the employer must make either

- Matching contributions—if the employee chooses to make salary reduction contributions—in an amount equal to the employee's contributions up to a maximum of 3 percent of the employee's annual compensation or

- Nonelective contributions—whether or not the employee chooses to make salary reduction contributions—in an amount equal to 2 percent of the employee's annual compensation

All contributions to a SIMPLE IRA must be fully vested in the employee. Generally, withdrawals from a SIMPLE IRA must comply with the same requirements imposed on withdrawals from other types of IRAs.

A *savings incentive match plan for employees (SIMPLE) 401(k)* is a special arrangement whereby an employer with 100 or fewer employees can establish a simplified 401(k) plan for employees. The SIMPLE 401(k) functions in much the same way as a regular 401(k) plan—both the employer and the employee can make contributions to the plan up to a specified maximum.

Under the SIMPLE IRA and the SIMPLE 401(k), the employee's and employer's contributions are excluded from the employee's current income. The employer's contributions are tax deductible to the employer as a business expense, and investment earnings accumulate on a tax-deferred basis. Withdrawals of contributions and investment earnings are taxable as income.

## Keogh Plans

A *Keogh plan*, also known as an *HR 10 plan*, is a qualified retirement plan set up by a self-employed individual, sole proprietorship, or partnership to which the business or individual can make annual tax-deductible contributions, subject to certain limits and conditions. Contributions are excluded from the employee's current income, and earnings are tax deferred. Withdrawals of contributions and investments earnings are taxable as income. Withdrawals may begin as early as age 59½ and must begin by age 70½.

# Components of a Retirement Plan

A retirement plan consists of three components: (1) the plan, which describes how benefits will be funded and paid to participants; (2) a method for administering the plan; and (3) the funding vehicle into which the plan assets are invested. Insurance companies are involved in activities related to all three of these components—designing and developing retirement plans, administering retirement plans, and providing retirement plan funding vehicles.

## The Plan

The plan sponsor must determine the type of plan to establish and the terms of that plan, which are spelled out in a plan document. A *plan document* is a detailed legal agreement that establishes the existence of an employer-sponsored retirement plan and specifies the rights and obligations of various parties to the plan. Among other things, the plan document must describe the benefits that are provided by the plan, how the plan will be funded, and the procedure that will be followed to amend the plan. In addition, plan participants must receive a summary plan description that informs them of their rights under the plan. In this section, we describe some of the types of provisions that a plan document must contain.

### Coverage, Eligibility, and Participation Requirements

The plan document must describe which group members are covered by the plan. The covered group typically is defined in terms of job class, location of the work site, salary, and/or occupation. For example, a plan may cover all non-union employees.

The plan document must specify which group members are eligible to participate in the plan. The most common eligibility requirement is a service requirement, which states a minimum required length of service a group member must have to be eligible for plan participation. Some plans also impose an age requirement that states a minimum age a group member must be to be eligible to participate. In the United States, employees who are 21 years of age or older and who have at least one year of employment typically are eligible to participate in a pension plan. Eligibility requirements are limited by law in some jurisdictions. In the United States, for example, a retirement plan may not set a maximum age for participation.

The plan document also must specify when employee participation in the plan becomes effective. Employer-sponsored retirement plans typically specify a start date, which is the date that participation in the plan becomes effective. The start date usually is the first day of the month or the first day of the calendar year following the person's completion of the plan's eligibility requirements. Participation in an employer-sponsored retirement plan can be automatic or voluntary.

- If participation is *automatic*, all eligible group members are automatically enrolled as plan participants. Typically, noncontributory plans are automatic plans.

- If participation is *voluntary*, eligible group members have a choice between participating or not participating in the plan. Typically, contributory plans are voluntary plans.

Thus, participants in an employer-sponsored retirement plan are members of the covered group who are eligible to participate in the plan and who actually choose to take part in the plan or whose participation is automatic.

## Benefit Formulas

A retirement plan's **benefit formula** describes the calculation of the plan sponsor's financial obligation to plan participants. Two types of benefit formulas are common—*defined benefit formulas* and *defined contribution formulas*. A **defined benefit formula** specifies the amount of retirement benefit a plan sponsor promises to provide to each plan participant. A retirement plan structured according to a defined benefit formula is referred to as a **defined benefit plan**. All defined benefit plans are pension plans, and these are the only retirement plans that provide a specific and guaranteed lifetime income benefit at retirement.

A **defined contribution formula** specifies the level of contributions that the plan sponsor promises to make to the plan. A retirement plan structured according to a defined contribution formula is referred to as a **defined contribution plan**. The benefit that a participant will receive is not determined in advance of the participant's retirement but depends on the investment performance of the funds in the plan. Savings plans, profit sharing plans, and stock bonus plans are defined contribution plans.

In recent years, the defined contribution plan has become increasingly popular among plan sponsors establishing pension plans. The reason for this rise in popularity is that when an employer establishes a defined contribution plan, it knows in advance what it will cost to fund the plan each year. By contrast, an employer that is funding a defined benefit plan must rely on actuarial estimates of what it will cost each year to fund the plan. There also is no guarantee that the costs will not go beyond what is estimated. In addition, ERISA imposes more complex requirements on defined benefit plans than it imposes on defined contribution plans.

## Plan Administration

The plan sponsor usually names a *plan administrator* who becomes responsible for a variety of aspects of the plan's operation. Although the plan administrator usually is a named individual, the administrator may be the sponsoring employer or it may be a board or committee established by the employer. The plan administrator is responsible for maintaining service records on all participants. These records ensure that the plan's eligibility and vesting requirements are met. Records also are needed to determine the amount of benefits payable to participants. The plan administrator uses these records to prepare all required reports for governmental agencies and for providing the plan participants with information about the plan.

In many cases, the services of various professionals are required to operate a retirement plan according to its terms; the plan administrator is responsible for hiring these professionals. For example, the services of an actuary typically are required to determine the amount of contributions that are needed to fund a defined benefit plan. The plan administrator also may need to obtain the services of other professionals, such as accountants, attorneys, and consultants. Life insurers often provide such administrative services for retirement plans. In some cases, a life insurer provides only administrative services to a plan. In other cases, the insurer provides both administrative services and a funding vehicle for the plan.

## Funding Vehicles

The sponsor of a retirement plan must choose a funding vehicle for the plan. A *funding vehicle*, also known as an *investment vehicle* or *funding instrument*, is an arrangement for investing a retirement plan's assets. Retirement plan funding vehicles can be classified according to whether they are allocated or unallocated.

- An *allocated funding vehicle* is one in which all of the plan sponsor's contributions are credited to individual participants in a manner that gives the participants a legally enforceable claim to the benefits related to those contributions. In practice, life insurance companies are the only financial institutions that can provide for individual allocation of assets.

- An *unallocated funding vehicle* is one in which some or all contributions are pooled together and not assigned to individual participants until each participant begins to collect benefits. Under an unallocated investment contract, the plan sponsor's contributions are credited to a pooled account. Any type of financial institution can provide unallocated investment contracts.

A defined benefit plan would be more likely to use an unallocated funding vehicle rather than an allocated funding vehicle. A defined contribution plan could use either type of vehicle, but typically such plans use an unallocated funding vehicle. The most common funding vehicles are trusts and group insurance contracts. Insight 14.3 describes trust arrangements for retirement plans.

Life insurers offer a variety of products that are designed as retirement plan funding vehicles, and insurers are quite flexible in tailoring their products to meet the specific needs of a plan sponsor. We describe the most common types of retirement plan funding vehicles that are offered by U.S. life insurance companies, including deposit administration contracts, immediate participation guarantee contracts (IPGs), separate account contracts or riders, guaranteed investment contracts (GICs), group annuity contracts, group deferred annuity contracts, and individual policy pension trusts.

## Deposit Administration Contracts

Although no longer offered by most insurance companies, deposit administration contracts are still in force. A *deposit administration contract* is a type of retirement plan funding vehicle in which a plan sponsor deposits plan assets with an insurance company, which places the assets in its general account. When a plan participant retires, the insurer withdraws sufficient funds from the general account to provide an immediate annuity for the plan participant. The insurance company usually provides the plan sponsor with guarantees against investment loss, as well as guarantees

---

 **INSIGHT 14.3** | Trusts as Retirement Plan Funding Vehicles

Most employer-sponsored retirement plans use a trust agreement to facilitate investment arrangements. Such a trust is based on the same legal principles as trusts used for other purposes. (See Insight 12.1 for a description of trusts.) With a retirement plan trust, the grantor of the trust is the plan sponsor, and the plan assets are placed into the trust. The trustee is typically the plan sponsor when the sponsor is a small company; a larger employer typically hires a bank or trust company to act as the trustee of its retirement plan. The trust beneficiaries are the plan participants.

The trust agreement specifies the terms under which the trust operates. Plan trustees bear the responsibility for receiving and investing plan contributions and paying benefits under the plan. Plan trustees are fiduciaries who are responsible for carrying out their duties solely for the benefit of the plan participants. Although plan trustees are responsible for investing plan assets, they may delegate that duty to investment managers. In all cases, those individuals responsible for investing plan assets must act in accordance with the plan document and the plan's investment policies. Plan assets may be invested in a variety of investment instruments, including deposit accounts, certificates of deposit, stocks, bonds, or mutual funds.

regarding minimum investment returns. Further, the insurer usually guarantees, in advance, the price of the immediate annuity to be purchased at the time of a plan participant's retirement. When the immediate annuity is purchased, the insurance company guarantees the amount of the periodic annuity benefit that will be paid to the plan participant.

A deposit administration contract is an unallocated funding vehicle that is suited for use with defined benefit plans.

## Immediate Participation Guarantee (IPG) Contracts

Under an *immediate participation guarantee (IPG) contract*, the retirement plan's assets are held in an investment account in the name of the plan sponsor and deposited in the insurer's general account on behalf of the plan sponsor. Typically, IPG contracts do not provide the full guarantees against investment loss or the guarantees regarding the minimum investment returns that are provided through deposit administration contracts. Instead, an IPG contract is designed to allow the plan sponsor to share in the gains or losses experienced by the life insurance company as it invests and pays benefits from its general account. Many IPG contracts, however, guarantee that the plan sponsor will not share in losses greater than a stated amount. When a plan participant retires, funds may be withdrawn to purchase an immediate annuity for that retiree, or the retirement benefit may be paid directly each month from the IPG account to the retired person.

IPGs are unallocated funding vehicles. Although IPGs may be used for defined contribution plans, they typically are used for defined benefit plans.

## Separate Account Contracts

Under a *separate account contract* (or *rider*), the insurance company invests the retirement plan assets in its separate account. As described in Chapter 6, an insurer's separate account consists of a number of subaccounts; the insurer follows a different investment strategy for each subaccount. A separate account rider usually is used as an addition to a deposit administration or IPG contract. In either case, the plan sponsor chooses the subaccounts into which plan contributions are to be placed.

Separate account contracts and riders usually do not make any guarantees regarding investment returns or even preservation of the invested principal. When a plan participant retires, the plan sponsor is permitted, but is not required, to purchase an immediate annuity from the insurer to provide periodic retirement income benefits. Retirement income benefits also may be paid directly from one of the insurer's subaccounts.

A separate account contract or rider is an unallocated funding vehicle used for both defined benefit and defined contribution plans.

## Guaranteed Investment Contracts (GICs)

Under a basic **guaranteed investment contract** (**GIC**), also called a *guaranteed interest contract* or a *guaranteed income contract*, the insurer accepts a single deposit from the plan sponsor for a specified period of time, such as five years. Some GICs allow the plan sponsor to make monthly contributions rather than a single up-front deposit. GICs generally have a specified maturity date and guarantee the repayment at the maturity date of the amounts deposited under the contract, plus the amount of credited interest, less withdrawals.

The contract guarantees that at least a specified interest rate will be paid on deposited funds during the contract period. The plan sponsor can choose for interest earned to be (1) accumulated until the GIC expires or (2) paid annually. At the end of the contract period, the account balance—including any accumulated interest—is returned to the plan sponsor.

Like separate account contracts, GICs permit but do not require the plan sponsor to purchase an immediate annuity from the insurer at the time of a plan participant's retirement. GICs are unallocated funding vehicles used primarily for defined benefit plans.

## Group Annuity Contracts

Although IPGs, separate account contracts and riders, and GICs sometimes are referred to as *group annuity contracts*, defined contribution plans often use a type of contract that is called a group annuity contract. A **group annuity contract** operates much like an immediate participation guarantee contract with a separate account rider. The contract itself is unallocated but the insurance company typically offers a coordinating service package that includes allocation services to accommodate the individual participant recordkeeping requirements of defined contribution plans.

## Group Deferred Annuity Contracts

A **group deferred annuity contract** is a retirement plan funding vehicle that provides plan participants with annuities upon their retirement. The insurance company usually issues a master group contract to the plan sponsor and issues certificates to each individual plan participant. Each year, the plan sponsor uses the contributions made on behalf of each plan participant to purchase a single-premium deferred annuity for that plan participant. When the plan participant retires, benefit payments from these deferred annuities will provide the scheduled retirement benefits. Group deferred annuities are a type of allocated funding vehicle.

## Individual Policy Pension Trusts

An **individual policy pension trust**, also known as a *412(i) plan*, is a type of allocated funding vehicle that typically is used for small pension plans.

Under this arrangement, plan trustees annually purchase individual life insurance or individual annuity contracts for each participant in the plan. Note that this arrangement uses individual, not group, annuities. An individual policy pension trust is one instance in which a defined benefit plan uses an allocated funding vehicle.

Figure 14.1 summarizes our discussion of insurance company contracts used as retirement plan funding vehicles.

| FIGURE 14.1 | Features of Insurance Contracts Used for Retirement Plan Funding | | | | |
|---|---|---|---|---|---|
| **Type** | **Principal Guaranteed** | **Interest Guaranteed** | **Purchase of Annuity(ies) at Guaranteed Rates** | **Allocated Funding Vehicle** | **Unallocated Funding Vehicle** |
| **Deposit administration contract** | ✔ | ✔ | ✔ | | ✔ |
| **Immediate participation guarantee contract** | Some contracts | | ✔ | | ✔ |
| **Separate account contract or rider** | | | Some contracts | | ✔* |
| **Guaranteed investment contract** | ✔ | ✔ | Some contracts | | ✔* |
| **Group annuity contract** | | | Some contracts | | ✔* |
| **Group deferred annuity contract** | ✔ | ✔ | ✔ | ✔ | |
| **Individual policy pension trust** | ** | ** | ** | ✔ | |

\* Defined contribution plans use a service agreement for allocations.
\*\* Depends on the nature of the underlying life insurance policy or annuity contract.

**Source:** Adapted from Mary C. Bickley, *Principles of Financial Services and Products* (Atlanta: LOMA, © 2004), 318. Used with permission; all rights reserved.

# Government-Sponsored Retirement Plans

The governments of many countries have established plans that provide periodic retirement income benefits to qualified residents. Many employer-sponsored retirement plans determine the amount of plan benefits by factoring in the amount of benefits that will be payable under government-sponsored plans. In the United States, government retirement income benefits are provided under several programs, including (1) the Civil Service Retirement Act, (2) the Railroad Retirement Act, and (3) the Old Age, Survivors, Disability and Health Insurance (OASDHI) Act, or, as it is better known, Social Security. *Social Security* is a federal program that provides specified benefits, including monthly retirement income benefits, to people who have contributed to the plan during their income-earning years. The program also provides a benefit to qualified disabled individuals, as well as to the surviving spouses and dependent children of qualified deceased workers.

Nearly all people employed in the United States, including those employed by the armed forces, are covered under Social Security. The only sizable groups not covered are federal civil service workers who are covered by the Civil Service Retirement Act, railroad workers who are covered by the Railroad Retirement Act, and some state and municipal civil service workers. Participation in the Social Security system is not mandatory for state civil service workers at this time, and several states provide their own retirement programs for their civil service workers. Other states, however, have voluntarily joined the Social Security system, and their civil service employees are covered by the Social Security program. Because Social Security covers far more people than do the other government plans, we limit our discussion to the pension plan provided through Social Security.

Social Security provides a monthly income benefit to people who have contributed to the system during their income-earning years. Social Security retirement benefits are available to covered persons who are age 62 or older, although people retiring before their full retirement age of 65 or older typically receive a lesser monthly benefit amount than they would receive if they retired at age 65 or older. The federal government administers the Social Security system and makes frequent changes in the system's funding and benefits.

The Social Security plan is funded by mandatory contributions from covered workers and their employers. During their working years, each covered worker must contribute a stated percentage of her earned income, up to a specified maximum yearly contribution amount. An individual's employer contributes an amount equal to that contributed by the employee. A self-employed participant must contribute a higher percentage of earnings than does an employee because a self-employed person's contributions are not matched by any employer contributions.

The amount of monthly benefit a person receives depends on the wages earned during the contribution period and is also subject to a specified maximum amount. However, the amount of retirement benefit is increased periodically to reflect increases in the cost of living, as measured by the Consumer Price Index (CPI) in the United States. The *Consumer Price Index (CPI)* measures the change in the price of a fixed basket of goods and services bought by a typical consumer. The goods and services included in the CPI include food, transportation, housing, utilities, clothing, and medical care.

In Canada, retirement income benefits are provided to retirees through three separate government plans, which are described in Insight 14.4.

---

 **INSIGHT 14.4** Canadian Government Pension Plans

Pensions are provided to Canadian retirees through three separate government plans: (1) the Old Age Security Act, which is in effect throughout Canada; (2) the Canada Pension Plan, which operates in all Canadian provinces except Quebec; and (3) the Quebec Pension Plan, which operates only in Quebec.

**Old Age Security Act**
The federal *Old Age Security (OAS) Act* is a universal public pension plan that provides a pension to virtually all Canadian residents who are age 65 or older. The right to receive a pension under the OAS Act is not depen-

dent on a person's preretirement wages, current employment, or marital status. Each person who has reached age 65 and has met certain residency requirements receives the same pension amount; this pension amount is tied to the Canadian Consumer Price Index and increases along with increases in that index. The money to fund these pensions is taken from federal government general tax revenues.

**Canada Pension Plan and Quebec Pension Plan**
The *Canada Pension Plan (CPP)* is a federal program that provides a pension for wage earners who have contributed money into the plan during their working years. The CPP covers workers in all provinces except Quebec, which has elected to establish its own provincial plan. The *Quebec Pension Plan (QPP)* functions in the same manner as the CPP except that the QPP applies only to wage

earners in Quebec. The CPP and QPP are closely coordinated and tend to operate as one plan. In addition to pension benefits, the CPP and the QPP provide survivorship benefits, lump-sum death benefits, benefits for orphans, and long-term disability income benefits.

Participation in these plans is mandatory for employees covered by the plans, and virtually all employees and self-employed persons in Canada are covered. Benefits are funded through compulsory contributions from employees, their employers, and self-employed persons. The amount of the monthly benefit paid following retirement is related to the amount contributed to the plan by or on behalf of the person; the amount is also limited to a legislatively established maximum amount. Benefit amounts are adjusted annually to reflect any cost-of-living increases.

# Key Terms

plan sponsor
plan participant
registered plan
vesting
pension plan
pension
registered pension plan (RPP)
savings plan
401(k) plan
group RRSP
profit sharing plan
stock bonus plan
simplified employee pension (SEP)
savings incentive match plan for employees (SIMPLE) IRA
savings incentive match plan for employees (SIMPLE) 401(k)
Keogh plan
plan document
benefit formula
defined benefit formula
defined benefit plan
defined contribution formula
defined contribution plan
plan administrator
funding vehicle
allocated funding vehicle
unallocated funding vehicle
deposit administration contract
immediate participation guarantee (IPG) contract
separate account contract or rider
guaranteed investment contract (GIC)
group annuity contract
group deferred annuity contract
individual policy pension trust
Social Security
Old Age Security (OAS) Act
Canada Pension Plan (CPP)
Quebec Pension Plan (QPP)

# Part 4:
# Health Insurance

# Medical Expense Coverage

## objectives

*After reading this chapter, you should be able to*

- Identify the most common types of basic medical expense coverage and describe the benefits that each provides

- Identify the purpose of expense participation features in major medical expense policies and give examples of commonly used expense participation methods

- Recognize the types of medical expenses that major medical policies commonly cover and those that are commonly excluded from coverage

- Identify and describe the most common types of supplemental medical expense coverage

- Explain the differences between Medicare and Medicaid

- Describe the primary types of managed care plans and the techniques they use to manage the costs, utilization, and quality of health care services

- Describe the three primary forms of consumer-driven health care plans

**M**ost people cannot afford to pay the full costs of their medical treatment should they become seriously ill, nor can most people afford a loss of income when they are unable to work because of an illness or injury. Life and health insurance companies market a range of individual and group health insurance products designed to protect against the risk of financial loss insureds are likely to experience as the result of an illness or injury. As noted in Chapter 1, the two major forms of health insurance coverage are as follows:

1. *Medical expense coverage*, which provides benefits to pay for the treatment of an insured's illnesses and injuries. This chapter describes medical expense insurance coverage.

2. *Disability income coverage*, which provides income replacement benefits to an insured who is unable to work because of sickness or injury. We describe disability income coverage in the next chapter.

In the United States and Canada, most people are covered by some form of medical expense insurance. Medical expense insurance coverage in the United States is provided to individuals and groups primarily by a private system of commercial life and health insurance companies and other private health insurance providers. Government-sponsored medical expense insurance programs are designed to cover only specified people, including the elderly and the poor. Figure 15.1 shows the percentages of individuals in the United States who have various types of health insurance coverage.

By contrast, virtually everyone residing in Canada has medical expense insurance coverage provided by government-sponsored programs. Life and health insurance companies market products designed to supplement the coverages provided by governmental programs, but such private coverage represents only a small portion of the medical expense insurance coverage in force in Canada.

Medical expense insurance coverage in the United States is available in three basic forms: (1) traditional medical expense insurance policies, which offer indemnity benefits, (2) government-sponsored health care programs, and (3) private managed care plans. Medical expense coverage also is available in the form of consumer-driven health plans.

## Traditional Medical Expense Insurance

Traditional medical expense insurance products provide ***indemnity benefits***, or *reimbursement benefits*, which are contractual benefits that are provided

| FIGURE 15.1 | Health Insurance Coverage in the United States, 2003 |
| --- | --- |

| Type of Coverage | Percentage of Total U.S. Population |
| --- | --- |
| Covered by some form of health insurance (private or government) | 84.4% |
| Private coverage | 68.6% |
| Employment-based private coverage | 60.0% |
| Direct-purchase private coverage | 9.0% |
| Government-provided coverage | 26.6% |
| Medicare coverage | 13.6% |
| Medicaid coverage | 12.4% |
| Military plan coverage | 3.5% |
| No health insurance coverage | 15.6% |

**Source:** U.S. Census Bureau, "Historical Health Insurance Tables," 26 August 2004, http://www.census.gov/hhes/hlthins/historic/hihistt2.html (15 October 2004).

based on the actual amount of the insured's financial loss. Under traditional medical expense insurance policies, insureds are reimbursed for the covered medical expenses they incur up to a stated maximum dollar amount. When an insured receives medical treatment for an illness or injury from any licensed provider of recognized medical services, the insured is responsible for paying the medical care provider's charges. The insured then files a claim with the insurance company for policy benefits. If the insurer determines that the charges are covered under the policy, the insurer reimburses the insured for the expenses according to the terms of the insurance policy. Alternatively, the medical care provider can file a claim with the insurer for the total cost of treatment and then bill the insured for any amount that remains after the insurer pays its share of the claim.

Traditional medical expense insurance provides three types of coverage: (1) basic medical expense coverage, (2) major medical expense coverage, and (3) supplemental medical expense coverage. These coverage options can be offered under separate policies or combined under a single policy, and the coverage can be offered on a group or individual basis.

# Basic Medical Expense Coverage

When insurance companies first offered medical expense policies, most policies provided *basic medical expense coverage*, which consisted of separate benefits for each of the following types of medical expenses:

- *Hospital expenses*, which include charges for specific inpatient and outpatient hospital services, such as room and board, medications, laboratory services, and other fees associated with a hospital stay

- *Surgical expenses*, which include charges for inpatient and outpatient surgical procedures

- *Physicians' expenses*, which include charges associated with physicians' visits both in and out of the hospital

Coverage for each of these expenses can be provided by separate policies, or several types of expenses can be covered under one policy.

Basic medical expense coverage typically provides *first-dollar coverage*—that is, the insurer begins to reimburse the insured for eligible medical expenses without first requiring an out-of-pocket contribution from the insured. However, benefits provided under basic medical expense policies typically are limited, and many types of medical expenses are not covered.

# Major Medical Expense Coverage

Today, rather than offering basic medical expense coverage, most health insurers offer *major medical expense coverage*, which provides substantial benefits for (1) basic hospital, surgical, and physician expenses, (2) additional medical services related to illness or injuries, and (3) preventive care.

### Types of Major Medical Expense Coverage

Two types of major medical coverage are commonly available: (1) supplemental major medical and (2) comprehensive major medical. A *supplemental major medical policy* is a policy issued in conjunction with an underlying basic medical expense insurance policy. The supplemental policy is designed to provide benefit payments for expenses that exceed the benefit levels of the underlying basic plan and, often, for expenses that are not covered by the underlying plan.

A *comprehensive major medical policy* is a single policy that combines the coverages provided by both a supplemental major medical policy and an underlying basic medical expense policy. A comprehensive major medical policy provides substantial medical expense coverage under one policy, and that policy covers most of the medical expenses the insured may incur. Today, the majority of medical expense insurance policies are issued as comprehensive major medical policies.

**FAST FACT**

During 2002, Canadian insurance companies paid almost $9 million in health insurance benefits.

**Source:** CLHIA, *Canadian Life and Health Insurance Facts*, 2003 ed. (Toronto: Canadian Life and Health Insurance Association Inc., 2003), 14.

## Covered Expenses

The benefits provided by major medical expense coverage include payment for many different types of medical treatments, supplies, and services. Major medical expense policies usually cover a wider range of medical expenses than do basic medical expense policies. The covered services and treatments typically include all or some of the following medical expenses:

- Hospital charges for room and board in a semiprivate room

- Miscellaneous inpatient hospital charges, such as laboratory fees, X-rays, medications, and the use of an operating room

- Surgical supplies and services

- Anesthesia and oxygen

- Physical, occupational, and speech therapy

- Surgeons' and physicians' services

- Registered nurses' services

- Specified outpatient expenses, such as laboratory fees, X-rays, and prescription drugs

- Preventive services, such as childhood immunizations and periodic screening and diagnostic tests

Major medical policies allow the insured to seek medically necessary treatment from any licensed provider of recognized medical services.

## Benefit Amounts

Major medical expense policies, like all health insurance policies, pay benefits only for allowable expenses—that is, those expenses the insured incurs that are covered under the policy. Most policies specify a maximum benefit amount that the insurer will reimburse for any allowable expense. In most cases, the maximum benefit amount payable for a particular service is based on the usual, customary, and reasonable fee for that service. The *usual, customary, and reasonable (UCR) fee* is the amount that medical care providers within a particular geographic region commonly charge for a particular medical service. For example, an insurer might set its maximum benefit amount for an appendectomy in a given state at 90 percent of the UCR fee for the procedure in that state. If an insured files a claim for an amount that is equal to or less than the maximum benefit for the treatment received, then the insurer will allow the entire amount of the claim. If the amount of the claim is greater than the maximum benefit, then the insurer will allow expenses up to the maximum and the insured is responsible for paying fees that exceed the maximum benefit amount.

Most major medical expense policies also include a maximum lifetime benefit amount, such as $1 million. Under such a policy, benefit payments cease after the insured person has received the maximum benefit amount specified in the policy.

## Expense Participation Requirements

Under most major medical expense policies, allowable expenses are subject to expense participation, or cost-sharing, requirements that are designed to encourage insureds to control the amount of their medical expenses. The two most common forms of expense participation requirements are deductibles and coinsurance, and most major medical expense policies include both a deductible and a coinsurance feature.

A **deductible** is usually a flat dollar amount of eligible medical expenses, such as $200 or $500, that the insured must pay before the insurer begins making any benefit payments under a medical expense insurance policy. Most major medical expense policies contain a **calendar-year deductible**, which is a deductible that applies to the total of all allowable expenses an insured incurs during a given calendar year. An insured's payments toward the deductible are calculated separately for each year, and partial deductibles generally are not carried forward. In other words, an insured is required to pay the deductible specified in the policy each calendar year in which he submits claims.

> **Example.** Michael DuPont is covered by a comprehensive major medical expense policy that specifies a $500 calendar-year deductible. During 2004, Mr. DuPont incurred a total of $400 in allowable expenses. In 2005, he incurred a total of $800 in allowable expenses.
>
> **Analysis.** Because Mr. DuPont's allowable expenses for 2004 did not meet the $500 calendar-year deductible specified in his policy, he was required to pay the entire $400 in expenses he incurred that year. In 2005, he was required to pay $500 of the $800 in allowable expenses he incurred to satisfy the policy deductible, but he was eligible to receive reimbursement from the insurer for at least a portion of the remaining $300.

The amount of the deductible specified in group major medical expense policies is generally lower than the amount specified in individual major medical expense policies.

**Coinsurance** is an expense participation requirement imposed by many medical expense plans; the requirement generally is a specified percentage of all allowable expenses that remain after the insured has paid the deductible and that must be paid by the insured. Most major medical expense policies set the coinsurance amount at 10, 20, or 30 percent of allowable expenses that remain after the insured has paid the deductible amount.

> **Example.** Suppose that, in addition to a $500 calendar-year deductible, Mr. DuPont's policy included a 20 percent coinsurance requirement.
>
> **Analysis.** Of the $800 he incurred in allowable expenses for 2005, Mr. DuPont was responsible for paying the $500 deductible and coinsurance equal to $60 (0.20 × $300). His total out-of-pocket costs, therefore, were $560 ($500 + $60). The insurer paid the remaining $240 ($800 − $560).

Most major medical expense policies limit the amount of money the insured must pay under the coinsurance provision by including a stop-loss provision. The *stop-loss provision* specifies that the policy will cover 100 percent of allowable medical expenses after the insured has paid a specified amount out-of-pocket to satisfy deductible and coinsurance requirements.

> **Example.** Maria Alvarez is covered by a comprehensive major medical policy that specifies a $500 calendar-year deductible, a 20 percent coinsurance requirement, and a $5,000 stop-loss provision. Ms. Alvarez incurred a total of $2,500 in allowable expenses in January when she was hospitalized for treatment of an illness. In May of that same year, Ms. Alvarez incurred an additional $30,000 in allowable expenses when she underwent surgery.
>
> **Analysis.** Of the $2,500 in allowable expenses Ms. Alvarez incurred in January, she was required to pay $500 to meet the policy's calendar-year deductible and an additional $400 (0.20 × $2,000) in coinsurance. The insurer paid the remaining $1,600. Because she had satisfied her deductible in January, Ms. Alvarez was required to pay only coinsurance on the allowable expenses she incurred in May. The amount of this coinsurance was $6,000 (0.20 × $30,000). However, the stop-loss provision in her policy requires Ms. Alvarez to pay only $5,000 of her expenses for the year. Because she had already paid $900 in deductible and coinsurance amounts in January, she paid only $4,100 of her May expenses ($5,000 − $900). The insurer paid the remaining $25,900.

## Exclusions

Although major medical expense policies cover most medical expenses, they commonly exclude from coverage any medical expenses that result from the following treatments:

- Cosmetic surgery other than corrective surgery required as a result of an accidental injury or other medical reasons

- Treatment of an illness or injury that occurs while the insured is in military service or that results from an act of war

- Treatment of intentionally self-inflicted injuries

- Treatment that is provided free-of-charge in a government facility or that is paid for by other organizations

- Routine dental treatments, routine eye examinations, and corrective lenses

An insured who incurs expenses for excluded services or for services not covered under the policy is required to pay the full amount of those expenses. In addition, excluded or non-allowable expenses are not counted toward the insured's deductible.

# Supplemental Medical Expense Coverage

Insurance companies offer a range of supplemental medical expense coverages to provide benefits for expenses that exceed the benefit levels covered by major medical expense policies or for expenses that are not covered under those policies. The supplemental medical expense coverages that are most commonly offered are dental expense coverage, prescription drug coverage, vision care coverage, dread disease coverage, critical illness coverage, and long-term care coverage. U.S. insurers also offer a variety of Medicare supplements, which we describe in the next section of this chapter. Most types of supplemental coverage are provided in stand-alone policies.

## Dental Expense Coverage

Basic and major medical expense policies typically do not provide benefits for expenses incurred in obtaining routine dental work and dental treatments. As a result, *dental expense coverage*—which provides benefits for routine dental examinations, preventive work, and dental procedures needed to treat tooth decay and diseases of the teeth and jaw—typically is provided under a separate supplemental dental expense policy.

Most dental expense policies include both a deductible and a coinsurance feature. Most policies also provide different levels of coverage for different types of treatment. For example, because early detection and treatment of dental problems can result in significantly lower expenses overall, most dental policies provide full coverage for routine examinations and other preventive work to encourage insureds to obtain regular dental checkups. Policies provide lower amounts of coverage for basic services, such as fillings, and major services, such as root canals or crowns. Deductibles typically also are required for basic and major services. A common benefit structure used in dental expense policies is a "100-80-50" structure, in which the insurer pays 100 percent of expenses incurred for preventive services, 80 percent of expenses of basic services, and 50 percent of expenses for major services.

## Prescription Drug Coverage

Another common supplemental benefit is *prescription drug coverage*, which provides benefits for the purchase of drugs and medicines that are prescribed by a physician and are not available over-the-counter. Prescription drug coverage usually requires the insured to pay part of the cost of the prescription out-of-pocket at the time of purchase. The insured, or in some cases the pharmacy, then submits a claim for the remainder of the cost of the prescription to the insurer or an organization that administers the prescription benefits. To encourage physicians and patients to help control costs, some policies now provide benefits for over-the-counter drugs, as long as they are prescribed by a physician for treatment of a specific condition.

Benefit levels and expense participation requirements for prescription drug coverage usually vary according to the type of drug. For example, some policies require insureds to pay one out-of-pocket amount for generic drugs and a higher amount for brand-name drugs. As an alternative, some medical expense policies and most managed care plans include a *formulary*, which is a listing of drugs by therapeutic category or disease class, that are considered preferred therapy and that are to be used by providers in prescribing medications. The insured's out-of-pocket expenses depend on whether a prescribed drug is included in the formulary. Some medical expense policies and managed care plans provide no benefits for non-formulary drugs; others cover drugs not included in the formulary, but at a lower level than for formulary drugs. Coverage also can be structured to include three expense participation levels—the insured is required to pay (1) a stated amount for generic drugs included in the formulary, (2) a higher amount for brand-name drugs included in the formulary, and (3) a still higher amount for non-formulary drugs.

## Vision Care Coverage

*Vision care coverage* provides the insured with benefits for expenses incurred in obtaining eye examinations and corrective lenses. Vision care coverage generally provides benefits to cover one routine eye examination per year for each insured. Policies also specify the maximum benefit amount the insurer will pay for eyeglass lenses and frames or contact lenses.

## Dread Disease Coverage

In some states in the United States, insurers offer **dread disease coverage** to provide benefits for medical expenses incurred by an insured who has contracted a specified disease. The most commonly offered form of coverage is cancer insurance. Supplemental dread disease coverage typically is issued in combination with basic medical expense coverage and serves the same purpose as major medical expense coverage if the insured should incur medical expenses as a result of having the disease named in the policy.

## Critical Illness Coverage

As an alternative to dread disease coverage, some insurers offer **critical illness (CI) coverage** that pays a lump-sum benefit if the insured is diagnosed with a critical illness while the policy is in force. The conditions that are considered critical illnesses are specified in the policy and usually include heart attack, stroke, and life-threatening cancer. Other conditions generally are listed, but the specific conditions covered vary from insurer to insurer. CI coverage typically includes a return-of-premium benefit that is payable if the insured dies without having a critical illness.

## Long-Term Care Coverage

An increasing number of insurers offer **long-term care (LTC) coverage**, which provides benefits for medical and other services needed by insureds who, because of their advanced age or the effects of a serious illness or injury, need constant care in their own homes or in a qualified nursing facility. To encourage taxpayers to purchase LTC coverage, U.S. and Canadian federal income tax laws allow taxpayers to deduct premiums paid for LTC coverage as a medical expense, subject to certain limitations. In addition, benefits received from an LTC policy are nontaxable.

The specific benefits provided by long-term care policies vary widely depending on the policy, but most policies offer coverage for both skilled nursing home care and in-home custodial care to help insureds perform normal daily activities. Benefit levels also vary depending on the policy, but most policies give insureds the option to add an inflation protection feature that allows benefit levels to increase with increases in the cost of living. Figure 15.2 lists some of the typical features of LTC policies.

| Figure 15.2 | Typical Features of Long-Term Care Insurance Policies |

| Feature | Details |
|---|---|
| Basic services | Nursing home care (includes skilled, intermediate, and custodial care)<br>Home health care<br>Assisted living |
| Optional services/benefits | Alternate care<br>Hospice care<br>Respite care<br>Care coordination/case management<br>Homemaker/chore assistance<br>Bed reservation<br>Medical equipment coverage<br>Spousal discount |
| Daily benefit | Nursing home care: $75-$250/day<br>Home health care: Percentage of nursing home rate or specified amount/day |
| Benefit eligibility | Medical necessity, cannot perform activities of daily living (bathing, continence, dressing, eating, toileting, and transferring), or cognitive impairment |
| Benefit period | 1 year–lifetime |
| Deductible period | 0–100 days |
| Pre-existing condition exclusion | 0–6 months, for conditions disclosed on the application |
| Renewability | Guaranteed renewable |
| Alzheimer's disease coverage | Yes |
| Age limits for purchasing | 18–99 years |
| Waiver of premium | Yes |
| Free-look period | 30 days |
| Inflation protection | Yes |
| Nonforfeiture benefits | Shortened benefit period, return of premium, or reduced paid-up coverage |

**Source:** Health Insurance Association of America, Long-Term Care Market Survey, 1996. Used with permission.

# Government-Sponsored Medical Expense Coverage

In many countries, governments or public agencies provide citizens with comprehensive medical expense coverage of core health care services, including hospital care and physician services. The scope of such government-sponsored coverage varies greatly from country to country. In Canada, for example, the federal *Canada Health Act* affirms the Canadian government's commitment to providing a universal, accessible, comprehensive, portable, and publicly administered health insurance system.[1] Provinces that establish medical expense insurance plans that meet the conditions set out in the Act qualify to receive federal funding for their plans. Each province and territory provides a medical expense insurance plan that provides benefits to qualified residents. Insight 15.1 describes these provincial medical expense plans and the coverages that commercial insurers offer to supplement the benefits provided by the provincial plans.

Although the U.S. government provides medical expense insurance benefits through several government programs, such programs provide coverage only to specified individuals. The most important of these programs are Medicare and Medicaid.

## Medicare

*Medicare* is a federal government program established by the *Old Age, Survivors, Disability and Health Insurance (OASDHI) Act* that provides medical expense benefits to elderly and disabled persons. Medicare benefits are available to the following groups:

- Persons age 65 or older and eligible for Social Security or Railroad Retirement benefits

- Persons with qualifying disabilities (regardless of age)

- Persons with end-stage renal disease or their dependents

Certain persons not meeting these requirements can purchase benefits.

Medicare consists of three components: Medicare Part A and Part B, which provide services and benefits to program enrollees, and Medicare Advantage, which addresses delivery of services and program administration.

*Medicare Part A* provides basic hospital insurance that covers the costs of inpatient hospital services, confinement in nursing facilities or other extended care facilities after hospitalization, home care services following hospitalization, and hospice care. Individuals who satisfy Medicare eligibility requirements are automatically enrolled in Medicare Part A and pay no premiums for coverage. However, Medicare Part A has deductible and coinsurance requirements, which are reviewed annually. Medicare Part A is funded primarily from a payroll tax imposed on employees and employers.

*Medicare Part B* provides benefits to cover the costs of physicians' professional services, whether the services are provided in a hospital, a physician's office, an extended-care facility, a nursing home, or an insured's home. Benefits under Medicare Part B also cover ambulance services,

## INSIGHT 15.1 — Canada's Provincial Medical Expense Insurance Plans

Although the insured services provided by Canada's provincial medical expense insurance plans vary somewhat from plan to plan, the following services are generally provided:

- Hospital services that are medically necessary to maintain health, prevent disease, or diagnose or treat an injury, illness, or disability

- Physician services, which include specifically defined medical services provided by medical practitioners

- Surgical-dental services, which include specifically defined surgical-dental procedures performed in a hospital

Some provincial plans also provide certain residents with additional coverages, including benefits for preventive dental care and prescription drugs.

Provincial laws allow commercial insurers to offer health insurance coverages to supplement the coverages provided by the provincial health plans. As a result, many employers offer extended health care coverage to their employees under group health insurance policies offered primarily by traditional health insurance companies. Individual health insurance policies are also available.

The benefits provided under supplemental, extended health care insurance policies vary widely. Many policies, for example, provide supplemental hospital benefits. The hospital benefit provided by the provincial government plans is based on the cost of a bed in a hospital ward; a supplemental policy usually provides a benefit to make up the difference in cost between a bed in a ward and a semiprivate room. Private health insurance policies often include coverage of the cost of prescription drugs and out-of-country emergency care. Some policies also cover vision care expenses, such as the cost of eyeglasses or corrective lenses, and dental care expenses, such as preventive dental care. Supplemental health insurance policies also may cover any number of other miscellaneous medical expenses. For example, many health insurance policies provide benefits to reimburse the insured for expenses incurred for ambulance services, hearing aids, private-duty nursing care, and care in a convalescent home.

Many of the features of major medical policies described earlier in this chapter are also found in policies in Canada. For example, policies issued in Canada typically include expense participation features—deductibles and coinsurance. The deductible amount, however, tends to be much lower in Canada than in the United States. Policies issued in both countries contain the same types of exclusions; in Canada, however, policies also exclude all services that the provincial health plans cover. Unlike major medical policies issued in the United States, health insurance policies issued in Canada usually contain no overall maximum benefit amount.

medical supplies and equipment, hospital outpatient services, diagnostic tests, and other services necessary for the diagnosis or treatment of illness or injury. Unlike Medicare Part A, Medicare Part B is a voluntary program and enrollment is not automatic. Eligible beneficiaries must enroll for Part B coverage; participants pay monthly premiums, which are deducted from their Social Security benefits, plus an annual deductible and coinsurance. Although Medicare Part B is funded primarily from participant premiums, additional funding is provided from the federal government's general tax revenues.

*Medicare Advantage* is a relatively recent alternative to Medicare Part A and Part B and is available in most areas of the United States. Medicare beneficiaries who are enrolled in both Medicare Part A and Part B may elect to enroll in a Medicare Advantage plan provided by a participating insurance company or managed care plan and to receive coverage under that private plan rather than under the traditional Medicare plan. Figure 15.3 lists the service delivery options that Medicare Advantage offers to enrollees.

All Medicare Advantage plans must cover at least Medicare Part A and Medicare Part B benefits. The federal government pays a set amount to the private plan for those services regardless of the number of services used by enrollees. Additional services may be offered as part of the benefit package or as a supplement for which enrollees may be required to pay extra.

---

 **FIGURE 15.3** | Medicare Advantage Service Delivery Options

- **Traditional fee-for-service**, under which the federal government reimburses providers for the actual services they deliver to enrollees.

- **Private fee-for-service (PFFS) plans**, under which coverage is provided by private insurance carriers rather than by the federal government.

- **Coordinated care plans (CCPs)**, which are managed care plans that include (1) health maintenance organizations, with or without an out-of-network benefit component, (2) preferred provider organizations, and (3) provider-sponsored organizations.

**Source:** Adapted from Mary C. Bickley, *Principles of Financial Services and Products* (Atlanta: LOMA, © 2004), 169. Used with permission; all rights reserved.

In December, 2003, the *Medicare Prescription Drug, Improvement, and Modernization Act* was signed into law. The Act calls for prescription drug plans to be available to Medicare recipients in 2006. In the meantime, in 2004 Medicare began contracting with private companies to offer drug discount cards that can help Medicare recipients save 10 to 25 percent on prescription drugs.

Because Medicare Part A and Part B cover only a portion of enrollees' expenses, Medicare recipients frequently purchase supplemental Medicare coverage. These supplements are private medical expense insurance policies that reimburse insureds for out-of-pocket expenses, such as deductibles and coinsurance payments, or provide benefits for medical expenses excluded from Medicare coverage.

Two major forms of Medicare supplement coverage are available: Medigap insurance policies and Medicare SELECT plans. A ***Medigap policy*** is an individual medical expense insurance policy sold by an insurance company to supplement Medicare Part A and Part B coverage. A ***Medicare SELECT plan*** is a managed care plan that supplements Medicare Part B coverage. Medicare SELECT does not apply to Part A benefits.

Federal laws contain extensive rules to prevent overlap or duplication of the benefits provided by Medicare and private Medicare supplement policies. These rules define the individuals for whom Medicare will be the primary payer and secondary payer of benefits. Private insurance plans include similar provisions to integrate their medical benefits with those provided by Medicare and prevent insureds from receiving more in benefits than the actual expenses incurred.

## Medicaid

***Medicaid*** is a joint federal and state program that provides basic medical expense and nursing home coverage to the low-income population and certain aged and disabled individuals. The federal government establishes broad guidelines for Medicaid programs, provides partial funding for states, and sets minimum standards for eligibility, benefits, and provider participation and reimbursement. Individual states provide additional funds and administer the programs.

Each state is free to customize its Medicaid program as long as the program satisfies minimum federal requirements. For example, states can expand benefits beyond federal guidelines by offering coverage for services such as prescription drugs, dental care, or vision care. States also can expand eligibility to include certain other groups. In all cases, Medicaid is considered the secondary payer of benefits. Thus, Medicaid benefits are paid only after benefits from all other available sources have been exhausted.

# Managed Care Plans

Over the last several decades, medical expense insurance coverage in the United States has changed dramatically. In the past, most medical expense insurance coverage was provided by traditional medical expense insurance, which dealt only with financing health care services. In other words, traditional medical expense insurance was concerned only with an individual's medical bills.

Today, most insureds in the United States are covered by some type of managed care plan. *Managed care* is a method of integrating the financing and delivery of health care services within a system that manages the cost, accessibility, and quality of care. A *managed care plan* is an arrangement that integrates the financing and management of health care with the delivery of health care services to a group of individuals who have enrolled in the plan. *Managed care organizations* (*MCOs*) are the entities that operate managed care plans, and the terms *managed care plans* and *managed care organizations* are often used interchangeably.

## Principles of Managed Care

Managed care plans differ from traditional medical expense insurance plans in a number of ways, including the ways in which they manage (1) health care services, (2) access to those services, (3) utilization of services, and (4) costs of services.

### Medical Management

MCOs oversee the types of health care services offered to plan members to ensure that members receive medically necessary and medically appropriate services and that resources are not used for unnecessary or excessive services. This process is referred to as medical management. Most managed care plans define *medically necessary services* as those services that are considered to be

- Consistent with the symptoms, diagnosis, and treatment of the member's condition

- In accordance with the standards of good medical practice

- Not solely for the convenience of the plan member, member's family, physician, or other health care provider

- Furnished in the least intensive type of medical care setting required by the plan member's condition[2]

*Medically appropriate services* are diagnostic or treatment measures for which the expected health benefits exceed the expected risks by a margin wide enough to justify the measures.[3] In general, questions of medical necessity apply to the needs of particular plan members and drive case-by-case decisions. For example, a question may arise concerning the medical necessity of a specific surgical procedure for a specific plan member. Questions of medical appropriateness apply to a plan's member population and drive decisions that affect segments of that population. For example, the medical appropriateness of a certain prescription drug for treatment of a specific medical condition is a question that might be considered as it affects all plan members.

Within the framework of medically necessary and appropriate services, managed care plans offer a menu of basic medical benefits, many of which are mandated by federal and state laws. In addition, managed care plans typically offer

- Extensive preventive care programs, including prenatal and well-baby care, routine physical examinations, screening programs, 24-hour telephone line access to a nurse, and childhood immunizations

- Access to wellness programs, including smoking cessation, weight management, and stress management programs

- Patient education programs, including seminars, newsletters, and medical self-help booklets

## Network Management

Managed care plans seek to control health care costs through the use of provider networks. A *network* is a group of physicians, hospitals, and ancillary services providers that a specific managed care plan has contracted with to deliver health care services to plan members. Ancillary, or supplemental, services providers include laboratories, radiologists, home health care providers, and physical, speech, and occupational therapists. Provider contracts specify how providers will be paid by the managed care plan and include certain risk sharing elements, which we describe in the next section.

Managed care plans typically require plan members to choose providers from within the network or offer financial incentives to members who choose network providers. Some plans also include in their networks *primary care providers* (*PCPs*), also referred to as *primary care physicians*, who coordinate members' medical care and treatment. In a PCP-based system, a plan member selects a PCP from among the network of providers and receives basic medical care, preventive care, and wellness care directly from the PCP, without obtaining authorization from the plan. To receive specialized care, however, the plan member usually must obtain authorization or a referral from the PCP. The PCP thus serves as a plan member's point of entry into the managed care system and as a gatekeeper to additional services. Plans typically encourage members to obtain services through PCPs by requiring little or no out-of-pocket cost for PCP-based care.

## Utilization and Quality Management

Managed care plans also manage costs through a process of ***utilization management***, which is designed to help ensure that plan members receive the most appropriate care from the most appropriate provider in the most appropriate and most cost-effective setting. In most managed care plans, utilization review, case management, and disease management are important components of the utilization management process. These components are described in Figure 15.4.

| FIGURE 15.4 | Components of the Utilization Management Process |
|---|---|

***Utilization review (UR)*** is a process that managed care plans use to evaluate the medical necessity, appropriateness, and cost-effectiveness of health care services and treatment plans. Although the specific details of UR vary from plan to plan, most UR programs include the following components:

- ***Prospective review***, which is the review and possible authorization of proposed treatment plans for a plan member before the treatment is implemented

- ***Concurrent review***, which is the review of treatment plans and services provided to a plan member while he is in the hospital or receiving ongoing treatment

- ***Retrospective review***, which involves evaluating the treatment and services that a plan member received

***Case management*** is a process by which a managed care plan (1) identifies plan members who require extensive, complex health care, (2) develops an appropriate treatment strategy based on medical necessity and appropriateness and the availability of alternative care solutions, and (3) coordinates and monitors patient care. Case management is most often used in situations in which the plan member has an illness or injury that is likely to require very expensive treatment.

***Disease management*** is a coordinated system of preventive, diagnostic, and therapeutic measures intended to provide cost-effective, quality health care for a patient population who have or are at risk for a specific chronic illness or medical condition. Disease management programs focus on specific conditions and coordinate care for those conditions across different providers and health care delivery settings.

**Source:** Excerpted from Mary C. Bickley, *Principles of Financial Services and Products* (Atlanta: LOMA, © 2004), 175. Used with permission; all rights reserved.

Quality management and improvement programs are designed to ensure that plan members receive high-quality care. Such programs include peer review for PCPs and specialists, accreditation standards for hospitals and ancillary services providers, overall plan accreditation standards, and performance evaluation.

## Cost Sharing

Managed care plans seek to manage health care costs by requiring plan members and medical care providers to share the cost of health care services. In most managed care plans, plan members receive comprehensive health care in exchange for payment of a fixed, periodic—usually monthly—premium. This premium covers the cost of most health care services, no matter how often the member uses those services. In addition, when a plan member receives services from a network provider, the plan member generally pays a specified, fixed amount, known as a *copayment*, to the provider.

> **Example.** Vincent Morgan is a member of a managed care plan that requires a $15 copayment for physician office visits and a $20 copayment for prescription drugs. On February 1, Mr. Morgan visited his PCP for treatment of a sprained ankle. During the office visit, X-rays were taken of Mr. Morgan's ankle. The PCP also wrote Mr. Morgan a prescription for pain medication.
>
> **Analysis.** Before leaving the PCP's office, Mr. Morgan paid a $15 copayment to cover the office visit. The remaining charges for the office visit, including the X-rays, were covered by the managed care plan. When Mr. Morgan took his prescription to the pharmacy, he paid a $20 prescription copayment. The pharmacy billed the managed care plan for the remaining cost of the prescription.

Although copayments are significantly lower than deductibles and coinsurance requirements included in traditional medical expense insurance policies and managed care plans, they provide an incentive for plan members to manage the utilization, and therefore the cost, of health care services.

Managed care plans also encourage medical care providers to deliver necessary care in a cost-effective way by requiring them to share in the financial risk of providing medical care. Managed care plans achieve risk sharing by negotiating fee arrangements with medical care providers and making other contractual agreements that encourage cost-effective care. Negotiated fee arrangements for in-network providers generally include salaries, fee schedules, fee caps, and capitation payments. A *capitation payment* is a flat amount a provider receives from an MCO each month for each plan member who is under the provider's care, regardless of the number or cost of services provided to the plan member. If the costs of medical services exceed the provider's negotiated fee, the provider must absorb the loss. Out-of-network providers typically are reimbursed on a fee-for-service basis.

## Types of Managed Care Plans

Several types of managed care plans have been developed in response to consumer needs and rising health care costs, and employers may offer their employees a choice of plans. The distinctions among the plans often hinge in part on how they manage plan members' access to health care services. As noted earlier, managed care plans manage access through the use of provider networks.

Although classifying managed care plans is not easy, they generally fall into one of the following basic categories: health maintenance organizations, point-of-service plans, preferred provider organizations, and managed indemnity plans. These basic plan types are part of a health care continuum, shown in Figure 15.5, that is anchored at one end by traditional indemnity medical expense insurance and at the other end by pure managed care.

### Health Maintenance Organizations

In the United States, a **health maintenance organization (HMO)** is a health care financing and delivery system that provides comprehensive health care services to plan members—often referred to as *subscribers*—in a particular geographic area. HMOs typically require subscribers to gain access to services through a primary care provider, and subscribers must use in-network providers; no benefits are provided for services rendered by

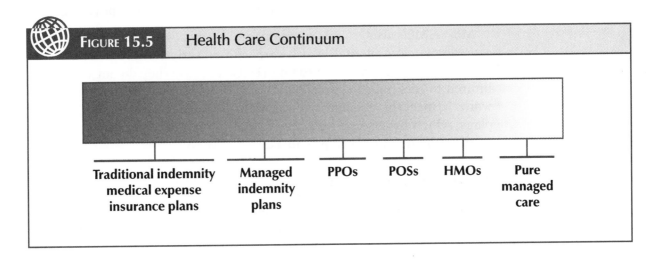

**FIGURE 15.5** | Health Care Continuum

Traditional indemnity medical expense insurance plans | Managed indemnity plans | PPOs | POSs | HMOs | Pure managed care

non-network providers. Subscribers are required to pay a small copayment at the time of service, but they do not pay deductibles or coinsurance, and they are not required to file claims for benefits.

Several types, or models, of HMOs have been created. HMOs usually can be broadly classified as either an open panel HMO or a closed panel HMO, depending on how the HMO staffs its network of participating health care providers.

- An **open panel HMO** is one in which any physician or provider who meets the HMO's specific standards can contract with the HMO to provide services to subscribers. The HMO contracts with physicians who agree to provide services to the HMO's subscribers. The physicians are independent practitioners who have established their own offices with their own supplies and support staff and provide services for their own patients as well as the HMO's subscribers. The HMO compensates participating physicians with capitation payments, or they pay them on a discounted fee-for-service basis whereby physicians are paid a stated percentage of their normal fees. These payment structures place much of the financial risk of providing medical care on the participating physicians.

- A **closed panel HMO** is one that provides health care services to subscribers by either (1) directly employing physicians in an arrangement known as a **staff model HMO** or (2) contracting with one or more physicians' group practices in an arrangement known as a **group model HMO**. In a staff model HMO, the HMO employs physicians who are paid a salary and operate out of offices in the HMO's facilities. The HMO also may own or contract with hospitals, laboratories, pharmacies, and other organizations to provide ancillary medical services. A group model HMO functions much like a staff model HMO, except that the physicians are employees of a physicians' group practice and typically the HMO pays a negotiated capitation rate to the group practice, which in turn pays salaries to the physicians.

Most HMOs also provide supplemental medical services, such as vision care, dental care, mental health care, and prescription drugs. Many consumers have been unwilling to join HMOs because they do not want to be limited to seeking care from only those providers within the HMO network. To meet this consumer concern, HMOs created point-of-service (POS) plans, which have some features of an HMO but extend coverage to care provided by non-network providers.

## Preferred Provider Organizations

A **preferred provider organization (PPO)** is a health care benefit arrangement that provides incentives for plan members to use network providers, but also provides at least some coverage for services rendered by non-network providers. PPOs do not provide health care directly to plan members; instead, they act as brokers or middlemen by contracting with health care providers to deliver medical services to a specific group of covered individuals. The PPO negotiates discounted fees with the network providers and generally requires providers to follow strict utilization management procedures to achieve cost-effective patient care. PPOs resemble traditional indemnity plans in that they typically reimburse in-network health care providers on a fee-for-service basis, though network providers agree to discount those fees for plan participants.

As noted, PPOs offer plan members financial incentives to receive medical care services from network providers. For example, a PPO plan may cover 90 percent of the cost of a specific medical expense—usually without a deductible—if the plan member uses a network provider. On the other hand, the plan may cover only 70 percent of the expense if the plan member uses a non-network provider and may also require the member to pay a deductible. More than half of the PPOs in the United States are owned by insurance companies. The remainder are owned by physician or hospital groups, Blue Cross and Blue Shield plans, third-party administrators, or employers. A *third-party administrator (TPA)* is an organization other than an insurance company that provides administrative services to the sponsors of group benefit plans.

## Point-of-Service Plans

A *point-of-service (POS) plan* is a managed care plan that combines features of HMOs and PPOs. A plan member generally must select a primary care provider who is responsible for coordinating the member's medical care within the plan's network of providers. Plan members who need medical care choose, at the point of service, whether to seek care in-network or out-of-network. The plan, however, provides a much lower level of coverage for services received from non-network providers. For example, a plan member may be required to pay only a copayment when he receives services from a network provider, but may be required to pay both a deductible and coinsurance when receiving care from a non-network provider. POS plans are among the fastest growing form of managed care today.

## Managed Indemnity Plans

A *managed indemnity plan* is a plan that is organized and administered like a traditional medical expense insurance plan to provide indemnity benefits but that uses managed care techniques, such as precertification and utilization review, to control plan costs. Such plans allow insured members to use the providers of their choice and do not offer provider networks.

# Consumer-Driven Health Care Plans

Although the methods used by managed care plans have helped reduce some of the costs of providing health care coverage, they also have drawn complaints from employers, employees, providers, and insurance companies. A variety of alternative health care options have been proposed in response to these complaints. The most promising alternative falls under the general heading of consumer-driven health plans. A *consumer-driven health plan* (*CDHP*) is an employer-sponsored health benefit plan that gives individuals freedom to choose health care providers and benefits, but also requires them to assume financial risk for their choices. The two key components of consumer-driven health care are (1) financial incentives for individuals to manage health care costs and utilization and (2) information—usually in the form of Internet-based medical information tools—to enable individuals to make informed decisions about basic health care.

Financial incentives for managing health care costs are built into plan funding mechanisms. Most consumer-driven health plans are structured as defined-contribution plans under which the employer contributes a fixed dollar amount (the defined contribution) toward health care coverage for each participating employee, and the employee then uses that amount to pay for selected medical services. Because the amount of funding is defined in advance, employees assume the financial risk if the costs of their health care selections exceed the employer's contribution. As a result, employees have a considerable incentive to manage their use of medical services and to ensure they have a complete and accurate picture of the quality and cost of those services.

Information provided through Internet sites allows customers to (1) track and manage health care bills, (2) manage and improve their health through health education and preventative services, (3) gather information about provider quality and services, and (4) receive group-rate prices from providers. As providers upgrade to electronic medical records, information to support consumer decision making will increase.

Consumer-driven health plans take one of three basic forms: tax-advantaged personal health spending accounts, individually designed network and benefit plans, and customized package plans.

## Tax-Advantaged Personal Health Spending Accounts

A *tax-advantaged personal health spending account* is an account established with contributions from an employer and/or employee to pay the employee's medical expenses. Employer contributions to the account are exempt from employee state and federal income taxes and Social Security taxes. Employee contributions are exempt from income taxes, but are subject to Social Security taxes. Withdrawals used to pay substantiated medical expenses also are tax exempt for employees. Withdrawals for non-medical purposes are allowed, but such withdrawals are subject to income taxes and a 15 percent penalty tax.

Most personal health spending accounts are accompanied by a high-deductible medical expense insurance policy, and the amount that can be contributed to the account is linked to the amount of the policy deductible. For example, most plans limit contributions to the health spending account to a percentage of the policy deductible. If the account is employer-funded, the employer can either include the amount of the premium for the policy in the employee's account or pay the policy premium separately. If the account is employee-funded, the employee is responsible for paying the policy premium. In plans that do not require an accompanying insurance policy, account contributions typically may not exceed a specified dollar amount.

If an employee's medical expenses exceed the amount in the employee's account, the employee must pay the excess costs out-of-pocket. In plans accompanied by a high-deductible medical expense policy, the employee must pay costs out-of-pocket until the policy deductible is satisfied. After the deductible is paid, the medical expense policy pays benefits according to the policy terms. In plans not accompanied by a high-deductible insurance policy, the employee's out-of-pocket costs are not limited. If the account has remaining funds at the end of the year, those funds "roll over" to future years. In addition, accounts generally are portable and move with employees who change employment.

Currently, three basic types of tax-advantaged personal health spending accounts are available: medical savings accounts (MSAs), health reimbursement arrangements (HRAs), and health savings accounts (HSAs). The basic features of these personal health spending accounts are described in Figure 15.6. Alternatively, some employers offer *flexible spending accounts* that allow employees to set aside a predetermined amount of pre-tax wages for qualified, mostly health-related expenditures. An employee must use the amounts set aside in her flexible spending account each year; an employee loses any amounts that she does not use within the year.

## Individually Designed Network and Benefit Plans

Individually designed network and benefit plans require a defined contribution from the employer, usually in an amount equal to the amount that would otherwise have been spent for medical expense insurance. Employees design their own insurance coverage, including provider networks, benefit packages, and copayment levels, and use the money set aside by the employer to pay plan premiums. The plan provides informational

**FIGURE 15.6** | Personal Health Spending Accounts

A ***medical savings account (MSA)*** can be funded by employers or employees, but not both, and can be established by employers with fewer than 50 employees or by self-employed individuals. MSAs are portable.

A ***health reimbursement arrangement (HRA)*** can be funded only by employer contributions and may be established by employers of any size. HRAs are not portable unless specifically allowed by the employer.

A ***health savings account (HSA)*** can be established by individuals under age 65 and employers. HSAs have (1) no restrictions on employer size; (2) no restrictions on source of contributions (both the employer and the employee can contribute to the account); and (3) deposits into an HSA are 100 percent tax deductible by employees. HSAs are portable.

**Source:** Excerpted from Mary C. Bickley, *Principles of Financial Services and Products* (Atlanta: LOMA, © 2004), 178. Used with permission; all rights reserved.

software and services to help employees make selections. The monthly premiums that individuals pay for their insurance coverage are based on their selections and can change from month to month. Employees bear the financial risk if personalized premiums exceed the amount of the employer's fixed contribution.

## Customized Package Plans

Under a customized package plan, an employer contributes a fixed amount for health care coverage for each employee. The employee, using Internet-based medical information tools, chooses from a predetermined set of network and benefit options and pays the premiums for the options selected with funds set aside by the employer. Premium amounts vary according to the network and benefit options the employee selects. Most customized package plans offer tiered network and benefit options based on charges, discounts, and, in some cases, quality of care and service. Different tiers require different premiums and cost-sharing requirements. For example, care delivered at a hospital would require a higher copayment than care delivered at a doctor's office or community health care center. Similarly, care delivered by a specialist would require a higher copayment than care delivered by a primary care provider.

# Key Terms

indemnity benefits
basic medical expense coverage
hospital expenses
surgical expenses
physicians' expenses
first-dollar coverage
major medical expense coverage
supplemental major medical policy
comprehensive major
    medical policy
usual, customary, and
    reasonable (UCR) fee
deductible
calendar-year deductible
coinsurance
stop-loss provision
dental expense coverage
prescription drug coverage
formulary
vision care coverage
dread disease coverage
critical illness (CI) coverage
long-term care (LTC) coverage
Canada Health Act
Medicare
Medicare Part A
Medicare Part B
Medicare Advantage
Medigap policy
Medicare SELECT plan
Medicaid
managed care
managed care plan

managed care organization (MCO)
medically necessary services
medically appropriate services
network
primary care provider (PCP)
utilization management
utilization review (UR)
prospective review
concurrent review
retrospective review
case management
disease management
copayment
capitation payment
health maintenance
    organization (HMO)
open panel HMO
closed panel HMO
staff model HMO
group model HMO
preferred provider organization
    (PPO)
third-party administrator (TPA)
point-of-service (POS) plan
managed indemnity plan
consumer-driven health plan
    (CDHP)
tax-advantaged personal health
    spending account
medical savings account (MSA)
health reimbursement arrange-
    ment (HRA)
health savings account (HSA)

# Endnotes

1. R.S. 1985, c. C-6 (2004).

2. Bruce W. Clark, "Negotiating Successful Managed Care Contracts," *Healthcare Financial Management* (August 1995): 28.

3. Mark A. Schuster, Elizabeth A. McGlynn, and Robert H. Brook, "Why the Quality of U.S. Health Care Must Be Improved," National Coalition on Health Care, October 1997, http://www.nchc.org/emerge/quality.html (1 March 2000).

# Disability Income Coverage

**objectives**

*After reading this chapter, you should be able to*

- Identify the various definitions of *total disability* that have commonly been included in disability income insurance policies and distinguish among those definitions

- Identify the criteria used to classify disability income coverage as either short-term coverage or long-term coverage

- Explain the purpose of including an elimination period in a disability income insurance policy and identify the length of the typical elimination period

- Identify and describe some supplemental benefits that may be included in a disability income insurance policy

- Recognize the causes of disability that a disability income insurance policy may exclude from coverage

- Identify three types of specialized disability coverage that are designed to meet the needs of closely held businesses for disability coverage of owners, partners, and key people

- Identify and describe the disability income coverage provided by government-sponsored plans in the United States

**W**hen a person is unable to work because of disability, the financial effect on the individual's family is potentially much greater than if the individual had died. When a wage earner dies, the family is left without a source of income. When a wage earner is disabled, the family not only loses a source of income, but they also face additional expenses resulting from the disability. To help relieve the financial stress created by disability, insurance companies and government programs offer income replacement benefits in the form of disability income coverage. In this chapter, we describe the primary sources of disability income coverage—private insurers and the government—and the key features of individual and group disability income policies.

## Disability Income Insurance

Private insurance companies issue both individual and group disability income insurance policies. The coverage provided by such policies is classified as either short-term or long-term coverage, depending on the length of the benefit period. The *benefit period* is the time during which the insurer agrees to pay income benefits to the insured, and the criteria used to classify the benefit period are different for individual and group coverages. Individual disability income coverage is seldom offered with a maximum benefit period of less than one year.

- *Short-term individual disability income coverage* provides a maximum benefit period of from one to five years.

- *Long-term individual disability income coverage* provides a maximum benefit period of five years or more. The maximum benefit period provided by individual long-term coverage for illnesses commonly extends until the insured reaches age 65; for accidents, benefits often are provided for the insured's lifetime.

Group disability income coverage generally specifies shorter benefit periods than those included in individual policies.

- *Short-term group disability income coverage* provides a maximum benefit period of one year or less; such coverage commonly specifies a maximum benefit period of 13, 26, or 52 weeks.

- *Long-term group disability income coverage* provides a maximum benefit period of more than one year. Many policies extend the maximum benefit period to the insured's normal retirement age or to age 70.

To receive periodic income benefits under a disability income insurance policy, an insured person must meet the policy's definition of total disability. In addition, the insured person generally must be disabled for a certain period of time—known as the elimination period—before benefits become payable. In this section, we describe typical definitions of disability, the elimination period, benefit amounts, and supplemental disability benefits.

## Definitions of Total Disability

Each disability income policy specifies the definition of **total disability** that the insurer uses to determine whether a covered person is entitled to receive disability income benefits. Although the definition of total disability varies from policy to policy, we describe the definitions that insurance companies have most commonly included in disability income policies.

### Any Occupation

At one time, disability income policies defined total disability as a disability that prevented the insured from performing the duties of *any occupation*. Because a strict interpretation of this definition would prevent most people from ever qualifying for disability income benefits, most insurers now define total disability more liberally.

### Current Usual Definition

Most disability income policies issued today use a two-part definition of total disability. An insured is considered totally disabled if at the start of disability, the disability prevents him from performing the essential duties of his *regular occupation*. At the end of a specified period after the disability begins, usually two to five years, an insured is considered totally disabled only if the disability prevents him from working at *any occupation for which he is reasonably fitted by education, training, or experience.*

> **Example.** Samuel Tyler, a surgeon, is insured under a disability income policy that contains the current usual definition of total disability; the policy's definition of total disability changes after the insured has been disabled for two years. Samuel was involved in an accident and lost his right arm. Although Samuel is unable to perform surgery, he has been hired to teach in a medical college.
>
> **Analysis.** Because Samuel's injury prevents him from working as a surgeon, he meets the policy's initial definition of total disability and, thus, will be eligible to receive disability income

benefits for up to two years. At the end of that time, Samuel will no longer be considered totally disabled because his disability does not prevent him from working at an occupation for which he is reasonably fitted by his education and training.

Some policies that use this definition of total disability also state that the insured is not considered to be totally disabled if he is working in a gainful occupation. Thus, no total disability income benefits are payable if the person insured by such a policy voluntarily returns to work at any occupation.

## Own Previous Occupation

Some insurers have further liberalized the definition of total disability included in disability income policies sold to members of certain professional occupations. This definition, which is included more often in individual policies than in group policies, specifies that an insured is totally disabled if she is unable to perform the essential duties of her *own previous occupation*. In fact, policies using this "own previous occupation" definition specify that benefits will be paid even while the insured is gainfully employed in another occupation, as long as she is prevented by disability from engaging in the essential duties of her own previous occupation.

> **Example.** Suppose that Samuel Tyler from our last example is insured under a disability income policy that contains this "own previous occupation" definition of total disability. Because of his accident, Samuel is unable to perform surgery and has begun teaching at a medical school.
>
> **Analysis.** Samuel is unable to perform surgery and, thus, will never be able to work in his own previous occupation. Therefore, the insurance company will pay Samuel the full disability income benefit until the end of the policy's benefit period.

## Income Loss

A type of disability income coverage, often called **income protection insurance**, has gained popularity primarily in the upper-income professional market. The definition of total disability included in income protection policies specifies that an insured is disabled if she suffers an income loss caused by the disability. As a result, such a policy provides an income benefit both while the insured is totally disabled and unable to work and while she is able to work but, because of a disability, is earning less than she earned before being disabled. Income protection policies specify (1) a maximum benefit amount that will be paid when an insured is completely unable to work and (2) a method for determining the benefit amount payable when the disabled insured is working but is earning less than she previously earned.

> **Example.** Catherine Reiner, a professional athlete, is insured under an income protection policy. Ms. Reiner injured her knee in an accident and was forced to retire from active competition. Later, she was hired as a coach at a local university. However, her current income is significantly less than her previous income.
>
> **Analysis.** Under the terms of an income protection policy, Ms. Reiner received the maximum benefit specified by the policy during the period when she was unable to work because of her disability. After that, she became eligible for a policy benefit based on the difference between her income as a professional athlete and her salary as a coach. These partial payments will continue until the end of the policy's maximum benefit period.

### Presumptive Disabilities

Some disability income policies classify certain conditions as presumptive disabilities. A **presumptive disability** is a stated condition that, if present, automatically causes the insured to be considered totally disabled; thus, the insured receives the full income benefit amount provided under the policy, even if he resumes full-time employment in a former occupation. Presumptive disabilities include total and permanent blindness, loss of the use of any two limbs, and loss of speech or hearing.

## Elimination Period

Although some forms of disability income coverage are designed to provide benefits beginning on the first day of an insured's disability, most policies specify an elimination period. An **elimination period**, often referred to as a *waiting period*, is the specific amount of time that the insured must be disabled before becoming eligible to receive policy benefits.

Like the deductible amount found in medical expense policies, the purpose of the elimination period is to reduce the cost of coverage. By specifying an elimination period, the insurer can substantially reduce the expenses involved in processing and paying claims for disabilities that last for only a very short time. This expense savings is reflected in the cost of the coverage; the longer the elimination period, the lower the cost for otherwise equivalent disability income coverage.

The length of the elimination period included in both short-term and long-term individual disability income policies is typically from 30 days to 6 months. The elimination period in a group policy is typically related to the length of the maximum benefit period.

- Group short-term disability income policies typically specify no elimination period for disabilities caused by accidents and an elimination period of one week for disabilities caused by sickness.

- Group long-term disability income policies typically specify an elimination period of from 30 days to 6 months, though such plans also typically coordinate their short-term and long-term coverages. That is, the length of the elimination period before long-term benefits are payable is designed to ensure that short-term coverage ends at the same time that long-term benefits become payable.

## Benefit Amounts

As a general rule, the benefit amount provided by disability income coverage is not intended to fully replace an individual's pre-disability earnings. Instead, disability income benefits are limited to an amount that is lower than the individual's regular earnings when not disabled. Without restrictions on the income amounts available through disability income coverage, a disabled insured could receive as much income as he received when working. In such a case, the disabled insured has no financial incentive to return to work.

Disability income benefit amounts, however, should not be so low that a disabled insured suffers a drastic reduction in income and lifestyle; the purpose of disability insurance is, after all, to provide protection against the economic consequences of income loss. Therefore, the benefit amount paid to a disabled insured should bear a relationship to the amount of the individual's income before disability.

Disability income providers use two methods to establish the amount of disability income benefits that will be paid to a disabled person: (1) an income benefit formula or (2) a flat benefit amount. The method used generally depends on whether the coverage is provided by a group or an individual policy and on whether the coverage is short-term or long-term.

### Income Benefit Formula

Group disability income policies typically include an income benefit formula that the insurer uses to determine the amount of the periodic benefit that is payable to a disabled insured. An income benefit formula usually expresses the disability income benefit amount as a stated percentage of the insured's pre-disability earnings and considers all sources of disability income that the disabled insured receives.

The amount of the stated percentage in the formula varies from policy to policy. The percentage typically included in group long-term disability income policies ranges from 60 to 75 percent. For example, the formula may specify that the insured will receive a disability income benefit amount equal to 75 percent of her pre-disability earnings and that the benefit amount will be reduced by the amount of any disability income benefit she receives from other sources. Group short-term policies often specify a higher percentage than do group long-term policies, and it is not uncommon for group short-term policies to provide from 90 to 100 percent income replacement benefits.

## Flat Amount

Individual disability income policies usually specify a flat benefit amount that the insurer will periodically pay to an insured who becomes totally disabled. The specified benefit amount is based on the amount of the insured's income when the policy was purchased. Unlike the benefit paid under group disability income policies, the specified benefit amount typically is paid to a disabled insured regardless of any other income benefits the insured receives during the disability.

Insurers carefully limit the maximum amount of disability income benefit that a particular applicant can purchase. When determining the maximum amount of disability income available to an applicant, the insurer considers the following factors:

- The amount of the applicant's usual income earned from employment, before taxes

- The amount of the applicant's unearned income, such as dividends and interest, that will continue during a disability

- Additional sources of income available to the applicant during a disability, such as disability income benefits provided through group disability income coverage and government-sponsored disability income programs

- The applicant's current income tax bracket, because the applicant's usual earned income is taxable income, whereas disability income benefits provided under an individual policy usually are not taxable income

In general, the maximum amount of disability income benefit that insurers will provide to an applicant is 50 to 70 percent of her usual pre-tax earnings at the time of the application for the policy. Note that the amount of an insured's disability income benefit will be lower than the amount of after-tax income the insured earned before becoming disabled.

# Buy-Up Options

As we discussed, most group disability income policies limit benefit amounts to a specified percentage of an insured employee's earnings. A **buy-up option** is individually purchased supplementary disability income coverage that increases the benefit amount available to the insured. An employee typically purchases a buy-up option under a separate policy. For example, an employee covered by a group disability income policy that provides 60 percent income replacement benefits could increase benefits to 80 percent of earnings by purchasing a buy-up option. These individually purchased supplemental coverages are becoming increasingly popular as employers reduce benefit levels in an effort to control costs.

---

**FAST FACT**

During 2002, Canadian insurance companies paid $33 million in disability claims.

**Source:** CLHIA, *Canadian Life and Health Insurance Facts*, 2003 ed. (Toronto: Canadian Life and Health Insurance Association Inc., 2003), 14.

---

# Supplemental Disability Benefits

A variety of supplemental benefits are available in connection with disability income policies. These supplemental benefits—which include partial disability benefits, future purchase option benefits, and cost-of-living adjustment (COLA) benefits—may be automatically included with the basic coverage or may be available on an optional basis for an additional premium amount.

### Partial Disability Benefits

Some disability income policies provide benefits for periods when the insured person has a **partial disability**—a disability that prevents the insured either from performing some of the duties of his usual occupation or from engaging in that occupation on a full-time basis. The amount of the disability income benefit paid when an insured has a partial disability is described in the policy. Typically, this amount is either a specified flat amount, often 50 percent of the total disability income benefit amount, or an amount established according to a formula specified in the policy. Using the formula method, the amount of the income benefit will vary according to the percentage of income that the insured has lost because of the partial disability.

### Future Purchase Option Benefit

Some disability income policies that specify a flat benefit amount contain a **future purchase option benefit**, which grants the insured the right to increase the benefit amount in accordance with increases in the insured's earnings. This benefit provision generally specifies that benefit increases can be made only if the insured can prove a commensurate increase in income; further, the amount of such increases is generally limited to a specified maximum. The insured, however, usually is permitted to increase the benefit amount without providing evidence of insurability.

### Cost-of-Living Adjustment Benefit

A *cost-of-living adjustment (COLA) benefit* provides for periodic increases in the disability income benefit amount that the insurer will pay to a disabled insured; these increases usually correspond to increases in the cost of living. When a policy or rider provides a COLA benefit, it usually defines an *increase in the cost of living* in terms of a standard index, such as the Consumer Price Index (CPI).

## Exclusions

Disability income policies often specify that income benefits will not be paid to a disabled insured if the insured's disability results from certain causes. The causes of disability that may be excluded from coverage include the following:

- Injuries or sicknesses that result from war, declared or undeclared, or any act of war

- Intentionally self-inflicted injuries

- Injuries received as a result of active participation in a riot

- Occupation-related disabilities or illnesses for which the insured is entitled to receive disability income benefits under some government program

# Specialized Types of Disability Coverage

In addition to disability income coverage, insurers market several specialized types of disability coverage. These specialized coverages are designed to provide benefits for specific expenses—other than loss of income—that may result from an insured's disability. Businesses are subject to certain financial risks if an owner, partner, or key person dies. Likewise, such businesses could suffer a financial loss if an owner, partner, or key person becomes unable to work because of a disability. We describe three types of disability coverage that are available to closely held businesses: key person disability coverage, disability buyout coverage, and business overhead expense coverage.

## Key Person Disability Coverage

Just as businesses that rely on the work of a key person may need to purchase key person life insurance, businesses also may need *key person disability coverage*, which provides benefit payments to the business if an insured key person becomes disabled. When a key person is unable to work because of disability, the business loses the person's services and, thus, loses money. Such losses can be offset by key person disability benefits.

## Disability Buyout Coverage

In Chapter 5, we described buy-sell agreements and how they can be funded by life insurance policy death benefits. A buy-sell agreement also may include provisions concerning the purchase of a partner's or owner's interest in the business should the partner or owner become disabled. *Disability buyout coverage* provides benefits designed to fund the buyout of a partner's or owner's interest in a business should he become disabled.

## Business Overhead Expense Coverage

Should a business owner become disabled, she still may incur expenses to operate the business. For example, office rent or mortgage payments continue and office utility bills come due. Some insurers sell *business overhead expense coverage* that provides benefits designed to pay the disabled insured's share of the business' overhead expenses. Policies typically define *overhead expenses* as usual and necessary business expenses, including employee salaries, rent, mortgage payments, telephone, electric and gas utilities, and other expenses required to keep the business open.

# Government-Sponsored Disability Income Programs

In many countries, government-sponsored programs provide disability income benefits to specified individuals. Insight 16.1 describes such programs in Canada.

In the United States, workers who are disabled as a result of work-related accidents or illnesses are eligible to receive wage replacement benefits, as well as medical expense benefits, under state-mandated workers' compensation programs. Each state has adopted a *workers' compensation program* that is designed to ensure that workers who are injured or disabled on the job receive fixed monetary awards without requiring the workers to pursue legal action against their employers. Programs are funded by mandatory employer contributions, and the amount of awards and benefits vary from state to state. The federal government has created similar programs that cover federal employees.

In addition, two federal programs—Social Security Disability Income and Supplemental Security Income—provide disability benefit payments to qualified individuals. Workers who are under age 65 and who have paid a specified amount of Social Security tax for a prescribed number of

| FAST FACT |
| --- |
| In June 2004, the U.S. Social Security Administration paid $5.6 billion to disabled workers and their dependents. |
| **Source:** U.S. Social Security Administration, Press Office Fact Sheet, 21 July 2004, http://www.ssa.gov/pressoffice/basicfact.htm (18 October 2004). |

**INSIGHT 16.1    Government-Provided Disability Income Coverage in Canada**

Several government-sponsored programs in Canada provide disability income benefits to covered residents. Short-term disability income benefits are available under the federal *Unemployment Insurance Act* for all employees who have worked a stated minimum number of weeks during the preceding 52-week period. These taxable benefits are available for up to 15 weeks after a short waiting period if absence from work was caused by accident or sickness; maternity benefits are available for up to one year. The benefit amount is a percentage of the worker's average weekly earnings, up to a stated maximum amount. The plan is financed by compulsory employer and employee contributions.

Employers can reduce their premium contributions by establishing a qualified, private disability income plan, and many employers have established such plans. For individuals who are covered under such a private plan that provides weekly benefits for short-term disabilities, the private plan is always the "first payor" before benefits are available under the federal program.

Long-term disability income benefits are provided through the Canada Pension Plan (CPP) and the Quebec Pension Plan (QPP). To qualify for disability income benefits under one of these plans, a worker must (1) have made contributions to the plan for a stated minimum number of years, (2) be under the age of 65, and (3) be afflicted with a *severe and prolonged disability*. A *severe disability* is defined as a disability that prevents the worker from engaging in any substantially gainful occupation. A *prolonged disability* is defined as a disability that is expected to be of long, continued, and indefinite duration or that is likely to result in the covered worker's death.

A disabled worker who meets the foregoing requirements receives a monthly income benefit. The amount of the benefit is based on the amount of the worker's pre-disability earnings and the amount he contributed to the plan. These taxable benefit payments begin 4 months after the onset of the disability and continue until the person (1) is no longer disabled, (2) dies, or (3) reaches age 65, when normal retirement benefits provided through the CPP or QPP become payable. Dependent children of disabled workers are also eligible to receive income benefits under both the CPP and the QPP.

quarter-year periods are eligible to receive **Social Security Disability Income (SSDI)** benefit payments if they become disabled. For purposes of SSDI, *disability* is defined as a person's inability to work because of a physical or mental sickness or injury; this sickness or injury must have lasted or be expected to last for at least one year, or it must be expected to lead to the person's death.

SSDI provides a disabled worker with a monthly disability income benefit equal to the monthly benefit that would normally have become payable when the worker retired. SSDI benefit payments do not begin until the insured has been disabled for at least five months and, hence, begin approximately six months after the onset of disability. As a general rule, benefit payments continue until (1) two months after the disability ends,

(2) the insured worker dies, or (3) the insured worker reaches the age when regular Social Security retirement income benefits become payable.

The spouse and dependent children of a disabled worker may also receive an income benefit while the worker is disabled. Their income benefits are equal to a percentage of the amount received by the disabled worker. Benefits, however, are subject to an overall family maximum benefit amount.

The **Supplemental Security Income (SSI)** program provides periodic benefit payments to people with limited incomes who are disabled, blind, or age 65 or older. Unlike SSDI payments, SSI payments are not limited to individuals who have paid a specified amount of Social Security tax; instead, recipients must have low incomes. For purposes of SSI, *disability* is generally defined as it is for SSDI purposes for individuals who are at least age 18. In most states, individuals who receive monthly SSI benefits also qualify for Medicaid. Figure 16.1 summarizes some of the differences and similarities between the SSDI and SSI programs.

**FIGURE 16.1    Comparison of SSDI and SSI Programs**

| Social Security Disability Income Program | Supplemental Security Income Program |
|---|---|
| Benefits are based on the individual's payment of Social Security taxes | Benefits are based on the individual's financial need |
| Beneficiaries receive monthly income payments | Beneficiaries receive monthly income payments |
| Beneficiaries younger than age 65 qualify for Medicare after they have received SSDI benefits for 24 months | Beneficiaries in some states qualify for Medicaid |
| Program is financed through a dedicated payroll tax paid by employers and employees | Program is financed by general funds of the U.S. Treasury |
| Program is administered by the federal Social Security Administration | Program is administered by the federal Social Security Administration |

# Key Terms

benefit period
short-term individual disability income coverage
long-term individual disability income coverage
short-term group disability income coverage
long-term group disability income coverage
total disability
income protection insurance
presumptive disability
elimination period
buy-up option
partial disability
future purchase option benefit
cost-of-living adjustment (COLA) benefit
key person disability coverage
disability buyout coverage
business overhead expense coverage
overhead expenses
workers' compensation program
Social Security Disability Income (SSDI)
Supplemental Security Income (SSI)

# Individual Health Insurance Policies

objectives

*After reading this chapter, you should be able to*

- Explain how the state and federal governments regulate health insurance in the United States

- Identify and describe the provisions that are typically included in individual health insurance policies

- Identify the factors that affect the degree of morbidity risk presented by an applicant and explain how each factor affects morbidity risk

- Identify ways in which health insurance pricing differs from life insurance pricing

- Explain how insurers calculate net premium rates for health insurance coverage

The health insurance coverages—including medical expense and disability income coverages—we described in the previous two chapters are provided under both individual and group health insurance policies. In this chapter, we describe the features of traditional individual health insurance policies issued by commercial insurance companies.

An individual health insurance policy is an enforceable contract between an insurance company and the policyowner. The policy describes the coverages provided, the benefits payable, and the premium amounts and their due dates. A copy of the application for insurance the policyowner completed typically is attached to the policy when it is issued. The policyowner and the insured usually are the same person, and the insurer typically pays benefits directly to that person or to a medical care provider on behalf of that person.

To create a valid health insurance contract, the applicant must submit the initial premium for the contract along with the application for insurance. The policyowner then must pay periodic renewal premiums to keep the policy in force. How often and in what manner renewal premiums are to be paid depend on the terms of the contract. Most individual health insurance policies require monthly renewal premiums. These premiums can be paid in cash, by money order, or by check. An increasing number of insurers also allow policyowners to pay renewal premiums online by charging the premium amount against a credit card. Renewal premiums also can be paid using automatic premium payment techniques. If a premium is not paid in cash, however, the insurer's acceptance of payment is contingent on the actual collection of the money.

In this chapter, we describe individual health insurance policies. We begin with a description of how such policies are regulated. Then we describe the policy provisions that insurers typically include in individual health insurance policies. We also describe individual health insurance underwriting and how insurers price individual health insurance policies. Remember that the term *health insurance* includes both medical expense and disability income coverage. Throughout the chapter, we point out ways in which medical expense insurance policies differ from disability income policies.

# Regulation of Health Insurance

As we described in Chapter 1, insurance regulation in the United States is shared between the state and federal governments. The states have enacted laws and regulations that govern a wide range of life and health insurance company operations. State laws, for example, regulate the licensing of insurers and their agents, seek to ensure the solvency of insurers, and regulate the advertising and sale of insurance policies. However, many state and federal laws apply specifically to health insurance and not life insurance, and we describe some of these laws in this section.

## State Regulation of Health Insurance

The National Association of Insurance Commissioners (NAIC) has adopted a number of model laws designed to regulate individual and group health insurance. The regulation of *individual* health insurance is somewhat uniform throughout the United States because almost all of the states have enacted laws patterned on NAIC model laws. In contrast, state regulation of group health insurance is much less uniform. Most states, however, require both individual and group health insurance policies to contain specified provisions. Figure 17.1 lists the provisions that typically must be included in individual health insurance policies; we describe these provisions later in the chapter.

Laws in most states also require all health insurance policies—individual and group—to provide specific benefits. The benefits that are mandated, however, vary widely from state to state. In some states, such laws apply only to policies that are issued within the state. In other states, the laws apply to any policy that insures a resident of the state. The benefits that have been mandated include, among others, coverage of newborn children; treatment of alcoholism and drug addiction; coverage of services provided by medical practitioners such as chiropractors, psychologists, and podiatrists; and coverage of certain diagnostic tests, such as mammograms.

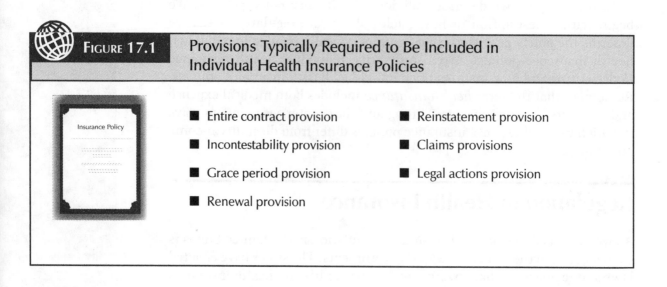

**FIGURE 17.1** Provisions Typically Required to Be Included in Individual Health Insurance Policies

- Entire contract provision
- Incontestability provision
- Grace period provision
- Renewal provision
- Reinstatement provision
- Claims provisions
- Legal actions provision

In addition to regulating the insurance industry and traditional health insurance policies, the states regulate HMOs, PPOs, and other alternative health care plans. Most states have enacted comprehensive laws to regulate all aspects of how HMOs operate, including a requirement that each such organization qualify to operate as an HMO before beginning operations. To qualify, an HMO must provide certain basic health care services and must meet a number of statutory requirements designed to ensure the financial and operational viability of the plan. Most states also regulate PPOs with laws and regulations designed to ensure that insureds have reasonable access to medical services and that those services adequately meet their medical needs.

Other state laws have affected the development of managed care plans. For example, some states regulate hospital rates; such regulation affects a health insurance plan's ability to negotiate discounted rates with those providers. Many states now impose numerous requirements on utilization review, and some states regulate third-party administrators (TPAs).

# Federal Regulation of Health Insurance

For many years, federal regulation of health insurance was limited primarily to regulation of health insurance plans provided as an employee benefit. Thus, little federal regulation affected individual health insurance policies. Over time, Congress has gradually expanded federal regulation of health insurance. Currently, several federal laws impose requirements on all types of health insurance policies, as well as on health insurers and managed care plans. We describe some of these federal laws in this section.

### Health Insurance Portability and Accountability Act

The *Health Insurance Portability and Accountability Act (HIPAA)* imposes a number of requirements on insurers that issue individual medical expense insurance policies, as well as on employer-sponsored group medical expense insurance plans.[1] Policies that provide accident-only coverage or only disability income coverage are exempt from HIPAA. Some of HIPAA's requirements overlap requirements imposed by state insurance laws, but HIPAA does not preempt state insurance laws that are more favorable to insureds than the minimum requirements imposed by HIPAA.

To protect insureds' access to medical expense coverage, HIPAA imposes a general requirement that insurers must renew or continue an individual medical expense insurance policy in force at the option of the policyowner. Insurers, however, have the right to discontinue or not renew coverage of an individual in specified situations, such as when premiums are not paid or the individual has committed fraud or made an intentional misrepresentation of a material fact under the terms of the coverage.

HIPAA also requires the guaranteed availability of individual medical expense coverage to certain individuals, referred to as *eligible individuals*, who have had group medical expense coverage. For purposes of this requirement, an eligible individual is a person who has had a specified minimum amount of coverage under a health plan and who is not eligible for coverage under a group health plan, Medicare, or Medicaid; an individual, however, is not considered an eligible individual if his most recent coverage was terminated because of fraud or nonpayment of premium. An insurer is prohibited from declining to cover such an eligible individual and may not impose any pre-existing condition exclusion on the coverage of an eligible individual. Health insurers, however, are exempt from this requirement if the state in which they conduct business implements an acceptable alternative mechanism by which such eligible individuals may obtain coverage. Currently, 48 states have implemented an acceptable alternative mechanism.

## Health Maintenance Organization Act of 1973

The *Health Maintenance Organization (HMO) Act of 1973* was passed to encourage the establishment and development of health maintenance organizations.[2] It provided federal funds to HMOs that met the requirements to become federally qualified. (See Figure 17.2, which lists benefits that federally qualified HMOs are required to provide.) Today, HMOs have

---

**FIGURE 17.2**    Benefits That Federally Qualified HMOs Are Required to Provide

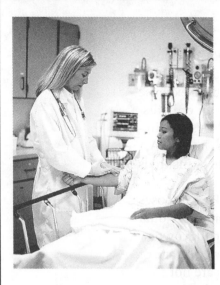

- Physician services

- Inpatient and outpatient hospital services

- Medically necessary emergency health services

- Preventive health services

- Short-term outpatient mental health care

- Medical treatment and referral for alcohol and drug abuse and addiction

- Home health services

- Diagnostic laboratory services

- Diagnostic and therapeutic radiological services

the option of becoming federally qualified, and many HMOs seek such qualification. To become federally qualified, an HMO must comply with a range of requirements established by the HMO Act and subsequent amendments to that Act. These requirements include standards concerning plan solvency, plan design and benefits, and plan administration.

## Mandated Benefits

A number of federal laws mandate that certain benefits be provided by individual and group medical expense insurance policies. The following are some examples of such mandates:

- The ***Mental Health Parity Act*** imposes requirements on group health plans, health insurance companies, and HMOs that offer mental health benefits.[3] Individual and group policies that provide mental health benefits may not set an annual or lifetime maximum mental health benefits limit that is lower than any such limits for medical and surgical benefits. A policy that does not impose an annual or lifetime limit on medical and surgical benefits may not impose such a limit on mental health benefits.

- The ***Newborns' and Mothers' Health Protection Act of 1996*** imposes requirements on individual and group health insurance policies that provide benefits for maternity and newborn care.[4] Such policies must provide coverage for at least a 48-hour hospital stay following a normal vaginal delivery and at least 96 hours for a cesarean section.

- The ***Women's Health and Cancer Rights Act of 1998*** requires individual and group health insurance policies that provide coverage for mastectomies to provide certain mastectomy-related benefits or services.[5] Insureds who receive benefits in connection with a mastectomy and who elect to have breast reconstruction following the mastectomy must be entitled to receive benefits for the reconstruction.

# Individual Health Insurance Policy Provisions

Individual health insurance policies include a number of provisions that are the same as provisions included in individual life insurance policies. For example, both types of policies include an *entire contract provision* that specifies the documents that constitute the insurance contract. With the exception of open contracts issued by fraternal insurers, the entire contract consists of the policy and any endorsements or other documents attached to the policy, including the application for insurance and policy riders.

Some provisions are included in both individual life and individual health insurance policies, but the provisions contain some differences. In addition, individual health insurance—both medical expense and disability income—policies contain some provisions that are not found in individual life insurance policies. In this section, we describe some of the provisions typically included in individual health insurance policies.

# Incontestability Provision

All individual health insurance policies include an incontestability provision that, like the incontestability provision included in individual life insurance policies, limits the time during which the insurer has the right to avoid the contract based on misrepresentations made in the application. However, the policy provisions included in individual medical expense policies and individual disability income policies are not identical.

### Contestability of Individual Medical Expense Policies

Most individual medical expense policies contain a provision entitled *time limit on certain defenses*. This time limit on certain defenses provision, commonly referred to as the *incontestability provision* or *incontestable clause*, states that after the policy has been in force for a specified period—usually two or three years—the insurer cannot use a material misrepresentation in the application either to contest the policy or to deny a claim *unless* the misrepresentation was fraudulent. This provision typically states the following:

> **Incontestability.** After coverage on a covered person has been in force during the lifetime of that person for two years, only fraudulent misstatements in the application shall be used to void the coverage on that person.
>
> No claim for a covered charge that is incurred after those two years will be denied because of a pre-existing condition, unless that pre-existing condition was excluded from coverage, by name or specific description, on the date that charge was incurred.
>
> This provision does not have any effect on nor does it bar any other defenses under this policy.

The word *defenses* refers to any reasons that the insurer may use to deny liability under the policy. Thus, the provision specifically notes that the insurer retains the right to deny a claim on the basis of another policy provision. For example, the insurer may deny a claim on the basis that the expenses are specifically excluded from coverage.

### Contestability of Individual Disability Income Policies

Most individual disability income policies include an incontestability provision which states that after the policy has been in force for a stated period—usually one or two years—the insurer cannot contest the policy's validity on the ground of material misrepresentation in the application. Note that, unlike the provision included in individual medical expense policies, the incontestability provision included in individual disability income policies does not include a reference to fraudulent misstatements. Consequently, the incontestability provision included in individual disability income policies is essentially the same as the incontestability provision included in individual life insurance policies in the United States.

## Grace Period Provision

Like individual life insurance policies, individual health insurance policies contain a *grace period provision* that allows the policyowner to pay a renewal premium within a stated grace period following the premium due date. Coverage remains in force during the grace period. If the premium is not paid by the end of the grace period, the policy lapses and all coverage ends.

The length of the grace period included in individual health insurance policies varies, depending on how frequently renewal premiums are payable. For example, policies for which renewal premiums are paid monthly typically contain a 10-day grace period. The grace period is usually 31 days if premiums are payable less often than monthly, although many insurers provide a 31-day grace period even when premiums are payable monthly.

## Reinstatement Provision

Individual health insurance policies typically include a *reinstatement provision*, which states that if certain conditions are met, the insurer will reinstate to in-force status a policy that has lapsed for nonpayment of premiums. To reinstate an individual health insurance policy, the policyowner usually must complete a reinstatement application, pay any overdue premiums, and satisfy any other requirements specified in the provision.

The insurer has the right to decline to reinstate the policy on the basis of statements in the reinstatement application. If the insurer does not complete its evaluation of the application within a stated number of days after receiving the reinstatement application—in most states, 45 days—or if the insurer accepts an overdue premium without a reinstatement application, then the policy is usually considered to be automatically reinstated.

Coverage under a reinstated policy is limited to accidents that occur after the date of reinstatement and to illnesses that begin more than 10 days after the date of reinstatement. Thus, the insurer can protect against antiselection by excluding from coverage those losses that occur after the policy lapses and before it is reinstated. As we discussed in Chapter 2, antiselection is the tendency of those individuals who believe they have a greater-than-average likelihood of loss to seek insurance protection to a greater extent than do those who believe they have an average or a less-than-average likelihood of loss.

## Renewal Provision

A provision that is unique to individual health insurance policies is the *renewal provision*, which describes (1) the circumstances under which the insurer has the right to cancel or refuse to renew the coverage and (2) the insurer's right to increase the policy's premium rate. Individual health insurance policies can be classified on the basis of the type of renewal provision included in the policy, as follows:

- A *cancellable policy* gives the insurer the right to terminate the policy at any time, for any reason, simply by notifying the policyowner that the policy is cancelled and by refunding any advance premium that has been paid for the policy.

- An *optionally renewable policy* gives the insurer the right to refuse to renew the policy for any reason on certain dates specified in the policy—usually either the policy anniversary date or any premium due date. The insurer also is allowed to add coverage limitations and to increase the premium rate if it does so for a class of optionally renewable policies. A *class of policies* consists of all policies of a particular type or all policies issued to a particular group of insureds. For example, a class of policies may be defined as all policies in force in a particular state or as all policies issued to insureds who are a particular age or who fall into a specific risk category.

- A *conditionally renewable policy* gives the insurer a limited right to refuse to renew an individual health policy at the end of a premium payment period. The insurer may refuse to renew a policy only if its decision is based on one or more specific reasons stated in the policy. The reasons *cannot* be related to the insured's health. The age and employment status of the insured are often listed as reasons for possible nonrenewal. For example, an individual disability income policy may state that the insurer will renew the policy until the insured reaches a certain age or until the insured retires from gainful employment. A conditionally renewable policy also gives the insurer the right to increase the premium rate for any class of conditionally renewable policies.

- A *guaranteed renewable policy* must be renewed at the policyowner's option—as long as premium payments are made—at least until the insured attains the age limit stated in the policy. Most individual guaranteed renewable policies are renewable until the insured reaches age 60 or 65; some are renewable until age 70 or for the insured's lifetime. The insurer has the right to increase the premium rate for such a policy only if it increases the premium rate for an entire class of policies.

- A **noncancellable policy** is guaranteed to be renewable until the insured reaches the limiting age stated in the policy. In addition, an insurer does not have the right to increase the premium rate for a noncancellable policy under any circumstances; the guaranteed premium rate is specified in the policy.

The renewal classification of a health insurance policy affects the premium rate that the insurer charges for the coverage. For example, premium rates for noncancellable policies—which provide guarantees not found in policies in other renewal classifications—are higher than the premium rates charged for otherwise equivalent policies in the other classifications.

The types of renewal provisions insurers can use in individual health insurance policies depend on legal requirements and regulations. In the United States, HIPAA imposes a general requirement that insurers must renew or continue an individual medical expense insurance policy in force at the option of the policyowner. As a result, individual medical expense insurance policies in the United States must be either noncancellable or guaranteed renewable policies. In the common-law jurisdictions of Canada, most individual medical expense policies are cancellable and most individual disability income policies are noncancellable. By contrast, most insurers in the Canadian province of Quebec offer individual health insurance policies in several classifications, and the applicant can choose which classification of policy to purchase.

## Pre-Existing Conditions Provision

Most individual health insurance policies include a **pre-existing conditions provision** stating that until the insured has been covered under the policy for a certain period—typically two years after the policy issue date—the insurer will not pay benefits for a pre-existing condition unless the condition has been specifically excluded. A sample pre-existing conditions provision follows.

> **Pre-existing conditions.** Benefits for a charge that results from a covered person's pre-existing condition, as defined in this policy, will be provided only if that charge is a covered charge and is incurred by that person after coverage for that person has been in force for two years. However, if a condition is excluded from coverage by name or specific description, no benefits will be provided for any charges that result from that condition even after those two years.

Individual health policies usually define a ***pre-existing condition*** as an injury or illness that (1) occurred or manifested itself within a specified period—usually two years—before the policy was issued and (2) was not disclosed on the application. The second part of this two-part definition is especially important. A condition that is disclosed on the application is never considered pre-existing for purposes of this exclusion. The insurer has the opportunity to evaluate such a condition and, thus, can specifically exclude the condition from the policy's coverage. If the insurer does not exclude a disclosed condition from the policy's coverage, then the policy covers that condition. Any specific exclusions, however, remain in effect throughout the life of the policy; a condition that is excluded is never covered by the policy.

> **Example.** Mark Spellman was treated for a back injury one year before he applied for an individual medical expense policy. Six months before completing the application, Mr. Spellman was diagnosed with, and treated for, allergies. When he completed the application, Mr. Spellman disclosed that he had been treated for allergies, but inadvertently omitted the fact that he had been treated for the back injury. The insurer issued the policy, which did not specifically exclude allergies from coverage.
>
> **Analysis.** Because Mr. Spellman did not disclose that he had been treated for a back injury, the insurer did not have the opportunity to evaluate the risks associated with that injury. Thus, that condition is considered a pre-existing condition, and the insurer has the right to exclude the condition from coverage for two years after the policy issue date. If Mr. Spellman has continuing problems related to the back injury and submits claims related to his back injury during the first two years after the policy was issued, the insurer can deny benefits because of the pre-existing condition provision. In contrast, Mr. Spellman's allergies are not considered a pre-existing condition because that condition was disclosed on the application, and the insurer was able to evaluate the risks associated with that health condition. When evaluating Mr. Spellman's application, the insurer decided not to exclude allergies from the policy's coverage. Thus, expenses incurred for treatment of allergies are covered throughout the life of the policy.

In most jurisdictions, two years is the maximum period during which an insurer is permitted to exclude pre-existing conditions from coverage. Insurers, however, are permitted to specify a shorter exclusion period because a shorter exclusion is more favorable to the insured. As noted earlier in the chapter, HIPAA prohibits U.S. insurers from including a pre-existing conditions provision in an individual health insurance policy issued to an eligible individual.

When an applicant fails to disclose a condition on the application for insurance, the insurer must determine whether that nondisclosure constitutes a material misrepresentation. If the insurer decides that the misrepresentation was not material, then it applies the policy's pre-existing conditions provision. If the insurer determines that the nondisclosure constitutes a material misrepresentation—or, in the case of medical expense coverage, a fraudulent misrepresentation—the insurer can apply the policy's incontestability provision and use the misrepresentation as grounds to avoid the policy.

## Claims Provisions

Individual health insurance policies, like individual life policies, typically include provisions that define both the insured's obligation to provide timely notification of loss to the insurer and the insurer's obligation to make prompt benefit payments to the insured. In Canada, for example, the policy usually requires the insured to notify the insurer of a claim in writing within 30 days from the date the claim arose and to furnish the insurer with proof of the loss within 90 days from the date the claim arose. The insurer must pay benefits within 60 days of receipt of proof of loss for a medical expense claim and within 30 days of receipt of proof of loss for a disability income claim. Policies issued in the United States contain similar requirements.

## Legal Actions Provision

Individual health insurance policies typically include a *legal actions provision*, which limits the time during which a claimant who disagrees with the insurer's claim decision has the right to sue the insurer to collect the amount the claimant believes is owed under the policy. The length of this time period varies from jurisdiction to jurisdiction, but it typically ranges from one to three years after the claimant provides the insurer with proof of the loss.

## Overinsurance Provision

To prevent an insured from profiting from an illness or injury, many individual health insurance policies contain an *overinsurance provision*, which states that the benefits payable under the policy will be reduced if the insured is overinsured. An *overinsured person* is one who is entitled to receive either (1) more in medical expense benefits than the actual costs incurred for treatment or (2) a greater income amount during disability than the amount that would have been earned from working.

An overinsurance provision takes effect *only* if the insurer was not notified of existing coverage at the time of application. In cases of overinsurance, the insurer reduces the amount of the benefits that would otherwise be payable under the policy and refunds any premium amount paid for the excess coverage.

## Change of Occupation Provision

Because occupation has a direct effect on an insured's risk of illness or injury, many individual disability income insurance policies contain a ***change of occupation provision*** that permits the insurer to adjust the policy's premium rate or the amount of benefits payable under the policy if the insured changes occupation. The provision typically permits the insurer to reduce the maximum benefit amount payable under the policy if the insured changes to a *more* hazardous occupation. If the insured changes to a *less* hazardous occupation, the provision permits the insurer to reduce the policy's premium rate. The amount of the benefit payable under a disability income policy is based on the insured's income at the time of application. Thus, many individual disability income policies give the insurer the right to adjust the maximum benefit amount if a change of occupation results in an insured's earning a significantly different amount of income. All benefit amount and premium rate changes take effect as of the time the insured changes occupation.

For example, if a teacher were to enter the more dangerous occupation of coal miner, then the insurer would reduce the maximum benefit amount available under the policy to the benefit amount that the premium charged would have purchased for a coal miner; the policy's premium rate would not change. Alternatively, if a coal miner were to change occupations and become a teacher, the insurer would reduce the premium rate to the premium rate that would be charged to a teacher for the same level of benefits; the policy's maximum benefit amount would remain the same.

## Physical Examination Provision

Individual disability income insurance policies usually include a ***physical examination provision***, which states that the insurer has the right to have an insured who has submitted a claim examined by a doctor of the insurer's choice, at the insurer's expense. Such an examination allows the insurer to verify the validity of disability income claims. The provision also gives the insurer the right to require that a disabled insured undergo medical examinations at regular intervals so that the insurer can verify that the insured is still disabled.

Figure 17.3 provides a comparison of the provisions that typically are included in individual life, individual medical expense, and individual disability income policies.

| | FIGURE 17.3 | Comparison of Provisions Included in Individual Life, Medical Expense, and Disability Income Policies | |

| Policy Provision | Individual Life Insurance Policy | Individual Medical Expense Insurance Policy | Individual Disability Income Policy |
|---|:---:|:---:|:---:|
| Incontestability provision | ✔ | ✔ | ✔ |
| Grace period provision | ✔ | ✔ | ✔ |
| Reinstatement provision | ✔ | ✔ | ✔ |
| Renewal provision | | ✔ | ✔ |
| Pre-existing conditions provision | | ✔ | ✔ |
| Claims provisions | ✔ | ✔ | ✔ |
| Legal actions provision | | ✔ | ✔ |
| Overinsurance provision | | ✔ | ✔ |
| Change of occupation provision | | | ✔ |
| Physical examination provision | | | ✔ |

# Individual Health Insurance Underwriting

Underwriters evaluate each application for individual health insurance to determine the degree of morbidity risk that a proposed insured represents. As noted in Chapter 2, morbidity refers to the incidence of illnesses and injuries, by age, occurring among a given group of people. The health insurance underwriting process is very similar to the process that insurance companies use to evaluate applications for life insurance.

# Morbidity Factors

The primary factors that affect the degree of morbidity risk presented by a proposed insured are the individual's (1) age, (2) current and past health, (3) sex, (4) occupation, (5) avocations, (6) work history, and (7) habits and lifestyle. We examine how each of these factors affects an individual's morbidity risk.

## Age

Morbidity rates generally increase with age. As people grow older, they are more likely to become ill, and the average duration of their illnesses increases. Further, the length of time required to recuperate from an injury also increases with age.

## Health

An individual's health history and current health are both important factors in determining morbidity risk. Many illnesses have a tendency to recur, and an individual's future health is strongly affected by her past and current illnesses and injuries.

## Sex

A person's sex has an effect on the degree of that person's morbidity risk. Because females generally experience a higher morbidity rate than males of the same age, the cost of providing health insurance coverage to females is generally higher than the cost of providing coverage to males.

## Occupation

A person's morbidity risk also depends on his occupation. Factors about a person's occupation that affect the degree of morbidity risk include the hazards inherent in the occupation, the stability of the occupation, and the amount of recovery time that people in that occupation usually need to resume their normal job duties. To reflect these differences in morbidity, health insurance underwriters establish several occupational classes and rank these classes according to morbidity rate. An individual's risk classification and corresponding premium rate correspond to the individual's occupation class. Figure 17.4 includes an example of an insurer's occupational rating classes, which range from least hazardous to most hazardous. Note that health insurers consider some occupations, such as experimental aircraft testing, to be so risk prone that applicants who work in those occupations are usually classified as uninsurable.

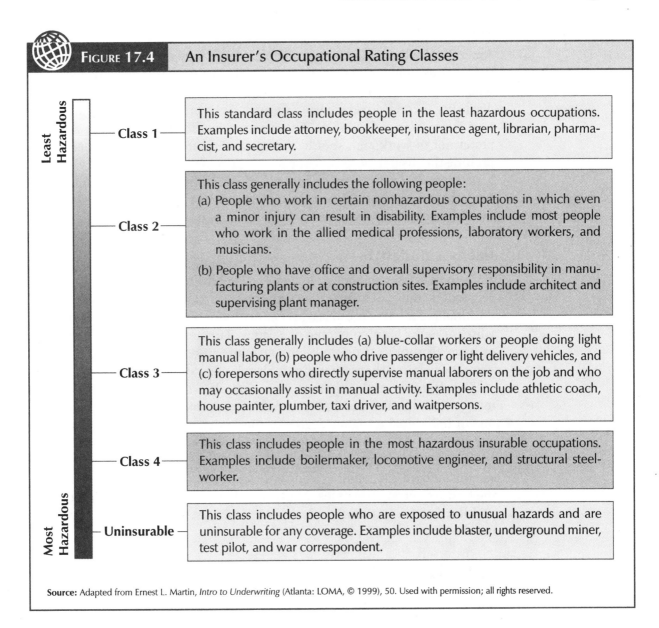

**FIGURE 17.4    An Insurer's Occupational Rating Classes**

Least Hazardous → Most Hazardous

**Class 1** — This standard class includes people in the least hazardous occupations. Examples include attorney, bookkeeper, insurance agent, librarian, pharmacist, and secretary.

**Class 2** — This class generally includes the following people:
(a) People who work in certain nonhazardous occupations in which even a minor injury can result in disability. Examples include most people who work in the allied medical professions, laboratory workers, and musicians.
(b) People who have office and overall supervisory responsibility in manufacturing plants or at construction sites. Examples include architect and supervising plant manager.

**Class 3** — This class generally includes (a) blue-collar workers or people doing light manual labor, (b) people who drive passenger or light delivery vehicles, and (c) forepersons who directly supervise manual laborers on the job and who may occasionally assist in manual activity. Examples include athletic coach, house painter, plumber, taxi driver, and waitpersons.

**Class 4** — This class includes people in the most hazardous insurable occupations. Examples include boilermaker, locomotive engineer, and structural steelworker.

**Uninsurable** — This class includes people who are exposed to unusual hazards and are uninsurable for any coverage. Examples include blaster, underground miner, test pilot, and war correspondent.

**Source:** Adapted from Ernest L. Martin, *Intro to Underwriting* (Atlanta: LOMA, © 1999), 50. Used with permission; all rights reserved.

## Avocations

An individual's avocations also have a strong bearing on his potential health insurance risk. Engaging in certain sports or hobbies may expose an individual to a significant chance of injury or disease. For example, a mountain climber is more prone to accidental injury than is a stamp collector. Hence, the manner in which a person spends leisure time may have a bearing on his exposure to health risks.

## Work History

An individual's work history also can have a bearing on her morbidity risk. For example, a person with a number of gaps in her work record or who has a history of temporary jobs might be deemed to be a poor risk for disability income coverage because such a person might lack the incentive to recover from a disability. The person may, for one reason or another, prefer not to work and, should she become disabled, might be inclined to prolong the disability so that she can continue receiving disability income benefits and avoid returning to work. Such an individual's morbidity risk is likely to be greater than the morbidity risk of an individual with a history of regular employment.

## Habits and Lifestyle

A person's habits and lifestyle can expose him to a high degree of risk of accidental injury or illness. For example, an individual who has a recent criminal record may present a higher degree of risk than does an individual who has never been convicted of a crime. Further, individuals who smoke or have alcohol or drug problems also are more likely to present health insurance claims than are individuals who do not abuse drugs or alcohol.

The degree of risk inherent in various lifestyles is often difficult to measure, and health insurance underwriters must be careful when assigning an individual a higher degree of morbidity risk on the basis of habits and lifestyle. Many jurisdictions have enacted antidiscrimination legislation to prevent health insurance underwriters from classifying individuals as substandard risks and charging them higher premium rates solely on the basis of certain lifestyles. Many jurisdictions, for example, specifically prohibit insurers from considering an applicant's sexual orientation during the underwriting process.

# Risk Classifications

Underwriters evaluate each applicant for individual health insurance to determine the degree of morbidity risk presented by the proposed insured. Using this evaluation, the underwriter usually places the applicant into one of three categories of risk—standard, substandard, or declined.

## Standard Risk

An applicant who is classified as a standard risk will be issued a policy at standard premium rates. The policy will not contain any special exclusions or reductions in benefits. Most applicants for individual health insurance are classified as standard risks.

## Substandard Risk

Those applicants who may be expected to present a higher-than-average morbidity risk are classified as substandard health insurance risks. Rather than decline such applicants for coverage, health insurers have developed several ways to modify health insurance policies to compensate for the extra risk represented by applicants in this category.

- Health insurers sometimes charge a higher premium rate to applicants who are classified as substandard risks.

- Health insurers sometimes modify the benefits available under a policy issued to insure a substandard risk. For example, the policy might include a longer elimination period or a lower maximum benefit amount than a policy issued to a standard risk.

- If an applicant presents a specific and definable extra morbidity risk, the insurer might attach an exclusion rider to the policy issued to that applicant. An **exclusion rider**, which is also called an *impairment rider*, specifies that benefits will not be provided for any loss that results from the condition specified in the rider. In this way, health insurers can often provide coverage at standard premium rates to an applicant who would otherwise be charged a higher rate because she has a known health problem or engages in certain activities that increase morbidity risk. For example, an insurer may be able to offer an individual who has a history of back disorders an individual disability income policy at standard premium rates by excluding from coverage any disability that results from the back disorders. (See Figure 17.5, which shows a sample exclusion rider.)

## Declined Risk

Applicants are declined coverage if they have very poor health or engage in extremely dangerous occupations or activities. Additionally, health insurers may decline to issue disability income coverage to applicants who would not suffer a substantial income loss during a disability either because the applicant has adequate disability income coverage through another provider or because a large percentage of the applicant's income would continue during a disability.

Many jurisdictions have issued regulations that prohibit insurers from declining coverage to physically disabled persons, unless such action can be supported by morbidity statistics. When insuring a disabled person, however, insurers are permitted to exclude coverage of the person's existing disability.

**Figure 17.5**     Sample Exclusion Rider

---

### ABC Life Insurance Company
New York, NY 00000
### WAIVER-RIDER

In consideration of the premium at which this policy is issued, it is agreed and understood, by and between the company and the insured, that the terms of this policy shall not apply to any disability or loss on the part of  Doris Holden
caused directly or indirectly, wholly or in part, anything in the policy to the contrary notwithstanding, by or from the following:

Any disease of or injury to the lumbosacral region of the spine or its underlying nerve structures, including intervertebral discs, any complications thereof, treatment or operation therefor.

In all other respects the provisions and conditions of the policy remain unchanged.

Attached to and forming
part of the policy number:
00000

This rider is effective at
12:00 noon standard time on:
September 19, 2004

*Allison Jones*
Secretary

*John Stevens*
President

**Issued to:**  Doris Holden      **Accepted by Insured:**      **Date:**

_____      _____

Countersigned at:    Authorized Representative:

_____      _____

# Pricing Health Insurance

To provide the funds it will need to pay health insurance claims as they come due, an insurance company must collect premiums from the people to whom it provides health insurance coverage. As in the case of life insurance, the insurance company uses those premiums to create a fund from which to pay benefits as claims are incurred.

The fundamental principles underlying the pricing of health insurance are the same as those underlying life insurance pricing. That is, health insurance premiums must be adequate to provide the promised benefits and must be equitable to all policyowners. Nevertheless, life insurance and health insurance have significant differences, and most of these differences affect how insurance companies price these two products. Before we describe how health insurance is priced, let's look at some of these differences between life insurance and health insurance.

- Whereas the amount payable for a life insurance claim is definitely defined by the policy, the amount payable for a health insurance claim is often much less definite. For example, medical expense claims range from fairly small amounts to very large amounts, depending on the severity of the covered illness or injury.

- An insurer is likely to pay a number of covered claims from each person insured by a health insurance policy, but it will pay only one death claim for each person insured by a life insurance policy.

- Inflation, changes in the economy, and changes in medical practice affect the amount of benefits paid for health insurance claims much more dramatically than such factors affect life insurance claims.

- Because of the variation in medical costs in different geographic areas, certain health insurance premiums must be calculated separately for different geographic areas. By contrast, life insurance premium rates at given ages generally do not vary by geographical location within North America.

As noted earlier, insurers use morbidity rates to calculate health insurance premium rates, just as they use mortality rates to calculate life insurance premium rates. The insurance company uses this information about morbidity rates to calculate its *claim costs*—the costs the insurer predicts that it will incur to provide the policy benefits promised. For example, medical expense insurance typically provides benefits to pay the following types of expenses: (1) hospital expenses, (2) surgical expenses, (3) physicians' fees, and (4) major medical expenses. The insurer must estimate its claim costs for each type of benefit provided.

Let's look at how an insurer might project its claim costs for benefits it will pay for hospital room and board expenses.

$$\left( \begin{array}{c} \text{Claim} \\ \text{costs} \end{array} \right) = \left( \begin{array}{c} \text{Frequency of the} \\ \text{expected claim} \end{array} \right) \times \left( \begin{array}{c} \text{Average amount of} \\ \text{each claim} \end{array} \right)$$

The *frequency* of the expected claim is the number of claims for hospital room and board expenses that the insurer will receive.

> **Example.** The Hathaway Insurance Company expects to receive 100 claims for hospital room and board. The average amount of each claim will be $1,600.
>
> **Analysis.** Hathaway's claim costs for hospital room and board will equal $160,000 (100 claims × $1,600 per claim).

The insurer uses its projected claim costs to calculate the net annual premium rates that will be sufficient to pay the promised health insurance benefits. The insurer then adds a loading factor that it estimates will be sufficient to cover all of its expenses and unforeseen contingencies. Because the risk is more uncertain for health insurance than for life insurance, insurance companies usually include in their loading for health insurance premiums a greater amount for unforeseen contingencies than they include in their loading for life insurance premiums. Recall that the net annual premium plus the loading equals the gross annual premium that the insurer charges for a policy.

Insurers generally calculate health insurance premium rates on an annual basis. If premiums are payable more frequently than annually, then the insurer adds a small amount to the gross annual premium to cover the additional expenses incurred in collecting premiums on this more frequent basis.

A number of states require gross premiums for health insurance policies to be "reasonable." As a measure of "reasonableness," insurers are generally required to calculate the anticipated loss ratio for a group of similar policies, and this loss ratio typically must be at least a minimum stated percentage. The **loss ratio** is the ratio of benefits an insurer paid out for a block of policies to the premiums the insurer received for those policies. The loss ratio measures the percentage of total premiums the insurer received for a block of policies and that the insurer paid out in policy benefits. Note that even if the loss ratio for a block of policies remains level over time, the amount of premiums required for those policies will increase if policy benefit costs increase.

The premium rate for an individual health insurance policy varies depending on the choices the applicant makes concerning the coverage the policy provides. For example, an applicant is permitted to make some choices concerning the benefit levels and renewal provisions that are included in an individual health insurance policy. Also, insurers usually offer an applicant for an individual medical expense policy several choices concerning the amount of the policy's deductible; the larger the deductible, the less the amount of premium required. Insurers generally offer an applicant for an individual disability income policy several possible combinations of elimination periods and maximum benefit periods. Applicants for individual disability income policies also may be able to purchase the supplemental disability income benefits that we described in Chapter 16.

## Key Terms

Health Insurance Portability and Accountability Act (HIPAA)
Health Maintenance Organization (HMO) Act of 1973
Mental Health Parity Act
Newborns' and Mothers' Health Protection Act of 1996
Women's Health and Cancer Rights Act of 1998
renewal provision
cancellable policy
optionally renewable policy
class of policies
conditionally renewable policy
guaranteed renewable policy
noncancellable policy
pre-existing conditions provision
pre-existing condition
legal actions provision
overinsurance provision
overinsured person
change of occupation provision
physical examination provision
exclusion rider
claim costs
loss ratio

## Endnotes

1. P.L. 104-191 (1996).
2. 42 U.S.C. 300e *et seq.* (2004).
3. P.L. 104-204 (1996).
4. 42 U.S.C. 300gg-4 (2004).
5. P.L. 105-277 (1998).

# Group Health Insurance Policies

## objectives

*After reading this chapter, you should be able to*

- Identify and describe the provisions that typically are included in group health insurance policies

- Calculate the amount of benefits payable when an insured is covered by two group health insurance policies that both contain a coordination of benefits (COB) provision

- Identify the factors that group underwriters use to determine a group's expected morbidity rate

- Identify and describe three funding mechanisms used in connection with fully insured group health insurance plans

- Explain why an employer might decide to self-insure a group health insurance plan

- Describe the operation of a self-insured group health insurance plan, including the use of stop-loss insurance and plan administration

M ost health insurance issued by commercial insurers is provided by group health insurance policies. In this chapter, we describe the features of traditional group health insurance plans provided by commercial insurance companies. Although we focus on traditional group health insurance policies, many of the features we describe also are included in group managed care plans. We begin by describing the provisions typically included in group health insurance policies. Then we describe group health insurance underwriting and group health insurance premiums.

# Group Health Insurance Policy Provisions

As we described in Chapter 12, a group health insurance policy is an enforceable contract between an insurer and the group policyholder that purchased the group insurance coverage. The insured members of the group are not parties to the insurance contract and are not given individual policies. Instead, each insured group member is given a certificate or benefit booklet that provides information about the group health insurance coverage and the insureds' rights under the policy.

An insurer can provide all of a group's coverage under one group health insurance policy, or the insurer can issue separate master policies to the group policyholder for each type of coverage provided. For example, an insurer could issue both a group major medical policy and a group disability income policy to the group policyholder. In addition, a group policyholder can choose to purchase various types of health insurance coverage from one or more providers.

In Chapter 12, we also described the provisions that are included in both group life and group health insurance policies. The policy provisions we described—eligibility requirements, grace period provision, incontestability provision, and termination provisions—are summarized in Figure 18.1.

Many policy provisions are substantially the same in all group life and group health insurance policies. Some health insurance policy provisions, however, vary depending on the type of coverage they provide.

- Group medical expense insurance policies specify the types of medical expenses they cover, the benefit maximums (if any), the deductible amount, and the coinsurance features. Group disability income policies specify the definition of total disability, the elimination period, the method of determining the amount of the disability income benefit payable, and the length of the maximum benefit period.

- Most employer-employee group medical expense policies provide that an insured employee's family and dependents are eligible for group insurance coverage. Such dependent coverage is generally available at the option of the insured group member, who usually must pay an additional premium amount for dependent coverage. In contrast, most group disability income policies do not provide coverage for dependents of group members.

In Chapter 17, we described the provisions that typically are included in individual health insurance policies. Many of these provisions also are included in group health insurance policies. For example, both individual and group health insurance policies include an incontestability provision and a grace period provision. Both individual disability income policies

---

## FIGURE 18.1    Provisions Common to Group Life and Group Health Insurance Policies

**Eligibility requirements**

Every group policy describes who is eligible for coverage under the policy.

**Grace period provision**

Group policies typically provide a 31-day grace period during which insurance coverage remains in force even if the premium is not paid. If the required premium is not paid by the end of the grace period, the group policy terminates, and the group policyholder is legally obligated to pay the premium for the coverage provided during the grace period.

**Incontestability provision**

Group policies contain an incontestability provision that limits the period during which the insurance company may use statements in the group insurance application to contest the validity of the master group insurance contract. Generally, the insurer may contest the validity of a group contract within two years after the issue date of the policy.

If a group insured makes material misrepresentations about his insurability in a written application, then the incontestability provision allows the insurer to contest the group insured's coverage on the ground of material misrepresentation in the application. The period during which the insurer has the right to contest the validity of a group insured's coverage usually is one or two years after the date of that group insured's application for insurance.

**Termination provisions**

Group policies contain provisions that govern (1) when the group insurance policy will terminate and (2) when a group insured's coverage will terminate.

and group disability income policies include a physical examination provision. Figure 18.2 provides a comparison of the provisions that typically are included in individual medical expense, individual disability income, group medical expense, and group disability income policies.

| FIGURE 18.2 | Comparison of Provisions Typically Included in Individual and Group Health Insurance Policies | | | |
|---|---|---|---|---|
| Policy Provision | Individual Medical Expense Insurance Policy | Individual Disability Income Policy | Group Medical Expense Insurance Policy | Group Disability Income Policy |
| Incontestability provision | ✔ | ✔ | ✔ | ✔ |
| Grace period provision | ✔ | ✔ | ✔ | ✔ |
| Reinstatement provision | ✔ | ✔ | | |
| Renewal provision | ✔ | ✔ | | |
| Pre-existing conditions provision | ✔ | ✔ | ✔ | ✔ |
| Claims provisions | ✔ | ✔ | ✔ | ✔ |
| Legal actions provision | ✔ | ✔ | ✔ | ✔ |
| Overinsurance provision | ✔ | ✔ | | |
| Change of occupation provision | | ✔ | | |
| Physical examination provision | | ✔ | | ✔ |
| Coordination of benefits provision | | | ✔ | |
| Conversion provision | | | ✔ | |

In this section, we describe how the pre-existing conditions provision included in group health insurance policies differs from the provision included in individual health insurance policies. We also describe the coordination of benefits provision and the conversion provision, which are unique to group health insurance.

## Pre-Existing Conditions Provision

Like individual health insurance policies, many group health insurance policies contain a *pre-existing conditions provision* stating that benefits are not payable for pre-existing conditions until the insured has been covered under the policy for a specified length of time. Group health insurance policies define a pre-existing condition in a variety of ways. Group policies usually specify that a condition is no longer considered pre-existing—and, thus, the condition is eligible for coverage—if the insured (1) has not received treatment for that condition for a specified period of time following the effective date of coverage or (2) has been covered under the policy for a specified number of consecutive months, such as 12 months.

Most group policies give the insurer the right to waive the requirements of the pre-existing conditions provision for any group member who was eligible for coverage when the policy became effective if (1) the group was previously covered by a group health insurance policy issued by another insurer and (2) the group member was covered by that prior policy. Thus, if a group policyholder decides to switch insurance carriers, the pre-existing conditions provision in the new carrier's policy will not apply to group members who were covered under the earlier plan.

In the United States, the federal Health Insurance Portability and Accountability Act (HIPAA) imposes a number of requirements on employer-sponsored group health insurance plans, health insurance companies, and health maintenance organizations. As a general rule, the requirements imposed by HIPAA are designed to provide wider access to health insurance coverage and to provide greater portability of benefits between group health insurance plans. Specifically, HIPAA places restrictions on the pre-existing conditions provision included in group medical expense insurance plans. These limits are designed to allow group insureds who have a pre-existing condition to change jobs without losing coverage for the condition.

## Coordination of Benefits Provision

In the United States, many people are eligible for coverage under more than one group medical expense plan. For example, spouses who both work typically are eligible for coverage under their own employers' group policy and under their spouses' group policy. If benefits payable under such duplicate coverage were not coordinated, the insured could receive full benefits from both policies and, consequently, would profit from an illness or injury. The *coordination of benefits (COB) provision* is designed to prevent a group member who is insured under more than one group medical expense insurance policy from receiving benefit amounts that are greater than the amount of medical expenses the insured actually incurred. The COB provision prevents duplicate benefit payments by defining the group health plan that is the primary provider of benefits and the plan that is the secondary provider of benefits for insured group members who have duplicate group medical expense coverage.

A plan defined in the COB provision as the primary provider of benefits is the plan that is responsible for paying the full benefit amounts promised under the plan. When the plan designated as the primary plan has paid the full benefit amounts promised, then the insured can submit the claim to the secondary plan along with a description of the benefit amounts the primary plan paid. The provider of the secondary plan then determines the amount payable for the claim in accordance with the terms of that plan.

A plan's COB provision may take one of several approaches to determining the amount of benefits payable when the plan is functioning as the secondary provider of benefits. Under the most common approach, the secondary provider first calculates the amount of the insured individual's total allowable expenses and the amount of those expenses that the insurer would pay if it were the primary provider. *Allowable expenses* are those reasonable and customary expenses that the insured incurred and that are covered under an insured's group medical expense plans. The secondary provider then looks at the amount the primary provider paid. If payment of the full benefit amount provided by the secondary plan would result in the insured receiving more in benefit payments from both plans than the total amount of allowable medical expenses, then the secondary plan pays only the difference between the amount of allowable expenses incurred and the amount the insured already received from the primary plan. Under this type of COB provision, the insured individual typically pays no portion of her covered medical expenses; the primary plan pays all benefits in excess of the deductible and coinsurance requirements, and the secondary plan pays the portion of allowable medical expenses not paid by the primary plan, including reimbursing the insured for any deductible and coinsurance amounts paid by the insured.

> **Example.** Sean Poe is covered by two group medical expense plans; both plans include a coordination of benefits provision. Each plan also specifies a $250 deductible and a 20 percent coinsurance requirement. In May, Mr. Poe incurred $5,100 in allowable medical expenses. He submitted a claim for his expenses to the plan designated as his primary plan. Mr. Poe later submitted the claim, along with a description of the benefit paid by the primary plan, to his secondary plan.

**Analysis.** The plan designated as the primary plan will pay benefits equal to $3,880. The calculations used to determine this benefit amount are as follows.

| | |
|---|---|
| $5,100 | Total allowable expense |
| – 250 | Deductible |
| $4,850 | |
| – 970 | Coinsurance (0.20 × $4,850) |
| **$3,880** | **Amount payable by the primary plan** |

Because both plans contain the same deductible and coinsurance features, Mr. Poe's secondary plan normally also would pay him $3,880 in benefits. Under the COB provision, however, the secondary plan will pay Mr. Poe only $1,220; that is, the secondary plan will pay the difference between the total allowable expenses ($5,100) and the amount the primary plan paid in benefits ($3,880). Mr. Poe incurs no out-of-pocket costs.

Some group medical expense insurance policies contain another type of coordination of benefits provision, generally called a nonduplication of benefits provision, that limits the amount payable if the plan is defined as the secondary plan. A **_nonduplication of benefits provision_** is a COB provision that, if included in a secondary provider's plan, limits the amount payable by the secondary plan to the difference, if any, between the amount paid by the primary plan and the amount that would have been payable by the secondary plan had that plan been the primary plan. A nonduplication of benefits provision requires the insured individual to pay a portion of the cost of covered medical expenses and, thus, more strictly limits the amount of benefits payable than does the COB provision we discussed previously.

**Example.** Let's return to our example in which Sean Poe is covered under two group medical expense plans that contain the same deductible and coinsurance features. In this example, however, assume that the plan designated as Mr. Poe's secondary plan contains a nonduplication of benefits provision.

**Analysis.** As in the earlier example, Mr. Poe's primary plan would pay a $3,880 policy benefit. Under the nonduplication of benefits provision, however, the secondary plan would pay no benefit because the primary plan had already paid the full $3,880 benefit amount to which Mr. Poe was entitled under the secondary plan.

Most COB provisions include rules for determining which plan is primary. First, most COB provisions state that when an insured also is covered by another group plan that does not include a COB provision, the plan without a COB provision is the primary provider of benefits; the plan with the COB provision is secondary. In addition, if more than one group plan covering an individual includes a COB provision, then the primary plan is usually defined as the plan under which the insured is covered as an employee rather than as a dependent.

> **Example.** Jeanette and Norm Langer are married and have a young daughter, Lacey. Both Jeanette and Norm work full time for employers that provide group medical expense coverage to employees and their spouses and dependents.
>
> **Analysis.** If only one plan covering the Langers includes a COB provision, then the plan without the COB provision is considered the primary payer of benefits for both Jeanette and Norm. Alternatively, if both plans contain a COB provision, then Jeanette's primary provider is her employer's plan, and her secondary provider is the plan provided by Norm's employer; Norm's primary provider is his employer's plan, and his secondary provider is the plan provided by Jeanette's employer.

Insurers use a variety of methods to define which plan is the primary payer if an individual is covered as a dependent under more than one group plan. A common method, known as the *birthday rule* or the *earlier birthday method*, states that the plan covering the employee whose birth date falls earlier in the calendar year will be considered the primary provider of benefits for a dependent. Note that the employees' actual ages are not a factor in determining the primary provider under the birthday rule.

> **Example.** Let's look again at the medical expense plans covering Jeanette and Norm Langer and their daughter, Lacey. Jeanette Langer's birthday falls in March, and Norm Langer's birthday falls in September.
>
> **Analysis.** According to the birthday rule, the plan provided by Jeanette's employer would be considered the primary provider of benefits for Lacey because Jeanette's birthday falls earlier in the year than Norm's birthday.

## Conversion Provision

The laws of most states in the United States require group medical expense insurance policies to include a conversion provision. Even in jurisdictions that do not require insurers to do so—Canada, for example—insurers often include a conversion provision in their group medical expense policies. The **conversion provision** grants an insured group member who is leaving the group a limited right to purchase an individual medical expense insurance policy without presenting evidence of insurability. The right is limited in that the insurer can refuse to issue the individual policy if the coverage would result in the insured group member becoming overinsured. For example, an employee who is changing jobs and will be eligible for group medical expense insurance from his new employer would probably be overinsured if he were also issued an individual medical expense insurance policy.

When an insured group member elects to convert his group coverage to an individual medical expense insurance policy, he will find that the individual policy differs from the group policy in several respects. For example, the insured generally will be charged a higher premium rate for the individual policy than he paid for group coverage, and the benefits provided by the individual policy probably will be more restricted than those provided by the group policy. Requirements regarding the specific coverages that a conversion policy must provide vary from jurisdiction to jurisdiction.

## COBRA Continuation Coverage

Many events can result in an individual no longer being eligible for coverage under a group policy. Often, people who lose their group medical expense coverage cannot afford the cost of an individual medical expense policy. To protect such individuals, the U.S. federal **Consolidated Omnibus Budget Reconciliation Act (COBRA)** requires all group insurance plans that provide medical expense benefits and are sponsored by employers with 20 or more employees to allow certain covered employees and their dependent spouses and dependent children the right to continue their group insurance coverage for a limited time in specified situations, known as *qualifying events*, in which their group coverage would otherwise terminate.[1] For example, when an employee terminates his employment, he ceases to be a member of the group and, thus, is no longer eligible to participate in the group insurance plan. As a result of COBRA, termination of employment that results in loss of coverage is a qualifying event; the employee must be allowed to continue his group medical expense coverage for up to 18 months following termination of employment. The employee's spouse and dependent children also may continue their group coverage for up to 18 months. In addition, the spouse and dependent children of a covered employee are given the right to continue their group medical expense coverage for up to 36 months following either the employee's death or a divorce or legal separation from the employee. COBRA also gives a dependent child who ceases to be an eligible dependent under a group medical expense plan the right to continue group coverage for up to 36 months.

A person who elects to continue group medical expense coverage under COBRA must pay the full cost of continuation coverage, including any portion of the premium that was paid by the employer. In addition, the insurer can add an administrative fee of 2 percent. Thus, the premium generally is 102 percent of the actual premium that would be charged for the person's group medical expense coverage if he were eligible for the group coverage.

The plan administrator of a group medical expense plan must notify covered individuals of their rights under COBRA when they become covered under the plan and when a qualifying event occurs. Upon the occurrence of a qualifying event, the affected individuals have a specified time within which they can elect to continue their group medical expense insurance coverage. This continuation coverage must be identical to that provided to individuals who are eligible for coverage under the group plan.

# Group Health Insurance Underwriting

When an insurer evaluates a group for group health insurance coverage, the insurer applies the group underwriting principles we described in Chapter 12. Usually, the group as a whole—rather than the individual members of the group—must meet the insurer's underwriting requirements. If the size of the group is small, however, the insurer may require the individual members of the group to submit evidence of insurability. We described individual health insurance underwriting in Chapter 17.

The group's risk classification—standard, substandard, or declined—is established on the basis of the group's expected morbidity rate. The expected morbidity rate for a group reflects a number of factors, including the following:

- **The nature of the industry in which the group members work.** Some industries, for example, present greater occupational hazards to employees than do other industries.

- **The age distribution of the group.** Morbidity rates generally increase as the group members get older.

- **The distribution of males and females in the group.** Females generally experience higher morbidity rates than do males of the same age.

If a sufficient amount of previous claim experience information is available, the group health insurance underwriter uses the group's own morbidity experience to estimate the group's expected morbidity experience. As in group life insurance, there are three possible rating methods: *manual rating*, *experience rating*, and *blended rating*. In calculating manually rated premiums, the insurance company generally derives the amount of its projected annual claim costs from the actual morbidity experience of all those groups it expected to have normal morbidity. In calculating experience-rated premiums, the morbidity experience of a particular group is the basis for that group's net annual premiums. Sometimes an insurer combines the experience of several small groups to produce experience-rated premiums.

# Funding Mechanisms

The way in which a group insurance plan's claim costs and administrative expenses are paid is known as the plan's *funding mechanism*. A number of funding mechanisms are available for group insurance plans. At one extreme is a *fully insured plan* for which the group policyholder makes periodic premium payments to the insurance company, and the insurance company bears the responsibility for all claim payments. At the other extreme is a *fully self-insured plan* for which the group policyholder—usually an employer—takes complete responsibility for all claim payments and related expenses. Between these extremes are a number of alternative funding mechanisms. In this section, we describe the methods most often used to fund group health insurance coverage.

## Fully Insured Plans

A fully insured plan is the traditional funding arrangement for a group health insurance plan. The insurer issues the group health insurance policy on a one-year renewable term basis, and each year's premium pays for just that year's coverage. New premium rates are charged each year based on the sex and attained ages of the insured members of the group. These group health insurance premium rates are typically guaranteed for 12 months. At the end of the policy year, the insurance company may establish new premium rates for the group. Most group long-term disability income insurance plans are fully insured.

Premiums for group health insurance policies usually are payable monthly and can be paid by the group policyholder, the individuals insured under the group policy, or both. As noted in Chapter 12, if the group policyholder pays all of the premiums without requiring the individual insureds to pay anything, the group insurance plan is said to be *noncontributory*. If individual insureds pay any part of the premium, the plan is said to be *contributory*. Individual insureds' contributions generally are paid to the group policyholder, which then makes monthly premium payments to the insurer. For most employer-sponsored group health insurance plans, the employer collects required premium contributions from covered employees through payroll deductions.

The insurer bears all risk under a fully insured plan. If the dollar amount of the claims submitted exceeds the dollar amount of premiums collected, the insurer must absorb the loss. On the other hand, if the group experiences lower claim expenses than anticipated and the dollar amount of the claims submitted is less than the dollar amount of premiums collected, the insurer retains the difference as profit.

To enable employers to reduce the total cost of providing health insurance coverage for employees, insurers and employers have developed a number of alternatives to the traditional fully insured plan to modify the manner in which premiums are paid. Figure 18.3 explains three of these alternatives—retrospective rating arrangements, premium delay arrangements, and minimum premium plans—which modify the manner in which a group policyholder pays premiums for group health insurance. Under these fully insured plans, however, the employer still must pay premiums for the group insurance policy, and the insurer remains responsible for paying all covered claims.

---

 **FIGURE 18.3**   Alternative Funding Mechanisms

- A ***retrospective rating arrangement*** is a group health insurance funding mechanism under which the insurer agrees to charge the group policyholder a lower monthly premium than it would normally charge for the group health insurance plan based on the group's prior claim experience. The group policyholder agrees that it will pay an additional amount to the insurer if, at the end of the policy year, the group's claim experience has been unfavorable. By reducing its monthly premium cost, the employer is able to increase the amount of funds it has available to it throughout those months. A retrospective rating arrangement also usually includes an experience refund feature. If the group's claim experience during the policy year is favorable, the insurer will pay the group policyholder an experience refund.

- A ***premium delay arrangement*** is a group health insurance funding mechanism that allows the group policyholder to postpone paying monthly group insurance premiums for a stated period of time beyond the expiration of the policy's grace period. As a result, the group policyholder has the use of those funds during the premium delay period. Typically, the group policyholder has the right to delay premium payments up to 60 or 90 days beyond the end of the grace period. When the group insurance contract terminates, the group policyholder must pay any deferred premiums.

- A ***minimum premium plan (MPP)*** is a group health insurance funding mechanism under which the group policyholder deposits into a special account funds that are sufficient to pay a stated amount of expected claims. For example, the group policyholder may deposit the amount needed to pay 80 or 90 percent of expected claims. The insurer administers the plan and pays claims from that special account until the allocated funds are exhausted. Thereafter, the insurer is responsible for paying claims from its own funds, and it charges the group policyholder a premium for the coverage it provides. By using this funding arrangement, the premium that the insurer charges for the coverage it provides can be greatly reduced; the amount of premium taxes is also thereby reduced.

## Self-Insured Plans

Many employers are taking an active role in providing health insurance benefits by choosing to partially or fully self-insure, or self-fund, the medical expense or disability income coverage they provide for their employees. As a result, the employers bear some or all of the risk of paying claims and the risk that claims may be excessive.

Many employers, for example, fully self-insure short-term disability income coverage for their employees by means of a salary continuation plan. A *salary continuation plan* typically provides 100 percent of the insured employee's salary, beginning on the first day of the employee's absence resulting from illness or injury and continuing for some specified time.

Alternatively, most group medical expense insurance plans are partially self-insured. Under such an arrangement, the employer is financially responsible for paying a certain level of claims, and the risk for claims above that level is transferred to a traditional health insurance provider. For example, an employer might self-insure the plan's basic medical expense benefits and purchase supplemental major medical insurance coverage from an insurance company.

Many employers believe that self-insuring can help them better control increasing health care costs by allowing them to avoid some of the costs that are built into traditional insurance premium rates. For example, a self-insured employer can avoid paying agent commissions and the insurer's overhead expenses. Likewise, premium taxes are imposed on the premium income an insurer receives from its business within a jurisdiction during a given calendar year; because such taxes are an expense that insurers incorporate into their premium rates, an employer can avoid paying those expenses by self-insuring. Another benefit an employer may receive from self-insuring is an improved cash flow because the employer retains the money it would have paid in premiums and can earn interest on that money.

Self-insured plans offer another advantage to some employers in the United States. Because self-insured plans are exempt from state laws that apply to insurance policies, employers that self-insure have more freedom in designing their group insurance plans. For example, insurance laws in many states require health insurance policies to include certain coverages. The cost of those mandated coverages must be reflected in any plan an insurer offers in those states. A self-insured plan is not subject to these state insurance laws, and, thus, an employer offering a self-insured plan does not have to include state-mandated coverages. Employer-employee plans, nevertheless, must comply with state and federal laws that regulate employee benefit plans. Such plans, for example, must comply with requirements imposed by ERISA.

## Stop-Loss Coverage

If a self-insured group experiences several catastrophic medical claims in one year, the employer may not have the financial resources to pay all of the claims. For this reason, many employers that self-insure purchase from an insurance company *stop-loss insurance*, which enables employers to place a maximum dollar limit on their liability for paying health insurance claims. Several forms of stop-loss coverage are available.

- Under *individual stop-loss coverage* or *specific stop-loss coverage*, the stop-loss insurer pays a portion of each claim that exceeds a stated amount.

- Under *aggregate stop-loss coverage*, the stop-loss insurer becomes responsible for paying claims when the employer's total claims exceed a stated dollar amount within a stated period of time.

Stop-loss coverage typically is provided under a contract entered into between the stop-loss carrier (the insurer) and the employer. The contract defines the relationship between the carrier and the employer and includes a schedule of benefit payments for which the carrier will reimburse the employer. The agreement is typically for a 12-month period. Note that the stop-loss carrier does not make benefit payments directly to the insured group members; instead, the carrier reimburses the employer, which retains responsibility for making claim payments to insureds.

## Plan Administration

Self-insured plans are administered by a variety of methods. Some employers that self-insure their plans are able to fully administer their own plans. For other employers, having an outside organization provide some or all administrative services for the plan is more cost-effective. These employers usually purchase an *administrative services only (ASO) contract* from an insurance company or other organization, such as a third-party administrator (TPA). Under an ASO contract, the employer pays a fee in exchange for the administrative services provided by the insurer or TPA. These fees are not subject to state premium taxes.

## Key Terms

coordination of benefits (COB) provision
allowable expenses
nonduplication of benefits provision
conversion provision
Consolidated Omnibus Budget Reconciliation Act (COBRA)
funding mechanism
fully insured plan
fully self-insured plan
retrospective rating arrangement
premium delay arrangement
minimum premium plan (MPP)
salary continuation plan
stop-loss insurance
individual stop-loss coverage
aggregate stop-loss coverage
administrative services only (ASO) contract

## Endnote

1. 26 U.S.C. 4980D (2000).

# Glossary

**401(k) plan.** In the United States, a special type of savings plan that allows employees to make pre-tax contributions to the plan. [14]

**412(i) plan.** *See* **individual policy pension trust**.

**absolute assignment.** An assignment of a life insurance policy under which the policyowner transfers all of his policy ownership rights to an assignee. [9]

**accelerated death benefit.** A supplemental life insurance policy benefit that gives a policyowner-insured the right to receive all or part of the policy's death benefit before her death if certain conditions are met. Also known as a *living benefit*. [7]

**accidental death and dismemberment (AD&D) benefit.** A supplemental life insurance policy benefit that provides an accidental death benefit and provides a dismemberment benefit payable if an accident causes the insured to lose any two limbs or sight in both eyes. [7]

**accidental death benefit.** A supplemental life insurance policy benefit that provides a death benefit in addition to the policy's basic death benefit if the insured dies as a result of an accident. [7]

**accumulation at interest dividend option.** A policy dividend option under which the policy dividends are left on deposit with the insurer to accumulate at interest. [9]

**accumulation period.** The period between the contract owner's purchase of a deferred annuity and the beginning of the payout period. [11]

**accumulation unit.** An ownership share in selected subaccounts of the separate account held during the accumulation period of a variable deferred annuity. [11]

**accumulation value.** During the accumulation period of a deferred annuity, the amount paid for the annuity, plus interest earned, less the amount of any withdrawals and fees. [11]

**actively-at-work provision.** A group insurance policy provision which requires that to be eligible for coverage, an employee must be actively at work—rather than ill or on leave—on the day the insurance coverage is to take effect. [12]

**actuarial assumptions.** The estimated values on which an insurer bases its product pricing calculations. [4]

**actuary.** A specialist who is responsible for calculating the premium rates an insurance company charges for its products. [4]

**AD&D benefit.** *See* **accidental death and dismemberment benefit**.

**ADA.** *See* **Americans with Disabilities Act**.

**additional insured rider.** *See* **second insured rider**.

**additional term insurance dividend option.** A policy dividend option under which the insurer uses each policy dividend as a net single premium to purchase one-year term insurance on the insured's life. Also known as the *fifth dividend option.* [9]

**ADEA.** *See* **Age Discrimination in Employment Act**.

**administrative services only (ASO) contract.** A contract under which an insurer or other organization agrees to provide some or all administrative services for a self-insured group health insurance plan. [18]

**Age Discrimination in Employment Act (ADEA).** A U.S. federal law that protects older workers from being discriminated against because of their age. [13]

**aggregate stop-loss coverage.** Stop-loss insurance under which the insurer becomes responsible for paying claims when the employer's total claims exceed a stated dollar amount within a stated period of time. [18]

**aleatory contract.** A contract for which one party provides something of value to another party in exchange for a conditional promise. *Contrast with* **commutative contract**. [3]

**allocated funding vehicle.** A retirement plan funding vehicle in which all of the plan sponsor's contributions are credited to individual participants in a manner that gives the participants a legally enforceable claim to the benefits related to those contributions. [14]

**allowable expenses.** Those reasonable and customary expenses that an insured incurred and that are covered under the insured's group medical expense plans. [18]

**Americans with Disabilities Act (ADA).** A U.S. federal law that requires disabled employees of certain employers to have equal access to the life and health insurance coverages that are available to other employees. [13]

**Annual Statement.** An accounting report each U.S. insurer prepares each calendar year and files with the insurance department in each state in which the insurer operates. [1]

**annuitant.** The person whose lifetime is used to determine the amount of benefits payable under an annuity contract. [11]

**annuitization.** Exercising the right to receive periodic income payments from a deferred annuity. [11]

**annuity.** A series of periodic payments. [11]

**annuity certain.** *See* **period certain annuity**.

**annuity contract.** A contract under which an insurer promises to make a series of periodic payments to a named individual in exchange for a premium or a series of premiums. [1]

**annuity date.** The date on which an insurer begins to make periodic income payments under an annuity contract. Also known as the *income date.* [11]

**annuity mortality rates.** The mortality rates experienced by persons purchasing life annuities. [11]

**annuity period.** The time span between each of the payments in the series of periodic income payments made under an annuity contract. [11]

**annuity unit.** A share in the subaccounts of an insurer's separate account that determines the size of future periodic income payments under a variable annuity contract after the contract has been annuitized. [11]

**antiselection.** The tendency of individuals who believe they have a greater-than-average likelihood of loss to seek insurance protection to a greater extent than do those who believe they have an average or a less-than-average likelihood of loss. [2]

**APL option.** *See* **automatic premium loan option**.

**applicant.** The person or business that applies for an insurance policy. [2]

**APS.** *See* **Attending Physician's Statement**.

**ASO contract.** *See* **administrative services only contract**.

**assessment method.** A method used in the past to fund life insurance in which the participants in an insurance plan prepaid an equal portion of the estimated annual cost of the plan's death benefits. If actual costs were less than expected, then participants received refunds. If costs were more than expected, then participants paid an additional amount. [4]

**assets.** All things of value owned by a company. [1]

**assignee.** The party to whom property rights are transferred in an assignment. [9]

**assignment.** An agreement under which one party transfers some or all of his ownership rights in a particular property to another party. [9]

**assignment provision.** A life insurance policy provision that describes the roles of the insurer and the policyowner when the policy is assigned. [9]

**assignor.** The property owner who makes an assignment. [9]

**attained age.** The age an insured has reached (attained) on a specified date. [5]

**attained age conversion.** A conversion of a term life insurance policy to a cash value life insurance policy in which the renewal premium rate is based on the insured's age when the coverage is converted. *Contrast with* **original age conversion**. [5]

**Attending Physician's Statement (APS).** A document reporting the care given by a physician who has treated a person. [10]

**automatic dividend option.** A specified policy dividend option that an insurer will apply if the policyowner does not choose an option. [9]

**automatic nonforfeiture benefit.** A specific nonforfeiture benefit that becomes effective automatically when a renewal premium for a cash value life insurance policy is not paid by the end of the grace period and the policyowner has not elected another nonforfeiture option. [8]

**automatic premium loan (APL) option.** A cash value life insurance policy nonforfeiture option under which the insurer will automatically pay an overdue premium for the policyowner by making a loan against the policy's cash value as long as the cash value equals or exceeds the amount of the premium due. [8]

**back-end load.** An amount charged to a contract owner when she withdraws money from an annuity contract. Also known as a *surrender charge*. [11]

**bargaining contract.** A contract in which both parties, as equals, set the terms and conditions of the contract. *Contrast with* **contract of adhesion**. [3]

**basic medical expense coverage.** Medical expense insurance coverage consisting of separate benefits for each specific type of covered medical care cost. Basic coverage typically provides benefits for hospital, surgical, and physicians' expenses. [15]

**beneficiary.** The person or party the owner of an insurance policy names to receive the policy benefit. [2]

**benefit formula.** A formula that describes the calculation of a plan sponsor's financial obligation to participants in a retirement plan. [14]

**benefit period.** The time during which an insurer will pay income benefits to an insured under a disability income insurance policy. [16]

**benefit schedule.** A schedule included in group life insurance policies to define the amount of life insurance the policy provides for each group insured. [13]

**bilateral contract.** A contract for which both parties make legally enforceable promises when they enter into the contract. *Contrast with* **unilateral contract**. [3]

**blended rating.** A method of setting group insurance premium rates under which the insurer uses a combination of experience rating and manual rating. [12]

**block of policies.** A group of policies issued to insureds who are all the same age, the same sex, and in the same risk classification. [4]

**business continuation insurance plan.** An insurance plan designed to enable a business owner (or owners) to provide for the business' continued operation if the owner or another key person dies. [5]

**business overhead expense coverage.** Disability income coverage that provides benefits designed to pay a disabled insured's share of a business' overhead expenses. [16]

**buy-sell agreement.** An agreement in which (1) one party agrees to purchase the financial interest that a second party has in a business following the second party's death and (2) the second party agrees to direct her estate to sell her interest in the business to the purchasing party. [5]

**buy-up option.** Individually purchased supplementary disability income coverage that increases the benefit amount available to an insured under a group disability income policy. [16]

**calendar-year deductible.** A deductible that applies to the total of all allowable expenses an insured incurs during a given calendar year. [15]

**Canada Health Act.** A Canadian federal law that affirms the Canadian government's commitment to providing a universal, accessible, comprehensive, portable, and publicly administered health insurance system. [15]

**Canada Pension Plan (CPP).** In Canada, a federal program that provides a pension for wage earners who have contributed money into the plan during their working years. The CPP covers workers in all provinces except Quebec. [14]

**cancellable policy.** An individual health insurance policy that gives the insurer the right to terminate the policy at any time, for any reason, simply by notifying the policyowner that the policy is cancelled and by refunding any advance premium that has been paid for the policy. [17]

**capital.** The amount of money invested in a company by its owners. [1]

**capitation payment.** A flat amount a medical care provider receives from a managed care organization each month for each plan member who is under the provider's care, regardless of the number or cost of services provided to the plan member. [15]

**case management.** A process by which a managed care plan (1) identifies plan members who require extensive, complex health care, (2) develops an appropriate treatment strategy based on medical necessity and appropriateness and the availability of alternative care solutions, and (3) coordinates and monitors patient care. [15]

**cash dividend option.** A policy dividend option under which the insurance company sends the policyowner a check in the amount of the policy dividend that was declared. [9]

**cash payment nonforfeiture option.** A nonforfeiture option that permits the owner of a cash value life insurance policy to discontinue premium payments and surrender the policy in exchange for a lump-sum payment of the policy's cash surrender value. [8]

**cash surrender value.** The amount, before adjustments for factors such as policy loans, that the owner of a cash value life insurance policy is entitled to receive upon surrendering the policy. Also known as *surrender value*. [6]

**cash value.** The savings element of a cash value life insurance policy, which represents the policyowner's ownership interest in the policy. [1, 6]

**cash value life insurance.** Insurance that provides life insurance coverage throughout the insured's lifetime and also provides a savings element. Also known as *permanent life insurance*. [1]

**CDHP.** *See* **consumer-driven health plan**.

**cede.** To obtain reinsurance on insurance business by transferring all or part of the risk to a reinsurer. [2]

**ceding company.** In a reinsurance transaction, the insurance company that purchases reinsurance. [2]

**certificate holder.** An individual who is insured under a group insurance contract and who has received a certificate of insurance. [12]

**certificate of insurance.** A document that a group policyholder delivers to each group insured and that describes the coverage provided by the group insurance contract and the group insured's rights under the contract. [12]

**change of occupation provision.** A disability income insurance policy provision that permits the insurer to adjust the policy's premium rate or the amount of benefits payable under the policy if the insured changes occupation. [17]

**children's insurance rider.** A supplemental life insurance policy benefit that provides term life insurance coverage on the insured's children. [7]

**CI coverage.** *See* **critical illness coverage**.

**civil laws.** Laws that are concerned with private—that is, nongovernmental—rights and remedies. *Contrast with* **criminal laws**. [10]

**claim.** A request for payment under the terms of an insurance policy. [2]

**claim analyst.** *See* **claim examiner**.

**claim approver.** *See* **claim examiner**.

**claim costs.** For purposes of calculating health insurance premium rates, the costs an insurer predicts that it will incur to provide the policy benefits promised. [17]

**claim examiner.** An insurance company employee who is responsible for carrying out the claim examination process. Also known as a *claim approver, claim analyst,* or *claim specialist*. [10]

**claim specialist.** *See* **claim examiner**.

**class designation.** A life insurance policy beneficiary designation that identifies a certain group of persons as beneficiaries, rather than naming each person who is a beneficiary. [9]

**class of policies.** All policies of a particular type or all policies issued to a particular group of insureds by a given insurance company. [17]

**closed contract.** A contract for which only those terms and conditions that are printed in—or attached to—the contract are considered to be part of the contract. *Contrast with* **open contract**. [8]

**closed panel HMO.** An HMO that provides health care services to subscribers by either (1) directly employing physicians in an arrangement known as a staff model HMO or (2) contracting with one or more physicians' group practices in an arrangement known as a group model HMO. [15]

**closely held business.** A sole proprietorship, a partnership, or a corporation that is owned by only a few individuals. [5]

**COB provision.** *See* **coordination of benefits provision**.

**COBRA.** *See* **Consolidated Omnibus Budget Reconciliation Act**.

**coinsurance.** An expense participation requirement imposed by many medical expense plans; the requirement generally is a specified percentage of all allowable expenses that remain after the insured has paid the deductible and that must be paid by the insured. [15]

**COLA benefit.** *See* **cost-of-living adjustment benefit**.

**collateral assignment.** A temporary assignment of the monetary value of a life insurance policy as collateral—or security—for a loan. [9]

**community-property state.** A U.S. state in which, by law, each spouse is entitled to an equal share of the income earned by the other and, under most circumstances, to an equal share of the property acquired by the other during the period of their marriage. [9]

**commutation right.** The right of the owner of a payout annuity to withdraw all or part of the contract's remaining periodic income payments in a lump sum. [11]

**commutative contract.** An agreement under which the parties specify in advance the values that they will exchange; moreover, the parties generally exchange items or services that they think are of relatively equal value. *Contrast with* **aleatory contract**. [3]

**compound interest.** Interest paid on both an original principal sum and on accrued interest. *Contrast with* **simple interest**. [4]

**comprehensive major medical policy.** A medical expense insurance policy that combines the coverages provided by both a supplemental major medical policy and an underlying basic medical expense policy. [15]

**concurrent review.** A component of a utilization review program, which involves the review of treatment plans and services provided to a plan member while he is in the hospital or receiving ongoing treatment. [15]

**conditional promise.** A promise to perform a stated act if a specified, uncertain event occurs. [3]

**conditionally renewable policy.** An individual health insurance policy that gives the insurer a limited right to refuse to renew the policy at the end of a premium payment period. [17]

**conservative mortality table.** A mortality table that shows higher mortality rates than an insurer anticipates for a particular block of policies. [4]

**consideration.** A requirement for the formation of a valid informal contract; the requirement is met when each party gives or promises to give something of value to the other party. [3]

**Consolidated Omnibus Budget Reconciliation Act (COBRA).** A U.S. federal law that requires all group insurance plans that provide medical expense benefits and are sponsored by employers with 20 or more employees to allow certain covered employees and their dependent spouses and dependent children the right to continue their group insurance coverage for a limited time in specified situations, known as qualifying events, in which their group coverage would otherwise terminate. [18]

**consolidation.** As it relates to the financial services industry, the combination of financial services institutions within or across sectors. [1]

**consumer-driven health plan (CDHP).** An employer-sponsored health benefit plan that gives individuals freedom to choose health care providers and benefits, but also requires them to assume financial risk for their choices. [15]

**contingency reserves.** Reserves insurers sometimes maintain to protect themselves against unusual conditions that may occur. [4]

**contingent beneficiary.** The party designated to receive the proceeds of a life insurance policy following the insured's death if the primary beneficiary should die before the insured. Also known as a *secondary beneficiary* or *successor beneficiary*. [9]

**contingent payee.** The person or party who will receive any life insurance policy proceeds still payable at the time of the payee's death. Also known as a *successor payee*. [9]

**continuous-premium whole life policy.** A whole life insurance policy for which premiums are payable for the life of the policy. Also known as a *straight life insurance policy* or an *ordinary life insurance policy*. [6]

**contract.** A legally enforceable agreement between two or more parties. [3]

**contract of adhesion.** A contract that one party prepares and that the other party must accept or reject as a whole, generally without any bargaining between the parties to the agreement. *Contrast with* **bargaining contract.** [3]

**contract of indemnity.** An insurance policy under which the amount of the policy benefit payable for a covered loss is based on the actual amount of financial loss that results from the loss, as determined at the time of loss. [2]

**contract owner.** The person or business that owns and exercises all rights and privileges of an annuity contract. [11]

**contractual capacity.** The legal capacity to make a contract. [3]

**contributory plan.** A group insurance plan for which insured group members are required to contribute some or all of the premium for their coverage. [12]

**convergence.** As it relates to the financial services industry, the movement toward a single financial institution being able to serve a customer's banking, insurance, and securities needs. [1]

**conversion privilege.** (1) A term life insurance policy provision that allows the policyowner to change—convert—the term insurance policy to a cash value life insurance policy without providing evidence that the insured is an insurable risk. [5] (2) A group life insurance policy feature that allows a group insured whose coverage terminates for certain reasons to convert her group insurance coverage to an individual policy of insurance, without presenting evidence of her insurability. [13]

**conversion provision.** A group medical expense insurance policy provision that grants an insured group member who is leaving the group a limited right to purchase an individual medical expense insurance policy without presenting evidence of insurability. [18]

**convertible term insurance policy.** A term life insurance policy that gives the policyowner the right to convert the term policy to a cash value life insurance policy. [5]

**coordination of benefits (COB) provision.** A group health insurance policy provision designed to prevent a group member who is insured under more than one group medical expense insurance policy from receiving benefit amounts that are greater than the amount of medical expenses the insured actually incurred. [18]

**copayment.** A specified, fixed amount that a member of a managed care plan pays to a network provider when the plan member receives services from the provider. [15]

**corporation.** A legal entity that is created by the authority of a governmental unit and that is separate and distinct from the people who own it. [1]

**cost of benefits.** For purposes of pricing an insurance product, all of the insurer's potential payments of benefit obligations to customers multiplied by the expected probability that each benefit will be payable. [4]

**cost-of-living adjustment (COLA) benefit.** A disability income benefit that provides for periodic increases in the benefit amount the insurer will pay to a disabled insured; these increases usually correspond to increases in the cost of living. [16]

**CPP.** *See* **Canada Pension Plan.**

**credit life insurance.** A type of term life insurance designed to pay the balance due on a loan if the borrower dies before the loan is repaid. [5]

**criminal laws.** Laws that define certain acts as crimes and provide a specific punishment for each crime. *Contrast with* **civil laws.** [10]

**critical illness benefit.** *See* **dread disease benefit.**

**critical illness (CI) coverage.** Supplemental medical expense insurance coverage that pays a lump-sum benefit if the insured is diagnosed with a critical illness while the policy is in force. [15]

**current assumption whole life insurance.** *See* **interest-sensitive whole life insurance.**

**custodial account.** An account set up at a depository institution or other financial institution for a minor or other person who lacks legal capacity. [11]

**damages.** The most typical remedy available to the injured party in a civil action; the remedy consists of monetary compensation that is recovered by the injured party from the party whose wrongful conduct caused the injured party's loss or injury. [10]

**DD benefit.** *See* **dread disease benefit.**

**death benefit.** A benefit that equals at least the amount of a deferred annuity's accumulation value and that is to be paid to a beneficiary designated by the contract owner if the contract owner dies before periodic income payments begin. Also known as a *survivor benefit*. [11]

**declined risk.** A proposed insured who is considered to present a risk that is too great for an insurer to cover. [2]

**decreasing term life insurance.** A plan of term life insurance that provides a policy benefit that decreases in amount over the term of coverage. [5]

**deductible.** A flat dollar amount of eligible medical expenses, such as $200 or $500, that an insured must pay before the insurer will begin making any benefit payments under a medical expense insurance policy. [15]

**deferred annuity.** An annuity under which periodic income payments are scheduled to begin more than one annuity period after the date on which the annuity was purchased. *Contrast with* **immediate annuity**. [11]

**defined benefit formula.** A benefit formula that specifies the amount of retirement benefit a plan sponsor promises to provide to each plan participant. [14]

**defined benefit plan.** A retirement plan structured according to a defined benefit formula. [14]

**defined contribution formula.** A benefit formula that specifies the level of contributions that a retirement plan sponsor promises to make to the plan. [14]

**defined contribution plan.** A retirement plan structured according to a defined contribution formula. [14]

**dental expense coverage.** Supplemental medical expense insurance coverage that provides benefits for routine dental examinations, preventive work, and dental procedures needed to treat tooth decay and diseases of the teeth and jaw [15]

**deposit administration contract.** A retirement plan funding vehicle in which a plan sponsor deposits plan assets with an insurance company, which places the assets in its general account. When a plan participant retires, the insurer withdraws sufficient funds from the general account to provide an immediate annuity for the plan participant. [14]

**disability buyout coverage.** Disability income coverage that provides benefits designed to fund the buyout of a partner's or owner's interest in a business should she become disabled. [16]

**disability income benefit.** A supplemental life insurance policy benefit that provides a monthly income benefit to the policyowner-insured if he becomes totally disabled while the policy is in force. [7]

**disability income coverage.** A type of health insurance coverage that provides income replacement benefits to an insured who is unable to work because of illness or injury. [1]

**disease management.** A component of a utilization review program, which consists of a coordinated system of preventive, diagnostic, and therapeutic measures intended to provide cost-effective, quality health care for a patient population who have or are at risk for a specific chronic illness or medical condition. [15]

**dividend options.** Specified methods by which the owner of a participating life insurance policy may receive policy dividends. [9]

**divisible surplus.** The amount of an insurer's surplus available for distribution to owners of participating policies. [4]

**domestic insurer.** From the perspective of a given state, an insurer incorporated by that state. [1]

**double indemnity benefit.** A supplemental life insurance policy benefit that provides an accidental death benefit that is equal to the face amount of the policy. [7]

**dread disease (DD) benefit.** An accelerated death benefit under which the insurer agrees to pay a portion of the life insurance policy's face amount to the policyowner if the insured suffers from one of a number of specified diseases. Also known as a *critical illness benefit*. [7]

**dread disease coverage.** Supplemental medical expense insurance coverage that provides benefits for medical expenses incurred by an insured who has contracted a specified disease. [15]

**EFT method.** *See* **electronic funds transfer method**.

**EIA.** *See* **equity-indexed annuity**.

**electronic funds transfer (EFT) method.** An insurance premium payment method in which policyowners authorize their banks to pay premiums automatically on premium due dates. [9]

**eligibility period.** The time during which a new group member may first enroll for group insurance coverage. Also known as the *enrollment period*. [12]

**elimination period.** The specific amount of time that an insured must be disabled before becoming eligible to receive disability income benefits. Also known as a *waiting period*. [16]

**Employee Retirement Income Security Act (ERISA).** A U.S. federal law designed to ensure that certain minimum plan requirements are contained in employee welfare benefit plans. [13]

**endorsement.** A document that is attached to an insurance policy and is a part of the policy contract. [9] *See also* **policy rider**.

**endorsement method.** (1) A beneficiary change procedure under which the name of the new beneficiary must be added to the policy itself for the beneficiary change to be effective. *Contrast with* **recording method**. [9] (2) A method of transferring ownership of a life insurance policy under which the ownership change becomes effective when the policyowner notifies the insurer, in writing, of the change and the insurance company notes the ownership change in its records. [9]

**endowment insurance.** Insurance that provides a policy benefit that is paid either when the insured dies or on a stated date if the insured lives until then. [1]

**enrollment period.** *See* **eligibility period**.

**entire contract provision.** An insurance and annuity policy provision that defines the documents that constitute the contract between the insurance company and the policyowner. [8, 11]

**equity-indexed annuity (EIA).** A type of annuity contract that offers certain principal and earnings guarantees, but also offers the possibility of additional earnings by linking the contract to a published index. [11]

**ERISA.** *See* **Employee Retirement Income Security Act**.

**estate.** All things of value—the assets—owned by a person when she died. [5]

**estate plan.** A plan that considers the amount of assets and debts a person is likely to have when he dies and how best to preserve those assets so that they can pass to the person's heirs as he desires. [5]

**evidence of insurability.** Proof that a given person is an insurable risk. [5]

**exclusion.** An insurance policy provision that describes circumstances under which the insurer will not pay the policy benefit following an otherwise covered loss. [8]

**exclusion rider.** A rider attached to an individual health insurance policy which specifies that benefits will not be provided for any loss that results from the condition listed in the rider. Also known as an *impairment rider*. [17]

**executive branch.** The branch of government that is responsible for administering, enforcing, or carrying out the jurisdiction's laws. [1]

**expected mortality.** The number of deaths that have been predicted to occur in a group of people at a given age according to a mortality table. Also known as *tabular mortality*. [4]

**experience rating.** A method of setting group insurance premium rates under which the insurer considers the particular group's prior claims and expense experience. [12]

**extended term insurance nonforfeiture option.** A nonforfeiture option that permits the owner of a cash value life insurance policy to discontinue premium payments and use the policy's net cash surrender value as a net single premium to purchase term insurance for the full coverage amount provided under the original policy for as long a term as the net cash surrender value can provide. [8]

**face amount.** The amount of the policy benefit listed on the first page of a life insurance policy. Also known as *face value*. [2]

**face value.** *See* **face amount**.

**facility-of-payment clause.** A provision included in some life insurance policies that permits the insurance company to pay all or part of the policy proceeds either to a relative of the insured or to anyone who has a valid claim to those proceeds. [9]

**family income coverage.** A plan of decreasing term life insurance that provides a stated monthly income benefit amount to the insured's surviving spouse if the insured dies during the term of coverage. [5]

**family income policy.** A whole life insurance policy that includes family income coverage. [5]

**family policy.** A whole life insurance policy that includes term life insurance coverage on the insured's spouse and children. [6]

**federal system.** A system of government in which a federal government and a number of lower level governments, known as state or provincial governments, share governmental powers. [1]

**fiduciary.** A person who holds a position of special trust. [12]

**fifth dividend option.** *See* **additional term insurance dividend option**.

**financial institution.** A business that owns primarily financial assets, such as stocks and bonds, rather than fixed assets, such as equipment and raw materials. [1]

**financial intermediary.** An organization that channels funds from those people, businesses, and governments that have a surplus of funds (savers) to those who have a shortage of funds (borrowers). [1]

**financial services industry.** The industry made up of various kinds of financial institutions that help people, businesses, and governments save, borrow, invest, and otherwise manage money. [1]

**Financial Services Modernization Act.** *See* **Gramm-Leach-Bliley Act**.

**first beneficiary.** *See* **primary beneficiary**.

**first-dollar coverage.** Medical expense insurance coverage under which the insurer begins to reimburse the insured for eligible medical expenses without first requiring an out-of-pocket contribution from the insured. [15]

**first-to-die life insurance.** *See* **joint whole life insurance**.

**fixed annuity.** An annuity contract under which the insurer guarantees that (1) the contract's accumulation value will experience no loss of principal and will earn at least a minimum guaranteed interest rate and (2) the periodic income payments will not fall below a stated minimum amount. *Contrast with* **variable annuity**. [11]

**fixed subaccount.** A subaccount that guarantees payment of a fixed rate of interest for a specified period of time. [11]

**fixed-amount annuity.** An annuity that guarantees the payment of periodic income payments of a specified minimum dollar amount for as long a period as the annuity's accumulation value will provide, regardless of whether the annuitant lives or dies. [11]

**fixed-amount option.** A life insurance policy settlement option under which the insurance company pays the policy proceeds in equal installments of a stated amount until the proceeds, plus the interest earned, are exhausted. [9]

**fixed-period option.** A life insurance policy settlement option under which the insurance company agrees to pay policy proceeds in equal installments to the payee for a specified period of time. [9]

**flexible-premium annuity.** An annuity that is purchased by the payment of periodic premiums that can vary between a set minimum amount and a set maximum amount. [11]

**flexible-premium deferred annuity (FPDA) contract.** A deferred annuity that is purchased with an initial premium of some minimum amount and thereafter the contract owner may make additional payments at any time in the future, usually subject to some smaller minimum amount. [11]

**flexible-premium variable life insurance.** *See* **variable universal life insurance**.

**foreign insurer.** From the perspective of a given state, an insurer incorporated under the laws of another state. [1]

**formal contract.** A contract that is enforceable because the parties to the contract met certain formalities concerning the form of the agreement. [3]

**formulary.** A feature of some medical expense insurance policies that consists of a listing of prescription drugs by therapeutic category or disease class; listed drugs are considered preferred therapy and are to be used by providers in prescribing medications. [15]

**FPDA contract.** *See* **flexible-premium deferred annuity contract**.

**fraternal benefit society.** An organization formed to provide social, as well as insurance, benefits to its members. [1]

**fraud.** An act by which someone intentionally deceives another party and induces that other party to part with something of value or to give up a legal right. [9]

**fraudulent claim.** An insurance claim in which the claimant intentionally attempts to collect policy proceeds by providing false information to the insurer. [10]

**fraudulent misrepresentation.** A misrepresentation that was made with the intent to induce the other party to enter into a contract and that did induce the innocent party to enter into the contract. [8]

**free-examination provision.** *See* **free-look provision**.

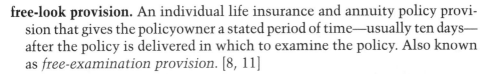

**free-look provision.** An individual life insurance and annuity policy provision that gives the policyowner a stated period of time—usually ten days—after the policy is delivered in which to examine the policy. Also known as *free-examination provision*. [8, 11]

**front-end load.** An amount charged to the contract owner at the time she pays for an annuity. The front-end load compensates the insurer for sales commissions and other expenses associated with acquiring the business. [11]

**fully insured plan.** A group health insurance plan for which the group policyholder makes periodic premium payments to an insurance company, and the insurance company bears the responsibility for all claim payments. [18]

**fully self-insured plan.** A group health insurance plan for which the group policyholder—usually an employer—takes complete responsibility for all claim payments and related expenses. [18]

**funding instrument.** *See* **funding vehicle**.

**funding mechanism.** The way in which a group health insurance plan's claim costs and administrative expenses are paid. [18]

**funding vehicle.** An arrangement for investing a retirement plan's assets. Also known as an *investment vehicle* or *funding instrument*. [14]

**future purchase option benefit.** A benefit that is sometimes provided by a disability income policy with a flat benefit amount and that gives the insured the right to increase the benefit amount in accordance with increases in the insured's earnings. [16]

**general account.** An undivided investment account in which an insurer maintains funds that support its contractual obligations to pay benefits under its guaranteed insurance products, such as whole life insurance and other nonvariable products. [6]

**GI benefit.** *See* **guaranteed insurability benefit**.

**GIC.** *See* **guaranteed investment contract**.

**GIO option.** *See* **guaranteed insurability benefit**.

**GLB Act.** *See* **Gramm-Leach-Bliley Act**.

**GMAB.** *See* **guaranteed minimum accumulation benefit**.

**GMDB.** *See* **guaranteed minimum death benefit**.

**GMIB.** *See* **guaranteed minimum income benefit**.

**GMWB.** *See* **guaranteed minimum withdrawal benefit**.

**grace period.** A specified length of time within which a renewal premium that is due may be paid. [8]

**grace period provision.** An insurance policy provision that specifies a length of time following each renewal premium due date within which the premium may be paid without loss of coverage. [8]

**graded-premium policy.** A whole life insurance policy that calls for three or more levels of annual premium payment amounts, increasing at specified points in time—such as every three years—until reaching the amount to be paid as a level premium for the rest of the life of the policy. [6]

**Gramm-Leach-Bliley (GLB) Act.** A U.S. federal law that removed regulatory barriers to affiliations among financial institutions. Also known as the *Financial Services Modernization Act*. [1]

**gross premium.** The premium amount an insurer charges a policyowner to keep the policy in force. The gross premium equals the net premium plus the loading. [4]

**group annuity contract.** A retirement plan funding vehicle that operates much like an immediate participation guarantee contract with a separate account rider. The contract itself is unallocated, but the insurance company typically offers a coordinating service package that includes allocation services to accommodate the individual participant recordkeeping requirements of defined contribution plans. [14]

**group creditor life insurance.** Insurance issued to a creditor, such as a bank, to insure the lives of the creditor's current and future debtors. [13]

**group deferred annuity contract.** A retirement plan funding vehicle that provides plan participants with annuities upon their retirement. The insurer usually issues a master group contract to the plan sponsor and issues certificates to each individual plan participant. Each year, the plan sponsor uses the contributions made on behalf of each plan participant to purchase a single-premium deferred annuity for that plan participant. [14]

**group insurance policy.** A policy that is issued to insure the lives or health of a specific group of people, such as a group of employees. [1]

**group insured.** An individual covered by a group insurance policy. [12]

**group model HMO.** An HMO that provides health care services to subscribers by contracting with one or more physicians' group practices. [15]

**group policyholder.** The person or organization that decides what types of group insurance coverage to purchase for a specific group, negotiates the terms of the group insurance contract, and purchases the group insurance coverage. [3]

**group RRSP.** In Canada, an employer-sponsored registered retirement savings plan in which an account is established for each participating employee into which the employer and employee can make contributions. [14]

**guaranteed income contract.** *See* **guaranteed investment contract**.

**guaranteed insurability (GI) benefit.** A supplemental life insurance policy benefit that gives the policyowner the right to purchase additional insurance of the same type as the basic life insurance policy—for an additional premium amount—on specified option dates during the life of the policy without supplying evidence of the insured's insurability. Also known as a *guaranteed insurability option (GIO)*. [7]

**guaranteed insurability (GIO) option.** *See* **guaranteed insurability benefit**.

**guaranteed interest contract.** *See* **guaranteed investment contract**.

**guaranteed investment contract (GIC).** A retirement plan funding vehicle in which the insurer accepts a single deposit from the plan sponsor for a specified period of time, such as five years. GICs generally have a specified maturity date and guarantee the repayment at the maturity date of the amounts deposited under the contract, plus the amount of credited interest, less withdrawals. Also known as a *guaranteed interest contract* or a *guaranteed income contract*. [14]

**guaranteed minimum accumulation benefit (GMAB).** A variable annuity contract feature that guarantees a return of premiums paid if the contract remains in force for a specified period of time. [11]

**guaranteed minimum death benefit (GMDB).** A variable annuity contract feature that guarantees that if the contract owner dies before periodic income payments begin, the beneficiary will receive at least the amount that was paid into the contract, less any withdrawals, even if poor investment performance causes the contract's accumulation value to be less than the premiums paid. [11]

**guaranteed minimum income benefit (GMIB).** A variable annuity contract feature that guarantees that variable periodic income payments will not fall below a certain amount—usually a specified percentage of the first periodic income payment—even if investments drop in value as a result of poor performance. [11]

**guaranteed minimum withdrawal benefit (GMWB).** A variable annuity contract feature that guarantees that up to a certain percentage of the amount paid into the contract will be available for withdrawals annually, even if subaccount investments perform poorly. [11]

**guaranteed renewable policy.** An individual health insurance policy that must be renewed at the policyowner's option—as long as premium payments are made—at least until the insured attains the age limit stated in the policy. [17]

**health insurance policy.** An insurance contract that provides protection against the risk of financial loss resulting from the insured person's illness, accidental injury, or disability. [1]

**Health Insurance Portability and Accountability Act (HIPAA).** A U.S. federal law that imposes a number of requirements on insurers that issue individual medical expense insurance policies, as well as on employer-sponsored group medical expense insurance plans. [17]

**health maintenance organization (HMO).** A health care financing and delivery system that provides comprehensive health care services to plan members in a particular geographic area. [15]

**Health Maintenance Organization (HMO) Act of 1973.** A U.S. federal law that provided federal funds to HMOs that met the requirements to become federally qualified. [17]

**health reimbursement arrangement (HRA).** A personal health spending account that can be funded only by employer contributions and may be established by employers of any size. [15]

**health savings account (HSA).** A personal health spending account that can be established by individuals under age 65 and employers. [15]

**HIPAA.** *See* **Health Insurance Portability and Accountability Act.**

**HMO.** *See* **health maintenance organization.**

**home service agent.** A commissioned insurance sales agent who conducts business within a home service distribution system. [6]

**home service distribution system.** A method of selling and servicing insurance policies through commissioned sales agents who sell a range of products and provide specified policyowner services, including the collection of renewal premiums, within a specified geographic area. [6]

**hospital expenses.** Charges for specific inpatient and outpatient hospital services, such as room and board, medications, laboratory services, and other fees associated with a hospital stay. [15]

**HR 10 plan.** *See* **Keogh plan.**

**HRA.** *See* **health reimbursement arrangement.**

**HSA.** *See* **health savings account.**

**immediate annuity.** An annuity that provides periodic income payments that generally are scheduled to begin one annuity period after the date the contract is issued. *Contrast with* **deferred annuity.** [11]

**immediate participation guarantee (IPG) contract.** A retirement plan funding vehicle in which plan assets are held by an insurer in an investment account in the name of the plan sponsor and deposited in the insurer's general account. The plan sponsor shares in the gains or losses experienced by the insurer as it invests and pays benefits from its general account. [14]

**impairment rider.** *See* **exclusion rider.**

**income date.** *See* **annuity date.**

**income protection insurance.** A type of disability income insurance coverage that provides disability income benefits to an insured who is disabled and has suffered an income loss because of the disability. [16]

**incontestability provision.** An insurance and annuity policy provision that describes the time limit within which the insurer has the right to avoid the contract on the ground of material misrepresentation in the application. [8, 11]

**increasing term life insurance.** A plan of term life insurance that provides a death benefit that starts at one amount and increases by some specified amount or percentage at stated intervals over the policy term. [5]

**indemnity benefits.** Contractual benefits that are provided under insurance policies and that are based on the actual amount of the insured's financial loss. Also known as *reimbursement benefits*. [15]

**indeterminate premium life insurance policy.** A nonparticipating whole life insurance policy that specifies two premium rates—both a maximum guaranteed premium rate and a lower premium rate. The insurer charges the lower rate when the policy is issued and guarantees that rate for at least a stated period of time. After that time, the insurer periodically uses its actual mortality, interest, and expense experience to establish a new premium rate, which cannot exceed the maximum guaranteed rate. Also known as a *nonguaranteed premium life insurance policy* or a *variable-premium life insurance policy*. [6]

**index.** A statistical measurement system that tracks the performance of a group of similar investments. [11]

**individual insurance policy.** A policy that is issued to insure the life or health of a named person. Some individual policies also insure the named person's immediate family or a second named person. [1]

**individual policy pension trust.** A type of allocated retirement plan funding vehicle that typically is used for small pension plans and under which plan trustees annually purchase individual life insurance or individual annuity contracts for each participant in the plan. Also known as a *412(i) plan*. [14]

**individual retirement account.** An IRA that takes the form of a trust or custodial account created in the United States for the exclusive benefit of an individual and his beneficiaries. [11]

**individual retirement annuity.** An IRA that takes the form of an individual annuity issued by an insurance company. [11]

**individual retirement arrangement (IRA).** In the United States, a retirement savings plan that allows a person with taxable compensation to deposit a stated amount of that compensation into a savings arrangement that meets certain requirements specified in the federal tax laws and, thus, receives favorable federal income tax treatment. *See also* **individual retirement account** and **individual retirement annuity**. [11]

**individual stop-loss coverage.** Stop-loss insurance under which the insurer pays a portion of each claim that exceeds a stated amount. Also known as *specific stop-loss coverage*. [18]

**informal contract.** A contract that is enforceable because the parties to the contract met requirements concerning the substance of the agreement rather than requirements concerning the form of the agreement. [3]

**initial premium.** The first premium paid for an insurance policy. [3]

**insurable interest.** The interest an insurance policyowner has in the risk that is insured. A policyowner has an insurable interest if she is likely to suffer a genuine loss or detriment should the event insured against occur. [2]

**insured.** The person whose life or health is insured under an insurance policy. [2]

**insurer-administered plan.** A group insurance plan for which the insurer is responsible for handling the administrative and recordkeeping aspects of the plan. *Contrast with* **self-administered plan**. [12]

**interest.** Money that is paid for the use of money. [4]

**interest option.** A life insurance policy settlement option under which the insurance company invests the policy proceeds and periodically pays interest on those proceeds to the payee. [9]

**interest-sensitive whole life insurance.** A type of indeterminate premium life insurance policy which provides that the policy's cash value can be greater than that guaranteed if changing assumptions regarding mortality, investment, and expense factors warrant such an increase. Also known as *current assumption whole life insurance*. [6]

**interpleader.** In the United States, a procedure under which an insurance company that cannot determine which claimant is entitled to receive policy proceeds may pay such proceeds to a court and ask the court to decide the proper recipient. *Compare to* **payment into court**. [10]

**investment earnings.** The money that an insurance company earns from its investment of premium dollars. [4]

**investment management fee.** A fee charged the owner of a variable annuity to cover professional investment management services. [11]

**investment vehicle.** *See* **funding vehicle**.

**IPG contract.** *See* **immediate participation guarantee contract**.

**IRA.** *See* **individual retirement arrangement**.

**irrevocable beneficiary.** A life insurance policy beneficiary who has a vested interest in the policy proceeds even during the insured's lifetime because the policyowner has the right to change the beneficiary designation only after obtaining the beneficiary's consent. *Contrast with* **revocable beneficiary**. [9]

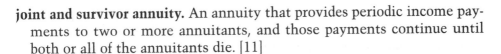

**joint and survivor annuity.** An annuity that provides periodic income payments to two or more annuitants, and those payments continue until both or all of the annuitants die. [11]

**joint and survivorship life income option.** A life insurance policy settlement option under which the policy proceeds are used to purchase a joint and survivor annuity. [9]

**joint mortgage insurance.** A variation of mortgage insurance that provides the same benefit as a mortgage insurance policy except the joint policy insures the lives of two people. [5]

**joint whole life insurance.** A plan of whole life insurance that has the same features and benefits as individual whole life insurance, except that it insures two lives under the same policy. Also known as *first-to-die life insurance*. [6]

**judicial branch.** The branch of government that is responsible for applying and interpreting the jurisdiction's laws. [1]

**juvenile insurance policy.** An insurance policy that is issued on the life of a child but is owned and paid for by an adult, usually the child's parent or legal guardian. [7]

**Keogh plan.** In the United States, a qualified retirement plan set up by a self-employed individual, sole proprietorship, or partnership to which the business or individual can make annual tax-deductible contributions, subject to certain limits and conditions. Also known as an *HR 10 plan*. [14]

**key employee life insurance.** *See* **key person life insurance**.

**key person.** Any person or employee whose continued participation in a business is necessary to the success of the business and whose death would cause the business a significant financial loss. [5]

**key person disability coverage.** Disability income coverage purchased by a business to provide benefit payments to the business if an insured key person becomes disabled. [16]

**key person life insurance.** Insurance that a business purchases on the life of a person whose continued participation in the business is necessary to its success and whose death would cause financial loss to the business. Also known as *key employee life insurance*. [5]

**lapse.** The effect on an insurance policy if a renewal premium has not been paid by the end of the grace period. [8]

**last survivor life insurance.** A variation of joint whole life insurance under which the policy benefit is paid only after both people insured by the policy have died. Also known as *second-to-die life insurance*. [6]

**law of large numbers.** A theory of probability which states that, typically, the more times we observe a particular event, the more likely it is that our observed results will approximate the "true" probability that the event will occur. [2]

**legal actions provision.** An individual health insurance policy provision that limits the time during which a claimant who disagrees with the insurer's claim decision has the right to sue the insurer to collect the amount the claimant believes is owed under the policy. [17]

**legal reserve system.** The modern method of pricing life insurance in which the insurer (1) specifies the amount of the death benefit payable before the insured's death, (2) collects the money needed to pay death benefits before the insured's death, and (3) ensures that the premium an individual pays for a policy is directly related to the amount of risk the insurer assumes when it issues the policy. [4]

**legal reserves.** *See* **policy reserves**.

**legislative branch.** The branch of government that is responsible for enacting laws to govern the applicable jurisdiction. [1]

**level premium pricing system.** A life insurance pricing system that allows the purchaser of a policy to pay the same premium amount each year the policy is in force. [4]

**level term life insurance.** A plan of term life insurance that provides a policy benefit that remains the same over the term of the policy. [5]

**liabilities.** A company's debts and future obligations. [1]

**life and health guaranty association.** In any given state, an organization that operates under the supervision of the state insurance commissioner to protect policyowners, insureds, beneficiaries, and specified others against losses that result from the financial impairment or insolvency of a life or health insurer that operates in the state. [1]

**life and health insurance company.** A financial institution that issues and sells products that insure against financial losses that result from the personal risks of death, disability, illness, accident, and outliving one's savings. [1]

**life annuity.** An annuity that provides periodic benefit payments for at least the lifetime of a named individual. [9]

**life annuity with period certain.** An annuity that guarantees that the insurer will make periodic income payments throughout the annuitant's life and guarantees that the payments will be made for at least a certain period, even if the annuitant dies before the end of that period. [11]

**life income option.** A life insurance policy settlement option under which the insurance company agrees to pay the policy proceeds in periodic installments over the payee's lifetime. [9]

**life income with period certain option.** A life insurance policy settlement option under which the policy proceeds are used to purchase a life income annuity with period certain. [9]

**life insurance policy.** An insurance contract under which the insurer promises to pay a benefit upon the death of a named person. [1]

**life with refund annuity.** An annuity that provides periodic income payments throughout the lifetime of the annuitant and guarantees that at least the purchase price of the annuity will be paid out. Also known as a *refund annuity.* [11]

**limited-payment whole life policy.** A whole life insurance policy for which premiums are payable only until some stated period expires or until the insured's death, whichever occurs first. [6]

**liquidation.** The process of selling off for cash a business' assets, such as its building, inventory, and equipment, and using that cash to pay the business' debts; any funds remaining are then distributed to the owners of the business. [5]

**liquidation period.** *See* **payout period.**

**living benefit.** *See* **accelerated death benefit.**

**loading.** An amount added to a net premium amount to cover all of the insurer's costs of doing business. [4]

**long-term care (LTC) coverage.** Supplemental medical expense insurance coverage that provides benefits for medical and other services needed by insureds who, because of their advanced age or the effects of a serious illness or injury, need constant care in their own homes or in a qualified nursing facility. [15]

**long-term care (LTC) insurance benefit.** An accelerated death benefit under which the insurer agrees to pay a monthly benefit to a life insurance policyowner if the insured requires constant care for a medical condition. [7]

**long-term group disability income coverage.** Group disability income coverage that provides a maximum benefit period of more than one year. [16]

**long-term individual disability income coverage.** Individual disability income coverage that provides a maximum benefit period of five years or more. [16]

**loss ratio.** The ratio of benefits a health insurer paid out for a block of policies to the premiums the insurer received for those policies. [17]

**LTC coverage.** *See* **long-term care coverage.**

**LTC insurance benefit.** *See* **long-term care insurance benefit.**

**M&E charge.** *See* **mortality and expense charge.**

**maintenance fee.** *See* **periodic fee.**

**major medical expense coverage.** Medical expense insurance coverage that provides substantial benefits for (1) basic hospital, surgical, and physician expenses, (2) additional medical services related to illness or injuries, and (3) preventive care. [15]

**managed care.** A method of integrating the financing and delivery of health care services within a system that manages the cost, accessibility, and quality of care. [15]

**managed care organization (MCO).** An entity that operates a managed care plan. [15]

**managed care plan.** An arrangement that integrates the financing and management of health care with the delivery of health care services to a group of individuals who have enrolled in the plan. [15]

**managed indemnity plan.** A medical expense insurance plan that is organized and administered like a traditional medical expense insurance plan to provide indemnity benefits but that uses managed care techniques, such as precertification and utilization review, to control plan costs. [15]

**manual rating.** A method insurers use to calculate group insurance premium rates without considering the particular group's prior claims and expense experience. [12]

**market conduct laws.** State insurance laws that regulate how insurance companies conduct their business within the state. [1]

**market value adjusted (MVA) annuity.** A type of annuity contract that offers multiple guarantee periods and multiple fixed interest rates. Also known as a *modified guaranteed annuity*. [11]

**master group insurance contract.** An insurance contract that insures a number of people. [12]

**material misrepresentation.** A misrepresentation that would affect an insurance company's evaluation of a proposed insured and, thus, gives the insurer grounds to avoid an insurance contract. [8]

**maturity date.** The date on which the insurer will pay the face amount of an endowment policy to the policyowner if the insured is still living. [6]

**McCarran-Ferguson Act.** A U.S. federal law under which Congress agreed to leave insurance regulation to the states as long as Congress considers state regulation to be adequate. Also known as *Public Law 15*. [1]

**MCO.** *See* **managed care organization.**

**MDO policy.** *See* **monthly debit ordinary policy.**

**Medicaid.** In the United States, a joint federal and state program that provides basic medical expense and nursing home coverage to the low-income population and certain aged and disabled individuals. [15]

**medical expense coverage.** A type of health insurance coverage that provides benefits to pay for the treatment of an insured's illnesses and injuries. [1]

**medical savings account (MSA).** A personal health spending account that can be funded by an employer or employee, but not both, and can be established by employers with fewer than 50 employees or by self-employed individuals. [15]

**medically appropriate services.** Diagnostic or treatment measures for which the expected health benefits exceed the expected risks by a margin wide enough to justify the measures. [15]

**medically necessary services.** Services that are considered by a managed care plan to be (1) consistent with the symptoms, diagnosis, and treatment of a plan member's condition, (2) in accordance with the standards of good medical practice, (3) not solely for the convenience of the plan member, member's family, physician, or other health care provider, and (4) furnished in the least intensive type of medical care setting required by the plan member's condition. [15]

**Medicare.** In the United States, a federal government program established by the Old Age, Survivors, Disability and Health Insurance (OASDHI) Act that provides medical expense benefits to elderly and disabled persons. [15]

**Medicare Advantage.** A component of Medicare that is available in most areas of the United States. Medicare beneficiaries who are enrolled in both Medicare Part A and Part B may elect to enroll in a Medicare Advantage plan provided by a participating insurance company or managed care plan and to receive coverage under that private plan rather than under the traditional Medicare plan. [15]

**Medicare Part A.** A component of Medicare, which provides basic hospital insurance that covers the costs of inpatient hospital services, confinement in nursing facilities or other extended care facilities after hospitalization, home care services following hospitalization, and hospice care. Individuals who satisfy Medicare eligibility requirements are automatically enrolled in Medicare Part A. [15]

**Medicare Part B.** A component of Medicare, which provides benefits to cover the costs of physicians' professional services, and other services necessary for the diagnosis or treatment of illness or injury. Eligible Medicare beneficiaries must enroll to receive benefits and must pay monthly premiums. [15]

**Medicare SELECT plan.** A managed care plan that supplements Medicare Part B coverage. [15]

**Medigap policy.** An individual medical expense insurance policy sold by an insurance company to supplement Medicare Part A and Part B coverage. [15]

**Mental Health Parity Act.** A U.S. federal law that imposes requirements on group health plans, health insurance companies, and HMOs that offer mental health benefits. [17]

**minimum premium plan (MPP).** A group health insurance funding mechanism under which the group policyholder deposits into a special account funds that are sufficient to pay a stated amount of expected claims. An insurer administers the plan and pays claims from that special account until the allocated funds are exhausted. Thereafter, the insurer is responsible for paying claims from its own funds, and it charges the group policyholder a premium for the coverage it provides. [18]

**minor.** A person who has not attained the age of majority. [3]

**misrepresentation.** A false or misleading statement in an application for insurance. [8]

**misstatement of age or sex provision.** A life insurance and annuity policy provision that describes the action the insurer will take to adjust the amount of the policy benefit in the event that the age or sex of the insured or annuitant is incorrectly stated. [8, 11]

**mistaken claim.** An insurance claim in which the claimant makes an honest mistake in presenting the claim to the insurer. [10]

**model bill.** A sample law that state insurance regulators are encouraged to use as a basis for state insurance laws. [1]

**modified coverage policy.** A whole life insurance policy under which the amount of insurance decreases by specific percentages or amounts either when the insured reaches certain stated ages or at the end of stated time periods. [6]

**modified guaranteed annuity.** *See* **market value adjusted annuity**.

**modified-premium whole life policy.** A whole life insurance policy that functions in the same manner as a traditional whole life policy except that the policy's annual premium changes after a specified initial period, such as 5, 10, 15, or 20 years. [6]

**monthly debit ordinary (MDO) policy.** A whole life insurance policy that is marketed under the home service distribution system and is paid for by monthly premium payments. [6]

**moral hazard.** A characteristic that exists when the reputation, financial position, or criminal record of an applicant for insurance or a proposed insured indicates that the person may act dishonestly in the insurance transaction. [2]

**morbidity tables.** Charts that show the incidence of sickness and accidents, by age, occurring among a given group of people. [2]

**mortality.** The incidence of death among a specified group of people. [4]

**mortality and expense risk (M&E) charge.** A fee charged the owner of a variable annuity to cover the benefit guarantees provided by the contract. [11]

**mortality experience.** The number of deaths that actually occur in a given group of insureds. [4]

**mortality rate.** The rate at which death occurs among a specified group of people during a specified period, typically one year. [4]

**mortality tables.** Charts that show the death rates an insurer may reasonably anticipate among a particular group of insured lives at certain ages. [2]

**mortgage insurance.** A plan of decreasing term life insurance designed to provide a benefit amount that corresponds to the decreasing amount owed on a mortgage loan. [5]

**MPP.** *See* **minimum premium plan**.

**MSA.** *See* **medical savings account**.

**mutual assent.** A requirement for the formation of a valid informal contract that is met when the parties reach a meeting of the minds about the terms of their agreement. [3]

**mutual benefit method.** A method used in the past to fund life insurance in which the members of a mutual benefit society each agreed to pay a specified amount of money after the death of any other member. Also known as *post-death assessment method*. [4]

**mutual insurance company.** An insurance company that is owned by its policyowners, and a portion of the company's operating profits are from time to time distributed to these policyowners in the form of policy dividends. [1]

**MVA annuity.** *See* **market value adjusted annuity**.

**NAIC.** *See* **National Association of Insurance Commissioners**.

**National Association of Insurance Commissioners (NAIC).** In the United States, a nongovernmental organization consisting of the insurance commissioners or superintendents of the various state insurance departments. [1]

**net amount at risk.** The difference between the face amount of a life insurance policy and the policy reserve at the end of any given policy year. [4]

**net cash surrender value.** The amount the owner of a cash value life insurance policy will receive upon surrendering the policy. The value is calculated by adjusting the amount of the cash surrender value for amounts such as paid-up additions, advance premium payments, and policy loans. [8]

**net premium.** The amount of money an insurer needs to provide benefits for a given policy. [4]

**network.** A group of physicians, hospitals, and ancillary services providers that a specific managed care plan has contracted with to deliver health care services to plan members. [15]

**Newborns' and Mothers' Health Protection Act of 1996.** A U.S. federal law that imposes requirements on individual and group health insurance policies that provide benefits for maternity and newborn care. [17]

**noncancellable policy.** An individual health insurance policy that is guaranteed to be renewable until the insured reaches the limiting age stated in the policy. [17]

**noncontributory plan.** A group insurance plan for which insured group members are not required to contribute any part of the premium for their coverage. [12]

**nonduplication of benefits provision.** A coordination of benefits provision that, if included in a secondary provider's health insurance plan, limits the amount payable by the secondary plan to the difference, if any, between the amount paid by the primary plan and the amount that would have been payable by the secondary plan had that plan been the primary plan. [18]

**nonforfeiture provision.** A cash value life insurance policy provision that sets forth the options available to the policyowner if the policy lapses or if the policyowner decides to surrender—or terminate—the policy. [8]

**nonguaranteed premium life insurance policy.** *See* **indeterminate premium life insurance policy**.

**nonpar policy.** *See* **nonparticipating policy**.

**nonparticipating policy.** An insurance policy under which the policyowner does not share in the insurer's surplus. Also known as *nonpar policy*. *Contrast with* **participating policy**. [4]

**nonqualified annuity.** An annuity that is not part of a qualified plan. [11]

**OAS Act.** *See* **Old Age Security Act**.

**Old Age Security (OAS) Act.** In Canada, a federal law that established a universal public pension plan that provides a pension to virtually all Canadian residents who are age 65 or older. [14]

**open contract.** A contract that identifies the documents that constitute the contract between the parties, but the enumerated documents are not all attached to the contract. *Contrast with* **closed contract**. [8]

**open panel HMO.** An HMO in which any physician or provider who meets the HMO's specific standards can contract with the HMO to provide services to subscribers. [15]

**Option 1 plan.** *See* **Option A plan**.

**Option 2 plan.** *See* **Option B plan**.

**Option A plan.** A universal life insurance policy under which the amount of the death benefit is level; the death benefit payable is always equal to the policy's face amount. Also known as an *Option 1 plan*. [6]

**Option B plan.** A universal life insurance policy under which the amount of the death benefit at any given time is equal to the policy's face amount plus the amount of the policy's cash value. Also known as an *Option 2 plan*. [6]

**optional insured rider.** *See* **second insured rider**.

**optional modes of settlement.** *See* **settlement options**.

**optionally renewable policy.** An individual health insurance policy that gives the insurer the right to refuse to renew the policy for any reason on certain dates specified in the policy—usually either the policy anniversary date or any premium due date. [17]

**ordinary life insurance policy.** *See* **continuous-premium whole life policy**.

**original age conversion.** A conversion of a term life insurance policy to a cash value life insurance policy in which the renewal premium rate is based on the insured's age when the original term life insurance policy was purchased. *Contrast with* **attained age conversion**. [5]

**overhead expenses.** For purposes of business overhead expense coverage, usual and necessary business expenses, including employee salaries, rent, mortgage payments, telephone, electric and gas utilities, and other expenses required to keep the business open. [16]

**overinsurance provision.** An individual health insurance policy provision which states that the benefits payable under the policy will be reduced if the insured is overinsured. [17]

**overinsured person.** A person who is entitled to receive either (1) more in medical expense benefits than the actual costs incurred for treatment or (2) a greater income amount during disability than the amount that would have been earned from working. [17]

**owners' equity.** The difference between the amount of a company's assets and the amount of its liabilities. [1]

**ownership of property.** The sum of all the legal rights that exist in a given piece of property. [3]

**paid-up additional insurance dividend option.** A policy dividend option under which the insurer uses any declared policy dividend as a net single premium to purchase paid-up additional insurance on the insured's life; the paid-up additional insurance is issued on the same plan as the basic policy and in whatever face amount the dividend can provide at the insured's attained age. [9]

**paid-up additions option benefit.** A supplemental life insurance policy benefit that allows the owner of a whole life insurance policy to purchase single-premium paid-up additions to the policy on stated dates in the future without providing evidence of the insured's insurability. [7]

**paid-up policy.** A life insurance policy that requires no further premium payments but continues to provide coverage. [6]

**par policy.** *See* **participating policy**.

**partial disability.** A disability that prevents the insured either from performing some of the duties of his usual occupation or from engaging in that occupation on a full-time basis. [16]

**partial surrender provision.** *See* **policy withdrawal provision**.

**participating policy.** An insurance policy under which the policyowner shares in the insurance company's divisible surplus. Also known as *par policy. Contrast with* **nonparticipating policy**. [4]

**partnership.** A business that is owned by two or more people, who are known as the partners. [1]

**payee.** (1) The person or party who is to receive life insurance policy proceeds under a settlement option. [9] (2) The person or entity named to receive the periodic income payments under an annuity contract. [11]

**payment into court.** In most Canadian provinces, a procedure under which an insurance company that cannot determine which claimant is entitled to receive policy proceeds may pay such proceeds to a court and ask the court to decide the proper recipient. *Compare to* **interpleader**. [10]

**payout annuity.** An annuity in the payout period. [11]

**payout options.** The choices a contract owner has as to how the insurer will distribute annuity benefits during the payout period. Also known as *settlement options.* [11]

**payout options provision.** An annuity contract provision that lists and describes each of the payout options from which the contract owner may select. [11]

**payout period.** The period during which an insurer makes periodic income payments under an annuity contract. Also known as *liquidation period.* [11]

**payroll deduction method.** An insurance premium payment method in which an employer deducts insurance premiums directly from an employee's paycheck and pays the premiums to the insurer. [9]

**PCP.** *See* **primary care provider**.

**pension.** A lifetime monthly income benefit that begins at retirement. [14]

**pension plan.** An agreement under which an employer establishes a plan to provide its employees with a pension. [14]

**period certain.** The stated period over which the insurer will make periodic income payments for a period certain annuity. [11]

**period certain annuity.** An annuity that is payable for a stated period of time, regardless of whether the annuitant lives or dies. Also known as an *annuity certain*. [11]

**periodic fee.** An amount charged the owner of an annuity contract at predetermined intervals; such fees typically compensate the insurer for its administrative expenses. Also known as a *maintenance fee*. [11]

**permanent life insurance.** *See* **cash value life insurance**.

**personal property.** All property other than real property. [3]

**personal risk.** The risk of economic loss associated with death, poor health, and outliving one's savings. [2]

**physical examination provision.** A disability income insurance policy provision which states that the insurer has the right to have an insured who has submitted a claim examined by a doctor of the insurer's choice, at the insurer's expense. [17, 18]

**physical hazard.** A physical characteristic that may increase the likelihood of loss. [2]

**physicians' expenses.** Charges associated with physicians' visits both in and out of the hospital. [15]

**plan administrator.** The party responsible for handling the administrative aspects of a retirement plan. [14]

**plan document.** A detailed legal agreement that establishes the existence of an employer-sponsored retirement plan and specifies the rights and obligations of various parties to the plan. [14]

**plan participant.** An employee or union member who is covered by a private retirement plan. [14]

**plan sponsor.** An employer or union that has established a private retirement plan. [14]

**point-of-service (POS) plan.** A managed care plan that combines features of HMOs and PPOs; plan members who need medical care choose, at the point of service, whether to seek care in-network or out-of-network. [15]

**policy.** A written document that contains the terms of the agreement between the insurance company and the owner of the policy. [2]

**policy anniversary.** The anniversary of the date on which coverage under an insurance policy became effective. [5]

**policy benefit.** A stated amount of money an insurance company agrees to pay under an insurance policy when a specific loss occurs. Also known as *policy proceeds*. [2]

**policy dividend.** The share of an insurer's divisible surplus the insurer pays to the owner of a participating policy issued by the insurer. [4]

**policy form.** A standardized form that shows the terms, conditions, benefits, and ownership rights of a particular type of insurance product. [1]

**policy loan.** A loan a policyowner receives from an insurer using the cash value of a life insurance policy as security. [6]

**policy loan provision.** A cash value life insurance policy provision that grants the policyowner the right to take out a policy loan for an amount that does not exceed the policy's cash value less one year's interest on the loan. [8]

**policy proceeds.** *See* **policy benefit**.

**policy reserves.** Liabilities that represent the amount an insurer estimates it needs to pay policy benefits as they come due. Sometimes known as *legal reserves* or *statutory reserves*. [4]

**policy rider.** An amendment to an insurance policy that becomes a part of the insurance contract and that either expands or limits the benefits payable under the contract. Also known as an *endorsement*. [5]

**policy term.** The specified period of time for which a term life insurance policy provides coverage. [5]

**policy withdrawal provision.** A universal life insurance policy provision that permits the policyowner to reduce the amount in the policy's cash value by withdrawing up to the amount of the cash value in cash. Also known as a *partial surrender provision*. [8]

**policyowner.** The person or business that owns an insurance policy. [2]

**portable coverage.** Group insurance coverage that can be continued if an insured employee leaves the group. [13]

**POS plan.** *See* **point-of-service (POS) plan**.

**post-death assessment method.** *See* **mutual benefit method**.

**PPO.** *See* **preferred provider organization**.

**pre-existing condition.** As defined by an individual health insurance policy, an injury or illness that (1) occurred or manifested itself within a specified period—usually two years—before the policy was issued and (2) was not disclosed on the application. Group health insurance policies define pre-existing condition in a variety of ways. [17, 18]

**pre-existing conditions provision.** A health insurance policy provision which states that until the insured has been covered under the policy for a certain period, the insurer will not pay benefits for a pre-existing condition unless the condition has been specifically excluded. [17, 18]

**preference beneficiary clause.** A provision included in some life insurance policies, which states that if the policyowner does not name a beneficiary, then the insurer will pay the policy proceeds in a stated order of preference. Also known as a *succession beneficiary clause.* [9]

**preferred provider organization (PPO).** A health care benefit arrangement that provides incentives for plan members to use network providers, but also provides at least some coverage for services rendered by non-network providers. [15]

**preferred risk.** A proposed insured who presents a significantly less-than-average likelihood of loss. [2]

**premium.** A specified amount of money an insurer charges in exchange for its agreement to pay a policy benefit when a specific loss occurs. [2]

**premium delay arrangement.** A group health insurance funding mechanism that allows the group policyholder to postpone paying monthly group insurance premiums for a stated period of time beyond the expiration of the policy's grace period. [18]

**premium payment mode.** The frequency at which insurance policy renewal premiums are payable. [9]

**premium rate.** The amount an insurer charges per unit of life insurance coverage. Typically, a coverage unit equals $1,000 of life insurance coverage, and thus, the premium rate is expressed as the rate per thousand. [4]

**premium reduction dividend option.** A policy dividend option under which the insurer applies policy dividends toward the payment of renewal premiums. [9]

**pre-need funeral insurance.** Whole life insurance that provides funds to pay for the insured's funeral and burial. Also known as *pre-need insurance.* [6]

**pre-need insurance.** *See* **pre-need funeral insurance**.

**prescription drug coverage.** Supplemental medical expense insurance coverage that provides benefits for the purchase of drugs and medicines that are prescribed by a physician and are not available over-the-counter. [15]

**presumptive disability.** A condition described by some disability income insurance policies that, if present, automatically causes the insured to be considered totally disabled and, thus, entitled to receive the full income benefit amount provided under the policy, even if the insured resumes full-time employment in a former occupation. [16]

**primary beneficiary.** The party designated to receive the proceeds of a life insurance policy following the death of the insured. Also known as *first beneficiary*. [9]

**primary care physician.** *See* **primary care provider**.

**primary care provider (PCP).** In a managed care plan, a physician or other health care provider who coordinates plan members' medical care and treatment. Also known as a *primary care physician*. [15]

**probability.** The likelihood that a given event will occur in the future. [2]

**probationary period.** The length of time—typically, from one to six months—that a new group member must wait before becoming eligible to enroll in a group insurance plan. [12]

**profit.** The money, or revenue, that a business receives for its products or services minus the costs it incurred to produce the goods or deliver the services. [1]

**profit sharing plan.** A retirement savings plan that is funded primarily by cash contributions payable from the employer's profits. [14]

**property.** A bundle of rights a person has with respect to something. *See* **real property** and **personal property**. [3]

**property/casualty insurance company.** A financial institution that issues and sells insurance policies to provide financial security from property damage risk and liability risk. [1]

**prospective review.** A component of a utilization review program, which involves the review and possible authorization of proposed treatment plans for a plan member before the treatment is implemented. [15]

**Public Law 15.** *See* **McCarran-Ferguson Act**.

**pure risk.** A risk that involves no possibility of gain; either a loss occurs or no loss occurs. [2]

**QPP.** *See* **Quebec Pension Plan**.

**qualified annuity.** An annuity contract purchased to fund or distribute funds from a qualified plan. [11]

**qualified plan.** In its strictest sense, a retirement plan that receives favorable income tax treatment by meeting the requirements imposed by U.S. federal tax laws and the Employee Retirement Income Security Act (ERISA). A broader, less formal usage of *qualified plan* includes other tax-advantaged savings plans such as IRAs. [11]

**Quebec Pension Plan (QPP).** In Canada, a provincial program that provides a pension for wage earners in Quebec who have contributed money into the plan during their working years. [14]

**real property.** Property that consists of land and whatever is growing on or affixed to the land. *Contrast with* **personal property**. [3]

**recording method.** A method of changing a life insurance policy beneficiary designation under which the change becomes effective when the policyowner notifies the company in writing of the change. *Contrast with* **endorsement method**. [9]

**redating.** A process by which an insurer reinstates a term life insurance policy that lapsed for nonpayment of premium and changes the policy date to the date on which the policy is reinstated. [8]

**reduced paid-up insurance nonforfeiture option.** A nonforfeiture option that permits the owner of a cash value life insurance policy to discontinue premium payments and use the policy's net cash surrender value as a net single premium to purchase paid-up life insurance of the same plan as the original policy. [8]

**refund annuity.** *See* **life with refund annuity**.

**refund life income option.** A life insurance policy settlement option under which the policy proceeds are used to purchase a life income with refund annuity. [9]

**registered pension plan (RPP).** In Canada, a pension plan that meets the requirements to qualify for favorable tax treatment. [14]

**registered plan.** In Canada, a retirement plan that meets the legal requirements to receive favorable income tax treatment. [14]

**registered retirement savings plan (RRSP).** In Canada, a qualified retirement account that may be established by any gainfully employed person, including a person who is covered by an employer-sponsored registered pension plan. [11]

**regular IRA.** *See* **traditional IRA**.

**reimbursement benefits.** *See* **indemnity benefits**.

**reinstatement.** The process by which an insurer puts back into force (1) an individual life or health insurance policy that was terminated because of nonpayment of renewal premiums or (2) an individual life insurance policy that has been continued under the extended term or reduced paid-up insurance nonforfeiture option. [8, 17]

**reinstatement provision.** An individual life and health insurance policy provision that describes the conditions the policyowner must meet to put the policy back into force after it has been terminated because of nonpayment of renewal premiums. The provision included in individual life insurance policies also describes when a policy that has been continued under the extended term or reduced paid-up insurance nonforfeiture option can be reinstated. [8, 17]

**reinsurance.** Insurance that one insurance company, known as the ceding company, purchases from another insurance company to transfer risks on insurance policies that the ceding company issued. [2]

**reinsurer.** An insurance company that accepts risks transferred from another insurer in a reinsurance transaction. [2]

**renewable term insurance policy.** A term life insurance policy that gives the policyowner the option to continue the policy's coverage for an additional policy term. [5]

**renewal premium.** Insurance policy premiums payable after the initial premium. [3]

**renewal provision.** (1) A term life insurance policy provision that gives the policyowner the right, within specified limits, to renew the insurance coverage at the end of the specified term without submitting evidence that the insured is an insurable risk. [5] (2) An individual health insurance policy provision that describes the circumstances under which the insurer has the right to cancel or refuse to renew the coverage and the insurer's right to increase the policy's premium rate. [17]

**representation.** A statement that will invalidate a contract if the statement is not substantially true. *Contrast with* **warranty**. [8]

**retention limit.** A maximum amount of insurance that an insurer is willing to carry at its own risk on any one life without transferring some of the risk to a reinsurer. [2]

**retrocession.** A reinsurance transaction in which a reinsurer cedes risks to another reinsurer. [2]

**retrospective rating arrangement.** A group health insurance funding mechanism under which the insurer agrees to charge the group policyholder a lower monthly premium than it would normally charge for the group health insurance plan based on the group's prior claim experience. The group policyholder agrees that it will pay an additional amount to the insurer if, at the end of the policy year, the group's claim experience has been unfavorable. [18]

**retrospective review.** A component of a utilization review program, which involves evaluating the treatment and services that a plan member received. [15]

**revocable beneficiary.** A life insurance policy beneficiary who has no right to the policy proceeds during the insured's lifetime because the policyowner has the unrestricted right to change the beneficiary designation during the insured's lifetime. *Contrast with* **irrevocable beneficiary**. [9]

**right of revocation.** A life insurance policyowner's right to change the policy's beneficiary designation. [9]

**risk class.** A grouping of insureds who represent a similar level of risk to an insurer. [2]

**Roth IRA.** An IRA that provides for nondeductible contributions annually, but tax-free qualified withdrawals. *Contrast with* **traditional IRA**. [11]

**RPP.** *See* **registered pension plan**.

**RRSP.** *See* **registered retirement savings plan**.

**salary continuation plan.** A fully self-insured group short-term disability income plan that typically provides 100 percent of the insured employee's salary, beginning on the first day of the employee's absence due to illness or injury and continuing for some specified time. [18]

**savings incentive match plan for employees (SIMPLE) 401(k).** In the United States, a special arrangement whereby an employer with 100 or fewer employees can establish a simplified 401(k) retirement savings plan for employees. [14]

**savings incentive match plan for employees (SIMPLE) IRA.** In the United States, a written salary reduction agreement between an employer with 100 or fewer employees and its employees; the agreement allows eligible employees (including self-employed individuals) to choose to reduce their compensation by a certain percentage each pay period and have the employer contribute the amount of the salary reduction to a SIMPLE IRA on the employee's behalf. [14]

**savings plan.** A retirement plan to which a plan sponsor may make contributions on behalf of a plan participant if the participant makes contributions to the plan. [14]

**second insured rider.** A supplemental life insurance policy benefit that provides term insurance coverage on the life of a person other than the policy's insured. Also known as an *optional insured rider* or an *additional insured rider*. [7]

**secondary beneficiary.** *See* **contingent beneficiary**.

**second-to-die life insurance.** *See* **last survivor life insurance**.

**Section 7702 corridor.** In the United States, the difference between an insurance policy's face amount and the policy's cash value, which amount is used to determine whether the policy qualifies as a life insurance policy rather than an investment product under federal tax laws. [6]

**segregated account.** *See* **separate account**.

**self-administered plan.** A group insurance plan for which the group policyholder is responsible for handling the administrative and recordkeeping aspects of the plan. *Contrast with* **insurer-administered plan**. [12]

**self-insurance.** A risk-management technique by which a person or business accepts financial responsibility for losses associated with specific risks. [2]

**SEP.** *See* **simplified employee pension**.

**separate account.** An investment account an insurer maintains separately from its general account to isolate and help manage the funds placed in its variable products. Also known as a *segregated account*. [6, 11]

**separate account contract or rider.** A retirement plan funding vehicle in which an insurance company invests the retirement plan assets in its separate account. [14]

**service fee.** A one-time fee charged for specific services. [11]

**settlement options.** Alternative methods that the owner or beneficiary of a life insurance policy can elect for receiving payment of the policy proceeds. Also known as *optional modes of settlement.* [9] *See also* **payout options**.

**settlement options provision.** A life insurance policy provision that gives a policyowner or a beneficiary several choices as to how the insurance company will distribute the policy proceeds. [9]

**short-term group disability income coverage.** Group disability income coverage that provides a maximum benefit period of one year or less [16]

**short-term individual disability income coverage.** Individual disability income coverage that provides a maximum benefit period of from one to five years. [16]

**SIMPLE 401(k).** *See* **savings incentive match plan for employees 401(k)**.

**simple interest.** Interest paid on an original principal sum only. *Contrast with* **compound interest**. [4]

**SIMPLE IRA.** *See* **savings incentive match plan for employees IRA**.

**simplified employee pension (SEP).** In the United States, a written plan that allows an employer to make contributions to an individual retirement arrangement (IRA) for each participating employee. [14]

**simultaneous death act.** A law that governs how insurance companies are to evaluate common disaster situations. [10]

**single-premium annuity.** An annuity that is purchased by the payment of a single, lump-sum amount. [11]

**single-premium deferred annuity (SPDA) contract.** A deferred annuity that is purchased with a lump-sum premium payment on the date the contract is issued. [11]

**single-premium immediate annuity (SPIA) contract.** An immediate annuity that is purchased with a lump-sum premium payment on the date the contract is issued. [11]

**single-premium whole life policy.** A type of limited-payment whole life insurance policy that requires only one premium payment. [6]

**social insurance program.** A welfare plan that is established by law and administered by a government and that provides the population with income security. [1]

**Social Security.** In the United States, a federal program that provides specified benefits, including monthly retirement income benefits, to people who have contributed to the plan during their income-earning years. [14]

**Social Security Disability Income (SSDI).** A U.S. federal program that provides disability income benefit payments to qualified individuals. [16]

**sole proprietorship.** A business that is owned and operated by one individual. [1]

**solvent.** A term used to describe an insurance company that is able to meet its debts and pay policy benefits when they come due. [1]

**SPDA contract.** *See* **single-premium deferred annuity contract**.

**special class rate.** *See* **substandard premium rate**.

**special class risk.** *See* **substandard risk**.

**specific stop-loss coverage.** *See* **individual stop-loss coverage**.

**speculative risk.** A risk that involves three possible outcomes: loss, gain, or no change. [2]

**SPIA contract.** *See* **single-premium immediate annuity contract**.

**spouse and children's insurance rider.** A supplemental life insurance policy benefit that provides term life insurance coverage on the insured's spouse and children. [7]

**SSDI.** *See* **Social Security Disability Income**.

**SSI.** *See* **Supplemental Security Income**.

**staff model HMO.** An HMO that provides health care services to subscribers by directly employing physicians. [15]

**standard premium rate.** A premium rate charged insureds who are classified as standard risks. [2]

**standard risk.** A proposed insured who has a likelihood of loss that is not significantly greater than average. [2]

**state insurance department.** A state administrative agency charged with making sure that insurers operating within the state comply with applicable state insurance laws and regulations. [1]

**statutory reserves.** *See* **policy reserves**.

**stock bonus plan.** A retirement plan into which a corporate plan sponsor makes contributions in the form of the corporation's stock. [14]

**stock insurance company.** An insurance company that is owned by the people and organizations that purchase shares of the company's stock. [1]

**stop-loss insurance.** Insurance purchased by an employer that self-insures a group health insurance plan to enable the employer to place a maximum dollar limit on its liability for paying health insurance claims. [18]

**stop-loss provision.** A major medical expense insurance policy provision which specifies that the policy will cover 100 percent of allowable medical expenses after the insured has paid a specified amount out-of-pocket to satisfy deductible and coinsurance requirements. [15]

**straight life annuity.** A life annuity that provides periodic income payments for only as long as the annuitant lives. [11]

**straight life income option.** A life insurance policy settlement option under which the policy proceeds are used to purchase a straight life annuity. [9]

**straight life insurance policy.** *See* **continuous-premium whole life policy**.

**subaccount.** One of several alternative pools of investments to which the owner of a variable life insurance policy or variable annuity contract allocates the premiums he has paid and the cash values that have accumulated under his policy. [6, 11]

**substandard premium rate.** A premium rate charged insureds who are classified as substandard risks. Also known as *special class rate.* [2]

**substandard risk.** A proposed insured who has a significantly greater-than-average likelihood of loss but is still found to be insurable. Also known as a *special class risk.* [2]

**succession beneficiary clause.** *See* **preference beneficiary clause**.

**successor beneficiary.** *See* **contingent beneficiary**.

**successor payee.** *See* **contingent payee**.

**suicide exclusion provision.** An individual life insurance policy provision that excludes suicide as a covered risk for a specified period—usually two years—following the date the policy is issued. [8]

**supplemental major medical policy.** An insurance policy issued in conjunction with an underlying basic medical expense insurance policy to provide benefit payments for expenses that exceed the benefit levels of the underlying basic plan and, often, for expenses that are not covered by the underlying plan. [15]

**Supplemental Security Income (SSI).** A U.S. federal program that provides periodic benefit payments to people with limited incomes who are disabled, blind, or age 65 or older. [16]

**surgical expenses.** Charges for inpatient and outpatient surgical procedures. [15]

**surplus.** The amount by which a company's assets exceed its liabilities and capital. [1]

**surrender charge.** A fee typically imposed if a deferred annuity contract is surrendered within a stated number of years after it was purchased. [11] *See also* **back-end load**.

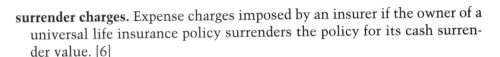

**surrender charges.** Expense charges imposed by an insurer if the owner of a universal life insurance policy surrenders the policy for its cash surrender value. [6]

**surrender value.** The accumulation value of a deferred annuity contract less any surrender charges included in the contract. [11] *See also* **cash surrender value**.

**survivor benefit.** *See* **death benefit**.

**survivor income plan.** An employee benefit plan that provides periodic income payments to specified dependents who survive a covered group member. [13]

**survivorship clause.** A life insurance policy provision which states that the beneficiary must survive the insured by a specified period, usually 30 or 60 days, to be entitled to receive the policy proceeds. [10]

**tabular mortality.** *See* **expected mortality**.

**tax-advantaged personal health spending account.** An account that is established with contributions from an employer and/or employee to pay the employee's medical expenses and that receives some tax advantages. [15]

**term life insurance.** Insurance that provides a policy benefit if the insured dies during a specified period of time. [1]

**terminal illness (TI) benefit.** An accelerated death benefit under which the insurer pays a portion of a life insurance policy's death benefit to a policyowner-insured who suffers from a terminal illness and has a physician-certified life expectancy of 12 months or less. [7]

**third-party administrator (TPA).** An organization other than an insurance company that provides administrative services to the sponsors of group benefit plans. [15]

**third-party policy.** An individual insurance policy that one person purchases on the life of another person. [2]

**TI benefit.** *See* **terminal illness benefit**.

**total disability.** A disability that meets the requirements of a disability benefit provision of an insurance policy or policy rider and that qualifies the policyowner or insured to receive specified disability benefits. [7, 16]

**TPA.** *See* **third-party administrator**.

**traditional IRA.** An IRA in which contributions may be deductible and investment earnings are tax deferred until the funds are withdrawn. Also known as a *regular IRA. Contrast with* **Roth IRA**. [11]

**trust.** A fiduciary relationship in which one or more persons hold legal title to property for the benefit of another person. [12]

**trust beneficiary.** The person for whose benefit a trustee holds legal title to property. [12]

**trust fund.** The property held in trust by one or more trustees. [12]

**trustee.** A person who holds legal title to property for the benefit of another person. [12]

**UCR fee.** *See* **usual, customary, and reasonable fee**.

**UL insurance.** *See* **universal life insurance**.

**unallocated funding vehicle.** A retirement plan funding vehicle in which some or all contributions are pooled together and not assigned to individual participants until each participant begins to collect benefits. *Contrast with* **allocated funding vehicle**. [14]

**underwriter.** An insurance company employee who is responsible for evaluating proposed risks. [2]

**underwriting.** The process of identifying and classifying the degree of risk represented by a proposed insured. [2]

**underwriting guidelines.** General rules of risk selection established by an insurer. [2]

**unilateral contract.** A contract for which only one party makes legally enforceable promises when entering into the contract. *Contrast with* **bilateral contract**. [3]

**universal life (UL) insurance.** A form of cash value life insurance that is characterized by its flexible premiums, its flexible face amount and death benefit amount, and its unbundling of the pricing factors. [6]

**universal life II.** *See* **variable universal life insurance**.

**UR.** *See* **utilization review**.

**usual, customary, and reasonable (UCR) fee.** For purposes of medical expense insurance, the amount that medical care providers within a particular geographic region commonly charge for a particular medical service. [15]

**utilization management.** A process used by managed care plans to help ensure that plan members receive the most appropriate care from the most appropriate provider in the most appropriate and most cost-effective setting. [15]

**utilization review (UR).** A process that managed care plans use to evaluate the medical necessity, appropriateness, and cost-effectiveness of health care services and treatment plans. [15]

**valid contract.** A contract that satisfies all legal requirements and, thus, is enforceable at law. [3]

**valued contract.** An insurance policy that specifies the amount of the policy benefit that will be payable when a covered loss occurs, regardless of the actual amount of the loss that was incurred. [2]

**variable annuity.** An annuity under which the amount of the accumulation value and the amount of the periodic income payments fluctuate in accordance with the performance of one or more specified investment funds. *Contrast with* **fixed annuity**. [11]

**variable life (VL) insurance.** A form of cash value life insurance in which premiums are fixed, but the face amount and other values may vary, reflecting the performance of the investment subaccounts selected by the policyowner. [6]

**variable universal life (VUL) insurance.** A plan of life insurance that combines the premium and death benefit flexibility of universal life insurance with the investment flexibility and risk of variable life insurance. Also known as *universal life II* or *flexible-premium variable life insurance*. [6]

**variable-premium life insurance policy.** *See* **indeterminate premium life insurance policy**.

**vested interest.** A property right that has taken effect and cannot be altered or changed without the consent of the person who owns the right. [9]

**vesting.** A retirement plan participant's right to receive partial or full plan benefits even if she terminates employment prior to retirement. [14]

**vision care coverage.** Supplemental medical expense insurance coverage that provides the insured with benefits for expenses incurred in obtaining eye examinations and corrective lenses. [15]

**VL insurance.** *See* **variable life insurance**.

**void contract.** A contract that does not satisfy one or more of the legal requirements necessary to create a valid contract and, thus, is never enforceable at law. [3]

**voidable contract.** A contract under which a party has the right to avoid his obligations without incurring legal liability. [3]

**VUL insurance.** *See* **variable universal life insurance**.

**waiting period.** *See* **elimination period**.

**waiver of premium for disability (WP) benefit.** A supplemental life insurance policy benefit under which the insurer promises to give up—to waive—its right to collect premiums that become due while the insured is totally disabled. [7]

**waiver of premium for payor benefit.** A supplemental life insurance policy benefit under which the insurer agrees to waive its right to collect a policy's renewal premiums if the policyowner dies or becomes totally disabled. [7]

**warranty.** A statement that will invalidate a contract if the statement is not literally true. *Contrast with* **representation.** [8]

**welfare benefit plan.** As defined by the Employee Retirement Income Security Act, any plan or program that an employer establishes to provide specified benefits to plan participants and their beneficiaries. [13]

**whole life insurance.** A plan of cash value life insurance that provides lifetime insurance coverage at a level premium rate that does not increase as the insured ages. [6]

**window premiums.** Additional premiums that a contract owner is permitted to pay during the first contract year of a single-premium deferred annuity. [11]

**withdrawal charge.** A charge imposed on the owner of a deferred annuity contract when the owner withdraws more than a stated percentage of the annuity's accumulation value in one year. [11]

**withdrawal provision.** A deferred annuity contract provision that gives the contract owner the right to withdraw all or a portion of the annuity's accumulation value during the accumulation period. [11]

**Women's Health and Cancer Rights Act of 1998.** A U.S. federal law that requires individual and group health insurance policies that provide coverage for mastectomies to provide certain mastectomy-related benefits or services. [17]

**workers' compensation program.** In the United States, a state program designed to ensure that workers who are injured or disabled on the job receive fixed monetary awards without requiring the workers to pursue legal action against their employers. [16]

**WP benefit.** *See* **waiver of premium for disability benefit.**

**yearly renewable term (YRT) insurance.** A plan of term life insurance that provides coverage for one year and gives the policyowner the right to renew the coverage. [5]

**YRT insurance.** *See* **yearly renewable term insurance.**

# Index

# A

# D

# H

# S

# T

**IMPORTANT—READ CAREFULLY BEFORE REMOVING THE INTERACTIVE CD FROM ITS JACKET. USE OF THE SOFTWARE PROGRAM ON THE ENCLOSED DISK IS SUBJECT TO THE TERMS OF THE LICENSE AGREEMENT PRINTED BELOW. BY REMOVING THE DISK FROM ITS JACKET, YOU INDICATE YOUR ACCEPTANCE OF THE FOLLOWING LOMA LICENSE AGREEMENT.**

## INTERACTIVE CD LICENSE AGREEMENT

This Interactive CD License Agreement (the "Agreement") is a legal agreement between You (either as an individual or a single entity) and LOMA (Life Office Management Association, Inc.) for the use of the Interactive CD software ("the Software") accompanying this Agreement. By removing the disk from its jacket, You are agreeing to be bound by the terms of this Agreement.

### Definition of in "Use"

The Software is in "use" on a computer when it is loaded into temporary memory (RAM) or installed into permanent memory (hard disk, CD-ROM, or other storage device) of that computer.

### Grant of License

**Rights of an Individual.** If You are an individual, LOMA grants to You a nonexclusive license to use one copy of the Software on your office computer and one copy on your home computer provided that You are the only individual using the Software.

**Rights of an Entity.** If You are an entity, LOMA grants to You a nonexclusive license to use the Software in only one of the following two ways, with the selection to be yours:

- You may designate one individual within your organization to have the sole right to use the Software in the manner provided above under "Rights of an Individual."
- Alternatively, You may install one copy of the Software on a single computer and allow multiple members of your organization to use the Software on that one computer. If You wish to use the Software on another computer, You must deinstall it from the computer it is on before installing it on another computer.

### Copyright

The Software is owned by LOMA and is protected by U.S. copyright laws and international treaty provisions. Therefore, You must treat the Software like any other copyrighted material (e.g., a book or musical recording) EXCEPT that You may either make one copy of the Software solely for backup or archival purposes or transfer the Software to a single hard disk provided You keep the original solely for backup or archival purposes. You may not copy the written material accompanying the Software. The questions and instructions and instructional material (hereinafter "the Content") contained in the Software are also owned by LOMA and protected by U.S. copyright laws and international treaty provisions. It is illegal to make any copy whatsoever of the content; to install the Software on a network, intranet, or Web site; to download the content to another computer or device EXCEPT as expressly allowed under "Grant of License" above; to print screens or otherwise cause the content to be printed EXCEPT as expressly allowed on several screens; or to in any other way reproduce the content contained in the Software.

### Other Restrictions

You may not rent or lease the Software. You may not reverse engineer, decompile, or disassemble the Software or in any way duplicate the contents of the code and other elements therein.

### Disclaimer of Warranty

LOMA MAKES NO WARRANTY EXPRESS OR IMPLIED INCLUDING, WITHOUT LIMITATION, NO WARRANTY OF MERCHANTABILITY OR FITNESS OR SUITABILITY FOR A PARTICULAR PURPOSE. UNDER NO CIRCUMSTANCES SHALL LOMA BE LIABLE TO YOU OR ANY THIRD PARTY FOR ANY INCIDENTAL OR CONSEQUENTIAL DAMAGES WHATSOEVER.

### Limitation of Liability

You agree to indemnify and hold harmless LOMA, its employees, its agents, and their successors and assigns against any loss, liability, cost or expense (including reasonable attorneys' fees) asserted against or suffered or incurred by LOMA as a consequence of, or in the defense of, any claim arising from or based upon any alleged negligence, act or failure to act whatsoever of You, its employees, their successors, agents, heirs, and/or assigns with respect to the aforementioned Software.